INNOCENTS

Jonathan Rose is a barrister who specialises
in criminal law. He has a particular interest
in defendants suffering from psychiatric,
psychological and mental illness and
mental handicap.

Steve Panter is a journalist on the *Manchester
Evening News* with responsibility for crime
reporting. He covered the Kiszko/Molseed
case from the outset.

Trevor Wilkinson is a retired Detective
Superintendent in the West Yorkshire Police.

INNOCENTS

JONATHAN ROSE WITH STEVE PANTER AND TREVOR WILKINSON

HOW
JUSTICE
FAILED
STEFAN
KISZKO
AND
LESLEY
MOLSEED

FOURTH ESTATE • London

This paperback edition published in 1998

First published in Great Britain in 1997 by
Fourth Estate Limited
6 Salem Road
London W2 4BU

1 3 5 7 9 10 8 6 4 2

A catalogue record for this book is available from
the British Library.

ISBN 1-85702-845-7

Typeset in ITC-NewBaskerville by
Avon Dataset Ltd, Bidford on Avon B50 4JH

Printed and bound in Great Britain by
Clays Ltd, St Ives plc, Bungay, Suffolk

Contents

Prologue

The punishment of a criminal is an example to the rabble;
But every decent man is concerned if an innocent man is condemned.

JEAN DE LA BRUYÈRE
LES CARACTÈRES, DE QUELQUES USAGES

On 10 November 1949, 1-year-old Geraldine Evans was strangled to death, but it was not her father, Timothy, who tightened the ligature around the baby's neck. Timothy Evans was executed for a crime he did not commit.

On 23 August 1961 Michael Gregsten was killed by a shot to the head, but is was not petty thief James Hanratty who pulled the gun's trigger. James Hanratty was executed for a crime he did not commit.

On 5 October 1975, Lesley Molseed was abducted and stabbed to death. Stefan Kiszko was innocent of her murder. Stefan Kiszko was imprisoned for sixteen years, for a crime he did not commit.

The terrible price of innocence.

The twentieth century has produced a significant number of cases in which innocent men have been convicted of murderous crimes of great repugnance. At least two men, Evans and Hanratty, paid with their lives for miscarriages of justice.

Consideration of such miscarriages tends to focus, almost exclusively and with much justification, on the innocent man. But to follow this path is to ignore those other people, equally innocent of any wrongdoing, who pay a high price for the failings of others. The families of those guiltless men whose lives are decimated by the imprisonment (or execution) of their loved ones, who then give years to clear the innocent's name. Iris Bentley, Anne Whelan, lives devoted to a single struggle. The victims are buried and forgotten to all but their relatives but how can they rest in peace whilst their killers live on unpunished? What rest is there today for the family of Michael Gregsten and the parents of Carl Bridgewater? And of Lesley Molseed?

Each time the scales of justice are unbalanced, by police misdemeanour, by inadequacies in the legal system or by the dishonesty of others, the implications extend far beyond the man or woman who has been wrongly convicted of the crime. Publicly there is criticism of 'the System', 'the Police' or 'the Law' but, as is evident from the case with which this book is concerned, such criticism has not resulted in positive change. Changes to systems have not eradicated miscarriages of justice, and there is little will to punish those who contribute to such miscarriages. The fact that innocent individuals, who have been convicted and punished for crimes they did not commit, have received compensation payments or pardons should bring little comfort to society, for each one of us remains at risk of wrongful accusation until the will for change and the momentum for change grow strong.

There lives today a man who took the life of Lesley Molseed. That he enjoys his liberty, his freedom and his life is cause enough to abhor the repercussions of the wrongful conviction of Stefan Kiszko. That he remains unpunished is reason enough for the family of Lesley Molseed to feel that justice has not been done. That he may kill again is quite sufficient for all to look at the case of Stefan Kiszko with anxiety and unease.

The Kiszko/Molseed case revealed painful truths about the inadequacies of the English legal system, and few of those truths have been adequately addressed more than twenty years after Kiszko was convicted. Many questions still remain unanswered:

i Why is there still no independent authority responsible for objective assessment of evidence prior to criminal charges being brought? Why has the procedure of 'Old Style Committals', whereby evidence may be assessed prior to Crown Court trial, been abolished, so that there are fewer, not more safeguards in place?

ii The Police and Criminal Evidence Act 1984 made failure to permit a suspect detained by the police access to a solicitor a 'breach of the Codes of Practice' which *might* render a confession inadmissible. Why, instead, did it not make it a mandatory requirement that such a suspect have legal representation, whereby any failure to provide such representation *would* render any confession obtained inadmissible?

iii Why is the Court of Appeal still reluctant to make incompetence of counsel a valid ground of appeal?

iv Why is there still no truly independent body to examine and take action on alleged miscarriages of justice?

This book is not about the innocence of Stefan Kiszko, nor the innocence of Lesley Molseed. It is not about the innocence of the families of that man and that child. It is about a series of events in 1975 and 1976 which destroyed the innocence of so many people.

And it should serve as a reminder that innocence remains a precious commodity, which can still be stolen.

As the twentieth century draws to a close, the innocents still suffer, the guilty still walk free.

CHAPTER ONE

The Ghost of Christmas Past

It was a snapshot of traditional Britain, Christmas Eve 1975. A small, neatly furnished room, its lighting dim, as if to enhance the atmosphere of peace. The green fir tree pointed symbolically heavenwards. Bedecked with tinsel and baubles, its myriad of fairy lights twinkled so much brighter in the half-gloom. Surrounded by gifts, brightly wrapped, unopened – as they would surely now remain. A solitary, poignant angel stood aloft, wings spread, embracing the scene below, gazing down, beatifically, upon the chair.

The chair. Where the man-child had sat until a few hours ago, staring at the presents with the same excitement he had shown as a young boy. His mother looked, without comprehension, at the vacant seat, as if staring upon some ancient royal throne. The king had gone, for surely he had been a king to her. Her only son, her only child. Her boy-child.

They had come for him earlier. Three wise men. Not kings, but surely men of power. He had risen from the chair, his massive frame dwarfing her, dwarfing them, but bent and stooped as if already shamed. Posing no threat, he had stood and listened, barely responsive to the words spoken.

'Stefan Ivan Kiszko. I must caution you that you do not have to say anything unless you wish to do so, but that anything you say will be taken down and may be given in evidence against you.'

He had said nothing.

'I would like you to accompany us to the police station at Rochdale.'

He had demurred, but for a moment only. Then he had nodded his bowed head. More of a shrug than a nod. He may have understood or he may not, but the nod was acquiescence and compliance, it was not agreement.

She had watched him leave with them. Leave the sanctuary of her home; leave the protection which she had always given him;

1

leave the safety which their family had always afforded him. Now, for the first time, he was alone.

CHAPTER TWO

Give Us this Day Our Daily Bread

On the spindly legs of a frail 11-year-old girl, Lesley Molseed skipped down to the corner shop on a simple enough errand for her mother. She would return home from that errand one month later, in an oak coffin.

She was a tiny girl, barely four feet tall, and so small that, as her mother would later say, you could push her over with your finger. Perhaps it was her heart defect which had contributed to the child's small stature. That Lesley had suffered ill health since birth was a fact of life with which she had already learned to cope. On days when she felt able to run a simple errand, like other children in the street, she was joyous, but Lesley also knew the torment of having to sit still by a window of her home, short of breath, watching other children playing tag or squabbling in the street. She had endured surgery for a faulty heart valve when only three years old, yet Lesley Susan Molseed was a cheerful, smiling, ordinary, happy child.

Her home, too, was not extraordinary. Her stepfather, Danny, was a working man, employed at an engineering factory where the vagaries of shift work meant that he had to work on Sundays. At seven forty-five he had put his head round the bedroom door, to see his sleeping stepdaughters Laura, aged 14, and Lesley, aged 11, before he left the house in Delamere Road, Rochdale, to catch the bus to work. It was not unusual for her mother to be washing in the kitchen of the family's council-owned home – not unusual on any day, not unusual on Sunday, 5 October 1975.

An ordinary Rochdale family, with the man working and the mother attending to the household chores. But in the middle of her work, with one eye on the laundry and one on the cleaning and somehow still finding a free hand to cook the Sunday lunch, April remembered that they had run out of bread.

With six mouths to feed you cannot wait until the next trip to the supermarket, nor do you need to. Just ask one of the kids to nip round the corner to Ryders grocers' shop, pick up a large loaf 'and don't dawdle coming back'. She shouted up to her daughter, ensconced in the bedroom she shared with sister Laura. They were doubtless listening to a Bay City Rollers record, whilst staring at a poster of the pop group both girls idolised. 'Lel!' came April's cry, using the family's name for Lesley. 'Lel,' shouted April for the second time, and then Lesley appeared, with her wide, tooth-filled grin, always eager to help, grasping the pound note in her tiny hand, Bay City Rollers tartan socks around those skinny legs, and shouting 'Back soon mam', the door slamming behind her. Clutching the money given to her as her reward for running the errand. Three pennies. Lel had wanted six, but her mother had haggled her down. It was really Freddie's turn to go, according to the family's errand rota, but he was at football practice. Lesley did not mind. She welcomed the chance to be outside when she was feeling well enough to take a walk. Perhaps the shopping ex-pedition would give her an opportunity to spot Jinxy, her missing cat. She had accepted the lesser sum with her usual impish grin. And then she was gone.

It was 1 p.m.

This was an era, after John Kilbride, after Lesley-Ann Downey, after Pauline Read, after Keith Bennett, when parents sent their children out to play alone, without fear.

Dinner-time passed, with no bread on the table and no Lesley at the table. Sister Laura is sent out to look for her: traces her likely routes along Delamere Road and Birkdale Road, crossing Turf Hill Road and into Ansdell Road. Lesley is not at Ryders corner shop, nor at the Spar shop, nor is she at Margaret's, the sweet shop on Broad Lane. Laura returns home. Brother Freddie joins the search, and when the two children can still find no trace of their sister, nor even anyone who has seen her, Freddie is sent to get Danny.

This was an era, before Susan Maxwell, before Caroline Hogg, before Sarah Harper, when mothers sent their children to corner shops, without concern.

Freddie finds Danny, his day's work as a maintenance electrician at an end, in the Plough public house, playing darts. The game is abandoned. Lesley is still not home, she has been gone for one and a half hours.

It had taken a far shorter time for Lesley to disappear. She had found Ryders closed, and had cut along a narrow dirt-path between Buersil Avenue and Ansdell Road, her navy-blue canvas shopping bag with the yellow Tweety Pie motif hanging from her bone-thin arm. She wore a blue coat with a white synthetic fur-lined hood, which she pulled over her head. Underneath, a blue woollen jumper, a red and white T-shirt, a pink skirt and brown shoes, and those blue and white hooped and tartan socks, em-blazoned with the name of her heroes, the Bay City Rollers. She was heading for the Spar shop on Ansdell Road, but she never arrived there.

It must have taken only seconds for Lesley to cross the short pathway, but in the few strides between Ryders and the Spar she was intercepted. Lesley Molseed was a quiet, shy and home-loving girl, well-disciplined by her parents not to talk to strangers. It was also true that Lesley was both vulnerable and suggestible. Robert Whittaker, Lesley's teacher at High Birch School was later to give his assessment of her mental age as being 'about 6', and he was to add his ominous opinion that 'She would have gone off with someone if they had approached her in the manner that suited her.' So what alluring bait was used by the man who took her? Did he tempt the child with sweets, or with the promise that he could help her find the missing Jinxy?

Of this Danny Molseed was then, of course, unaware. Alerted to Lesley's out-of-character disappearance he is swiftly out of the house again, searching. April Molseed had at first been vexed that her youngest child had ignored her directive to return quickly from the simple errand. Then, as the minutes passed, she grew ever more fretful for the girl's safety. By the time an hour had passed, her anxiety had become feverish, so that Danny's eventual return was to a woman verging on panic.

Danny Molseed was determined to bring Lesley home. In his own mind, indignation dominated. Unable to conceive that harm would come to her, he walked the route she had earlier taken. Surely she had become distracted, seen a friend, stopped to play, seen a cat and thought that it was Jinxy, and followed it away. He passed Ryders and turned on to the dirt path. Walking firmly, but unhurriedly, he paced towards Ansdell Road, calling her name, ever more strongly. As the ideas in his mind revolved to thoughts more sinister, to fears more real, the steps became shorter and the voice became a shout, until he was running running running, shouting Lesley Lesley LESLEY. In to every house along the lane, he demanded 'Have you seen her?' 'Is she here?' 'Did she go past?' 'A little girl in a raincoat?' but there was no reply to help him. At the end of the path he was greeted by an empty Ansdell Road: there was no sign of her.

Phone calls to the police brought an immediate response but no results. Julie Molseed, Lesley's older sister, came to the family home which she herself had left some eight months earlier, to live with her natural father after friction had developed between her, April and Danny. Now she was pregnant by her boyfriend James Hind, and they were planning to return to the Turf Hill Estate. The family gathered round in a show of collective security, collective strength, collective fear.

Danny ventured out again, believing that he and only he would find this child and bring her safely home. By daylight and by night he searched, alone or with others. No anxious father could have done more, still thinking first 'I'll tan her hide when I get her home' and then, 'Dear God let her be safe.'

The police search extended across the estate and the surrounding area. Photographs of the missing child were shown, and residents and passers-by were questioned. At the same time, news of the little girl's disappearance spread, along with tales of suspicious men in vans and cars loitering where local children met and played, trying to entice them into their vehicles.

As the police searched and Danny searched, small armies of neighbours and friends formed to play their own part, a spontaneous gathering of volunteers taking to the streets, with fear for the child and empathy for the family their only motivations. The armies became swollen, until scores of people were engaged in the chaotic and frantic covering of the streets and snickets.

A cluster of sightings was reported. Once those obviously not of Lesley were discounted, attention turned to the more likely reports. Julie Molseed ignored her heavily pregnant state to join her boyfriend and their friends in scouring the streets. Two of those friends, Steven Scowcroft and Brian Statham used their motorbikes to add speed and efficiency to the search.

At 8.30 p.m. Julie returned to her mother's home to telephone her father, Frederick Anderson, to break the news of Lesley's disappearance, and to assure him that she would keep him informed. Then Julie stepped back, whilst police officers spoke to April with delicacy and tact, prying into the family's background, squeezing out details of the missing child's character, habits and behaviour. Who were her friends? Where might she go? Was there any reason they could think of why Lesley might not return.

The police instituted a discreet search of the house, to ensure that the child was not, somehow, hidden there. It would not be the first time that a report had been made of a missing child, when in truth the child was trapped, hidden or even killed within the home, and the body secreted there. April confirmed that Lesley had not taken a change of clothing with her, and thus provided a complete answer to any suggestion that the little girl's failure to return was voluntary.

By 10 p.m. there was widespread and serious concern. The police officers' street searches had now condensed into house-to-house enquiries, looking for the child, looking for clues, looking for answers. At 11 p.m. the police called on John Conroy, Danny Molseed's best friend, at his home on Neston Road. Alerted of Lesley's disappearance, Conroy and his wife went immediately to their friends, where they joined a further search party of friends and neighbours which remained out on the streets until 4 a.m. the following day.

The night slowly passes. The younger children are put to bed, unaware of high drama and mounting fear. But there is no sleep for the parents, their minds filled with thoughts of Lesley, and of how she could never cope with being away from her family all night. She would certainly be unable to spend a night outdoors. Each tries to comfort the other, but true optimism is in short supply. Sunday runs into Monday.

At dawn, the police resume their searches, governed by routines honed by experience, experience which usually brings results. They are joined by community members who do not have to work that day, and even some who have elected not to go to work so that they can assist. The search is extended beyond the strict limits of the estate, to wasteland and farmland which border it, and to abandoned freezers and fridges where a body might be hidden. That evening, the expertise of the local youth was brought to bear, when club leader Dennis Wilkinson asked the youths to search those – mainly secluded – areas where they might sometimes go, including Kays Field, derelict houses and garages of the Deeplish and Ashfield Valley areas, and numerous hidden spots where young people wanting privacy would sometimes disappear. This fruitless search continued until 2 a.m. the following day.

The estate rumour machine continued to grind out its seemingly endless ribbon of tales, of men in vehicles on the estate trying to entice young children into their cars, of indecent exposure and of attacks on lone women. These tales, inevitable consequences of a crisis in such a close-knit community, served only to heighten the fears of the Molseed family. And as the tales spread, so did the fear, so that other families watched their children with more than

7

usual care, and an orchestrated curfew was imposed on local children. The searchers, whilst concentrating on their primary task of finding the child, now looked equally for the suspicious or out-of-the-ordinary. Find Lesley; protect the children. These were the priorities under which the Turf Hill Estate was now operating.

Day three: no sign, no word, and it is hard, even for optimists, to believe. All but the occupants of Delamere Road have given up hope. 'Any news?' the neighbours ask, or turn their heads to avoid having to frame that question, hear the reply, see the shaking head, notice the tired face and ragged looks that speak the words that no one dares to say.

Fred Anderson had arrived at the Delamere Road house on Monday morning, and he and April were to remain there throughout, neither wanting to take the chance of missing some news. Each member of the household is eager to reassure the others, but the ticking of the clock accompanies the growing fear that, unbelievably, this tiny child may not be seen again. That thought remains unspoken, but by Tuesday night such optimism as had once existed is strained to its limits.

Inevitably, the police operation was starting to wind down, although a police officer remained with the family throughout. The search was being downscaled, as all possible locations had been covered, every street searched, every house visited. The mobile loudspeakers stopped blaring Lesley's description, and the enquiry incident room was moved to Rochdale Police Station, away from the immediate vicinity of the estate. The incident room's role as the centre of a missing person enquiry was gradually being changed in anticipation of it being needed for an enquiry of a different kind.

Incredibly, Danny Molseed still walks and searches and asks. But as Tuesday reaches midnight, he and the neighbours and friends who have walked, unstintingly, since Sunday, looking for new areas to search, new stones to turn, come together and agree to meet the following morning to regroup and resume. With the thanks of the Molseed family in their ears and their hearts, they head off for much needed sleep.

That sleep remained in short supply for Lesley's family. The strain at last told on Julie, and problems developed with her pregnancy which required immediate hospital attention, but by Wednesday morning she was ignoring medical advice, and returned to be with her family once more. She telephoned Fred Anderson to come and collect her, and for a brief moment, the family rejoiced that the baby was well. It was Wednesday, 8 October 1975.

As dawn broke over Rishworth Moor, David Greenwell stirred from sleep and threw open the rear doors of his yellow 1965 BMC Mini van, which was parked in a lay-by off the A672 Oldham to Halifax Road at Ripponden, West Yorkshire. A night's sleep behind him and the early morning urge to relieve himself caused him to scramble upwards until the land became flat, changing from craggy hillside to moor.

Who was this man, who had spent the night sleeping in a lay-by? Why did he look up into the bleakness? What was it that first caught his eye, to draw it to the terrace twenty-five feet above his head, to see the folds of a blue raincoat, flapping in the air currents and swirling winds which never seem to abate across this grassy embankment.

David Arthur Greenwell, a joiner by trade, was at this time working for a firm of Birmingham shopfitters who were engaged in a jewellery shop refit in Rochdale. It was simply too far for him to travel daily from his Nottingham home, and, although he was paid an allowance to cover overnight expenses, Greenwell's tiny van sometimes became his home-away-from-home, with sleeping bag and mattress, kettle and primus stove, cup and plate. But no toilet.

And so at around six forty-five, rising to wash and cook breakfast, he first scurried upwards to find a secluded spot, where he could not be seen. After his task was completed, he turned and made his way back down the moorside. The wisp of cloth that had caught his eye on the ascent could be seen again as he headed back to his van, but this time he looked a little closer. The wisp then seemed part of a bundle of clothes. He took another pace towards it, then reeled backwards at the sight of what was clearly human flesh. The body of a child, of a little girl, face down on the grass. Still fully clothed, the Bay City Rollers socks visible, the blue canvas bag revealing the incomplete errand that had set her on the route which brought her here. But the trappings of childhood innocence were obscured by the obvious and appalling injuries, the bruising and the stab-wounds, and by the terrible stillness of the child, from whom all life had now departed.

For a moment only, he stood, transfixed, somehow unable to absorb the enormity of this sight. Then, slowly, he began to recall news reports over the previous weekend of a young girl missing from the Rochdale area, and that recollection sent him running to his van. The wash could wait, the breakfast was abandoned as shock turned to panic. He hurriedly drove to his work site and told his foreman, Michael McClean, and fellow employees of his grim discovery, and they in turn advised him that he must report the finding to the police.

Within the hour the grisly find had been reported at Rochdale Central Police Station to the desk officer, Constable Michael Roberts. The duty detective from Rochdale criminal investigations department required Greenwell to repeat his story, as he would be asked to repeat the story many times over the next few days.

Then DC Roberts asked Greenwell to accompany him back to the scene, to retrace his steps. Once more the Nottinghamshire shopfitter embarked on the climb up the moorside, this time with far more trepidation, followed by the officer. Did Greenwell hope that the body would have gone? That he had imagined it? That the nightmare would then be over? Had he yet realised that he would not be allowed simply to carry on with the day's work, before returning to the lay-by to sleep again that night? Could he comprehend that he was already being ear-marked, not merely as a witness, but as a suspect, a position he would have to hold until he could be, in the jargon, eliminated from police enquiries?

It was a matter of moments before he and the detective stood within sight of the child. Neither approached the body, it was obvious that the child was dead, and it was equally obvious to Roberts, who by this time had engraved on his mind the description of the frail 11-year-old child who had been missing since Sunday, 5 October, that he had found the body of Lesley Susan Molseed. The 'child missing from home' investigation had become a murder enquiry.

In April 1974 a major restructuring of the British police service had reduced the 115 county, city and borough forces to fifty-one larger forces covering England, Scotland and Wales. The series of amalgamations which took place created Greater Manchester police and West Yorkshire Metropolitan police as two of the largest police forces in the country. Rishworth Moor, remote and desolate, was situated between the Halifax and Huddersfield divisions of the West Yorkshire force, although it also bordered the Rochdale division of the Greater Manchester police area.

A radio message from Roberts' police car to senior officers at Rochdale was quickly relayed on to West Yorkshire police, on whose ground Lesley had been found. West Yorkshire officers were immediately dispatched to the location, and by 9 a.m. Detective Chief Inspector Richard (Dick) Holland of Halifax division, and Detective Chief Inspector John Stainthorpe of Huddersfield division were at the scene, trying to determine on whose 'patch' the body lay.

The murder enquiry fell within the jurisdiction of Detective Chief Superintendent Jack Dibb, head of West Yorkshire number one crime area, and his junior officer from the Halifax division, Dick Holland. And because all major murder enquiries in West Yorkshire were at that time handled by the Home Office Forensic Science Laboratory at Harrogate, near Leeds, the principal forensic scientist in the case would be one Ronald Outteridge.

Holland's immediate task was to establish an 'exclusion zone', the borders of which would preserve any evidence deposited at the scene by the offender or the victim. Within those borders fingertip searches would be made for clues. Within those borders the story of Lesley Molseed's death would begin to be told.

The extent of the crime scene, including any possible routes taken by the killer to or from the place where the body had been found, was also marked out. This would be a larger area than the exclusion zone and would include the lay-by and any vantage points from where witnesses might have overlooked the scene of Lesley's death. This, too, was taped off and guarded by local officers. It would be into these areas that there would come, first, the forensic scientists and the pathologist.

While waiting for the scientists and medical men, Holland began the task of structuring the major investigation, the early stages of which comprise time-honoured routines and procedures which remain common practice today. One key procedure is to attempt to establish the sequence of events at the immediate scene, including the identification of all movements of people (and, essentially, vehicles) and occurrences prior to, during and after the commission of the crime, up to the moment of the discovery of the body so that the exclusion zone can be established. In this way no evidence is lost or contaminated, the value of potential clues is identified and any unconnected material is correctly eliminated.

The experienced police officer, who had attended many, many murder scenes, was able to speculate, quite reasonably, on the circumstances which had brought Lesley to this moor. She had clearly been driven from the back-streets of Rochdale to the moors overlooking the M62 motorway, only twenty yards from the A672 Oldham to Ripponden Road. The frail child had been dragged or carried up forty feet of moorside, to a bracken and heather terrace where she was ultimately found. Had her journey to this final place been non-stop, or had the man taken her elsewhere first? That question would have to wait for an answer. Lesley had undoubtedly been alive when her killer laid her down on the damp ground, but for how long had she been kept there, terrified, before her so-short life was brought to such an unmerciful end?

The forensic scientists and pathologist would soon confirm that, mercifully, she had not been sexually abused, but that, although she had not been interfered with, her last companion had undoubtedly obtained some sexual pleasure from her final hours on earth. Upon her underwear forensic scientists were to find semen, but whether the man had ejaculated in some private, quiet place, or up in the winds and mists of the moors, whether he had done so when she was alive or dead, would also remain unknown. It is known only that the killer had masturbated on to Lesley, and that he had killed her, brutally, stabbing her twelve times in the chest and neck with a small knife, before wiping the blade on her thigh and leaving her, uncovered, to the elements.

The Rochdale police would soon receive many accounts of sightings of Lesley as she walked from her home to the shops, and then at various locations in Rochdale and the surrounding areas. In the initial stages Dick Holland only worked on those sightings of the child which clearly could be relied on, in the hope of piecing together Lesley's last movements and identifying the moment when her abduction took place. The first witness to confirm that Lesley had left Delamere Road at the time her mother claimed was a young girl called Dianne Reeves, who knew Lesley well. Dianne had seen Lesley turn from Delamere Road into Stiups Lane, passing right by her as Dianne swung on the garden gate at her own home. Mark Conroy, a schoolboy friend of Lesley, saw her further along Stiups Lane as he walked from Kingsway playing-fields across Stiups Lane into a snicket or walkway towards Ansdell Road. Four girlfriends of Lesley's were heading towards Kingsway playing-fields at this time, and noticed her as she walked along. They and Mark also saw a young ginger-haired girl with a scruffy grey dog, who was so close to Lesley that Mark had thought the two girls were together.

Bernadette Hegarty also saw Lesley walk towards Ansdell Road. She was swinging the blue shopping bag and Bernadette, a 10-

year-old neighbour of Lesley's, thought that she was 'dilly-dallying'. Bernadette was also heading for the Spar, but took an alternative route which ran parallel with Stiups Lane. She visited the Spar shop, but she did not see Lesley there.

Fifteen-year-old Stephen Tatters, who knew Lesley well, also visited the Spar shop at the same time as Bernadette, but he did not see Lesley there.

John Cooper, a newcomer to the area but one who recognised Lesley, remembered seeing her at twelve fifteen walking towards him on her way to Ansdell Road. He was sure of the time, because he had just asked it of an elderly lady who had been walking in the road ahead of him.

At that time, Anita Owen, aged 13, visited the Spar shop and, having bought some sweets, headed back to her home on Turf Hill Road. She walked along Ansdell Road and was just about to turn right into the snicket leading to Buxton Crescent when Lesley came out of the snicket opposite and to her left from Stiups Lane. The two girls were seen by Jane Jeffreys, a school friend of Anita, who described Lesley's clothing – especially her socks – with great accuracy. Anita and Lesley said hello. Anita walked on towards Buxton Crescent and last saw Lesley approaching the Spar shop.

Robert and Marion Ellidge, the proprietors of the Spar, were interviewed at 3 p.m. on the Sunday of Lesley's disappearance. They had closed the shop at 2.10 p.m., and had not seen Lesley all day. Steven Ellidge had worked in the shop with his parents until 12.30 p.m. that day, and had then gone to work on his blue Ford Escort car in a garage on Buxton Crescent. He had seen Danny Molseed searching for his stepdaughter at 2 p.m., and had shortly afterwards gone into the shop and asked his parents if they had seen her. Like them, he was unable to help the police, although he had been backwards and forwards across Ansdell Road several times between 12.30 and 3 p.m.

Frank and Edith Jones owned the tobacconist/confectioner's shop at 65 Broad Lane, known locally as Margaret's. Lesley was a regular visitor to that shop, particularly on a Sunday when most other shops were closed. Initially the Joneses said they believed Lesley had not been in the shop that afternoon, but after seeing a photograph of the child they changed their minds, saying that she might have been in around 2 p.m., but that they were not certain whether it had been on the Saturday or the Sunday.

Thus, almost all the sightings of Lesley which were to come to the attention of Dick Holland were for around twelve fifteen on the Sunday, and between Lesley's home address and the Spar shop. There was one further sighting, by Jacqueline Reilly, who saw Lesley from her kitchen window as she walked along Stiups Lane. Jacqueline Reilly had also seen a small yellow van which appeared to be following behind Lesley, and this fact was noted with some interest since there had already been a number of reports of a yellow van on the Turf Hill Estate acting suspiciously near to young children, in particular at the Kingsway Youth Club on the Friday night prior to Lesley's disappearance.

DC Roberts was debriefed to ascertain what, exactly, David Greenwell had told him, how both men had approached the scene, and whether either of them had touched or moved the body. But Greenwell could not, yet, be considered only as a witness, since it is not uncommon for the person 'finding' the body of a murder victim to be the perpetrator of the crime he claims to have discovered.

With this common occurrence in mind, and the knowledge of the description of Greenwell's van, Dick Holland ordered that the man be interviewed at length, and his movements between Friday, 3 October and Wednesday, 8 October checked and corroborated. Greenwell explained how he had been working in Rochdale for three weeks on the shopfitting job, saving money by sleeping in his van Monday to Thursday, before returning to his home in the Clifton area of Nottingham for the weekend. He had a perfect alibi, confirmed by his parents, Arthur and Siegrid, with whom he lived, who told the police that Greenwell had spent the relevant weekend at home with them, mostly working on the repair of his mobile home. Neighbours of the Greenwells, Iris Dennis, who lived next door, and George McClean, who lived opposite, also supported the man's account. The police also checked with the tyre company and scrap yard where Greenwell claimed to have gone that weekend to buy spare parts for his van.

Anthony Stych, a workmate, confirmed that Greenwell had given him a lift to his home in Sheffield on the Friday, and had picked him up again at 10.10 a.m. on the Monday. Together with the foreman, Michael McClean, he was able to vouch for Greenwell's whereabouts from the time he began work in the early morning through to the early hours of the next morning, for it was common practice for the six employees to work late, and then go out for a meal and a drink together, usually until about 1 a.m., since each of them was working away from home. The only exception to this routine had been the Tuesday night, when Greenwell had gone straight from work to his 'home' in the lay-by.

McClean described how Greenwell had arrived on site at about eight twenty on the Wednesday morning, looking shaken, pale and worried. He had immediately spilled out his terrible experience, and both Stych and McClean had urged him to report his find to the police.

The above accounts, coupled with reported sightings by passing motorists of the van in the lay-by between Monday night and Wednesday morning and with the information from his home town and his workmates – not least of which were descriptions of him as a good worker, though quiet and nervous – were sufficient to satisfy the police as to Mr Greenwell's movements. The alibi was accepted, and Mr Greenwell was no longer regarded as a suspect.

That said, there remained the question mark over the sightings of the yellow van; and, of course, Greenwell himself, although absolved of any part in the death of Lesley Molseed, remained a crucial witness in the case. This was not merely because of his discovery of the body, but because he had spent many hours at and around the area in which the police were interested, including hours when the child's body could have been dumped. He was interrogated further, in the hope of gleaning from him any strand of evidence which could later be woven into the rope with which the killer would be caught. The clothes he was wearing at the time of the discovery of the body and his small yellow van were also taken for forensic examination to eliminate any particles or traces which he might have left at the scene or, of equal importance, to obtain anything which he might inadvertently have removed from that terrible place.

Then, and only then, could the habitually nervous shopfitter go from the police station, free to resume his normal everyday life the best he could after what he had seen.

On the Turf Hill Estate enquiries were being made by officers anxious to achieve a result, but their questioning also revealed the effect which Lesley's disappearance had had on the local community and, in particular, the anguish being suffered by the parents. The community's desire to have the killer apprehended was based only in part on feelings of sympathy towards the Molseed family. It was also founded on the fear that an outsider had intruded into the communal safety of the estate, putting each of their own children at risk.

Turf Hill was once a rural farming area adjoining the mill town of Rochdale, but as the town became swollen with the increasing population which accompanied industrial expansion, the growing need for accommodation sent tentacles of urbanisation into the readily available and easily accessible land which lay, untouched, nearby.

It was a typical council housing estate, with brothers in every town and city of substance in Great Britain. Rows of (then) modern three-bedroomed terraced houses with small front and rear gardens were joined by a series of connecting roads and the intersecting walkways known as snickets. Two main roads, Broad Lane and Turf Hill Road, serviced the estate, giving access to a major arterial road in and out of Rochdale. The remaining farmland that surrounded the estate stretched towards the neighbouring town of Oldham, running along the edge of the M62, between junctions 20 and 21 of that great cross-country motorway, which served as the boundary line between the two towns.

The community of Turf Hill, not atypically, was self-contained and close-knit. Most of the children knew each other, as did their parents. The local availability of schools, shops and a youth club brought parents and children into regular contact with each other. Many socialised together, making use of the various pubs, clubs and sporting facilities available in the area.

A feature of such a community was that news, whether bad or good, travelled with great speed. Rumour and gossip mingle with fact and hard news, and exaggeration and distortion are inevitable features in the retelling. In the Molseed enquiry this feature was repeatedly to cause problems for the police, who were constantly required to sort fact from fiction, evidence from rumour, credible witnesses from gossip mongers. Conversely, out of the community spirit came the positive feature of the residents' willingness to help each other and the police (who were not the natural friends of many in that community) to find Lesley and, later, to find and catch the child's murderer.

Within hours of the discovery of the child, the grim mechanism of murder was grinding into action, starting with the knock on the door of 11 Delamere Road that the occupants had hoped would never come. As gently as possible, the parents were notified of the finding of a body, and before that shock had penetrated minds and hearts, they were taken on a journey, by police car, to a mortuary at Halifax Royal Infirmary, to identify the child, hoping against hope that it would not be Lesley, that a mistake had been made.

It was a duty for a mother to perform alone. Although she had steeled herself for the task ahead, April's nerves were strained by a delay in proceedings, and she and Danny waited together in a small room. But she became claustrophobic and left the room to pace up and down the corridor, leaving Danny alone with his thoughts.

At last, a policeman's footsteps on the hard, Victorian hospital floor, followed by 'They're ready for you now, Mrs Moleseed,' and she is escorted, one officer beside her and two behind. Inside the room are more policemen, in plain clothes. But while the uniformed officers had seemed considerate and caring, these men seemed to be avoiding her, or certainly avoiding her eyes. And then it became clear for her. There was no need to look. They had found Lesley, and these men knew it.

The mother has to be the one to speak: it is her duty. Words are hard to find and April struggles to make a sound, until she whispers, 'I'd like to hold her,' But as April steps forward to embrace the tiny frame, she is stopped from doing so. 'Don't touch her!' The command is barked, breaking the solemnity of the room, but instilling immediately the importance of not disturbing the child.

Lesley was no longer April's daughter, but police evidence, which must not be touched.

'Is this your daughter, Mrs Moleseed?' speaks an unknown voice, and she does not look to find the speaker, but replies 'It is, but she doesn't belong to me any more.' And then and only then the resolve of the woman is gone, the strength she had shown or tried to show throughout the three-day ordeal, disappears. At last she weeps, and her eyes blur with tears. She turns away.

April rejoined Danny. He did not have to ask her and she did not have to tell. He had 'inherited' Lesley as a 1-year-old, and she was the favourite of his four foster children. He had lost his own daughter, he felt, and his tears flowed down his face, its expression as desolate as that of his wife.

CHAPTER THREE

Of Science and Pounding Feet

In terms of the investigation of homicides, there are only two primary types. The first is where the killer is immediately identified or identifiable, and apprehended at or shortly after the event, and where the legal issues at any subsequent trial narrow down to those concerning state of mind at the time of the killing. The second is where the killer is completely unknown. In such a case, of course, the first task on the lengthy path to securing a conviction is ascertaining who is responsible for the killing. Obviously the investigation of the latter type is far more onerous than that of the first, because the police start, in effect, with a completely blank sheet of paper.

In any homicide it is necessary to establish a number of facts:

i identity of the victim;

ii manner and cause of death (for example, asphyxiation by strangulation);

iii time and place of death;

iv weapon used, if any;

v identity of killer;

vi motive;

vii state of mind of killer.

These facts must be determined in order that the investigation of the case be complete. Even if some of the facts (such as motive) do not, as a matter of law, require proof for a successful prosecution, it is obvious that they are each of great importance in the quest to establish how the victim died and at whose hand.

Once it is established that the police are concerned with a suspicious death and, more particularly, once the suspicion becomes that of an unlawful killing, the investigative process begins. Of the seven factors listed above, the identity of the killer becomes the most pressing. All other matters will be investigated as the enquiry proceeds, but the search for the killer must begin immediately, and before the trail begins to cool.

Whilst the public face of a murder investigation is the television news reports, showing police officers searching fields on hands and knees, scouring for the most minute of clues, and the further reports of house to house enquiries, there is, from the moment the body is discovered, a far more private aspect of the investigation. It takes place in the clinical sterility of the laboratory and in the case of Lesley Molseed, it was a side of the investigation which was to have substantial and profound implications.

High on the moors, away from the anguish of the Turf Hill Estate and the homeliness of 11 Delamere Road, Dick Holland presided over the murder scene, one eye on his watch as he awaited the arrival of the forensic and pathological support services. He was only too aware that the further away from the moment of killing he got, the more difficult it would be to find his man. Moreover, the passage of time accompanied intrusions into the evidence: a wind blowing across the moors could blow away a fragment or fibre, a rainstorm could destroy footprints, a less-than-careful bobby might obliterate some tyre tracks, or the killer himself could dispose of clothing, or a vehicle, or a weapon.

Anxious to preserve the murder scene in at least one respect, Holland had directed PC Stuart Akerman to take a series of photographs, of the features of the moorland and the area in which the child was found, and of Lesley's body itself, *in situ*, before there could be any further disturbance of the area. He was confident that the body had not been moved by Greenwell or DC Roberts, and therefore had no reason to suspect that the child was not in the same position as she had been left by the murderer. One further photograph. A seemingly innocuous print of a blue-grey coloured fibre-tipped pen, with a white cap and base, found on a rock about fifteen yards from the body, in a direct line between the body and the lay-by. If every picture does in fact tell a story, what tale would be told by the print of this harmless writing instrument?

Senior colleagues of Holland began to arrive at the lay-by. Awaiting the arrival of the pathologist, there were a number of officers of the West Yorkshire police force, among them Assistant Chief Constable Donald Craig, DCS Jack Dibb and Detective Chief

Superintendent George Oldfield (whose name would later become inextricably linked with the investigation into the crimes of the Yorkshire Ripper). Officers from the adjoining Greater Manchester force who covered the area from which Lesley had disappeared were also present.

At 10.30 a.m., the assembled officers witnessed the arrival of Home Office pathologist Professor David John Gee. Holland briefed Professor Gee with a thumbnail sketch: the identity and age of the victim, when and where she went missing, when and how she was found and that the body had not been moved since its discovery. The professor prepared to view the body. He was accompanied by trainee pathologists Dr Boateing and Dr Swaloganathan, and by Home Office forensic scientists Ronald Outteridge from the Harrogate laboratory, and a Mr Firth from the laboratory at Chorley. The forensic scientists would examine the scene, removing samples of grass and vegetation from around the body, and soil and stone samples both from the site where the body was found, and from the lay-by. Clear plans would indicate the exact location from which each sample was obtained, and the bags containing the samples would be marked accordingly. Later, they would examine the clothing of the deceased and any samples obtained by the pathologist.

Police officers continued to work, first with a finger-tip search of the immediate area, then with a wider, less-detailed rake over a more extensive area, hoping to find anything relevant but, in particular, the weapon used to end this tiny child's life.

The pathologist's work would primarily take place in the mortuary, after the body had been moved from the scene, but it was important for him to view the body *in situ* as it would help him to determine whether that was the place where the murder had taken place, or whether the child had died elsewhere and then been moved there. He would go on to consider the injuries, how they were inflicted and in what order, and which one or ones had been responsible for the death.

Times were vital factors for all the investigators, since they would attempt to provide a band of times within which death had occurred. These parameters would be crucial in eliminating suspects who were able (as Greenwell already had done) to account for their movements within those times.

An access route to the body had been created, so that the scientists could make their way to the corpse without fear of intruding upon any potential evidence. Ascending the steep grassy bank from the lay-by, the men reached a broad, grassed terrace from where they could see, beyond, a rock-strewn slope, steeply rising to the moorland proper far above. At the back of the terrace, some fifty yards from the roadside, they saw, as Greenwell had seen, mere cloth blowing in the stiffening breeze, which, only on closer inspection, became their ultimate objective: the body of a child lying face down in the coarse grass. It was still clad in the dark-blue gabardine raincoat, the hood raised over the back of the head so as to obscure the hair and other features. The left arm was bent up at the side of the body towards the face, the right arm was beneath the child. The thin legs were flexed at the hips, somehow twisted to the left, and the trunk was tilted slightly to its right. The skirt of the raincoat was somewhat displaced upwards, exposing an area of white padded lining, and beneath that could be seen a pink skirt and a pair of red knickers. The blue shopping bag lay across the feet, not quite obscuring the brown shoes, and the Bay City Rollers socks of which Lesley had been so proud.

A closer examination revealed a number of slit-like cuts in the material of the raincoat, running across the back of the body and between the shoulders, and one, similar cut, to the back of the head. Dark stains around the cuts of the material gave an overall appearance of stab wounds with slight blood-staining of the coat's material. The exposed parts of the body – the left hand and thighs – were not blood-stained, save for a single smear of blood approximately two inches (five centimetres) in diameter on the upper surface of the left thigh. There was blood soiling of the grassed area some three inches (seven centimetres) in diameter below the body, approximately one foot (thirty centimetres) beyond the lower end of the trunk. Behind the right side of the child's back lay an unzipped purple purse, and for a moment the thought entered many minds, 'Has this child been murdered for the sake of the meagre contents of her purse?' The body and clothing appeared not to have been disturbed since the child's death, but that did not prevent there being a collective theory that the motive for this crime had been sexual, not financial.

Then, for the first time since hands had taken her life from her, Lesley Molseed is touched again, but this time it is by people who care about her, at least in the sense of being anxious to help bring her killer to justice. They are gentle, not violent, deliberate, not frenzied, and they are painfully experienced in the performance of their various tasks. With minimum conversation they go about their macabre but necessary business. Detective Sergeant Kenneth

Godfrey has been appointed exhibits officer, responsible for the collection, collation and identification of every single item of physical evidence, whether seized by a scientist or police officer, whether taken from a witness or, in due course, a suspect. He receives the Tweety Pie-crested handbag and the purple purse, and places each into a separate polythene bag which is then sealed and labelled: a description of the item, the time, date and place of recovery and a unique reference number which relates to the person who recovered it. The items will remain protected in their polythene sheath until the time comes for forensic examination in the sterile atmosphere of the laboratory.

Sellotape lifts are taken from the child's left hand and legs, the simplest of tools to search for the tiniest fragment of evidence. A fragment of blue material is found stuck to the back of the left thigh.

Then, and only then, does Professor Gee begin to intrude on the body itself. He first removed the child's knickers. They did not appear to have been tampered with, giving at least an indication that there had been no sexual interference. Then the professor took anal and vaginal swabs, which were placed in exhibit tubes and handed to the exhibits officer.

To assist in determining the time of death, Professor Gee took the rectal temperature of the body. At 12.30 p.m. it was 46 degrees fahrenheit. The examination had by now taken over two hours, and though the weather was dry, there was a cold westerly wind blowing. The air temperature on the ground varied between 52 and 48 degrees fahrenheit, whilst the temperature three feet above the body varied between 47 and 48 degrees fahrenheit. Although the ground appeared to be dry, the upper clothing of the deceased was slightly damp, and a few beads of moisture had been visible on the upper surface of the raincoat when the men had first arrived at the body, but these had quickly disappeared due to the effects of the wind. The sky, which had been clear at the beginning of the examination, was now starting to cloud over.

Now, finally, the child could be removed from the exposed grass bank. With reverence and respect – and doubtless with thoughts of their own children and grandchildren never far away – the assembly of men watched Lesley Molseed as she was lifted on to a black polythene sheet. As her body was lifted, it was evident that rigor mortis was well developed in the limbs, although hypostasis[1]

---

1 Hypostasis is the process whereby blood accumulates in the lower parts of the body due to the effects of gravity. In Lesley's case this would be the front of her body, since she had been left lying face down.

was only faint. As Lesley was turned, they saw that she had bled from the nose and her facial features were distorted and flattened from their prolonged contact with the ground. There was no blood soiling at the back of the head, nor of the fleecy white lining of the interior of the hood of her raincoat. A small cut was visible to the left of the front of the raincoat, and there was a stab wound beneath. The front of the child's clothing was heavily blood-stained, as was that which covered the back of her shoulders, where blood had seeped into the right-hand side of the clothing due to the position in which the body had lain. These early indications lead to a hypothesis that Lesley had been repeatedly stabbed where she lay, and left to bleed to death. She had been alive when brought to this desolate place, and her life had ebbed away in lonely isolation, her screams only partially drowned by the high-pitched whistling of the winds which swirled through the peaks and vales of the moors.

Then she had been left. The skin over the left hand was macerated, being sodden, white and wrinkled. The skin of the lower limbs was slightly grey, and a few fly eggs were found in the hair close to the left ear. These features, and the rectal temperature, indicated that the body had been exposed to the elements for some time, although a more precise time of death would only become clear after the post-mortem, and a more careful analysis of the temperature readings already taken.

After Lesley's hands and feet were encased in plastic bags to preserve any evidence which might cling to them, the black sheet was wrapped around the body, which was then placed into a coffin-shell and carried off the bleak moors with solemnity and dignity. Whatever vehicle had carried her on her last journey in life, she was now to be moved by a hearse which was waiting in the lay-by below. Her next journey led to the Halifax Royal Infirmary.

Removed from the wind and rain of the moor to the hospital mortuary, the child is received by Mr Seward, the mortuary attendant. He is experienced, and treats each corpse given to his charge with equal care and reverence. But his experience extends to victims of crime and, knowing that this child was said to be such a victim, he is instantly aware that his care of the body must extend beyond the norm. He knows from previous post-mortems in murder cases that the body is itself a source of evidence, and that whilst he must prepare the body for viewing by the relatives, so as to cause as little distress as possible, he has a second, but equally important, role in ensuring that any movement of the body will not contaminate or cause the loss of any evidence. These dual roles clashed at this point: whilst he had previously prepared bodies with extensive head or facial injuries so as to minimise the trauma to the relatives carrying out the identification, he was unable to do so with Lesley, whose face, although uninjured, was heavily stained with blood. That blood-staining would doubtless be of concern to the scientists, and so the best Mr Seward was able to do was to lay her body out in the black plastic sheet, now covered with a purple velvet cloth.

Mr Seward was assisted by Sergeant Appleyard, the coroner's officer, who performs a number of functions for the coroner. One such function is to ensure that an accurate identification of the deceased has taken place at an early stage. And so, the child is identified. April Molseed is brought by police officers to Halifax, the journey littered with her questions which those officers were unable to answer: were they sure it was Lesley? How had she died? Had she been sexually assaulted? These officers do not have the answers. Indeed, at this point, no one does.

Now Lesley is left to the scientists. Now is the white, sterile phase. The tiny child reduced to 'the deceased' whilst the cause of her death is sought. A grim and gruesome task in any case, made the more pitiful by the victim's age. A necessity, both for the detection of the criminal and for his prosecution, to know that she did not die from natural causes, to know the nature of the attack, the number of wounds and of blows, to know (if possible) the time and place of death, to know whether there has been indecent interference. Mercifully not. To draw from the child any clue which may yet help justice to be done.

Professor Gee and the forensic scientists work, methodically and in accordance with regulated and established procedures, under the watchful eyes of ACC Craig and DCS Oldfield. The participants agree an order in which to proceed, a necessity when some type of examination might secure one form of evidence whilst destroying others.

The first step is an examination of the body's external surfaces by Detective Chief Inspector Swann, a fingerprint expert, but he finds nothing upon the child and soon leaves, taking with him a set of the child's own fingerprints for use in comparison against any found in a culprit's home or car (although Lesley's prints were never found on any exhibit in the eventual case).

Then the child is undressed, and each item of clothing is handed to Sergeant Godfrey who, assisted by Detective Constable Robert

Shore, bags and labels each garment separately. Lesley is wearing precisely the same clothing that she was wearing when she left home.

The forensic scientists are provided with samples of Lesley's hair, both plucked and cut, and with finger-nail scrapings, and they then leave, to continue their work back on the moors, while they wait to receive all exhibits at the laboratory, where their own tests would be conducted. Samples would be taken from the body by Professor Gee in the course of the post-mortem, for later use by the professor and by the forensic scientists.

Finally Professor Gee is alone with the body. He will carry out his extensive examination whilst ensuring that he makes detailed notes, for in the information which the post-mortem will yield it is hoped to find, not merely the time of Lesley's death, but also the motive behind her death and the cause and, perhaps, some clue which might assist in the bringing to justice of the person responsible.

The external examination revealed the body of a thin, small, brown-haired girl, some four feet in length and weighing forty pounds. There was slight blood soiling of the skin at the front and back of the trunk and over the face. When this was removed post-mortem staining was found to be faint, pinkish in colour and mainly present at the front of the body, with some areas of pressure pallor in the skin over the knees. Rigor mortis, though confirmed had by this time begun to pass off. The effect of exposure to the elements, visible in the exposed parts of the body, by reason of a dark-grey coloration, particularly to the left hand and the thighs, was also confirmed.

The eyes appeared normal although the pupils were unequal, the right being larger than the left. The absence of petechial haemorrhages[2] in the lids or on the eyeballs enabled the professor to exclude strangulation or asphyxiation as the cause of death. The ears and nose were normal, whereas the mouth was slightly soiled by blood with the tip of the tongue protruding between the teeth, and although the teeth themselves showed several caries, none was loose or displaced, indicating that the face had not been subjected to violence.

The chest carried an old, healed, oblique surgical scar on the right side of the chest, some seven inches in length, with a second

---

2 Collections of red or purple spots caused by blood seeping into the skin.

and similar scar on the left side, both reminders of the surgical treatment for Lesley's heart complaint.

The external genitalia were normal, with no blood soiling and no evidence of injury. The hymen was intact and the anus normal. The child had not been raped nor subjected to any penetrative sexual attack.

Professor Gee found twelve stab wounds: one to the left front chest, one to the right front of the neck, one to the back of the left ear and nine to the upper part of the chest, at the back, principally on the left-hand side, all within an area measuring six inches by three inches.

As Professor Gee measured the dimensions, the angles, the tracks of entry of each stab wound, was he already constructing a scenario of blows driving the child to the ground, then the killer's orgy of violence as he stabbed her in the back. He might say it was violent, for several wounds had faint areas of bruising of a half-inch diameter. Were these bruises caused by the impact of the hilt of the knife against the child's body? It is not a scientific term, but the expression 'frenzied attack' hangs unspoken, like an uninvited guest at a wedding.

Her hands were unmarked. There were no defence wounds.[3] She had not had time, or had not been able to defend herself. Or she had been attacked from behind.

When the professor examined the child internally, the twelve stab wounds could be traced on their path into the body. Each had penetrated to different depths, and some had caused damage to bones and to internal organs, most notably the heart and lungs.

The hair was cut from Lesley's head to enable examination of the scalp, but there was no evidence of injury or blood-staining. It was then passed to PS Godfrey, along with a vaginal swab, a mouth swab, a blood sample and the stomach contents (which would show that Lesley had not eaten since leaving her home). The internal organs each yield further samples to be taken for further examination. They are taken to exclude any suggestion of death by natural causes.

From 2.30 p.m. until 6 p.m. Professor Gee went about his work, slowly, cautiously, meticulously and without regard to the silent staring of the police officers – including ACC Craig – who lined the walls of the mortuary, observing proceedings anxiously.

---

3 Victims of frontal stabbing attacks are frequently found to have wounds to their hands, caused when they, instinctively, raise their hands in an attempt to stave off the incoming blows.

The result of the post-mortem revealed that Lesley had died of bleeding from the twelve stab wounds, the heart, aorta and left lung having been penetrated. The wounds were caused by a knife, with a thin blade no more than half an inch broad and not less than two and a half inches long, with one edge sharp and the other rounded. Bruising adjacent to two of the wounds at the back of the left shoulder suggested that those blows had involved the knife being driven in with substantial force, the hilt or the attacker's hand having made forceful contact with the body. The wounds to the back of the body had been inflicted as the child lay in the position in which she had been found.

Whilst it was impossible to be certain as to the time of death, Professor Gee was of the opinion that Lesley had been dead more than twenty-four hours before she was found, and that she had possibly died up to three days earlier, namely on Sunday, 5 October 1975. There was a silent hope that his longest estimate was most accurate, so that the child had not had to endure days of captivity (and what else?) before her final, brutal death.

The inquest into the child's death which opened on 14 October 1975 would disclose only that Lesley had died from multiple stab wounds. There was no need to say more.

Her body has been mutilated, and the post-mortem necessarily adds to that defilement, but Mr Seward again applies his skills, and the body may now be prepared for burial.

But her clothes are neither discarded nor returned to her parents. In murder cases the victim's silence is compensated for: for her body speaks for her, and her clothes speak for her, and for Lesley Molseed her clothes shout loud.

DS Godfrey amasses his collection from the search team which has, throughout the day, continued to scour the moors and lay-by. He receives twenty-six items, including seven bottles, a Polaroid camera cartridge wrapped in silver foil, part of a plastic bag, a small tablet still in its foil (would that be the killer's medication?) and four photograph negatives. Had one of these items been discarded by the murderer and, if so, would even one yield up his fingerprint?

A pair of socks, a handkerchief, a packet of cigarettes and a high heel from a lady's shoe.

And, from the lay-by, a broken knife . . .

For nearly thirty-six hours PS Godfrey has collected exhibits, numerous and diverse. The collected materials are brought together, and then they are removed from Halifax to the laboratory at Harrogate, where they are handed to Ronald Outteridge, the principal scientific officer in the case and a highly respected member of the Home Office Forensic Science Service.

For now, the scientific material is mute, or, if not mute, it speaks in half-sentences only. It directs the scientists to look carefully, and note what they might find, but it can say no more until the time comes for comparisons. Until fibres from two sources lie alongside each other under a microscope, or two semen samples are observed together, the scientific material can tell only a fragment of the story. It will say that Lesley had been in contact with a cloth which shed fibres, but it cannot yet say from where that cloth came. It will certainly tell the investigators that, whilst the child had not been interfered with, the killer appeared to have derived some sexual pleasure from being with her. But it cannot, now, say who the murderer was. Or was not.

Each single item is removed from its shielding plastic bag and is examined closely. It is a critical and crucial examination, and it yields results. Peter Guise, a forensic scientist and Batchelor of Technology examines the clothing: each garment, as ever, on its own to prevent any contamination, lying on a sheet of brown paper to collect any matter which may fall away in the course of the examination. He looks for blood or fluid staining, and he notes the dimensions and directions of the cuts. He runs Sellotape over the garments to collect loose fabrics which might adhere.

Of the blood-stains, he finds no evidence of 'run down', supporting the already-held theory that the child had not been standing up when the principal injuries were inflicted. From the jumper, the vest, the skirt and a sock, tiny fibres of a certain hue, a certain type, a certain constituency. And a single blue fibre from the back of Lesley's neck. From the underwear, what appear to be semen stains. He makes up microscopic slides from these stains and looks further: his initial belief is confirmed. He can see sperm heads. He applies the test then in use to record the amount of heads: +H is the lowest, ++++H the highest. He writes '+H' in his notes. There is a low sperm count given the large area of seminal staining.

Outteridge was soon to provide an initial report, confirming Professor Gee's findings that Lesley had been murdered where she was found, and indicating Outteridge's belief that the murder had a sexual motive, based on the finding of semen on the lower garments. He has identified Lesley's blood as being group B,[4] but he wishes to continue to examine blood-staining on the clothing in the hope of finding blood of a different group, perhaps belonging to the murderer. Outteridge would therefore advise Dibb and Holland that any suspects should have blood specimens taken from them, and that their clothing should be seized for forensic examination. Any suspect vehicles should also be examined, for matching fibres, but also because Lesley's purse bore a sequined pattern, and the sequins appeared to be falling away. The appearance of any such sequins in a suspect's vehicle would be a matter of great interest.

Finally, Outteridge informs Dibb and Holland that the knife found in the lay-by is not, in his opinion, the murder weapon.

---

4 There are four primary blood groups: A, B, AB and O. There are, however, further methods of blood grouping, one being the PGM scale, so that Lesley had a PGM of 2-1. These two types of grouping were of particular importance in 1975 and throughout the era before the advent of DNA testing, which enables bloods to be identified with infinitely more accuracy, and without recourse to the A/B or PGM groupings which enabled identification only as part of a group which might contain many thousands of people. DNA testing enables identification to be expressed as accurately as, say, one in ten million.

CHAPTER FOUR

Needles in Haystacks

The work of Gee and Outteridge was, of course, limited to the materials already gathered from the scene of the crime and from Lesley herself. Clearly there was a great deal of available information which had to be obtained, and to this end Dibb, who had been appointed head of the enquiry, and Holland, his deputy, set in motion information 'seeks' on the Turf Hill Estate and the A672 near to the lay-by, searching for the elusive clues as to the identity of the killer.

High up on the moors officers were combing the grasses and shrubs around the site where the body was found, using metal detectors and electronic probes to try to find the small knife which had so cruelly slashed the child, and police scenes of crime officers took photographs of the still-untrampled area. At the direction of the supervising officers, other uniformed officers set up blocks at the Junction 22 exit of the M62 to ask questions of every motorist leaving the motorway at that point. Similar questions were asked of motorists passing the lay-by. Had they driven that route the preceding Sunday? Had they passed by the site? Had they seen a girl, a parked car, a man – alone or with a child – anything? A list of questions designed to squeeze information from people who might have seen something, yet not paid close attention or even noticed that they had seen something. A car parked up on the moors is not so rare a sight that it would be regarded as noteworthy, but if later asked perhaps the question will cause the brain to yield up that sighting, stored somewhere in the subconscious.

Professor Gee's findings tended to suggest that the police would be well advised to confine their questioning to the Sunday, since that, he believed, was most probably when Lesley was killed. But even if that were correct, it could not be taken as conclusive, since it is not unusual for a killer to return to the scene of the crime, particularly when the body has not been discovered immediately.

There are two notable aspects of this questioning of dozens of motorists (and, indeed, of the door-to-door questioning going on in Rochdale): the vast number of man-hours involved, and the enormous volume of information gleaned. The resource problems are, perhaps, obvious, but the difficulties caused by the sheer quantity of information gathered are perhaps less glaring. They would be painfully illustrated towards the end of the decade and the beginning of the eighties with the Yorkshire Ripper enquiry, when information gathered by dozens of police officers involved in a lengthy investigation was stored on thousands of cards in a file index, as one might find in a library. Each witness interviewed in the Molseed case had his details entered on to a card, and the card duly filed by name or date or some other point of reference. But the cards provide only a limited system of cross-reference. The facility did not exist to cross-reference all relevant aspects and, although there were different indices created according to names of persons and streets, type of motor vehicle, suspects etc, the time to carry out a manual cross-reference (and the obvious and real probability of human error both in filing and in making cross-references) made detection with such a system difficult and, occasionally, haphazard. The Ripper enquiry revealed this starkly: Peter Sutcliffe was interviewed on no less than six occasions before he was finally (and quite by chance) arrested. It is obvious now that a computerised system would enable cross-reference to take place, literally, at the push of a button. One beneficial effect of the errors of the Ripper enquiry was the bringing into use of the 'HOLMES'[1] computer system, which now plays a vital function in complex criminal investigations. But Lesley Molseed's death preceded the advent of HOLMES by several years, and so the investigation of her death was carried out in the time-honoured fashion. All information was duly recorded on file cards: an army of paper for the death of a tiny child.

Although already effectively eliminated from the enquiry, Greenwell and his yellow Mini van were 'assisted' by a number of witnesses, including Ralph Holden, who actually described seeing the shopfitter scrambling up the embankment at 7.30 a.m. on the day Lesley's body was discovered and Police Constable Robert Sendall, who, as a road traffic officer, had spoken with Greenwell in the lay-by at 9.30 p.m. the previous Thursday evening, confirming Greenwell's account that the lay-by was his usual sleeping area.

---

1 Home Office Large Major Enquiry System, which was introduced in the United Kingdom for the first time in 1984.

Amongst the plethora of witnesses who did come forward for elimination were Derek and Doreen Hollos from Blackley, Manchester, who had driven past the scene at 2.15 p.m. and 7.15 p.m. on the Sunday, on their way to and from visiting relatives in Halifax. Their assistance to the police at that time was regarded as minimal. But their vehicle was a red Renault 16TL, registration ADK 539 L, and those innocuously recorded details would, in due course, become of crucial importance.

As the questioning of motorists continued, so police activity in the town escalated. On the afternoon of 8 October a joint operation of West Yorkshire and Greater Manchester police officers was coming into effect, with a hundred officers involved in the investigation from the outset. Come the following day, they and others joining them would go out on to the streets of Rochdale to begin the house-to-house enquiries essential to such an investigation. Pounding feet along residential streets. Knocking on doors. The traditional methods of British policing.

The decision to base the incident room, the 'nerve-centre' of the investigation, at Rochdale had not been difficult to make, even though the operation was, strictly speaking, a West Yorkshire matter. Discussions between Dibb and a detective chief superintendent of the Greater Manchester police confirmed what was already known, namely that the majority of enquiries would take place within the Turf Hill Estate. It made practical and logistical sense to have the incident room as close to the main area of investigation as possible.

Dibb and Holland then addressed the practical needs of the investigating team: staffing needs, hours of work for the enquiry team and the incident room staff, an indexing policy for the card system and a documentation registration procedure suitable to officers from both forces. Usually each police force used its own system for the logging and filing of index cards. But now a 'common language' was essential.

Dibb decided that the enquiry officers and incident room staff would operate on shifts covering at least 8 a.m. and 11 p.m. each day in the initial stages, and longer if required, as the several lines of enquiry were identified and pursued. This was to cause problems for the incident room staff, since it meant that different people might be responsible for reading and collating incoming information to those responsible for directing officers to make further enquiries (which are known as 'Actions') resulting from that information. Pieces of information came in, from officers on the enquiry, officers not on the enquiry and from members of the public. The information was then analysed and, if appropriate, a further action was prescribed. That action would be allocated to a team, led by a detective inspector, who would allocate actions through a team leader to a pair of detectives. It was a chain of command with inherent potential for breakdown, and this would be amplified if there was a turnaround of incident room staff in between the receipt of the first information, the decision to action and the subsequent allocation of that action.

Dibb made a policy decision to adopt the West Yorkshire force's practice of taking full written statements from all persons interviewed. This would avoid the loss of pieces of information jotted down in an officer's notebook or on scraps of paper, but it carried with it the obvious difficulty that it would generate substantial amounts of documentation, requiring reading, analysing and indexing. The volume of paperwork would be large. Even so, it is obvious that both the brief note method and the full statement method carry a risk that information recorded, perhaps at the time without an appreciation of its importance, might be lost. Dibb's policy also added to the difficulty mentioned above, namely that the person reading and analysing a statement might not be the same person who would then decide an action on that statement, with a further opportunity for a breakdown in communications and a loss of continuity.

The investigation was not entirely dependent on the police seeking out information for themselves. The public were not slow to respond to the horror of this crime. By Friday, 10 October, with over 200 officers now involved, the investigators had received more than 400 telephone calls from members of the public who believed that they had seen something of importance. Not one of those calls could be overlooked, however trivial the information given might at first have seemed. The information may be fresh information, or a repetition of what an earlier caller had given, or a slight variation on such earlier-given information. The latter two types of call enable detectives to develop the picture as more detail is added to initial rough sketches. Each call required and received a follow-up.

Those telephone calls from the public were beginning to generate some sort of a pattern. There was what was described as a 'flood' of calls from a number of parents concerning a kerb-crawling driver, who, it was said, had accosted several girls under the age of 14 on Rochdale housing estates in the week preceding

Lesley's disappearance. No child had got into the man's car, and no reports had been made to the police whilst Lesley had been missing. With no harm done to their own child (if the child had at that time told its parents) and with Lesley's disappearance still open to any number of explanations, parents chose not to involve the police, but to be thankful that their own children were safe and well. With a child now dead – consciences were pricked, and the calls came in.

Suspicious motor cars became a topic raised in a number of calls, made by members of the public anxious to assist the police. Had these calls referred with any consistency to a single make, type or colour of vehicle, the common thread might have been of use. As it was, the genuinely made phone calls proffered a variety of descriptions of vehicles.

One car seen frequently in the two weeks preceding Lesley's disappearance, on and around the Turf Hill Estate where she lived was described as a yellow or cream-coloured van.

Another vehicle generating a number of reports was a cream car with grey primer paint on one door which had been seen twice on Sunday, 5 October in Well-i'-th'-Lane, Rochdale. The second sighting had been by two men, Martin Wellburn and Stanley Russ, who had identified it as an old – possibly 1965–Vauxhall Viva, but the men had been unable to say whether there were any people, or children, in the car. The first sighting was by an elderly lady who was unable to give much detail beyond the car being a cream-coloured four-door, with red primer on the passenger side doors. This witness claimed to have seen a girl in the car who she thought looked exactly like Lesley. A light-coloured vehicle with red primer paint on the bodywork had been seen at the lay-by between 6.15 p.m. and 6.45 p.m. by Sandra Chapman and by Colin Sutcliffe.

Yet another vehicle was also spotted parked in the lay-by. This was described as a dirty blue-green 5cwt Morris van, which had had a green check blanket draped over the windscreen and driver's window. It had been seen by a couple driving past on the Sunday of Lesley's disappearance, at 2 p.m. and again at 3.30 p.m. This vehicle was subsequently described as being a Morris Minor-type van, hand-painted in turquoise or light green. No fewer than fourteen people came forward to speak of this van, covering a period between 1.30 and 6.30 p.m. Press reports at the time indicated that the police believed that this vehicle was being used by a courting couple, although the failure of the driver to come forward to police appeals made the police proffer the opinion that the couple involved a man and 'someone else's wife or girlfriend'. The police so wanted to identify the driver of this vehicle that they were prepared to offer him anonymity should he come forward voluntarily, but the tone of Detective Chief Inspector Bill Little gave away the anxiety of the police when he said, 'Come forward, there will be no embarrassment and the matter will go no further,' before adding the warning, 'If [this] man does not come to us we will eventually find him and we can't make the same promises then.' It does appear that the police initially believed that this vehicle contained potential witnesses, rather than the abductor(s) and killer(s) of Lesley, but so determined were the investigating officers to move the enquiry along expeditiously, that they were not averse to making open threats. If the police did initially think this van contained an innocent courting couple, that view subsequently changed dramatically when DCS Dibb spoke to the press in these terms: '[This van] has got to be found even if we have to check every Morris or Austin five hundredweight van in this part of the country. It might well be a major breakthrough if we can trace this vehicle,' which was believed to be a 1967 or 1968 model.

The threats were replaced by a sense of urgency. DCS Dibb regarded it as 'absolutely necessary' that the van be traced, although he was concerned that the van had been disposed of in the used car trade, or resprayed. He had assembled a team of twenty officers, lead by Detective Inspector Brian Sidebottom, to work full-time on this one aspect of the enquiry, with motor taxation officers helping the search by covering scrap yards and garages. The details of over 6,000 vehicles were considered. But by the end of October 1975, although the police had somehow managed to trace every other vehicle seen in or near the lay-by, the blue-green van had still not been found.

A further car was sighted and referred to, this time a sports car of the Triumph Spitfire or MGB type. It had allegedly been seen, again in a lay-by not far from the moorland grave. This car had been parked at right-angles to the road, with two men standing not far from it, upon the moors themselves. The seemingly innocuous part of the description 'parked at right-angles to the road' barely concealed an obvious element: a car parked with its boot away from the road was perfectly positioned for unloading a body from the boot, without it being visible to motorists speeding past.

When officers set about taking statements from motorists who had driven along the A657 on Sunday, 5 October, and, in particular, from those who had seen anything at or around the lay-by, they were to obtain a plethora of information such that, had the investigation centred or been dependent upon finding a particular car, it would have rapidly foundered. Forty-six witnesses came forward to give statements concerning cars or vans seen in the lay-by between 1.20 p.m. and 11.45 p.m. on Sunday, 5 October. There was little or no unanimity, as to make, colour or the number of occupants. Indeed, a number of witnesses would claim to see different cars in the lay-by at any one time, so that, for example at 3 p.m., one witness claimed to have seen a dark Triumph Spitfire and another said that there was a pale-blue Mini in the lay-by. At 5 p.m., an orange Mini and a cherry/maroon Vauxhall 101 are described by one witness, but another witness claimed to have seen only a pale-green small van, whilst a third described having seen a green Bedford van. Between 9.55 p.m. and 10.15 p.m., a red Viva, a dark-red Mini and a dark Cortina were described by three separate witnesses as being the only car in the lay-by at the time of their sighting. At least five witnesses claimed to have seen something like a dark-coloured Morris 1000 van, possibly a shade of blue, but, again, there was no consistency. There can be no question but that these witnesses were doing their best to be helpful but, in providing the police with such a variable selection of information, they inadvertently added to the confusion and to the amount of police time which would have to be devoted to tracing and eliminating the vehicles mentioned.

DC Michael Roberts drove three possible routes from Rochdale to the lay-by. The three routes were of 9.6, 9.8 and sixteen miles and the police officer's journeys took between fifteen and twenty-nine minutes. If Lesley disappeared at a time between 12.30 and 1.30 p.m., then she would have arrived at the lay-by at some time between 1 p.m. (fifteen minutes maximum from leaving home to being abducted + the shortest journey time to the lay-by, being fifteen minutes) and 2.15 p.m. (fifteen minutes + longest journey time, taking 1.30 as the time of leaving home) or 2.30 p.m. The possible car sightings within that time are:

1	13.20	Light-blue/green Ford
2	13.20	Light-blue Hillman Hunter Estate
3	13.30	Dark saloon
4	13.30	Dark-blue or green Cortina or Vauxhall
5	14.00	Dark, similar to a Cortina

6	14.20	Light-cream or grey 1100
7	14.20	White car
8	14.30	Cream or white Sunbeam Alpine
9	14.30	Pale-yellow Hillman Minx
10	14.30	Light Hillman Hunter
11	14.30–15.30	White car
12	14.30–17.30	White Transit Van

Of those twelve cars, perhaps only numbers 3,4 and 5 allow of the possibility of confusion with the car owned by the man they would eventually charge: a bronze–brown Avenger. The best that the police had would have been the description 'dark, similar to a Cortina'.

It would therefore appear that there was virtually nothing which the police could usefully glean from the many statements regarding cars sighted at or near the lay-by, provided by members of the public in good faith. Eighty-four different vehicles and a number of people were made the subject of reports, but after three weeks Dibb had narrowed the field down to three which were of interest, could not be eliminated and had to be pursued. The white car with primer paint on the doors, the cream van and the blue/green 5cwt Morris 1000 van.

At 1.45 p.m. on the Sunday Christopher Coverdale, a self-employed contractor from Rochdale, drove past the scene. As he approached the lay-by he saw a man and a little girl on the embankment above the lay-by. His attention was on these people, so that he had not noticed any car, he thought it foolhardy to be on the moor in poor weather conditions, especially with a child. He recalled the child was wearing a blue, hip-length gabardine coat with the hood up. He believed the child to be a girl, because he could see uncovered legs. The man was facing towards the road, reaching down the embankment and pulling the child up by the hand. Coverdale described the man as being a 30- to 35-year-old white male, with light-brown or fair hair cut short and giving the appearance of being receding. He was five feet six to five feet eight, plump and dressed in a mid-brown jacket with a check pattern, matching trousers and a beige or mustard-yellow cardigan.

This was the first description obtained of a man and a child. Dibb was anxious to act, and he personally took Coverdale to the lay-by. It was not the cold which caused Jack Dibb to shiver when, asked to show the place where the man and child were standing,

Coverdale pointed out a spot within yards of the place where Lesley had been found.

Within a week of the investigation commencing, police had obtained the names of, and were taking statements from, over 14,000 people using a team of 300 officers. The names had been taken at the road stops on the M62 and from door-to-door enquiries on the Turf Hill Estate. But such a volume of information had its problems. In the absence of any computerised system which could scan the field of information and draw from it any repetitive concept (be it a type or colour of car, or a description of a person or persons) which might lead to a single identifiable source, it was virtually impossible for the police to use the information gleaned to assist in identifying a suspect. Whilst the information might be used *after* a suspect had been identified, to confirm the identification, it was apparent that the police needed assistance from some other source to find the man they were looking for.

The police had quickly formed the view, and DCS Jack Dibb had expressed that view in the media, that the motive for the killing was 'definitely sexual' and that the killer was a local man. Moreover, they believed the man to be 'mentally deranged with sexual deviations' and being in need of urgent treatment. This theory is, with hindsight, of great interest. The police, at an early stage, were speaking of a man whose sexual urges went beyond mere perversion. If there exists such a thing as a 'normal' paedophiliac, it appears to be quite clear that the person whom the police sought was regarded as being beyond that range of normality. He was mentally ill, to the point that his illness was in need of treatment.

The flow of information from the public related to a wide range of incidents considered suspicious and the geographical spread of these reported incidents was also enormous.

On Tuesday, 7 October 1975 a 6-year-old girl in Denton, Manchester, was lured into a car and given sweets, before the driver of the vehicle indecently assaulted her. The car had been driven on to an unmade road, only yards from the girl's home, and she had screamed and run away after the assault had taken place. This incident took place only two days after the abduction of Lesley, and a day before her body was found. The fact that Lesley's body had not yet been found, and so had not yet been publicised, tended to militate against the Denton attacker being of the 'copycat' variety. Conversely, the fact that the child in Denton had escaped from her attacker, apparently uninjured, represented an argument that it was a wholly unconnected attack, and a mere coincidence.

Nevertheless, Denton is only ten miles from the scene of Lesley's abduction and, with the evidence being equivocal as to whether the two attacks were linked or not, DCS Dibb understandably expressed the view that, 'It would be foolish to disregard the possible links.' He was speaking, of course, with the benefit of the full police report on the circumstances of the Denton assault. He had been provided with a sketchy description of the attacker: 30 to 40, tall and thin with short brown hair.

Of more interest was the description of the car involved. The young girl could only say that it was brown, but a local resident gave a more full description of a car which the police believed was involved. It was a four-door brown Cortina with patches of primer on the front offside wing and the driver's door, J or K registered.[2]

The report on the Denton attack was quickly followed by an alleged attack on a 13-year-old girl in Stockport, Manchester. An attempt was made to entice the girl into a car, and, when that failed, the man concerned had grabbed the girl and tried to drag her into the vehicle. She was able to escape and run away.

A further incident was then reported in Eccles, Greater Manchester, when a man, said to be aged about 30, drew his car alongside a 13-year-old girl as she walked along the street. He had opened the passenger door and attempted to drag the girl into the car, but she had struggled and freed herself before running off.

Although experience has told the police that a few murderers – particularly serial offenders – do travel about the country, it is clear that the vast majority live within a few miles of the victim or the scene of the killing.

It was, therefore, unsurprising that Dibb concentrated his initial enquiries on the Turf Hill Estate, from where the majority of calls were received. Naturally, there was no structure or format to the flow of information, and Dibb was anxious not to miss a potential witness. He had already seen, with Coverdale, that many witnesses were, until 'prodded' by police investigators, unaware of the significance of what they knew or what they had or had not seen. In this latter respect, those people who were on the estate on Sunday, 5 October, who knew Lesley, and had *not* seen her, particularly between twelve noon and 1 p.m., were of significant relevance to the investigation, for they reinforced the belief held by the police investigators that Lesley had already been abducted

---

2 The J registration suffix appeared on cars registered between 1970 and 1971, and the K registration suffix on cars registered between 1971 and 1972.

by 1.30 p.m., that is, before the Molseed family began their search for her.

Dibb would use the information from these people both to trace the last movements of Lesley and, he hoped, to trap the suspect or at least to create a list of potential suspects which might then be cut down. To tap the source of information which the estate represented, Dibb deployed teams of officers on the estate, some to conduct house-to-house enquiries and others to set up roadside check-points, questioning all motorists and pedestrians passing through the estate. Each officer was supplied with a carefully prepared pro forma questionnaire, thus ensuring continuity in questioning. Every house on the estate and the surrounding area was visited, as was every business, and every resident or employee was questioned. It was difficult to believe that, on such a close-knit estate, even on the Sabbath, not a single person would have seen the abduction of Lesley. Whereas houses had been visited before, during the search for Lesley, now their occupants and the business employees were being questioned in a desperate search for clues. Dibb had to know who was on the estate, including visitors, that Sunday, for each such person was a potential witness and, until eliminated, a potential suspect. This included women, although the findings of the post-mortem and early forensic investigations made the police more interested in adult and teenage male suspects. Details of their names, ages, dates and places of birth together with a full physical description were recorded on Personal Description Forms (PDFs). They were asked to account for their movements on that Sunday and, in certain instances, up to the morning of the day when the child was found. Where possible the accounts were independently verified or submitted to the incident room for further checks to be made. The killer was believed to be a driver, so details of any vehicles they owned or had access to were obtained. All this information was channelled into the incident room where specially trained staff carefully compiled indices, whilst others analysed the information received, comparing it with reported sightings of persons or vehicles at the scene or on the estate. Checks were made into the criminal records of those interviewed for, it has been found, sexually motivated murderers have often been found to have previous criminal convictions for other forms of violent behaviour.

Dibb wanted no person eliminated from the enquiry until the last piece of information had been drained from them, and until the research had proven them to be unconnected with the crime.

Dibb's first objective was to establish a picture of Lesley's last movements. Far from having insufficient reported sightings Dibb was now faced with a plethora of often conflicting sightings, and he needed to eliminate those which were false or inaccurate. To do this he needed to trace everyone who had seen Lesley on her last errand, for confirming genuine sightings is often less time-consuming than eliminating false ones. However, the latter not only complicate and slow down enquiries, but can, if not disproved or eliminated, seriously damage a prosecution.

Two teenage girls, Julie Cooper and Ann Jones, who both knew Lesley from the estate, told police that they had seen her off the estate, on Oldham Road, between 8 p.m. and 8.15 p.m. that Sunday. They described how they had spoken to her as they waited for their boyfriends near a local supermarket, and how she had walked off towards Rochdale town centre.

This simple tale could have had gross repercussions for the investigation:

i   it significantly altered the time of the last sighting of Lesley;

ii   it therefore opened a further time period of up to seven hours during which her movements would have to be discovered;

iii   it significantly altered the geographic location of Lesley's abduction, from a relatively small housing estate to an area substantially larger, from Oldham Road up to and including large parts of Rochdale;

iv   it raised substantial questions as to the type of girl Lesley really was, changing her from the quiet home-loving obedient child, to one who would strike out to a (to her) major town. In doing so it may have altered the profile of the killer from an abductor who had lured the child with, say, sweets or the promise of finding the cat, to any range of possibilities of a more malevolent kind;

v   it negated much of the investigation which had taken place as to the movement of vehicles in the lay-by, by dramatically altering the possible times at which the child could have been brought to the lay-by.

In the event, the girls, naturally, were re-interviewed and they completely retracted their previous statements. Cooper said that she thought she had seen a girl with Bay City Rollers socks, but knew it was not Lesley. Jones admitted the story was totally false, but neither she nor Cooper would ever say why they had invented their story. The phenomenon of children making up false accounts with no apparent motive save, perhaps, to involve themselves in the 'excitement' is further illustrated by three young boys, Philip Hinchcliffe, Mark Kirkham and Andrew Fletcher, who said that they had spoken to Lesley near to the Spar shop at 2.30 p.m., and that she had put her tongue out at them. The boys later admitted that they had made this story up.

The false and inaccurate reports were not restricted to the estate or to the Sunday. The incident room received a number of calls from the Greater Manchester and Yorkshire areas, with callers' memories having been triggered by photographs of Lesley released to and published by the media. There were sightings of Lesley, or at least lone little girls fitting Lesley's description, in vehicles, taxis or on the street accompanied by men, and these sightings were believed (usually genuinely) by the callers to be suspicious. Reports were even received of sightings of Lesley up until the Tuesday night. The fact that Lesley wore the distinctive Bay City Rollers socks became more of a hindrance than a help, since the group was one of the most popular of 1975, and was adored, in particular, by girls in the 10 to 15 age group. The socks featured in many of the calls. Each sighting had to be investigated: it was simply not possible, not safe, to overlook any call, and so Dibb was obliged to place officers on each call, to check and, where possible, eliminate the sightings. This increased the burden on police resources and enabled the 'trail' from the genuine sightings and the body of Lesley, to the true killer, to go cold.

Another approach taken by the police in their interviews was to ask whether the interviewee had any suspicions as to family members, neighbours, relatives, friends or acquaintances. Any such suspicions would be pursued with total confidentiality as to the source of the information. Dibb's need to glean information about any suspicious event in the area on or around 5 October made this an appropriate approach. He was particularly concerned where there were incidents of drivers of vehicles accosting women or children or attempting to entice them into cars, or where there had been minor sexual offences which had not been reported to the police, and he was particularly interested in any such case where a knife had been brandished. Results were forthcoming. In scenes reminiscent of Nazi Germany or Soviet Russia, people did 'inform' on individuals with whom they were acquainted, simply because of suspicions concerning their behaviour, lifestyle, or previous sexual behaviour. The number of these reports was such as to make the investigating officers wonder how so many incidents could take place in so small a geographical area.

There were numerous reports of men in vehicles following children and lone women. A yellow van, a bronze Cortina, a light-coloured Vauxhall Viva and a light blue-green GPO-type van figured prominently in these reports. The first two vehicles were traced and eliminated (elimination being achieved by forensic examination of the vehicles) but the Viva and the GPO-type van were never traced. None of these reports, however, involved the driver attempting to force the person accosted into the van, they merely involved offers of lifts. There were reports of an indecent exposure by a driver, and even of a man masturbating, but in each case some element of the report enabled elimination to take place.

Local schoolteachers reported to the police a man who had been disturbed on several occasions taking photographs of children in school playgrounds. When confronted he spoke English with a foreign accent, and purported to be a Canadian on holiday. He was 35 to 40 years old, six foot two, slim build with collar-length sandy hair. It is not believed that he was ever traced.

Thus the enquiry team was supplied with a steady stream of suspects. Just as any purported sighting of Lesley had to be investigated, just as any suspicious incidents had to be compared to what was then known, just as in all these cases there were mistakes, errors and complete fabrications, so too did the police have to investigate and eliminate any individual at whom the finger of suspicion had been pointed. In some cases this was difficult, when individuals were unable to provide information as to their movements that could be corroborated: how could a single man, living alone, 'prove' that he had spent Sunday, 5 October alone at home? In many cases, arrests were necessary to enable clothing and vehicles to be subjected to forensic examination, and this was particularly so where the index of suspicion was raised by previous convictions, type of vehicle or current unusual behaviour.

Professor Gee, having considered the results of his findings more carefully, contacted Dibb and Holland with information which was to open up a further avenue of investigation. He had come to the conclusion that the killer could have cut his own hand in the attack. The knife had struck underlying bones with force, and this might have caused his hand to slide off the handle on to the blade. Thus the enquiry team carried out checks with local hospitals, for men attending for treatment for any such injury.

Professor Gee also thought that the killer's clothing might have been stained with either his or Lesley's blood. Dibb therefore circulated surrounding police forces requesting enquiries be made of dry cleaners, a method which at one time was frequently utilised in murder enquiries.

Ronald Outteridge was also keeping the police abreast of his investigations, although, as yet, he had little to offer by way of assistance. He had found no traces of foreign blood on Lesley's clothing and the semen staining was of insufficient quantity to enable blood grouping to take place. He had, however, found traces of white powder on the clothing, and this was found to contain maize starch, which is an ingredient of wallpaper paste. The investigating team had been informed that workmen employed on local housing renovation were associating with and befriending local schoolgirls, who would visit the redevelopment site. All of these men were therefore interviewed, as were the employees of a local firm connected with painting and decorating.

As it was believed that the killer could have committed sexual offences previously, it was necessary for police records in surrounding areas to be searched for 'MO Suspects', that is persons who had committed offences with a *modus operandi* similar to that in the instant case. A similar search went on where the police held records of unsolved sexual offences or violence against children. Local mental hospitals and psychiatric units were checked for absconders and people on weekend release. 'Normal people would not do this' is such a common expression in the face of the killing of a child, that somehow great comfort is taken from the assertion that the killer must be mentally ill. It is an untrue proposition, and, like many propositions in the Molseed case, was to prove unhelpful. All that the sweeps and searches and enquiries achieved was an increase in the number of persons to be eliminated and in extra work for the police.

The senior officers held private meetings on a regular basis to assess progress and evaluate the direction being taken and what new lines were developing. From these private debates emerged the view that the killer, whether as a result of being injured in the attack or disturbed by the realisation of what he had done, had stayed off work, not attended school or college, or even moved away from his home temporarily, perhaps even moved out of the area. They also considered that local traders, ice-cream men, milkmen or a person who had worked at or near Lesley's home could have befriended Lesley, as could taxi and minibus drivers who were involved in taking Lesley and her school friends to their special school.

More interviews, more eliminations, more overstretched resources subjected to further strain, but nothing was discovered. For all the manhours invested in the case, for all Dibb's wish that no one be eliminated from the enquiry until the last piece of information had been drained from them and for all his intention to trace everyone who had seen Lesley on her last errand, Jack Dibb failed in his objectives. He was never able to trace a single witness who saw the abduction of Lesley that October day.

At the same time as the net of enquiry was swept across large sections of the community, those responsible for the investigation also turned their attentions to the central figures, Lesley Molseed's family. Lesley may have been known to many as a happy and friendly child, who would talk to passers-by, although there was also strong evidence to support the contention that she would not go off willingly with anybody that she did not know, nor would she get into a stranger's car. But unpalatable though it may have been, the enquiry had to look at the converse picture: that she had gone, not abducted by a stranger, but willingly with someone she knew, and that included her family. It is an unpleasant but true fact that over ninety per cent of murders in Britain are committed by persons who know the victim. The vast majority of those murders are committed in domestic or family circumstances. With those figures very much in mind, Dibb had little difficulty in ordering that the family would have to be considered, they would have to be eliminated, and this applied even to Lesley's sister Julie's former boyfriends and to Danny Molseed's best friend, John Conroy.

Officers were allocated to research the family, and Detective Constable Jim Butterworth was appointed family liaison officer. His function, besides attending to the family's welfare needs, was to obtain intimate details of their daily routines and relationships. The house-to-house team had reported the public face of the family, which portrayed Lesley as a friendly, happy-go-lucky child who came from a stable family background. The picture obtained by the family enquiry team was significantly different.

Lesley Molseed and her siblings were still, legally, called Anderson, and had assumed the name Molseed only when April began to live with the then-married Danny Molseed. The four children were the issue of April's marriage to Frederick Anderson, a marriage which was celebrated in Anderson's home town of Glasgow on 10 October 1958. Julie Jane Anderson was their first child, born on 2 July 1959. Next came Laura Agnes in December 1961, Frederick Augustin in August 1963, and Lesley herself on 7 August 1964.

Lesley had been born with a heart condition which caused her to be a weak and frail baby, who, at the age of 3, required an emergency pulmonary valvotomy operation. The Anderson family lived in the Springburn area of Glasgow, despite April being a Londoner by birth. Life in the household was far from tranquil. Frederick Anderson, six years older than his wife, was an acknowledged 'man's man', who did not adjust well to the role of being a father. The constant crying and demands of four children, and the extra attention required by Lesley caused friction, which invariably resulted in him storming out of the house in a temper.

In a not-atypical fashion, April, lacking the support of her husband, found both care and succour from another man, 31-year-old Danny Molseed, whom she had met in 1965. As their relationship developed, April was pleasantly surprised to find that Danny not only paid her unaccustomed attention, but that he also had a genuinely caring attitude towards the children, and in particular to Lesley. For April, life with Anderson continued to deteriorate whilst her relationship with Danny Molseed intensified, so much so that, in February 1966, when Frederick Anderson went on a government training course in Gloucester, April and Danny took Lesley and her brother Freddie and ran to Rochdale. Julie and Laura were left in Glasgow with their paternal grandparents. When Anderson returned to Glasgow to find his family disintegrated, he travelled to Rochdale in an attempt to effect a reconciliation. This failed, and he went back to Glasgow where he placed his two daughters in local authority care. This did not prevent him periodically visiting April to make further attempts to patch up their still-extant marriage, and in 1967 he took employment at Carrier Brothers in Rochdale and moved to the area, thus being able to be near to April and to Lesley and Freddie.

Whether the presence of Anderson caused April to become unsettled, she became unsure of her relationship with Danny Molseed and, in due course, she moved out of the flat she shared with Danny and set up home at 11 Delamere Road with her husband and their four children.

Unfortunately, April was pregnant with Danny's child, and even though Anderson believed there was a chance that the child was his he insisted that it be adopted, a course which was followed when a boy was born in May 1967. The relationship with Frederick began to break down again within five weeks of their reunion, and all attempts at reconciliation eventually failed when April was admitted to Birch Hill Hospital for psychiatric treatment. On her release, Danny moved into the house to look after her, and as the tenancy was in April's name Anderson had little choice but to move out, although he was to remain in touch with the children. This caused an unsettled environment, especially for Lesley and Freddie. Anderson responded to this by restricting his contact with the two older girls. Julie, Anderson's favourite, did not like living with Danny Molseed. It mattered little for Lesley: she had had little contact with Anderson and had come to regard Danny as her natural father. He had seen her in hospital immediately after her operation and had adopted a protective and fatherly stance towards her. April later said she believed it was Danny Molseed's paternal affection towards Lesley which motivated him to live with her.

Lesley's condition required ongoing treatment, and she was under the continuing care of Dr Watson, a consultant paediatrician at the Royal Manchester Hospital. At her last appointment in July 1975 she complained of feeling tired, and the doctor felt that this was due to a narrowing of the heart valves. But he decided the repair could be held in abeyance until she was older. Lesley had a particular syndrome which gave her an 'elfin-like' appearance, particularly facially, and a pleasant and very friendly disposition. She had a low IQ and attended High Birch Special School, for educationally disadvantaged children. There, despite her physical deficiencies, she took part in all normal recreational activities, including games, PE and swimming. At home she was equally active, regularly playing in the street with other children and attending the local youth club held in Kingsway School. Lesley Molseed had inadequacies, both physical and mental, but she quietly and without bother or drama dealt with them with the assistance of her family. In every other respect she was as a normal child: enjoying her schoolwork, enjoying her play, enjoying her innocence in the summer of 1975.

April and Frederick Anderson had finally divorced in September 1972, but April did not marry Danny until February 1975, an event which caused some surprise in the Turf Hill community, who believed them to be already man and wife. Despite the marriage, tension and turmoil remained substantial features of the family's life, particularly between Danny and Julie. Theirs was a relationship built on mutual dislike, particularly when, as he often did, Danny would express his disapproval of Julie's boyfriends.

Domestic circumstances deteriorated still further as both parents became heavy drinkers, alcohol being the mainstay of their social life, and further disharmony was inevitable when April, unable to derive sufficient comfort and love from Danny, began to seek the attentions of other men. The family was distant from other relatives and April made only occasional visits to her brother in London when circumstances in the family home became unbearable.

By 1974 the home was in turmoil. Danny had lost his job, the family was heavily in debt and rent arrears were beginning to mount up. As a result of allegations made by various neighbours about the welfare of the children, the social services visited the family, on one occasion finding Lesley and Freddie in the care of their 12-year-old sister Laura while Danny and April were in the pub. Julie had moved out to live with Fred Anderson. She had run away from home, and when interviewed by the police it became clear that she was petrified to return home. She cited violent arguments with Danny over her boyfriends as the reason for her running away.

Danny Molseed was not to find employment until November 1974, a job he was still holding at the time of Lesley's disappearance. Even this work, however, and the assistance of welfare agencies with financial help, did not alter their state of indebtedness. It appears to have been common knowledge that the Molseeds were in debt, so much so that Brent Davies, who had a bread round on the estate, refused to give April Molseed a loaf of bread 'on tick' on the Saturday afternoon preceding Lesley's disappearance, because he was owed money by her. Davies would later blame himself for Lesley's death, for it was his refusal that necessitated April sending Lesley to the shops on the Sunday.

Given the volatile relationship in the household, the assertions by Julie of Danny's temper, and the depth of affection which he had for Lesley, DCS Dibb considered it essential to add Danny Molseed's name to the ever-growing list of persons to be considered and eliminated. Dibb also ordered all of Lesley's clothing to be taken for forensic examination, to eliminate any question of previous sexual abuse on her.

By the end of October 1975 Dibb had so much, and so little. He had dozens of vehicles, cars and vans, hundreds of statements of sightings, movements, actions and circumstances, a plethora of exhibits, and only two really valuable pieces of information.

One was from Mrs Emma Tong who had seen a small girl in a cream car, parked on Well-i'-th'-Lane, Rochdale – some 800 yards from the Turf Hill Estate – on Sunday, 5 October at 1.30 p.m. Mrs Tong became convinced that the child was Lesley.

The other was Mr Coverdale's statement regarding his sighting of a man with a girl in a blue gabardine coat, at about 1.45 p.m. on Sunday, 5 October, climbing the embankment above the lay-by. Apart from her killer, he was, quite possibly, the last person to see Lesley Molseed alive.

Both of these statements illustrate the merits of turning the sweeping net inward on the Molseed family. The child in Well-i'-th'-Lane was sitting in the car, looking down. She was not struggling to get out of the car or otherwise make good her escape. She smiled at Mrs Tong, she did not open a car window and scream for help. The child at the lay-by was being helped up the embankment, she was not being dragged against her will. At worst these two statements show nothing more than that the child was being lured, duped and deceived into taking the car journey which lead to her death. At best, they showed that the child knew her killer, and had nothing to fear from him. The latter may not mean that the killer could only come from her immediate family (meaning Danny Molseed or Frederick Anderson, since the children had no contact with other relatives) but it would narrow the field to the family, to neighbours, to schoolteachers or youth group assistants.

But there was little to go on, despite the mass of information which was overwhelming the incident room. It had become apparent that a quick result to the enquiry would not be found. All the most obvious and common solutions to murder enquiries had been followed with no result.

In truth, there was little substantial evidence to pursue, apart from the enquiries flowing from the Tong and Coverdale statements and the suggestions of the car involved. Twenty-two vehicles had been swept and subjected to Sellotape lifts, fifteen suspects had had their clothing subjected to forensic examination, 335 other articles had been examined forensically, including fifteen knives which had been found on the moors or the estate, or in the possession of suspects. Nothing had been found.

Substantial numbers of men had been eliminated, including Danny Molseed and Frederick Anderson, family friends, local traders and other local suspects, but it had not enabled progress towards a positive identification. All that it had done was to create a profile of the murderer, a man who was believed to have used a knife which had a blade three and a half inches long and seven sixteenths of an inch wide. The police believed that the offender was a man who was sexually active and with a liking for children. He may have come to the attention of the police or other bodies in the past for sexual or other peculiar behaviour. He would be able to drive and would have access to a vehicle which might be a turquoise Morris 1000 van or a light-coloured Ford Anglia or Cortina – cars sighted at the lay-by but still not traced by police. He might be in his thirties and approximately five foot six inches tall, and it was also believed that he would be unable to verify his movements between twelve noon and 3 p.m. on the Sunday, and possibly for a longer period. He may have cut his hand and his clothing may have been stained, certainly with traces of Lesley's blood, possibly with wallpaper paste remnants. It was also felt, at least by the senior officers, that the person they were seeking had not merely behavioural problems, but mental health problems, too.

The officers thought the identity of the killer might be revealed by tracing the persons responsible for the numerous sexually related incidents reported to them, especially those of indecent exposure on the estate. They prioritised these enquiries and restructured the investigations in line with their review.

And then Dibb was called back to West Yorkshire to head another murder enquiry in the Bradford area. He would retain an overview of the Molseed case but essentially the case was now firmly in the hands of Dick Holland. Holland was immediately promoted from detective chief inspector to detective super-intendent, a great personal advance for him based entirely on his ability and on previous successes.

CHAPTER FIVE

Bye Bye, Baby

The undertakers, who had collected Lesley's cleaned and reconstructed body from a police mortuary, paid brief respects to April and Danny before gently closing the front door behind them. They would return later that morning to take the child for burial. April and Julie had selected a spot close to a clump of trees, where a family of wild rabbits played. In the bright October sunshine the place had seemed perfect, for Lel had loved all animals. Now she could rest among them.

For a couple of minutes after the men in black had gone, no one could muster the courage to enter the front room with its curtains closed, where the small coffin had been placed. Julie, the 16-year-old sister whom Lesley had called Jupes, had placed a tentative hand on the door to the room with the will of a teenager and, wondering if the lid of the coffin would be opened or not, she had eased the door open. Entering the darkened room, Julie saw the cat, Tiger, curled up on the coffin lid, settling down to sleep. It could have been seen as a desecration, but to Julie it was somehow natural that the family pet should be with her younger sister at this moment of passing. Julie crept up to the coffin, subliminally wondering whether she had done so to avoid disturbing the cat or Lesley, and she gazed at the inscription on the brass plate fixed to the lid. It read, simply, 'Lesley Molseed. Died October 8 1975.' Julie cried, because the inscription brought home grim reality. Lesley was not coming back. And Julie cried because the inscription was wrong. Lesley had been found on 8 October, but it was thought that she had died on the day she had gone missing, 5 October 1975. It was that date which would ever be fixed in the Molseed collective memory. The discrepancy, whatever the reason for it, greatly upset Julie and all her family who had cared so very deeply for the child who was now gone.

Julie stared at the coffin, yearning to see her beloved Lel, but afraid to move the lid. She had wanted to see Lesley before she came home from the undertaker's, but all the family had advised against it. 'Remember Lesley as she was in life,' the undertaker had solemnly said. She had wondered if that was because her sister's face had been distorted by the violence and stab wounds administered. She thought about that gap-toothed grin, and hoped that the memory of that smile would restore unity to the Molseed household.

In the darkened room the pregnant teenager was immersed in thought as she stood alone by the coffin, but on this day her thoughts were only of Lesley. It seemed that Lesley had never been destined for a long life; she had been blighted since birth. There was the operation on her heart and the fact that Lesley's growth had been suppressed, making her small and skinny, but Julie managed a half-smile as she recalled her mother's description of Lel. 'Lesley is not skinny, she is dainty.' A family plan to emigrate to Australia had been vetoed by the Australian Immigration Service because of Lesley's medical condition. But for the hole in the heart the family would have emigrated. 'Then I would not have been pregnant,' thought Julie, 'and Lesley's kidnapper would have murdered some other little girl, and I would not be watching this cat sitting on my sister's coffin.'

Julie recalled that Lesley had previously brushed with death, on three occasions. She had poked a hair clip into an electric socket and been blown across the room, somehow escaping serious injury. Lel explained that she had been copying a repair she had seen her electrician stepfather perform many times. Later, on a family holiday in Spain, the lightweight Lesley had been swept off her feet by a wave which would have had little effect on her more robust contemporaries. Only the speed of April dashing into the sea had saved the 7-year-old child from drowning.

The last occasion had been when Lesley's dressing gown had brushed against a fire, catching light and engulfing the child in flames. Again it had been April who had saved her, leaping from her bed when she had heard her daughter's screams and rushing to the child in time to smother the flames with a blanket. Lesley had suffered burns to her leg which required hospital treatment.

But this time there had been no one to hear the child's screams. This time there had been no April racing to the scene to rescue her daughter. This time had been the last time that Lesley would take on death. This time she had lost.

April's mind too had drifted. The family had been overwhelmed with comfort and sympathy and warmth from everyone they had come in contact with since Lesley's disappearance, save for one man. Inexplicably, when she came to gaze at the tiny coffin, April's thoughts went to that man. He had appeared at the Molseeds' door the day after April had identified Lesley's body. He was from the Department of Health and Social Security he explained, and whilst he apologised for intruding at a time of such grief, he wanted to collect Lesley's family allowance coupons. It was dutiful callousness, April had thought at the time. They have to make sure we don't steal their precious money, for a child on whom no further money will be spent. Why should she have to think of such things at this time?

The dozing Tiger was ushered off the coffin. Behind April was her previous husband Fred Anderson alongside Lesley's uncle, Bobby Garrett, who in turn comforted 12-year-old Freddie, the brother who had missed his turn on the chores duty rota that Sunday afternoon. Reverend Ramage recited the Lord's Prayer, then each member of the family laid a rose on the coffin.

Outside, the October garden was in full bloom, an appearance created by the plethora of wreaths, bouquets and single flowers which had been laid by Lesley's classmates at High Birch School, by friends, by family, by strangers, by the anonymous who felt the Molseeds' grief as if they themselves had borne the child. A solitary policeman guarded the sea of floral tributes. The curtains were drawn in every house in the street, a sign of respect which mirrored the drawn curtains of April's house. Behind those curtains Lesley's family enjoyed a last moment of privacy, on what was to be a day of grief shared by the whole town of Rochdale. Newspaper reporters and photographers had encamped on the opposite side of Delamere Road, separate huddles indicating separate newspapers, each anxious to secure both written and photographic memories of the day. Child murders remained mercifully rare, and it was because of that very scarcity that newspaper sales were increased when they occurred. Every reader, in Rochdale and in England, would feel in their heart for the pain of the Molseeds.

One evening newspaper reporter, anxious about his early deadline, had pre-penned the opening paragraphs of his story, anticipating the scene now unfolding. He had written: 'Murdered schoolgirl Lesley Molseed was carried from her home in a coffin today followed by her weeping mother.' But he was obliged to make a hasty change. April Molseed was not weeping. She had not wept since the day she had identified her daughter's body. No one could understand how that could be, but it is impossible for anyone who had not walked in April's shoes to know of the utter desolation and emptiness that pervaded her existence.

Lesley's small coffin, its size emphasising the cruelty of a young life cut short, was carried past the floral tributes lying either side of the garden path. Little Lel had been for a ride in a car on Sunday, 5 October 1975. Today she would take another ride. The coffin was slid into the back of the hearse, and Lesley Molseed's final journey began.

The cortège travelled slowly along roads lined by men and women, boys and girls. Rochdale does not hold many claims to fame. Gracie Fields, the entertainer and Cyril Smith, the outsize politician, had been the most famous of the town's sons and daughters. Now those names were joined by Lesley Molseed. Schoolchildren downed pens and rulers, and were allowed to stand in silence by the kerbside as Lesley went by. Workers downed tools, and men doffed caps in the traditional manner. The conscience of an entire town was on grim display, with its community refusing to admit out loud that a savage child killer was probably within its midst.

They sang Lesley's favourite hymn, 'Morning Has Broken' at Trinity Church, in a service relayed by tannoy to the crowd outside. Reverend Ramage recalled the words of Jesus: 'Suffer the little children to come unto me.' Julie Molseed, deeply emotional, felt anger welling inside her and wondered what sort of God would let her sister die so terribly. How could He let such good be killed this way? How could He let her killer continue with his evil and worthless life, when Lesley, who had endured so much in her life, was buried in a wooden casket?

Lesley was laid to rest, in the shade of the trees with the wild rabbits waiting to play, wearing a party dress and coffee-coloured coat with fluffy-edged cuffs and hood. Around her neck was a gold love-heart which Julie had given to the undertaker. On her finger was April's favourite dress ring which Lesley had always admired, hoping one day that she might wear it when she became a young woman. As the coffin was lowered into the ground, April stood with head bowed and eyes dry, her right hand clutching soil, which she slowly sprinkled after the daughter whose strong will to live had been so callously crushed on a carpet of moorland heather. Some days later, April told her local newspaper: 'No one knows until they have stood by their child's grave, how far down six feet seems.'

In the days following the revelation of Lesley's disappearance and death, Rochdale's, and in particular the Turf Hill Estate's, community moved towards the spirit which had in days gone by encapsulated the essence of a hundred English industrial towns. Immediate neighbours had sought to offer condolence and, if possible assistance to the grieving family, while together they and those more geographically distant had applied their minds and hearts to aiding the police in solving this horrendous crime. The feelings and emotions of Rochdale's citizens had swollen and grown as the days passed leading to the funeral of the child. Then came change. It was as if the community had done its best to render service to the family and to the police. Now that they could do no more, they settled back into their everyday existences. They retained an avid interest in any development in the case, and would frequently enquire of investigating officers whether any progress had been made, but with the passage of time came a relaxation of the fears which had guided their daily lives in the immediate aftermath of the murder.

At first the residents of the Turf Hill Estate protected their children with a passion. Children were escorted to and from school, and were forbidden to play on the streets. For a while, vigilante patrols roamed the streets in darkness. But then, perhaps inevitably, time passed, emotions subsided and guards were dropped . . .

Friday, 7 November 1975, a little over a month since the child's terrible passing. A white cross adorned her grave, and the photograph of April and Danny Molseed standing, heads bowed, adjacent to that grave soon adorned the pages of the local papers. It was published in accordance with the express wishes of April Molseed. Although only weeks had passed since her daughter's abduction and murder, Mrs Molseed wondered at the attitudes of parents living nearby. Their children had returned to playing outside in the dark, wintry streets, alone and without any parental supervision. Lesley's death appeared to have been forgotten. Mrs Molseed described the story of her daughter's tragic death as being 'a ten-day wonder', as she declaimed, 'I'm afraid [the children's] mothers don't understand it could happen to them,' and she had said that the graveside photograph should be published 'to show mothers it can and could happen to them'.

CHAPTER SIX

Of Sugar and Spice

As October had come to a close, it was clear that the case had reached something of a hiatus, and that some further impetus was needed if the investigation was to make further progress. It was with that in mind that Dick Holland renewed appeals to the public through the media. General information was still flowing into the incident room, but Holland did not want generalities, he needed specifics. He needed specific information concerning the Morris 1000 van, the light-coloured car and, importantly, concerning offences involving indecency. In addition, Holland made an appeal to one person, a person whom he did not know, but strongly believed existed. That person, in Holland's opinion, knew the identity of the killer, but was shielding him out of a misplaced sense of loyalty. Holland appealed to that unknown individual to come forward.

Use of the media was a carefully approached tactic. From the outset Dibb and Holland had to determine what information should be withheld, and two matters in particular remained only with the police: the fact that the killer had ejaculated over Lesley and that her underclothes had not been removed. Withholding this information had two purposes. Firstly, it enabled cranks, persons who made false confessions, to be eliminated. If they failed to mention the two withheld facts, it would be unlikely that they were genuinely confessing. The second reason was that these facts would enable the true killer to be identified, since only the actual killer would be able to specify these facts in the course of making a confession. In 1975 this was crucial, since it would enable a prosecutor to point to the two specific matters as irrefutable evidence that the confession was genuine.

As the appeals continued and information came in, the investigation team deliberately investigated every act of indecency which was brought to their attention. Many were discounted; others were pursued even though it was believed unlikely that anything useful to the murder enquiry would be found, but the investigative course was essential if no stone was to be left unturned, however remote the chances were.

In 1975 the principle of 'best chance' did not apply. Today, financial and human resource constraints imposed on investigators, together with increased and competing demands on the modern police force have brought a new discipline to murder enquiries. Officers are now committed to those enquiries which are regarded as having the best prospect of producing a detection, and investigations are structured on a computer which enables prioritisation of lines of enquiry, at any given time in the investigation. This methodology has to be compared with the systems in place only twenty years ago, when much depended on the personal knowledge of individual officers as to a particular line of enquiry, with no certainty that an officer would be aware of the stage other enquiries had reached. Curiously, this method had an advantage over the 'modern' system in that it enabled a substantial number of other crimes to be detected in the course of a murder investigation, a result lacking in the more refined approach of the 1990s.

Of course, even at that time enquiries were prioritised. Dick Holland used experience, personal knowledge and instinct to select what he considered to be the first priority, which were reports of indecency which were similar to those of Lesley's abduction or geographically proximate to the Molseed case. In the former category local detectives believed that the abduction of an 8-year-old girl earlier in 1975 might provide a link.

At 11 a.m. on Tuesday, 12 August 1975 'Jennifer'[1] was playing with her 7-year-old sister 'Francine' by the side of the Leeds Manchester Canal at Miles Platting, near Manchester. They were fishing for tiddlers using a small fishing net, keeping their catch in a little blue bucket. A man, who later called himself 'John' came and stood near them before looking down into the water at the fish, and then turning and smiling at the two girls. He said 'Hello' and the girls both answered him 'Hello', before Francine wandered off. John then engaged Jennifer in conversation about the fish, before offering to take her to a park where there were lots more fish. He took her in a white car, past a City of Salford road sign and to a shop, where he bought her mints and a can of Pepsi Cola. He had told her that he lived near the shop, but had then taken

---

1 The names used here have been changed to protect identities.

her by car to another place which he said was near Heaton Park. He had driven on, however, until he came to a car park and, from there, led the child on foot across a field and to a much larger field where they sat down. There, the man undressed Jennifer, removed his trousers and underpants and lay on top of her, kissing and sucking her body whilst he attempted to have intercourse with her. He failed to do so, but did ejaculate on to her stomach.

Even after he had dressed, John kept the child with him, she wearing only her underpants. He took her to swim in a nearby pond, after which he again took her to a field where he repeated the previous sexual assault, before taking her back to the canalside where he had first met her.

Jennifer had been abducted for a three-hour period, but, despite her ordeal, she was able to give police to whom her mother reported the incident a graphic and detailed account of the events of that day. So accurate were the details that the police were able to trace a man to whom Jennifer had spoken at the pond where she and John had swum, and he was able to confirm Jennifer's description of John as being a well-built, muscular man of 33 to 35 years of age, with short, well-groomed black hair. He was about five feet ten inches tall, had a distinctively hairy chest, a deep suntan and wore a silver watch. Despite the description, John was never caught.

The team investigating Lesley's murder considered this report, and believed that it gave them some possible insight into what may have happened to Lesley during the last hours of her life, and, in particular, how very easy it was to abduct, or take away, an un-suspecting and trusting child, even where, as in the case of John and Jennifer, other members of the public are in the immediate proximity.

In truth, it must be asked quite how useful the John/Jennifer case was to the investigating officers in the Molseed case. It was a child abduction case involving a little girl, and the perpetrator had ejaculated on to the child, but in many respects it was so very different. The obvious difference is that Jennifer was not subjected to any violence at all. Lesley was not undressed in what might be termed 'the sexual phase' of the incident, and her killer had ejaculated on to her clothing. John had attempted to rape Jennifer, but there was no evidence whatsoever that Lesley's killer had attempted to have sexual intercourse with her, or had interfered with her in any sexual way at all. As for the other features of the Jennifer case, they indicated only that a child abductor might use sweets and lemonade to lure a child, and that much must have been obvious to the experienced police officers.

It would appear, however, that the police were aware of the substantial differences between the two cases, and that their interest had been aroused simply by reason of the fact of abduction of a young girl and the fact of ejaculation. The case illustrates the methodology being used by the police at this stage in the investigation. It was a method with many merits, and those merits would become patently clear in two cases much closer to Lesley Molseed's home, lifestyle and the date of her death.

At about 8.15 p.m. on Friday, 3 October 1975 two girls called Ann Marie Storto and Sheila Woodhead, both aged 10, were walking home from the Kingsway Youth Club in Rochdale, of which Lesley was a member. As the girls approached the clinic on the corner of Stiups Lane and Kingsway, they saw a man in the clinic porchway, leaning against the wall with one hand in his pocket, who appeared to be staring at them. Through real or imagined fear, the girls walked away, at which point they were later to say that the man began to follow them, whereupon they both ran back to the youth club. They described the man as being about five feet ten inches tall, thin, with dark hair, wearing a dark overcoat and a dark wool knitted printed skull cap. They also described a large dark-green or yellow car in the area, parked with its radio playing very loud.

A part-time youth leader at the club, a Mr Alfred Sutcliffe, was told that a man had stopped the two girls, but that some older girls would walk Ann Marie and Sheila home. As a precaution Mr Sutcliffe walked behind the group of girls to Ann Marie's house, and then walked the older girls back to the club, where he telephoned the police. He did not see any men in the area, and Police Constable Stefan Kowal, who attended at the youth club at about 8.45 p.m. and conducted a search of the immediate vicinity was also unable to find anyone.

There is very little that is remarkable in the account of the two girls, or of the two adults who gave statements concerning this incident, but it began to take on rather different proportions and have yet more significance when statements were taken from other children who had been in the youth club that Friday night.

Debbie Brown, who was then 13 years old, told the police that Ann Marie Storto had said that the man at the clinic had followed and tried to stop her and Sheila, and that he had had a knife. She said that herself, Maxine Buckley and Debra Mills (both aged 12) then walked the younger girls home.

According to Debbie Brown, Maxine Buckley and Debra Mills, there then followed an incident in which one of these girls was to say that a man exposed himself, but the accounts of the three girls vary so much, and the incident itself has so much relevance in the later proceedings, that there is some value in examining the details. It should be borne in mind that neither Ann Marie Storto nor Sheila Woodhead reported any incident of indecent exposure on the night of 3 October 1975. Nor, of course, did Alfred Sutcliffe, the youth club worker who had walked behind the group of girls on the way home.

Debbie Brown gave two statements to the police, one made on 8 October and the second on 9 October.

In her first statement she said that she had been in the youth club with Ann Marie and Sheila, and that Ann Marie had gone outside (alone) and had then come running back in, whereupon all three of them – that is, herself, Ann Marie and Sheila – had gone outside and seen a man, aged 30 to 40, five foot nine inches tall, with a long thin face and receding hair, wearing a dark beret, grey trousers and black coat and shoes. The man had opened his coat and exposed himself, dropping his trousers to reveal a scar down his left leg which ran down to his knee. They had all gone back into the club and told Alfred Sutcliffe, *who had chased the man away*. Debbie Brown reported seeing a dark car with its window open and music coming from the radio.

In Debbie Brown's second statement, made only a day later, she said that after Ann Marie Storto had first told her about the man, they had told Alfred Sutcliffe and then herself, Debra Mills and Maxine Buckley had walked the younger girls home. Apart from the change in the sequence of events and the absence of any reference in the second statement to Mr Sutcliffe chasing the man, this later statement is remarkable in that it incorporates Debra Mills and Maxine Buckley as being present during and witnesses to the indecent exposure, for the first time.[2]

Debra Mills made two statements concerning this incident: on 9 October and then 2 January 1976. In those statements she spoke of leaving the youth club with Miss Brown, Miss Buckley and the two younger girls, when they saw a man standing on the footpath, 'staring at us'. Mr Sutcliffe had then approached and they had

2 Debbie Brown made a further statement, also dated 9 October, in which she related an incident during the summer of 1975 when a fat man in a blue van had shouted to her, 'Come on darling you can come for a ride.'

told him about the man, but the man had then disappeared. She made no reference at all to any incident of indecent exposure.

Maxine Buckley's first statement was made on 9 October, and she too spoke of leaving the club with Debbie, Debra and the two younger girls, and of seeing a thin man in a beret who had stared at them, but had disappeared before Mr Sutcliffe had come on to the scene. She too had seen a green car with loud music playing through an open window. She had telephoned her mother who had, in turn, telephoned the police. She made a further statement in December 1975, but that statement too made no reference to any indecent exposure on 3 October. Maxine was never to change her version of the night's events and police found her to be a consistent and reliable witness.

Other children made statements concerning Friday, 3 October. Beverley Mullins, aged 12, described seeing a man outside the clinic wearing 'a black mask with two eye holes, two nostril holes and a mouth hole', although in a later statement she amended this vivid and detailed description to 'a black beret . . . like girl guides wear'. Colin Peers, aged 12, spoke of the man wearing 'a dark trilby hat' and having a pair of binoculars around his neck. Sarah Lord, a 10-year-old girl, made no reference to either a hat or binoculars. Sarah spoke of seeing the man through the youth club windows at which time she thought he had a knife. Sarah's statement had made no reference to any peculiarity in the man's walk although, ominously perhaps, she had added that she had seen the man again the next day: in Delamere Road.

Only Debbie Brown, in her first statement to the police, made reference to an incident of indecent exposure on 3 October. It might be easier to dismiss her statement as merely wild exaggeration (such as those of Beverley Mullins concerning a ski-mask) or an error, rather than to assert that she was lying, but subsequent events might point more forcefully to her being deliberately misleading.

The officers involved in the investigation were doubtful concerning the statements given by the younger children, particularly since only those of Ann Marie Storto and Sheila Woodhead matched those given by Alfred Sutcliffe. Some support for Miss Brown's allegation of indecent exposure was to come, however, and that support came from a source apparently quite separate from and independent of the younger children. Three older girls, aged between 16 and 18, gave statements to the police concerning the night of 3 October.

Catherine 'Kitty' Burke, Gillian Cleave and Pamela Hind had approached the youth club at about 9.50 p.m., and had seen a man standing in the clinic doorway. He had jumped out in front of Kitty and Pamela and had then opened his coat. His trousers fell down to his ankles and his penis was exposed, and he had said, 'When I get you two bastards I'll shove this right up you.' The man was described as being aged 35 to 40, fairly tall and broadly built, with dark collar-length hair, and wearing a dark coat, trousers and a dark flat cap. Pamela Hind, in her statement, gave a version of events which differed slightly from that of her friend Kitty. Rather than the man dropping his trousers, she said that he had unzipped them and taken his erect penis out. He had shouted, 'Come here, let me ram this up you,' as the girls had run away. Gillian was not interviewed until some ten days later, and all that she was able to recall was Pamela and Catherine running up to her, saying, 'Run, he's got his thing out.' Her description was of a man between five feet ten and five feet eleven, 30 to 40 and well-built, but not fat, with dark collar-length hair. In merely repeating her friends' words, there was no suggestion that Gillian was lying about the event.

The incident of 3 October was not one which could readily be connected with any identifiable man, but it was the first of two similar incidents in the days immediately preceding the disappearance of Lesley Molseed which caused alarm to the children and parents living in the area around Lesley's home.

On Saturday, 4 October at about 12.50 p.m., Maxine Buckley and Debra Mills, two of the girls who had been part of the events of the night before, were walking along Vavasour Street when they saw a man on the corner of Jackson Street. He was between 20 and 30, five foot ten to six foot, broad build or fat, smooth complexion with light-brown hair and 'staring eyes'. He was wearing a light-green parka jacket, and he crossed the road to stand in front of the two girls, before opening his coat and exposing his erect penis. He then ran off along Vavasour Street towards Crawford Street.

Maxine ran straight home, from where her sister reported the matter to the police. When Maxine Buckley's mother arrived home a short time later, her daughter exclaimed, 'A man has exposed himself to me in Vavasour Street. *I think it was the man who lives in Crawford Street, the house with the plants in the window.*'[3] Maxine would remain insistent that this was what she had seen and her mother

---

3 Authors' italics.

was entirely convinced of the truthfulness of her daughter's account.

Police Constable Peter Sergeant responded to the call, but he was unable to find anyone in the area matching the description given by the girls. The officer then drove the girls to Crawford Street where Maxine pointed out number 31 as the house where she believed the man lived, but after waiting for some time, hoping to see the occupants, he formed the opinion that nobody was living in the premises as they appeared empty. Being unable to do anything further he took the girls home, only later referring the matter to the incident room.

In a little more than twenty-four hours, Lesley Molseed would be on her way to her death.

A further month was to pass before the third part of the trilogy of events which had as a central player Maxine Buckley. This matter again resulted in a telephone call to the police from her mother, but this call was rather more sinister, and did spur prompt action by the investigation team once it was linked to the alleged exposure of 4 October.

It was Wednesday, 5 November 1975. Bonfire Night. A night for fireworks and bonfires and children out on the streets long after their normal bedtimes, carried along by the excitement of the smells and noises and colours of this most exhilarating of evenings. Children chanting the traditional nursery rhyme, 'Remember remember the fifth of November, gunpowder, treason and plot.' How well would this Bonfire Night be remembered in years to come.

Maxine Buckley was walking home from a bonfire party, with a friend called Michael Rigby, along Vavasour Street, at about eight thirty in the evening, when she saw, she was to say, the same man who had exposed himself to her and Debra Mills on 4 October. He was walking towards her, wearing the same parka coat, and, whilst he did not expose himself to the girl, he stared at her and pulled faces, whilst grinding his teeth, such that the child was terrified. Michael Rigby had seen Maxine's expression change, from smiling and chattering to blank fear. He too saw the man's face then and, being equally afraid, he and Maxine both ran to find her mother. The police were called and took Maxine and Michael off in a car to try to find the man, with little success. But when the children returned, Carole Rigby took Mrs Buckley and the two children out in her van, and drove, at Mrs Buckley's direction, to a house in Crawford Street. It was a terraced house, with a profusion of plants in the window. The front door of the house was open and the open doorway was well illuminated. The adults saw in the doorway a big man and a small woman. The man matched the description which both children had given, including the dark trousers and light-coloured shirt which he was still wearing. They alighted from the van. The man began to shout 'What do you want me for, I've done nothing,' over and over, whilst Michael Rigby was brought from the back of the van. Maxine was too scared to leave the van, and she was crying, but she was able to see the man, and she spoke, 'That's him, mum.' 'It is him,' said Michael Rigby.

The house was at 31 Crawford Street. The man was Stefan Kiszko.

CHAPTER SEVEN

Stefan Ivan Kiszko

Charlotte Slawich had been born on 21 June 1923, on a farm in Slovenia, close to the Austrian border. She was the second daughter of Leopold and Hedwig Slawich. By 1945 the communists were taking vengeance on any German-speaking families, whom they regarded as collaborators with the vanquished Nazi occupiers. Charlotte's older sister, Alfreda, arrived home from work at the local council offices one day to find the family home deserted. A neighbour told her that a 'big lorry' had taken her family away. Alfreda had to follow and she caught a train to Austria where she searched for her family. By some miracle of fate, Alfreda found Charlotte sitting on a bench in Ogersteiermag. Charlotte had already decided to emigrate to England, where there were no communists and she could find stability and work. She was unable to persuade her sister to join her so, when Charlotte arrived in England in 1948, she was 24, a refugee, and alone.

Charlotte headed for the north-west cotton-town belt where she knew she would find work in the mill. She went first to Oldham, where she trained for six months as a spinner before she was sent to a mill in neighbouring Rochdale. There, she lodged with other immigrants in Drake Street, worked as a spinner during the day and learned English at night. In 1950, sister Alfreda joined Charlotte, learning spinning, English and lip-reading, an essential skill amongst the racket of the looms.

Charlotte met migrant worker Ivan Kiszko, a burly Ukrainian road repairer and began a courtship which culminated in marriage, on 10 February 1951 in Rochdale. They moved into their first home at 31 Crawford Street. Far from the horror of Nazis and communists and the poverty of her homeland, Charlotte had found work, then a husband. She now had the peace and stability she had longed for. Now she wanted a child. Her son, Stefan Ivan, was born on 24 March 1952 at Birch Hill Hospital, Wardle, Rochdale. Twelve days after his birth, the young Stefan Ivan Kiszko was taken to the house at Crawford Street, which was to be his home for the next twenty-four years.

Stefan was a healthy baby until he was six months old, when he developed breathing problems, diagnosed as asthma, a common ailment for those who lived in streets which were constantly blanketed with cotton dust. The child's condition worsened during the first five years of his life, and there were fears that he might die, which prompted specialists to advise the Kiszkos to move house or go abroad. It was a terrible dilemma for Ivan and Charlotte. They had found happiness, peace and a living in the north of England, an area chosen for the cotton process because its inherent dampness helped to prevent yarn from becoming brittle. Now the choice was to remain within the bliss they had found, with possible tragic consequences for their son, or abandon their home and their livelihood and move back to Eastern Europe for the sake of the life of their only child. At this time Stefan developed eczema, a common ailment accompanying asthma. The Kiszkos were prompted towards a short-term solution. Charlotte would take Stefan to her mother's home in Radbersburg in Austria for six months of clear air and medical treatment. Stefan was 5, and had not even started school because of the severity of his affliction. He and his mother spent the next six months in Austria where the boy received treatment under an asthma specialist, Dr Sollag. Charlotte too was developing chest problems which manifested later in her life as byssinosis, a potentially fatal consequence of her constant inhalation of cotton dust. The clean air of Austria provided welcome relief for both mother and son.

Whilst in Austria, however, Stefan suffered further health problems. He had his tonsils out and, because of an ensuing blood disorder, had to remain in hospital for eleven days, during which time he developed an abscess on his buttocks. When Stefan was 6, Dr Sollag forecast that the boy's asthma would alleviate as he grew older and stronger, and with the doctor's prognosis in mind, Charlotte decided it was time to return to England.

With the family reunited in Rochdale, Stefan finally started school, one year behind his contemporaries. He attended Newbold Junior School in Vavasour Street. His maternal grandmother, Hedwig, travelled to England in 1956, living in the Kiszko home while Charlotte went back to work in the mill. Hedwig stayed with the family for ten months of every year, until 1967 when Charlotte and Ivan were granted British nationality. Stefan became very close to his grandmother, a portent of things to come. He rarely played with children his own age, which served merely to emphasise Stefan's position as the strangest boy in the area. It was an image for which Charlotte had to take much of the blame, having sent him to school on his first day dressed, doubtless with touching pride, in traditional German dress. During the long summer holiday Stefan became even more alienated from the other children when, rather than enjoying the long school holiday running in the streets, playing football and getting into childish mischief, he went with his parents each year to spend six weeks in Austria, as an aid to his poor health.

Stefan's poor health was in marked contrast to that of his father: a massive man who utilised his great physical strength by helping to lay the M62, the great trans-Pennine cross-country motorway, which ran from Liverpool in the west to Hull in the east, passing close to the Kiszko home of Rochdale, and across the broad expanses of Manchester on its way. This was the great road which had to split for a distance of three miles, because a landowner refused to sell his farmhouse which lay directly in its path, obliging the road planners to direct the new motorway on either side of the house. This was the motorway which would carry speeding cars past Saddleworth Moor, drivers' eyes pulled inexorably towards the dark foreboding hillsides.

But as his father was strong, so was Stefan weak. Moving to St Peter's Junior School at the age of 8, Stefan received a total exemption from all physical activity because of his weak constitution, an exemption which can have done nothing to assist in his integration into the school community. But the sickly child combated his alienation by taking pride in his classwork. He passed his 11-plus exam and went on to Kingsway High School where he was remembered by the headmaster, Ronald De Courcey, as a boy who had few personal friends, but who got along well with everyone. He was a loner, probably because he had few of the qualities of his contemporaries, and was not attracted by their usual activities. He did not take part in sports, for he had no interest in them and was, in any event, limited by his medical condition, which had not resolved. He was not a 'boy's boy', but was generally friendly, well behaved and generous, although he dressed a little eccentrically, being a little old for his age. He tried hard to be reliable and trustworthy, and was on an academic par with his contemporaries. Still exempt from sports and physical activities, Stefan was encouraged by Ivan to learn to play the accordion, something no other child in Rochdale ever contemplated doing. Stefan learned to play the difficult instrument diligently, entertaining his family whenever they gathered in celebration, with his father beaming with pride. As each day passed, Stefan became more dependent on, and closer to, his parents, grandmother and aunt. Inevitably, he was taunted at school by his schoolmates, who accused him of skiving from sports. It was decided that, to escape the teasing, Stefan should transfer to Rochdale Technical College, where sporting games were not on the curriculum.

Stefan was 15. His last school report read: 'An average pupil who does not excel in any subject. On the physical side he is very weak. He has no aptitude for games. He was an oddity and a butt for bullies. Dressed differently from other children. Old-fashioned. Very kind and thoughtful and bore his physical disabilities well.'

The comments were made by head teacher, Mr De Courcey, whose wife would, coincidentally, work with the adult Stefan Kiszko at the tax office, and who described him as 'very conscientious and the only lad who ever carried heavy bags for ladies in the office'.

On leaving school in 1968 Kiszko completed a one-year full-time commercial course at Rochdale College followed by a two-year part-time course, receiving a certificate in office studies. He also attended evening classes in English and German. Following college, he obtained employment as a clerical assistant with the Inland Revenue, Newgate House, Rochdale, where he started on 29 September 1969. Edward Higham, the Inspector of Taxes in charge of his department regarded Kiszko as a satisfactory worker. Overnight, the family walked taller. It meant a greater social standing when a migrant family's child obtained a professional post, and the pride of the mill worker and the road layer was immeasurable. Ivan Kiszko wore a collar and tie only on Sunday, but his son Stefan wore one every day, including Saturday. His Aunt Alfreda was later to recall: 'He had studied hard and now he was dressing posh.' He remained a loner, but he did associate with staff at work – although not outside work hours. No complaints were ever received about him or his conduct, and female colleagues found him willing to assist by carrying heavy boxes and files which other male staff were often unwilling to do. His attendance record was good until February 1974 when he began to have long periods of absence due to ill health. Big Ivan believed his son was capable of higher office, and wanted him to study for more qualifications after a year's work with the Inland Revenue. But Ivan never got his wish, and Stefan never went back to college.

When Stefan Kiszko was 18, life dealt him a devastating blow with the death of the man he referred to as 'my dear dad'. It was to be a permanent setback for Stefan and, with the removal of the only effective male influence in his life, the female domination of the young man became total, and he was tied still closer by his mother's apron strings. Ivan Kiszko was only 56 when he collapsed in the street, suffering a heart attack as he and Stefan walked home from a visit to Alfreda's house. Unable to help his father, Stefan lumbered home to seek assistance. Ivan Kiszko was a giant of a man of massive build with a huge head and shovel-sized hands, and he had seemed to his son to be indestructible. Now he was gone, and the family unit, reduced to two, meant that Stefan became more dependent on his mother and she on him. She smothered Stefan with even more affection, to try to help to fill the void left by his father's death. Stefan Kiszko had been a boy of weak personality who had idolised his father and whose weakness sought compensation in his father's strength. With his father gone, Kiszko was obliged to seek that strength elsewhere, and he was fortunate to find it in the fortitude of his mother. Ivan's death meant that Stefan moved from the shadow of his father to the shadow of his mother.

The grieving son resigned himself to never going to college again. His mother now needed his wages, and he immersed himself in work at the tax office, intending that his labours should take his mind off his terrible loss. His grandmother Hedwig had died only ten months earlier, and he had in no way recovered from that bereavement before death had struck again.

Stefan's father had always promised him a car when he had passed his driving test. His death left the vow unfulfilled. But four days after Stefan passed his test, on 1 November 1971, Charlotte discharged her late husband's obligation, buying Stefan a bronze Hillman Avenger which he kept in the covered backyard of Crawford Street.

The devoted son and nephew was able to abandon the bus, for work each weekday and for pleasure at weekends. Now he was able to drive his mother and aunt to the garden centres which lay on the edges of town. Now he could take the car shopping – even to the local corner shop. Kiszko need never walk anywhere again, and rare it was that he did do. For a man already very overweight, the new car was both a blessing and a curse, for what little exercise he had previously obtained by a stroll to the shops, or even to the bus stop, was now replaced by the splendour of his car. Every weekday at 10 p.m. he drove to the mill and met his mother at the end of her 2 p.m. to 10 p.m. shift, to take her home in comfort.

Another blow was dealt when Stefan was 22. His mother's chest complaint worsened, confirmed as byssinosis. Typically, despite the fact that her work had almost certainly caused her illness, and continued to exacerbate it, Charlotte refused to heed the advice to retire. It ran against the grain, and anyway, she could not afford to. One concession she made was to obtain a job with Courtaulds at Castleton, where they worked only with man-made fibres.

One night in April 1974 Stefan failed to arrive for the 10 p.m. rendezvous with his mother who, after making a short search outside the mill, caught the bus home. Charlotte was anxious, knowing that her son would not willingly let her down. She fretted throughout the tedious bus journey, fearful that some terrible thing had caused her son to be unavoidably detained. Arriving home she found a note in Stefan's meticulous handwriting: 'Dear Mother,' it read, 'I have had a fall and think I may have broken my ankle. I have gone to Rochdale Infirmary . . .' Charlotte did not remove her coat, but headed back to the bus stop where she caught a bus to the hospital. She could not then have been aware how significant the injury would become in later years, and even had she known it would not have detracted from her primary concern, which was to ensure that the boy was all right.

In the casualty department she found Stefan with his leg heavily bandaged. His first words to her, typically, were an apology for failing to meet her at the mill. Charlotte pacified him, telling him that she had been fine, and that he would be fine once she had him in the comfort of their home. She would take a few days off until he was able to work. The bandage hid the true severity of the injury. X-rays soon revealed that Kiszko had sustained a complex break known as a Potts fracture which required surgery. Stefan was released after four days but, to Charlotte's chagrin, was transferred for convalescence to the local Springfield Hospital. He remained there for five weeks, gamely trying to master his crutches, which proved difficult for one who was normally so inept on his feet.

He returned home to hobble around the house, but was, of course, unable to drive his beloved Hillman car. He immediately secured a rebate on his motor tax and insurance payments, reasoning that the money saved would pay for transport on the now-hated bus. The injury proved more debilitating than Stefan had at first thought, and more plaster casts were fitted during the next six months. After seven months in the hospital and at home Kiszko was able to drive again and then to return to work, but the effects of the injury remained with him. When mother and son moved to a new house in Kings Road in 1975 Stefan tackled the wallpapering, but he was frequently in agony from leg pain, which consigned him again to the office sick list.

In August 1975 Kiszko had visited his GP, Dr George D'Vaz, complaining of tiredness. The doctor had immediately realised that there was something seriously wrong, for his patient had a grey pallor and, even whilst sitting down, was panting. He had the appearance of acute anaemia, but refused to be admitted to hospital despite the doctor's insistence. In the face of this refusal Dr D'Vaz gave Kiszko a prescription, and arranged for him to be seen at his home the following day, Tuesday, 5 August, by Dr Gerard Duffy, Consultant Physician.

Dr Duffy found Kiszko to be severely anaemic, and arranged for his immediate admission to Birch Hill Hospital in Rochdale. There, Dr Duffy also found Kiszko to be hypogonadal, in that he had no testicles in his scrotum and an immature penis.[1] The treatment administered for the anaemia was not successful, and Dr Duffy arranged for his patient to be transferred to Manchester Royal Infirmary, on 18 August, where he remained until 15 September.

At the Manchester hospital it was determined that Kiszko was the subject of long-standing hypogonadism and testosterone deficiency, and that the appropriate treatment for Kiszko would be replacement of the hormone testosterone. This was to be achieved by intramuscular testosterone injections administered once every three weeks.

Daily, Charlotte dutifully caught the bus for the fifteen-mile journey to the Manchester hospital. The consultant readily quashed her fears that the problem was leukaemia, but explained to Charlotte that her son could not have sexual contact with girls. For a woman of her background, who continued to regard her son as little more than a child, such information was bound to cause only confusion and embarrassment. Hence Charlotte did not ask the consultant to explain, and was equally unable to bring herself to

---

1 Kiszko's refusal to be admitted to hospital on 4 August was, apparently, due to a fear of having his underdeveloped genitals seen by nurses.

discuss this matter with her son. She shut the matter from her mind: Stefan had never needed girlfriends anyway and, most importantly, he was going to recover and be allowed home.

On 15 September 1975 Stefan was discharged from hospital and returned to the cloying bosom of his tiny family. Almost three weeks later he had to return for an injection, but he was home by tea-time. He told his mother only that it was a routine injection and that she need not worry. Charlotte had not forgotten the consultant's reference to a sexual problem, but had pushed it to the back of her mind. It surfaced again, but again she chose not to pry. Her son was home, and nothing else mattered. She did not know what the injection was and she did not ask. She did not know what her son's sexual problem was and she did not ask. She would never hear the details from Stefan but, in due course, would learn his intimate secrets along with millions of other people who would read of Stefan Kiszko in the papers.

Where the absence of exercise, controlled diet and self-control had failed to put a ceiling on Kiszko's ballooning weight, illness succeeded. He had lost two stones in weight whilst in hospital and his leg injury still required that he walk with a stick, but the person inside remained the same and Stefan was happy to be at home with his mother, helping wherever he could. Although he remained unable to return to work Stefan found that, as his recovery progressed, he was able to assist his mother more and more and, when the house move came about on 6 November Kiszko was to be found at the wheel of his Hillman Avenger, ferrying household items on a roof rack and in the boot. The ability to serve his mother contributed to Kiszko's recovery: he was doing what he liked best. They were together again, as close as ever. He recalled that, during his time of illness at Crawford Street Charlotte had moved a bed settee into his bedroom so that she could be near him at night, to keep an eye on him and to be close at hand should he need her. The bond, broken only by physical separation, was now restored.

At 23, he lived with his mother in a tight community, which regarded Stefan as being abnormally close to his mother. As he grew up into his teens he had become aware of the jibes about being tied to his mother's apron strings, but he had shrugged them off with more than a measure of bewilderment. People's curiosity about the relationship followed him from school to college to his first job at the tax office in Rochdale. 'It's a mother fixation,' he had overheard one clerk telling another. He had never fully understood his supposed fixation with his mother or whether the comments were designed to be hurtful, salacious or were possibly some sort of compliment.

Certainly he felt no shame for his love of and attachment to his mother, and the whispering campaign did not hurt him, for Stefan was never happier than in the company of his mother. He loved her, in the purest sense of that word. He respected her and admired her and paid heed to her advice, but she was also his friend. His best friend. Just about his only friend. He looked up to her, metaphorically at least, for at six feet two inches and weighing approximately seventeen stones, Stefan Kiszko towered in lumbering form over the bird-like lady who was his mother, Charlotte. Children had always found Stefan a figure of fun, an amiable giant with slightly popping eyes and turned-out feet. He waddled down the street like a bloated Charlie Chaplin. Even his name of Stefan marked him out as somebody 'offbeat'. At the tax office he was the only man of his age who did not shave. He had quite a high-pitched voice and, almost inevitably, he did not have a girlfriend. His teeth were brownish because of his near-addiction to sweets, which he always carried in his baggy trouser pockets and which made him a soft target for the neighbourhood children.

He was an object of amusement. His imposing physical shape contrasted starkly with his apparent meekness, high voice and closeness to his mother. The fear which his height and girth might otherwise have caused was completely dissipated by the knowledge that he was too shy to speak to girls, too interested in his mother to bother anyone else and, in particular, by reason of it being well-known that Stefan Kiszko had never in his life done harm to another living thing.

CHAPTER EIGHT

. . . And All Things Nice

Once Maxine Buckley and Michael Rigby had pointed out the man who they believed had scared them it was incumbent on their parents to take appropriate steps.

The police were notified and, at 10.20 p.m. on 5 November 1975 WPC Shaw and PC Oliver went to 31 Crawford Street where they spoke with Kiszko regarding the complaint of indecent exposure on 4 October 1975. For the first time in his twenty-three years Stefan Kiszko was to have experience of police officers as inquisitors.

This interview provides an interesting illustration of the power of Charlotte Kiszko compared to the weakness of her son. WPC Shaw's statement, which was read to the jury at the later trial, says that she 'spoke to Stefan Ivan Kiszko in the presence of his mother': it is, for a moment, difficult to believe that she is speaking not of a 14-year-old boy, but of a 23-year-old clerk in the Inland Revenue.

Not that he was, at first, able to say much. The officer explained the nature of their call, saying, 'I have received a complaint from two girls that a man fitting your description indecently exposed himself to them on Saturday, 4 October 1975, at about 12.45 p.m. in Jackson Street, Rochdale.' WPC Shaw administered the caution, telling Kiszko that he did not have to say anything unless he wished to do so, but that anything he did say would be taken down and might be given in evidence. But it was Charlotte Kiszko who spoke, saying, 'You have no right to accuse my son of such things, he is a sick boy, he has only been out of hospital a couple of days, after being in for six weeks,' and then, 'My son wouldn't do a thing like that and I don't like what you're saying about him.' Charlotte was exaggerating; she may not have intended her words to be taken as the literal truth. They would recur later to torment Stefan. The officers then asked Kiszko if he would go into another room with them, but even then they went so far as to ask Charlotte if they could interview him on his own. She, perhaps not entirely unnaturally, asked why the police did not want her there, but she then accepted the explanation that he might be embarrassed to talk in front of her, and let the police and her son go without her into the living room.

Once the police officers had taken Kiszko to a room away from his mother, they were able to direct his attention to 4 October, and to ask him where he had been that day. He replied that he had been with his mother until after lunch, and had later gone out with a friend to take some things to Kings Road, where they were moving. Boxes full of household items tended to confirm that the Kiszkos were indeed moving house. He said that he had been in hospital for six weeks, from 6 August 1975, and had not, therefore, been in hospital on 4 October. He calmly explained that he had been at home with his mother on 4 October, until 3 p.m., and was not, therefore, in the vicinity of Jackson Street at about 12.45 p.m. But when the officers tried gently to give him the opportunity to confess to indecent exposure, with PC Oliver saying, 'We appreciate that this type of offence is very embarrassing *but we understand*,'[1] Kiszko became highly agitated and jumped from his seat with the words, 'I am a civil servant, this is ridiculous, I want my mother here,' and Charlotte Kiszko, who had been waiting in the hall, doubtless listening in to the conversation, entered to defend her son. Kiszko turned to his mother and said, 'They have just accused me of exposing myself to some girls,' to which Charlotte retorted, 'That's stupid. He never would do a thing like that.'

Kiszko went on to tell the officers that he did own a car, and showed them his bronze Hillman Avenger, registration number VDK 157 K which was parked in the garage. He explained, however, that he had not driven that or any other car for several weeks, because of his bad leg. He denied owning a parka coat or jacket, but when the police searched the house and found a blue anorak with a hood, and said to him that that coat was just like a parka,[2] Kiszko replied, 'Yes, I suppose it is.'

The coat was not taken, and the officers, having heard him once more deny indecent exposure, left the house with a warning that they would be making further enquiries. These particular officers were to make no further enquiries in this matter. Instead, they notified the relevant police officers who were investigating the murder of Lesley Molseed, and the reports of Shaw and Oliver

---

1 Authors' italics.
2 Although Maxine Buckley had described the parka worn by the man on 4 October as being light green.

joined the forest of paperwork in the incident room, where they would lie, untouched, for several weeks.

Despite the events of late October and early November in Rochdale, the investigation proper (as it was at that time) remained very much on the track laid down by Holland, although by the middle of December it was becoming clear to Dibb and Holland that the flow of information had all but dried up, and that the enquiries in the Rochdale area were nearing completion. It was time for a further review of the entire investigation.

Three hundred and seventy-nine items, including knives, vehicles and clothing had been taken from the crime scene, the body of the child and from suspects, and had been submitted to Ronald Outteridge for examination. He had produced five interim reports. Hundreds of items had been fingerprinted. Photographic negatives found on the moor had been developed.

The data was overwhelming: 12,269 persons and 8,069 vehicles (including 5,700 Morris 1000s) had been recorded in the incident room indices, and a further 7,000 people had been interviewed at the road checks near the scene or in house-to-house enquiries on the estate; 10,070 actions had been raised in the course of the investigation, the majority of which had been completed, and 4,917 statements had been taken. Hospitals, doctors' surgeries, dry cleaners, local firms and vehicle taxation offices had also participated in the enquiry process, but by the end of 1975, the only outstanding enquiries were the untraced Morris 1000, the white car seen by Emma Tong, and the elimination of six people who were regarded as being strong suspects, although without any evidential basis existing for that suspicion.

As the enquiries on the Lancashire side of the Pennines were clearly nearing completion, a decision was taken on the grounds of cost efficiency to transfer the incident room to Harrison Road Police Station, Halifax. Detective Chief Inspector Little was charged with the transfer of all documentation and Detective Inspector Cooper would manage facilities and telecommunications in Halifax.

It is no criticism of Mr Dibb, Mr Holland, Mr Outteridge or any of the many officers, who had invested hard hours' work into the investigation, to say that as 1975 was drawing to a close, the prospect of catching the killer of Lesley Molseed did not appear to have improved by a single evidential iota. All that had come forward, from discussions between detectives and scientific staff, was a belief (and it was no more than a belief) that they could be looking for someone who was infertile or with a low or negligible sperm count.

It is quite clear that the incidents of 3 and 4 October and of 5 November represented the beginning of a transitional phase in that investigation. Whilst the police carried out their forensic tests and their examination of motor vehicles; whilst DCS Dibb was taking to the air in a helicopter to trace possible routes taken by the killer, and (more importantly) to add impetus to the publicity machine which was yielding a massive response from the public; and whilst that same officer was appealing to inmates in British jails to give information which might lead to the one type of offender loathed and despised by all 'normal' criminals, the transmogrification from the psychological profile reading 'mentally deranged with sexual deviations' to identifiable suspect was brought about by the alleged commission of relatively trivial sexual or quasi-sexual offences, and was due in large part to the efforts of the 12-year-old child Maxine Buckley and her mother Sheila.

As we have seen Maxine Buckley made a number of statements to the police. In her first, dated 4 October, she spoke only of the incident of that day. She said that she thought she had seen the man before, and would recognise him if she saw him again. Her second statement was dated 9 October, and dealt with both the Friday (third) and Saturday (fourth) incidents, although she did not think that the same man was involved. The man on the fourth was of a much heavier build. She said that she thought that she had seen this second man before in the area between Vavasour Street and Crawford Street.

Maxine Buckley, Debra Mills and Ann Marie Storto, Sheila Woodhead and the other very young children who gave statements and evidence regarding the three incidents in the autumn of 1975 have each maintained, from the moment of making their statements that what they said to the police and to the courts was, from beginning to end, the truth. They have adhered to their accounts throughout, notwithstanding any efforts to dislodge them, whether in cross-examination or otherwise. It is quite clear that each child believed that they had seen something improper and suspicious, and each was content that they had done their duty in reporting it to the police.

It is just possible that the incident alleged on the Friday night was little more than imagination on the part of young girls, but, whatever the perception of the girls who gave evidence concerning the events of that night, there was an entirely innocent explanation for what they might have seen.

There had been a man exposing himself that night in October 1975. His name was Maurice Helm. He was a milkman who had urinated near the youth club, not knowing that his hoped-for privacy had been interrupted by three young girls. They had seen his exposed penis and had run away, screaming that they had seen a flasher. It was an entirely innocent act by Mr Helm. He had disappeared by the time the police arrived in response to the call from the club, but he did not wait long before coming forward to explain the mistake. Although he was not, at that time, aware that his actions had brought about the arrest of a man innocent of any crime, he was soon to learn that Stefan Kiszko had been arrested. And he was to learn that Kiszko's arrest for the murder of Lesley Molseed had been precipitated by his arrest for the so-called 'flashing incident'. Maurice Helm did not know – could not know – whether or not Stefan Kiszko had murdered Lesley Molseed, but he was absolutely certain that Kiszko had not been the man whose private parts had been seen by the girls outside the youth club. Long before Kiszko's trial had even begun, Maurice Helm had explained to the police that he had been the man at the youth club. The police investigated Mr Helm as a suspect, not as a potential witness, and with little difficulty he was excluded from the murder enquiry.

The statement provided by Mr Helm was simply part of a huge bundle comprising thousands of pages that was served on the morning of the Kiszko trial. Although clearly important, the statement was not specifically drawn to the attention of the defence, nor was it referred to in court. It did not publicly emerge until 1991. Of course, providing an innocent explanation for this flashing incident would not have destroyed the entirety of the crown's case against Kiszko. But it would have been used, undoubtedly, to cast serious doubts upon the accuracy and the veracity of the girls, not merely as to the facts of that incident but as to the identification of Kiszko as the man responsible.

The full relevance of the evidence of the various girls, concerning the events of those three nights in October and November 1975, would become apparent at the trial of Stefan Kiszko, but one matter is immediately clear. Had Sheila Buckley and Carole Rigby not taken their children out on to the streets of Rochdale on the night of 5 November 1975, and had Maxine Buckley and Michael Rigby not made their identifications of Stefan

Kiszko on that particular night, it is perfectly possible that Stefan Kiszko might never have come to the attention of the police investigating the murder of Lesley Molseed.

In the event, police involvement with Stefan Ivan Kiszko did begin on the evening of Wednesday, 5 November 1975, albeit he was not arrested nor was he formally interviewed at that stage, and he was questioned only in respect of the events of 4 October. In due course his defence to the allegations of abduction and murder would incorporate an alibi: that, on the afternoon of 5 October, when Lesley disappeared, he was with his mother and aunt, visiting Rochdale Cemetery. By an eerie and macabre co-incidence, two days after this first police visit to Kiszko's home, Lesley Molseed's funeral took place at the very cemetery which would, in due course, be such a feature of Kiszko's defence.

CHAPTER NINE

Of Suits and Fear

When WPC Shaw and PC Oliver left 31 Crawford Street on the
night of 5 November, Stefan Kiszko no doubt felt that that was an
end to the matter. The police had made their allegations and he
had made his denials, and, whilst they had said that they would be
making further enquiries, he may well have assumed that, given
his denials and his respectable employment, he would be hearing
no more from them. In any event, there were other matters to
occupy himself and his mother. The address at 31 Crawford Street,
in which the Kiszko family had lived since the 1950s, had been
made the subject of a compulsory purchase order in 1974. After
twenty years, and the whole of Stefan's memory, he and Charlotte
were moving to a new home at 25 Kings Road in Rochdale. They
were to acquire the keys on 6 November, and there was much to be
done before they could move.

On Friday, 7 November 1975, whilst April and Danny Molseed
were burying their youngest child, Charlotte and Stefan Kiszko
were busy packing up their belongings for the impending removal.
Their activities – and any feeling that the events of 5 November
were at an end – were suddenly interrupted at a little before 5 p.m.
that afternoon, by the arrival at the door of Detective Sergeant
Mawson and Detective Constable Russell.[1]

These men were very different to the uniformed officers who
had called two days earlier. They were plain-clothes detectives, but
their appearance did not seem to cause fear in Stefan. The officers
noted that he was angry. Seeing that the house was in disarray, DS
Mawson assumed that Kiszko's anger was due to the inconvenience
of the moment, and he apologised in anticipation of that, but
Kiszko made it clear that he was annoyed at the fact of more police
officers coming to his home. 'Your lot have been here the other

---

1 DS Mawson was based with the drug squad at Bradford, under the West Yorkshire
Metropolitan police. DC Russell was a member of the Greater Manchester Constabulary.

day accusing me of things I haven't done,' he said, adding that the other officers had upset his mother.

DS Mawson was surprised that other officers had already spoken to Kiszko and asked him what it was that he had been accused of, and when Kiszko told him that it was 'something to do with a young girl in Vavasour Street' on Saturday, 4 October, Mawson asked Kiszko if he had been in that area on that day. The officer did so without administering the words of the caution, which in 1975 were these: 'You are not obliged to say anything unless you wish to do so but what you say may be put down in writing and given in evidence.'[2]

Of course, Kiszko was not being arrested at that stage, but it is certainly arguable that it would have been fair to him, and more appropriate given the true nature of the enquiries, had he been reminded that he was not obliged to say anything. His answer to DS Mawson's question was to the effect that he had been thinking hard as to his whereabouts on 4 October, and his best recollection was that he was still in hospital on that date, having had an operation on his foot. Had the officer cautioned him prior to this answer being given, Kiszko might not have given a reply which was capable of being proved to be false. He might have preferred to give no answer at that stage. But the officer then made clear that his enquiry was certainly not limited to 4 October. Whereas up to that point the young man had been aware that the investigation was about an allegation of indecent exposure on Saturday, 4 October, now it was revealed to him that a far more serious matter had brought these policemen to his home. 'I am making enquiries,' said DS Mawson 'into the murder of Lesley Molseed, which occurred on 5 October.' The officer did not pause. Notwithstanding the sudden and dramatic change in the subject-matter of the enquiries, the officer did not, even then, feel it appropriate to administer the caution to Kiszko. Instead he immediately asked, 'Were you still in hospital then?' and Kiszko replied that he had a discharge letter from the hospital which he would try to find for the officer.

The Judges' Rules of 1964 (Rule II) only required the caution to be administered, 'As soon as a police officer has evidence which would afford reasonable grounds for suspecting that a person has committed an offence,' and not when an officer is trying to discover whether a person has committed an offence (Rule I). 'He

---

2 See the Judges' Rules, Home Office Circular No 31/1964.

is not bound to caution until he has got some information which he can put before the courts as the beginnings of a case.'[3] Thus the rules then in force did not, it would seem, demand that Kiszko be cautioned at this stage, because the officers were still very much in the investigative stage. They did not have information which could be put before the court 'as the beginnings of a case', not concerning indecent exposure and certainly not concerning murder. And yet, observing the case with almost twenty years' hindsight – years that saw significant development of police practices and an arguably more restrictive approach by the courts to such practices – and knowing where the questioning was leading, one cannot help feeling that a caution should have been administered at least at the point where DS Mawson told Kiszko that the matter under investigation was murder.

Stefan Kiszko, although of some intelligence and in a position of some responsibility with the Inland Revenue, was an unworldly man, an immature man, who clearly could not – and did not – give much thought to the implications of the answers he was giving to the police. He, doubtless, thought at this stage that he had nothing to fear, because he had nothing to do with the abduction and killing of this child, and because, in the way in which the question had been phrased, DS Mawson had not made it crystal clear that the enquiry he making meant that Kiszko was himself at least of interest as a possible suspect in the murder investigation. Thus the young man would almost certainly have given no thought to the possibility that his answers could have repercussions for him. It is for that very reason that the caution should arguably have been administered at this point, even though DS Mawson was operating within the rules governing good police practice that applied at the time.

It is a curious feature of DS Mawson's account of 7 November that Kiszko appears to have registered no surprise at being told that the enquiry had switched to the murder of Lesley Molseed. The officer specifically observed that Kiszko had shown no surprise that the police had returned so soon after the fifth, but there appears to have been no response when Lesley's murder was mentioned, other than to send Stefan scurrying off to find the discharge letter. When he was unable to do so, he telephoned a friend to ask if that person could recall the date of his discharge. The officers heard Kiszko say, 'The police are here again, I know

---

3 See Lord Justice Lawton in R v Osborne and Virtue (1973).

my mother is very upset, can you remember what day I came out of the hospital?' There was then a long pause. The officers, of course, could only hear one end of the conversation, but they were taken aback when Kiszko said to the unknown party on the other end of the phone, 'Oh, it's just that I am supposed to have killed a little girl now.' To the officers it must have seemed an unusually callous or, at least carefree, response to the situation. It may have been a reflection of Kiszko's lack of concern or his lack of under-standing, but it was certainly a remark which, again, showed an absence of surprise on the part of this young man, where any reasonable person might have shown panic or alarm at even having the murder mentioned to him by officers who were anxious to know his whereabouts at the material time.

Mawson was told by Kiszko that his friend was unable to help, and Mawson then switched the conversation to Kiszko's car. Kiszko told them, with some impatience, that he owned the Hillman Avenger which was parked outside, and had access to no other vehicles. The anger which Kiszko had shown when DS Mawson and DC Russell had first arrived at the house had quickly dis-appeared, doubtless because of this less accusatory approach. DS Mawson asked Kiszko if he was willing to make a statement about his movements on Sunday, 5 October, the day of Lesley's disap-pearance. Kiszko offered no objection and a written statement was taken from him.

It was a short document, of only one page. In it, Stefan stated that he was the owner of a spice-coloured Hillman Avenger motor car, registered number VDK 157 K, which had been his only vehicle since 1971. As to 5 October he said this: 'As far as I can remember on Sunday, 5 October this year I was an in-patient . . . at Manchester Royal Infirmary, where I was receiving treatment for an ankle injury.' He went on 'I cannot remember the date of my discharge, but it was early October. If I had been discharged from hospital on 5 October[4] I would certainly have spent all that day at home, as I was almost unable to walk at that time.'

No caution was administered to Kiszko before he made this statement, although the statement itself was on a pro forma paper which had, below the name, address and occupation of the maker of the statement, a declaration in the following terms:

This statement (consisting of One page each signed by me) is

---

4 Kiszko probably meant by this 'If I had already been discharged from hospital by 5 October, that is, prior to 5 October.'

true to the best of my knowledge and belief and I make it
knowing that, if it is tendered in evidence, I shall be liable to
prosecution if I have wilfully stated in it anything which I
know to be false or do not believe to be true.

Immediately below that were the signatures of Kiszko and DS
Mawson.

Any statement made by a potential prosecution witness in a
criminal trial must have this declaration on the first page. But by
no stretch of the imagination was Kiszko being asked to give a
statement with a view to him becoming a prosecution witness.
What then was the purpose of taking a statement from him? The
statement reflected a policy decision by West Yorkshire police. In
the investigation into Lesley's murder it had been decided that
statements would be taken from everyone as part of a three-stage
process: trace; identify; eliminate. When Stefan gave his statement
on 7 November it reflected merely the routine in operation. He
was not yet considered a witness, less still a suspect. But the errors
made in the statement were to have lasting consequences. This
written statement was one which might be used against him in any
future proceedings, yet Stefan had not been told that he was not
obliged to make the statement at all.

What was in the statement was Kiszko's assertion that he
believed that he was in hospital at the time of the murder or, if not
in hospital, that he was unable to walk. The assertion that he was
in hospital amounted to a disclosure of his possible alibi, and whilst
defendants often disclose their alibis in interview or discussion
with the police, the normal position would be that that would
happen only after the defendant had been cautioned, and probably
also told that he could consult a solicitor if he wished. What this
amounted to in the case of Stefan Kiszko was a man who was
obviously suspected of at least indecent exposure, but more
probably of murder, being interviewed (at least in the general, if
not the legal sense of that word) without any of the protective
mechanisms which have become developed and established in the
English criminal procedure over hundreds of years.

With the statement as his 'proof' of the position which Kiszko
was taking in respect of 5 October, DS Mawson left Kings Road
with his colleague. They were at that point not clear of what 'status'
would be allocated to Kiszko. There was nothing of substance to
make him a suspect. Kiszko would either be eliminated from police
enquiries, or he would be further investigated. Mawson and

Russell's next stop was to be the Manchester Royal Infirmary, where they checked the records and discovered that Kiszko had in fact been discharged on 15 September, almost three weeks before the relevant weekend. They also traced the officers to whom Kiszko had referred, and obtained from WPC Shaw a full account of the earlier interview, an account which had yet to make its way through the incident room system.

The officers returned to Kings Road on 10 November, and they challenged Stefan Kiszko with the information they had gleaned. Kiszko was asked, again without the benefit of a caution, why he had told Shaw and Oliver that he had been moving furniture on Sunday, 5 October, but had told them that he was in hospital. Kiszko was unruffled by the question and replied, 'As far as I could remember I was in hospital then but if I wasn't I would certainly have been helping mother move furnishings from the old house.'

Mawson told him of their enquiries at the hospital, so that it was clear that he had been discharged in mid-September, and he then asked Kiszko whether there was anybody, other than his mother, who could confirm his whereabouts on the weekend of 4 and 5 October. Kiszko replied that he could not think of anyone. However, he did not stop at that, but went on to say that he and his mother had been talking the matter over and that:

> We remember visiting my father's grave on Sunday, 12 October and that was the first time I went out anywhere. I am sure I would have stopped in all day on 5 October. I know I was having difficulty walking then . . .

DS Mawson then asked Charlotte Kiszko if what her son had said was correct, and she replied that it was, adding, 'but it is a long time ago. I cannot remember fully.' Kiszko was then asked if he would provide a further written statement, and he again agreed. This statement was as short as his first, and it contained an admission by Kiszko that he had been mistaken about the date of his discharge from hospital. It went on to say, however, as Kiszko had said in the first statement, that he could hardly walk at the time of the incidents under investigation and, furthermore, that the first time that he had driven his car after his discharge had been on Sunday, 12 October, when he had taken his mother to the cemetery. He said that he had not left the house on Sunday, 5 October, and he concluded the statement with the words, 'I have never seen Lesley Molseed at any time.'

The difference between the two statements was not substantial.

In Kiszko's first statement he had not been certain about his date of discharge from hospital, and he had said that he was either still in hospital or incapacitated from walking. The admission of a mistake in his second statement is not particularly damning, adhering as he did to his assertion of incapacity.

What does stand out in the statement of 10 November is his assertion that he went to the cemetery on 12 October: read with DS Mawson's account of their discussions prior to the statement being taken, Kiszko's position on 10 November was that he did not leave the house on 5 October, and that the first time he left the house and the first time he visited the cemetery, was a week later, on the twelfth. Since Kiszko's case at the trial was to be that he had been at the cemetery on the day, and at the time, of Lesley's abduction, the statement of 10 November was bound to be recalled to show him either not to have been telling the truth in that statement, whether by way of an innocent mistake, or as a deliberate lie, or to be lying in his evidence to the jury.

Moreover, Charlotte Kiszko's assertion to DS Mawson that, in early November 1975 the events of 5 October 1975 were 'a long time ago' and were events which she could not fully remember, was an expression of poor memory which would be unlikely to support her evidence, in July 1976, that she and Stefan had indeed visited the cemetery on the day of Lesley's disappearance.

By the middle of November 1975 the police were still trying to construct a case. It was not a substantial structure. The probative evidence accumulated from hundreds of hours of policework was limited. The statements showing car movements around the lay-by had produced no element of uniformity, in that no single car had shown up, repeatedly, as a probable means of transport for the murderer and his victim. Certainly no car described by the many witnesses matched in any peculiar or individual manner the car driven by the man upon whom the police were now concentrating. To be sure, the police did have some evidence arising out of the incidents of 4 October and 5 November, but even taking that evidence at its highest it amounted to no more than a 12-year-old girl's and an 11-year-old boy's identifications. Michael Rigby's identification (of 5 November) was all but valueless: it was of Stefan Kiszko as a man he had seen earlier in the evening staring, pulling faces and grinding his teeth. Maxine Buckley's identification was of that same man, who she claimed had indecently exposed himself to her on 4 October. It is just possible that her evidence might have been sufficient for the police to prosecute Kiszko for an offence of indecent exposure, but it is highly unlikely that such a prosecution would be mounted on her evidence alone. In any event, the police were investigating a murder, and evidence of indecent exposure is in no way probative of murder, even a quasi-sexual murder of a girl of similar age to the alleged victim of the indecent exposure. Finally there were Kiszko's answers to the questions so far asked, in particular, by DS Mawson.

And yet, at the same time, the cumulative effect of these spider-web-thin strands of evidence was to begin to create a framework within which the cocoon of suspicion was spun.

Dibb and Holland were aware that the investigation, so far as they could tell, was running out of steam. For reasons already explained, the fact of the killer ejaculating over Lesley's clothing had remained a closely guarded secret. It was now decided to release the information within the police service, hoping to catalyse officers to a more productive course. It was, however, still not released into the public domain.

The spider-web gained strength on 16 December 1975, and the framework seemed more secure, for it was on that date, during the process of preparing the incident room documentation for transfer to Halifax that WPC Shaw's report concerning the indecent exposure and Kiszko came to light. The unusual name of Stefan Ivan Kiszko seemed to be repeated with much frequency, too much frequency to be mere coincidence. All the reports, statements and actions concerning Kiszko were passed to Holland, who immediately spoke to Shaw, and then caused further enquiries to be conducted about the man who still lived with his mother. He ordered that Kiszko be interviewed at a police station as soon as 31 Crawford Street, which was now known to be unoccupied, had been searched.

The task of searching Kiszko's former home fell to DS Godfrey, the exhibits officer, and he went to the property on 20 December. The house was completely empty, but Godfrey was aware of the results of the forensic examination of Lesley's clothing, and he gathered some white polystyrene, a piece of brown paper with a small footprint on it and samples of a white powder, all of which were scattered on the floor. From the fireplace he collected the debris not consumed by the last fire lit to warm Charlotte and Stefan before they left for their new home.

On Sunday morning, 21 December 1975 the senior officers investigating Lesley Molseed's murder moved their investigation into its next phase. They had nothing at all to link Stefan Kiszko with their investigation, only the slender threads which bound him to the spate of indecent exposures and incidents of children being frightened by an older man in the same area. In truth, they had only Maxine Buckley's identification and accounts to tie Kiszko even that far, and then only to 4 October.

Seemingly far removed from the police activity, Stefan Kiszko sat in his armchair and looked longingly at the presents under the twinkling Christmas tree in the corner of the spotless back living room. He looked forward to Christmas Day with all the enthusiasm of a child, which is how he had always been perceived by others, even his mother. He was a child in a man's frame – a man-child. Intelligent, but possessed with an odd maturity which no one could quite explain, although the doctors had provided some answers in recent months.

This was a particularly special Christmas for Stefan and Charlotte. They had moved into their splendid new semi-detached house at 25 Kings Road only six weeks earlier. It was a far grander affair than the terraced property at Crawford Street and the move meant that they were nearer to Charlotte's sister, Alfreda Tosic, whom Stefan dearly loved. In fact, Alfreda had made it all possible by dipping into her savings and helping Charlotte pay cash for the bigger semi-detached. Even though Stefan was pleased with the upward move, he would always fondly remember the comfortable plant-filled two-up two-down in Crawford Street as a haven from a world he perceived as sometimes hostile and sometimes simply incomprehensible. He knew that that home would soon be demolished.

It was Sunday morning, 21 December and Charlotte Kiszko was in the kitchen, tidying after breakfast and as usual, wearing an immaculate apron. She had been house-proud at Crawford Street, but she treated Kings Road in accordance with its name, as a palace, Stefan had told one of his very few friends. Those whom he called friends were always friends of, and the same age as his mother. He had no friends of his own, and he never went to the Ukrainian Club, as his late father had. Stefan preferred to drink fortified wine at home, with his mother. The Austrian cuckoo clock chimed on the living-room wall. Works like clockwork, just like mother. He chuckled at his own joke.

Tearing his eyes away from the Christmas presents in their gaudy wrappers, Stefan thought about what they would do that afternoon.

It was always 'them', never just him. Sunday had a set routine. Dinner, as he called it, was at noon, and then he would take his mother and Aunt 'Freda out in his 4-year-old Hillman Avenger. They always called at Rochdale Cemetery to place flowers on the graves of his father and maternal grandmother. He was always back before 2 p.m., when the pubs were closing, to avoid any risk of his cherished car being in collision with a drunken driver. Today, he might return from the cemetery and have a tipple of cider in the armchair. Or he might play his mother a traditional German tune on the piano accordion. German was his mother's native tongue and he spoke it fluently. Sometimes they went to the moors and dug peat for their many house plants. Thrift was something his mother had adopted in the war as a young woman living on the Yugoslav–Austrian border, and it remained a guiding factor in their lives. Whatever the option chosen, the afternoon ahead held any variety of delights, and then there would only be three more nights to Christmas Eve . . .

The officers who rapped loudly on the door of 25 Kings Road at ten thirty that winter's morning, breaking Kiszko's pre-Christmas reverie, were detectives from the Number 1 Operational Task Force in Bradford, West Yorkshire, and they had each been involved in the murder investigation since the Yorkshire force had been brought in shortly after the discovery of the body. Their brief was murder, but when Stefan Kiszko opened the door of his home to Detective Sergeant John Michael Akeroyd, Detective Constable Robert McFadzean and Detective Constable Anthony Melvyn Whittle, the most senior of those three men introduced himself and his colleagues by reference to the enquiries which were being made into the indecent exposure allegations, and by administering to Kiszko the words of the caution. 'Yes, what do you want?' said Kiszko. This time there was to be no short conversation and equally short written statement, for when DS Akeroyd next spoke it was to say the words which the young man had never heard before in his life. 'I would like you to accompany us to the police station at Rochdale,' said the officer, 'so that we can discuss the matter,' and Kiszko quickly agreed.

They had made clear that they were investigating an allegation of indecent exposure and the young man was confident that he could quickly deal with this trifling matter, and return to his restful Sunday and the preparations for Christmas. The police had made no mention of their real objective: to question Kiszko concerning the case of Lesley Molseed. Kiszko's confidence that he could deal with police officers without any assistance might not have been so pronounced had he known that he would be accused, not of indecent exposure, but of murder, once he was on the police officers' territory. Indeed, he might not have been so willing to accompany them to the police station at all.

Stefan Kiszko never resiled from his position that the police force existed for the protection of good people, like himself and his mother. Charlotte too had the utmost faith in the integrity of the police. Naive, innocent or simply trusting, Stefan went to Rochdale police station on 21 December 1975 willingly, because he could not imagine for one moment that he could be in any trouble or, more particularly, that he had anything to fear from the police. Charlotte had come to England from oppression in post-war Eastern Europe. England had provided a safe haven, and she had admired its stand against evil oppressors. Having come from a part of Europe where the police were the enemies of all civilians, and where it was impossible to respect the justice system or believe that it was anything other than a further arm of the state, designed to strangle the freedom of the individual, it was almost axiomatic that Charlotte would arrive in this country with the conviction that the system of justice in existence here was anything other than fair, legitimate, just and wholly honourable.

Whilst Kiszko was engaged with DS Akeroyd, other officers searched his bedroom, finding and taking away a soiled tissue and some girlie magazines from the side of his large double bed. They looked for a knife, but did not find one. At the same time, his Aunt Alfreda's house in nearby Kingsway was also being subjected to a meticulous search.

As DS Akeroyd waited for Kiszko to get ready, his colleagues went out into the garage to examine the Hillman Avenger. It was immaculately kept, save for the sweet wrappers which seemed to be everywhere. Unaware of the relevance of his car to the enquiry, Kiszko, when he saw the officers in the garage, asked if he could bring the vehicle with him to the police station. DC Whittle agreed that he could do this, and that he would ride with him on the journey. His brother officers went back to Rochdale Police Station together. DC Anthony Whittle accompanied Stefan Ivan Kiszko as he left his mother and his home.

Seventeen long years would pass before he next returned.

CHAPTER TEN

Three Days

In 1984 police procedures in dealings with suspects were subjected to a dramatic overhaul by the introduction of the Police and Criminal Evidence Act, known thereafter by the acronym PACE. Prior to 1984, the police were governed by a mixture of statutory rules, police internal regulations and decisions of the High Court and the Court of Appeal. The appellate courts had, over the years, dealt with complaints made by convicted men on topics as diverse as identification parades, search of property and the person, the right of a detained person to legal advice and the interviewing of suspects. Out of those decisions had developed a framework of law, but without a rigorous structure and with somewhat vague and fluctuating parameters.

The 1984 act was designed to introduce a more rigid statutory framework, providing certainty for the police, the defendant and the legal advisors. Whether it has done so is an area of debate and conjecture outside the scope of this book. In 1975, however, the main controls over police conduct were the common law rules and the so-called Judges' Rules of 1964.

The Judges' Rules required that a man be cautioned by police 'As soon as a police officer has evidence which would afford reasonable grounds for suspecting that a person has committed an offence.'[1] No caution had been administered to Kiszko by the officers who had seen him on 7 or 10 November. The only change in the case against Kiszko since he was seen on 10 November when he had *not* been cautioned was his making of a formal written statement that day which was slightly contradictory of his statement of 7 November. It has been suggested that the case against him at the end of 10 November had still been extremely thin. It was certainly not of sufficient strength to be described as containing evidence 'which would afford reasonable grounds for suspecting'

---

1 Judges' Rules Rule II.

him of murder. That may justify the police in not having cautioned Kiszko on 10 November, and perhaps it also explains why he was not arrested, nor even asked to go to the police station until 21 December.

Stefan Kiszko was not arrested on 21 December; he voluntarily accompanied the police officers to the police station. But when Stefan Kiszko arrived at Rochdale Police Station on that day, and was taken by the three detectives to an interview room, the first words spoken to him, repeating what DS Akeroyd had already said at the house, were the words of the caution.

Why it was that Kiszko was not cautioned on 10 November, but by 21 December was being asked to go to the police station and was being cautioned both at home and at the police station is not at all clear. There had not been any apparent dramatic change in the state of the evidence so as to transform Kiszko from someone who might possibly have indecently exposed himself, to a man who could be reasonably suspected of murder, and yet members of the squad dealing with the murder had come to take him to the police station, and were now engaged in interviewing him in formal circumstances.

When Stefan was taken away by the police, Charlotte reassured herself with the idea that they simply wanted to talk to her only son. They would soon realise that Stefan was a good and truthful boy whom she had brought up well and to whom she had taught right from wrong, and that a boy like that could not possibly murder a child. He would be home by that afternoon, she reasoned. But as the time passed, Charlotte had put on her Sunday coat and hat, and caught a bus to the police station.

The archetypical Eastern European woman asked the archetypical young policeman on the enquiry desk if she could speak with the policeman who had brought Stefan to the police station. He was not impolite. They are busy at the moment and cannot be interrupted. Perhaps she would care to telephone later. Charlotte left a message for her son and went home. The message never reached him.

Charlotte considered contacting a solicitor, but, with no experience of such things she did not think it was possible to speak to a solicitor on Sunday, even for money. Neither she nor Stefan had ever been involved with the police before, and she frankly had no idea what to do. She sought solace in her sister, staying with her for a few hours before returning home, to her empty house.

The first interview with Kiszko began very shortly after his arrival at the police station. The rules then in force required only that a person in custody should be allowed to speak on the telephone to his solicitor, whereas the 1984 act now demands that a person accused of an offence must be allowed access to a solicitor save in the most limited circumstances. Moreover, he must be told of his right to have a solicitor present. Kiszko did not have a solicitor present, and it is not clear whether he was asked whether he wanted one or whether he gave any intimation that he wished for one.

This interview was conducted by DS Akeroyd as the most senior of the officers present. DCs McFadzean and Whittle were also present, but their role was limited to taking a mental note of what was said.

Under systems introduced by the Police and Criminal Evidence Act 1984, all interviews at police stations are tape-recorded, whatever the crime under investigation, be it shoplifting or murder. It seems almost incredible that until those systems were introduced there was no system at all for ensuring accurate recording of the content of an interview. Common practice was for an officer to make a mental note of what was said in the interview, and later make a written record of his recollection. That record was not put to the interviewee for him to say whether or not the note accorded with his recollection, and the avenues and opportunities for error or dispute are obvious. Moreover, in every case where an issue arose as to the *content* of an interview, officers inevitably found their integrity and honesty being brought into question. In other words, it offered no security or support to the interviewing officers themselves. Nevertheless, this was the custom adopted during the interviews of Kiszko, and those considering the case some twenty or more years later are dependent on the written recollections of McFadzean and Whittle for an accurate account of what was said.

Although the first interview began with the officers referring to the indecent exposure allegations, it must have been obvious to all parties that it was the murder which was under investigation. At first the officers concentrated on the change of versions as to Kiszko's whereabouts on the weekend of 4 to 5 October. According to Akeroyd's version of the interview, Kiszko adhered to his account that he had not gone out on 5 October, but rather than making reference to the injury to his leg, he told the officers that he had not gone out because he was weak and could hardly walk. DS Akeroyd then asked him why he was feeling weak and he received the reply, 'I'd just been in hospital. I'd only just come out. *I'd had a blood transfusion*,'[2] thus switching the emphasis as to the cause of his claimed disability on that day. A little later he was to say, again, that he was very weak and depressed because of the blood transfusions and the injections he had been given. He was asked again what was the first day that he had gone out after his discharge from hospital on 15 September, and he repeated that it was Sunday, 12 October, when he had gone to the cemetery with his mother. Akeroyd wanted there to be no confusion here, nor would he allow of any possibility of claiming mistake at a later date. 'Was that the Sunday after you were discharged from hospital?' he asked. 'No, the Sunday after the girl went missing,' came the reply. 'Do you mean 12 October 1975?' asked the officer, to which Kiszko replied, with some certainty, 'Yes.' Again Akeroyd asked him if he was sure that that was the first day that he had gone out after being discharged from hospital, and Kiszko again replied, 'Yes, I'm sure.'

Akeroyd, unknown of course to Kiszko, was in the process of setting and closing a trap, and so he asked of Kiszko again, 'Are you saying that you never left your house at all until 12 October 1975?' and, without pausing to consider the implications of his reply, Kiszko replied, 'Yes, I never went out. I was too weak.' Having thus ensured that Kiszko had created an account of being at home until 12 October, so that any subsequent alibi would have to be limited to the confines of Crawford Street, Akeroyd gently closed the trap on his quarry. 'I want you to think very carefully before you answer this question,' he said. 'Where were you at about 12.45 p.m. on Saturday, 4 October 1975?' Kiszko paused for moments before replying, 'At home with my mother. I was very weak and depressed what with the blood transfusions and the injections.'

Asked about the night of 5 November he maintained that he had not gone out that night, and he claimed not to remember the visit of Mrs Buckley, Mrs Rigby and their children to his home that evening. The police persisted. 'You obviously went out [on Bonfire Night],' insisted DS Akeroyd, 'think very carefully. You were seen,' to which Kiszko made the curious response, 'Can I be identified?' When the officer said that Kiszko not only could be identified, but had been identified that very night, Kiszko's reaction was to assert that the witnesses might be lying: 'They might have it in for me because I work for the Inspector of Taxes,' he said. The police reaction was incredulity, and when Kiszko asked

2 Authors' italics.

what other reason there could be for the witnesses to make false allegations against him, DS Akeroyd suggested that it was not the witnesses who were lying, but Kiszko himself.

This was an experienced and skilled interrogator. The officer was relentless. The interviewee had come up with a ridiculous explanation as to why the witnesses against him should lie, and Mr Akeroyd knew this to be a sign of lying, and he told Kiszko that he did not believe him. To the interviewing officer any untruth told which is not obviously capable of being mere error has to be regarded as a lie. To the more simplistic Kiszko, he was not lying unless making a deliberate attempt to mislead the police.

DS Akeroyd now applied a modicum of pressure, simply by leaning forward to bring his face closer to that of Kiszko. 'You are telling lies,' he said. 'You did go out on Bonfire Night and you are the man that indecently exposed himself on 4 October 1975. Is that not the case?' Whatever bravado, real or imagined, that was within Kiszko was rapidly evaporating, for in his next reply the falsehood was revealed. 'Well I suppose I could have gone up to the house at Kings Road with some things and,' he continued, with no idea how damaging his replies were becoming, 'she must have seen me but she has mistaken me for someone else.'

A lie told in a criminal case can be damaging, but in itself it cannot prove anything. Proof is dependent on first the lie and then the truth, and Akeroyd had just secured his proof. Kiszko had lied by saying he had not gone out on 5 November. Akeroyd believed he could prove that lie by reference to Maxine Buckley and Michael Rigby. But he had gone one better, for he had managed to make Kiszko admit the lie, and concede that he had gone out on Bonfire Night.

Kiszko then went further. Prompted first by Akeroyd and then by McFadzean, he conceded not only that he had gone out, but that he also might well have gone to a bonfire. He insisted, however, that he had not got out of his car. 'I did stop,' he said, 'but I did not do anything wrong.'

The change was obvious. From asserting that he had not gone out at all on the night of 5 November he was now conceding, not that he *might* have gone out, but that he *did* go out in his car, and that he had stopped that car at or near a bonfire. He was moving backwards fast, unable to resist the questioning of the officers, and when he was asked whether he was quite sure that he had not got out of his car his response was one of the landmarks in the case: 'Well I may have done but I can't remember. It's all a bit hazy.

It's these damned injections, they make me feel a bit funny for a few days after I have had them.'

It was a turning point for sure, for now Kiszko was going slightly further than merely admitting going out and stopping the car at a bonfire. Now, without admitting any offence, specifically, he was putting forward a justification. It seemed to the assembled officers that the words Kiszko was using might be the beginnings of his justification or mitigation, not merely for an indecent exposure, but for something far more serious.

Kiszko was asked about the injections but refused to say more than that they were to help him with what he called his 'complaint'. Akeroyd left the topic alone.

When Kiszko was asked again where he had been on Saturday, 4 October at about twelve forty-five his answer was a rather lack-lustre. 'At home with my mother I suppose.' 'There's no suppose about it,' said Akeroyd, 'I know where you were on that Saturday dinner-time and so do you.' 'I don't know,' replied Kiszko. 'It is obviously someone trying to get me into trouble.' It was the sign of a man who had been beaten back. His position had changed substantially as to 5 November and, whereas his change in ex-planations – as to the date of his discharge from hospital – given at home on 7 and 10 November could be seen as a mistake on his part, his account given in this first interview was clearly false. He behaved as if he knew that he had lied, and he knew that he had been caught out. His meagre protestations that the witnesses 'had it in for him' amounted to nothing, and it is certain that the police now believed that he was trying to cover up for some wrongdoing.

The interview was brought to an end to enable the officers to confer with Holland. Whilst Kiszko had been shown to be a liar, and there was little doubt that those lies had been told to conceal guilt of one or more offences of indecent exposure, there was now a strand of suspicion, linking his lies to the murder, and that his last answers as to his 'damned injections' added strength to the link. Kiszko, it is true, did not fit the 'profile' of the man they were looking for, but he did fit the stereotype many held of sex offenders: large, awkward individuals who dress oddly and are obvious social misfits.

The profile which the officers had of Kiszko, based on know-ledge of his family, education and employment history, was of an intellectually bright loner, socially naive and inadequate, with few friends and none of the opposite sex, who lived for his mother, and who was a little strange but perfectly decent and, in every sense, respectable.

Whilst the interviewing process was continuing, Detective Constable John Merkin and Police Constables Booth and Akerman went to 25 Kings Road. Although distressed by the officers' request, Charlotte Kiszko did not object to them searching her son's bedroom and garage. Akerman went to the garage attached to the side of the house as Charlotte escorted Merkin and Booth upstairs. She watched as they pored over the neatly kept bedroom, filled with Stefan's personal possessions, but the only items taken by the officers were a small white-handled penknife from a box on the window sill, and a red-handled flick knife from the top drawer of the dressing table. Akerman, meanwhile, had taken samples from two white powders and pieces of asbestos which were in the garage. All three officers felt that a more thorough search of the home might prove productive, depending on the progress made in the interviews, and the knives were then handed to Akeroyd, the other items to the exhibits officer.

At a little after 2.30 p.m. the interviewing resumed, with the officers concentrating now on 4 October. It was DC Whittle who told Kiszko that he was satisfied that Kiszko had exposed himself to Maxine Buckley and Debra Mills, but Kiszko's reply in denial was to open up the whole murder case against him. 'I couldn't do anything like that,' he said, 'that's why I'm having these injections.' He now explained that he was having the injections because 'I don't fancy girls.' Whittle asked him what he meant by this, and Kiszko replied, 'Well, when I was in hospital I discussed my problem with a doctor and he gave me some injections to bring me on.'

It was Akeroyd who, immediately, realised the potential significance of what had just been said. Kiszko had not 'fancied' girls before he went into hospital. He had then been given injections for his particular complaint. But the offences of indecent exposure and, indeed, of the sexual murder of Lesley Molseed, had been committed after Kiszko had come out of hospital. After he had received the injections to 'bring him on'. Akeroyd was now proceeding cautiously, and he delicately approached his next question: 'This is a very personal thing, but are you telling us that you are impotent?'

Kiszko, of course, had no knowledge that the police harboured a belief that the killer of Lesley Molseed was infertile, and so he replied without further thought, 'Yes I am. That's why I couldn't have done these things they say I've been doing. My doctor will tell you so.'

Akeroyd then asked if he had understood correctly, that Kiszko was receiving treatment for his condition, and Kiszko confirmed that he was: 'Yes I am. I've no interest in girls at all but the injections will help me.' Akeroyd asked if he had girlfriends at work, and Kiszko said that he had not, that he had never bothered with them.

DC Whittle left the room to notify Holland of this development, clearly seeing the need to make further enquiries into Kiszko's condition and treatment. He then took the keys to the Hillman Avenger and, looking under the carpet in the boot, he found eleven magazines showing naked women. He returned to the interview room clutching his find, and said to Kiszko, 'You have just told us that you have no interest in girls whatsoever, so why do you have nude books in your car?' At this point the officer was later to report that Kiszko began to tremble violently and to bite his nails, before replying, 'It's those damned injections. I never did anything like this before.' DS Akeroyd took over the questioning from DC Whittle, applying a more sympathetic and gentle approach which was quickly picked up by the other officers. He told Kiszko that it was normal to buy magazines of this type, and Kiszko then said that he had started to be attracted to girls, and had developed sexual urges, after being discharged from hospital in September. It was put to him that he was responsible for the indecent exposure on 4 October, and this time Kiszko did not deny the offence but tamely and naively replied, 'I can't remember, can I go home now?'

He was then asked to empty his pockets, and when the contents were placed on the table the officers saw two knives, one with a black-handle and one with an imitation bone handle. He explained that the black-handled knife was for cleaning his car battery and the other was for cutting string.

The officers then returned to the night of 5 November and, wishing to know why Kiszko had changed his story about going out that night, DC Whittle asked him, 'If you'd done nothing wrong, why did you lie about the bonfire?' to which Kiszko, in an unexpected and entirely voluntary admission said, 'Well perhaps when I stopped I might have rubbed my trousers up and down.' Whittle asked only the briefest of questions, allowing Kiszko himself to develop the admission he was making. He said that it was one of the 'urges' he had referred to earlier, a sexual urge, and he said that he had had an erection and had ejaculated. He then explained that his impotence had been rectified by the injections, and he said that he had seen some little girls and, 'I got it out and wanked myself off.' The officers had known nothing about this: they had only known that the man Maxine and Debra had seen had exposed an erect penis, but they were even more surprised when Kiszko, asked if he had done anything like this before, replied, 'No, but I've done it twice since.' According to the police he went on to tell of two occasions in November when he had been sitting in his car and, seeing a girl walking towards him, had taken out his penis and masturbated, adding, 'It's these injections, they make me feel funny when I see girls, but I've never touched any of them. I wouldn't do that.'

Asked to give a reason for having the magazines in his car, Kiszko explained that if there was nobody about, he could park up and look at the magazines and masturbate.

By the end of this second interview the position had, therefore, come to this. From his blanket denial of having gone out between 15 September and 12 October and of being seen at the bonfire on 5 November, Kiszko was now admitting indecent exposure on 4 October and being at the bonfire on the fifth, as well as having sexual urges brought on by young girls which had caused him to masturbate in public places. The relevance was not merely in his having admitted either the sexual urges or some wrongdoing connected with those urges, but in the change of story showing him, apparently, to be a person capable of lying. Moreover, by admitting the indecent exposure of 4 October, Kiszko had broken his alibi, and had, in the mind of the police, moved himself one step closer to being in the frame for the murderous events of 5 October.

The magazines became exhibits, along with various other items recovered from Kiszko's car by Booth and Merkin. The footwells had been swept for soil and debris samples. Stained tissues and a piece of grey felt were found between the front seats. Under the front passenger seat of the car, which belonged to a clerical employee of the Inland Revenue, Booth found a pair of red industrial gloves. Two further pairs of plastic/imitation leather gloves were taken from the dashboard. The glove compartment yielded a syringe, the rear seat a blue nylon parka-type coat, and the ashtray, three balloons and two bags of sweets. It was, at this stage, mere speculation, but in the hooded parka, the industrial gloves and the alluring sweets and balloons, the officers thought they had recovered a kit for abducting and killing a child. All that was missing was a knife, and the search of Kiszko's home and his person had already yielded sufficient knives to complete the 'kit'.

There was, however, one more find. In the glove compartment of the car there were two small pieces of paper upon which was written a series of car registration numbers. On the first, in blue, three numbers: PWX 583 K, JNA 272 F, KNW 912 L and the word 'PAKIS'. In red was the single number ADK 539 L. On the second paper, in black, 47142, SMY 950, GPX 406 H, BDK 101 M, and in red 'Friday 7/4/75, NO NOT ISSUED, BELL RANG'. Both papers were placed in plastic bags, and the collected materials were placed before DSupt Dick Holland for his consideration.

Holland made contact with Dibb, and after discussions with his senior officer a course of action was agreed. It was determined that the time had come for Holland himself to take an active role in the interrogation of Stefan Ivan Kiszko. So it was that, later that day, when DS Akeroyd returned to interview Kiszko for a third time, he was accompanied by Holland. The detective superintendent had the items which had been seized from Kiszko's home and from his car, but he began the interview by returning to the incident of 4 October, which Kiszko had already admitted. Now the young man was to change his story again, for, far from admitting indecent exposure on that day, he insisted that what had happened had been an accident. 'I remember that now,' he said, 'but it's not like you think. I was moving a carpet and the carpet knocked my zip down on my trousers and my shirt tail came out. There weren't many people about anyway and I zipped myself up as soon as I had put the carpet down.'

Holland ignored this, and put to Kiszko that, on 5 November, two young girls had seen him and told one of their mothers and they had come down and identified him as being the person involved on 4 October. The superintendent's error – it had been Maxine Buckley and Michael Rigby who had come with their mothers on 5 November – was not noticed at the time, but Kiszko then appeared to revert to admitting indecent exposure on 4 October saying, 'Well, perhaps I did. I can't remember. Things keep going hazy.' He denied, however, any connection with the alleged incident of 3 October.

The superintendent then asked Kiszko questions about his knives and a number of pens. Kiszko proudly informed the officer that he was a civil servant who used many pens in the course of his work, but he denied that he had lost any. He likewise gave explanations for the ownership of three of the knives; two were gifts from his father, one was for cleaning the battery of his car. Holland then moved to some of the more interesting contents of the car. 'What is the point,' he asked, 'in carrying balloons in your car, other than to attract children?' 'It's Christmas,' came the reply 'and I had them for decorations.' 'What about the sweets?' asked the superintendent, receiving the reply, 'I eat a lot of sweets. I always carry sweets with me everywhere I go.'

Holland terminated the interview, leaving Whittle and McFadzean to sit with his suspect, which they did. In silence. Whether this was intended to unsettle Kiszko is unclear, but Kiszko's initial view of Holland as a more friendly policeman was rapidly beginning to change.

At nine o'clock that evening, Kiszko having already been interviewed on three occasions, DSupt Holland and DS Akeroyd returned, having examined Kiszko's car again. They had found some peaty soil in the back seat of the car, but Kiszko was able to offer no explanation for this. Holland then turned to the lists of car registration numbers. Kiszko explained that he had had some trouble with vehicles from a scrap yard, which had tried to run him down, when he and his mother had lived at Crawford Street. He had contacted the police, and been told by a PC Bell to make a note of the registration number of any vehicle with which he had an altercation. He was then shown the list, containing three car numbers in blue and a fourth – ADK 539 L – in red. He told the officers that the three numbers in blue were numbers of cars which he had seen and which appeared to be acting suspiciously at a house near to his home, but he was unable to explain the fourth number at all. '. . . I just can't remember anything when I've had my injections,' he insisted, 'I go all hazy.' Kiszko was never able to explain how this particular car number came to be in his possession, nor why it alone was written in red ink.

Stefan Kiszko spent the rest of the evening alone in Rochdale Police Station, whilst officers went back to his home and recovered, amongst other things, a box of ampoules of a drug containing testosterone and a number of articles of clothing. Charlotte had followed the officers round the house as they had conducted their search, anxiously enquiring as to the welfare of her son, but Merkin and Booth were unable to tell her anything, other than that Stefan was still being interviewed. The two officers then returned to the police station, showing Holland their haul, which included now a white and blue handkerchief found under Kiszko's pillow. The handkerchief and pillowcase were both heavily stained with a fluid.

Holland decided to return to Kings Road, and he arrived there at 11 p.m. The frightened woman who answered the door looked beyond the four police officers who now entered. She could see Holland, Merkin, Booth and Akeroyd. But she could not see Stefan. Dick Holland explained to her that her son was still assisting with enquiries, but that he had admitted offences of indecency involving children. With some evidence of the firebrand which she would prove to be, Charlotte leapt to her son's defence, accusing Holland of lying and of picking on her son. Holland repeatedly told her that it was true, and he then proceeded to search Kiszko's room, finding a white-handled knife and a pair of scissors, and four ampoules of testosterone which Charlotte confirmed were for Stefan's injections.

DSupt Holland wanted to know everything about the Kiszko family. He particularly wanted to know about Stefan, whom he regarded as a sex monster who had killed a child. Kiszko, he believed, would go down in history, and everything of the man's background would have to be recorded. The jury would expect to be told at his trial. It was from Charlotte that this information would come. Charlotte traced the family story, from her own birth to her migration to England, her marriage to Ivan and the birth of her beloved son. She detailed Stefan's health problems and his steadily progressing development, which had come to an abrupt halt when Ivan Kiszko had died.

Charlotte would recall, in later years, how her faith and trust in the police was decimated by Dick Holland. He had sat in an armchair in her pristine home, and had turned to this lady and said to her, 'I will get the fucking truth out of Stefan, one way or another.' For a woman as isolated as Charlotte, a woman of regimen and certainty, a woman of strict upbringing whose entire being was based on respect, the profanity of the police officer and the tone in which he had expressed his objective brought fear and terror. She began to shake, and her fears for Stefan began to grow.

As Charlotte recounted the story of the life and troubles of Stefan Kiszko, she was perturbed at what she perceived as the hardening attitude of the listening detectives. They repeatedly mentioned girlfriends. She told them, 'Even though Stefan has a sturdy body, he is very childish in his ways. He is very attached to me and to my sister. As far as I know he has never had a girlfriend.' After informing Charlotte that Kiszko would not be home that night, Holland and the other officers left. She was anxious and distressed, and she called on her sister, Alfreda Tosic, then 58, to come and stay with her for the night.

At one forty-five on the morning of Monday, 22 December Holland and Akeroyd returned to interview Kiszko again. He had been sitting in silence with McFadzean and Whittle since the end of the last interview, some three to four hours earlier. He had been in the police station since about ten thirty the previous morning, some fifteen hours earlier. He had been offered but had refused any food, although he had had a drink. He does not appear to have slept, and could not have slept, even if able, for more than about three hours. It must also be borne in mind that Kiszko was still not at that time under arrest. He had gone to the police station voluntarily, rather than as an arrested man. That said, he was quite clearly a 'suspected' man, whether of indecent exposure or of murder. Yet despite his apparent voluntariness, he had gone without food, sleep and legal advice. Now, in the early hours of the morning, Holland and Akeroyd returned to question him again.

Dick Holland showed him the ampoules, and asked him about the drugs. Kiszko told the superintendent that he had both injections and tablets, and he said of the drugs, 'They make me go all queer and hazy and I fancy girls when I've had my tablets and injections. I used to be all right before.' He was again asked about ADK 539 L and why he had written down that number, and it was at this point Dick Holland told Kiszko, 'I now know that car was at the scene of the murder at Ripponden at 2.30 p.m. on Sunday, 5 October 1975,' to which Kiszko replied, 'I just can't remember. I have been thinking all the time. I am hazy when I have had my injections and my tablets.' The relevance of this number was clear, even if Kiszko was failing to see its importance. If Kiszko had made a note of the number ADK 539 L and if that car was at the scene of the murder on Sunday, 5 October, the police were drawing the inference that Kiszko too must have been at that scene. This inference would be entirely appropriate unless and until Kiszko could tell the police that he had recorded the number at another time in another place, and that was something he could not do.

At last, Kiszko was allowed to sleep, and he remained undisturbed until the following morning.

Charlotte rang the police immediately after waking. She was told only that Stefan was 'helping police with their enquiries'. Concerned as she was, Charlotte did not overlook her necessary obligations. She was conscientious, as conscientious as her son, and she asked Alfreda to contact the tax office, to tell them that

Stefan would not be in for work that morning. The office suggested that they should consult a solicitor. Charlotte Kiszko did not act sufficiently expeditiously to be of much assistance to her son.

At eleven thirty on Monday, 22 December DSupt Holland and DS Akeroyd returned to interview Kiszko. He was still not under arrest, but he was surely by now firmly under suspicion, for the questioning began again about the note of the registration number ADK 539 L. The police account of the conversation began with Holland insisting, 'I know that that car passed the scene of the murder,' before he asked Kiszko, 'How did you come to write that number down? Have you ever been involved in an accident with the vehicle?' 'No,' came the reply, 'I just can't remember. I can't tell you anything about that, my mind's a blank.' 'Your job is being concerned with figures,' came back the senior officer, 'and your boss tells me you are most accurate and meticulous in your work.' 'Yes, I can remember most things but I just can't remember anything about that,' was the forlorn reply.

This questioning can only have taken a matter of a few minutes, but then, curiously, Dick Holland told Kiszko that he had to make further enquiries, and that he was going to leave Kiszko with DS Akeroyd.

It is not clear why Holland left. What was Akeroyd to do with Kiszko whilst his superior officer was out of the room? Was he to continue to question him or were they to sit in silence, or talk about matters unconnected with the enquiry? If he was to continue questioning Kiszko, how could this be 'safely' done with only one officer in the room, and why should he continue questioning Kiszko in the absence of the senior officer? If he was not to question Kiszko, what was the point in him remaining in the room with him? What enquiries had to be made, and why did Holland have to make them so soon after the beginning of the first interview of that day? (It would later be asserted by Holland that he had left to supervise the loading of Kiszko's car on to a transporter bound for the forensic science laboratory, but this cannot be correct, since that had been done the day before.) Why, if the interview had not commenced until eleven thirty that day, had Holland not made whatever enquiry had become so urgent prior to commencing interview with his only suspect? The questions concerning the conduct of this interview remain unanswered, but they require asking and answering in the light of what the police report as happening next.

As Akeroyd and Kiszko sat together in the room, it may be that

Kiszko had by now become sufficiently familiar with this particular officer to regard him as someone he could talk to. 'What is going to happen now?' he asked. 'When can I go home?' 'Mr Holland has just told you that he is going to make further enquiries into the matter,' said DS Akeroyd, and at that moment, according to the officer, Stefan Kiszko confessed to the killing of Lesley Molseed.

'Oh, this is terrible,' he said, 'it's those damn injections. All this would never have happened.'

'What has happened?' asked the sergeant.

'Well that thing at Kingsway Youth Club and that little girl I picked up,' was Kiszko's reply. He was asked which little girl and he went on:

'That little girl, Lesley. I don't know what happened. It's all a bit hazy. It's those damn injections.'

'Are you telling me that you picked Lesley Molseed up in your motor car?' asked DS Akeroyd, amazed by the developing conversation, but not losing sight of his objective as an investigating officer.

'Yes,' came the reply. 'You see I can't help myself when I've had my injection.'

'When did you pick Lesley up?' was the next question, and the sergeant was astounded to receive the reply

'On that Sunday dinner-time, the day that I killed her.'

DS Akeroyd had heard enough, but was clearly anxious not to break the flow of the admission by going for Dick Holland. He did, however, administer to Kiszko the caution once more, before asking this question, 'Are you telling me that you murdered Lesley Molseed?' Kiszko replied, 'Yes, I killed that little girl.'

DS Akeroyd then reports that he opened the door of the interview room and 'made a communication' as a result of which he was joined, 'almost immediately' by DSupt Holland and Chief Inspector Thomas Steele. Turning back to Kiszko Akeroyd said, 'Now Stefan, you just tell these two officers again what you have just told me,' and Kiszko immediately said, 'I killed that little girl, I stabbed Lesley.' This time it was Holland who administered the caution before asking Kiszko how it had happened.

The young man showed signs of the emotional strain he was, no doubt, labouring under, when he then told his story.

'I went out for a run on my own in the car and I went through Turf Hill towards Broad Lane. Lesley was on the side of the road near a pub. I stopped and I can't remember what I said to get her into the car but I drove up there. I had been to Ripponden once before. Soon after I got the car I went up the motorway and came off there and I went down into Ripponden and I sort of got lost. I had to turn round near some bollards and I finished up going back home to Rochdale another way. I went through Littleborough to get back but I didn't take her so far, I just took her off the road. I drove into the lay-by [. . .] I talked to her in the car and then something came over me. I go all hazy and queer when I've had my injections, like I keep telling you [. . .] I took her up the hillside on to the moor and she struggled a bit. I held her down and I played with myself on to her.'

Dick Holland asked him whether he masturbated a lot, and Kiszko replied, 'Not very much but only since I started with the injections. You will find a hanky near my bed.'

He was then asked what happened with the knife, and he replied, 'I got my knife out and stuck it in her neck.' He demonstrated how he had put his arm around the girl over her right shoulder with the knife to her throat, whilst they were lying down. Asked what happened after that he said: 'Look, I just went blank and hazy I just can't remember anything. I don't know what came over me. I don't remember driving home or leaving up there.' He did, however, remember wiping the knife, which he said was the bone-handled one, on the girl or her clothes.

He was asked, finally, about the matter outside the youth club and he told DSupt Holland that he would tell him everything: 'I just want to get it off my chest. I don't know what has come over me. It's the tablets and the injections.' DSupt Holland asked Kiszko if by this he meant that he wanted to make a statement and Kiszko replied, 'Yes, I want to get it all sorted out.'

Before supervising the written statement, Dick Holland paused to ensure the continuing investigations were being attended to. All too aware that a conviction could not be guaranteed if it were based on a confession alone, even one which was in the form of a statement signed by the accused, Holland wanted corroborative evidence. Kiszko's car had already been sent to Ronald Outteridge in Harrogate. The knives and the handkerchief would also go to Outteridge, to whom Holland had spoken by telephone when he had asked the scientist to examine the handkerchief to ascertain whether Kiszko had a low sperm count, and the knives for traces of blood.

At 3.20 p.m. on Monday, 22 December a statement was taken at Stefan Kiszko's dictation, which ran to nearly seven pages in handwritten form. He was cautioned first, and the statement was witnessed by Dick Holland and Detective Superintendent John Wheater.

He began by explaining the treatment he had received, both before and after his discharge from hospital on 15 September. Speaking of the injections and tablets he repeated what he had said during the interviews, namely that they made him feel dizzy and that they also made him 'fancy' girls. He said that these feelings lasted for three to four days after the injections.

He dealt first with the youth club incident on Friday, 3 October, although he could not recall whether it was the Friday or the Saturday, nor indeed the date, other than it being the beginning of October.

> It was fairly dark, there was a disco going on at the youth club and two girls came down the road towards the disco. Something came over me and I got out of my car unzipped my trousers and got my penis out. I had a knife in my hand but that was a mere triviality.

It is only clear that he was talking about the Friday because he then went on to deal with the incident in Vavasour Street, which we know happened on Saturday, 4 October.

> The following day about dinner-time I had put an old carpet into my car to take and dump on some spare ground near Vavasour Street. I stopped my car in one of the side streets near Vavasour Street. I got out, opened the boot up and took out the carpet, it was a pretty hefty one . . . I unzipped myself and my shirt flap came out. I put that back in and pulled my zip back up. There was an old lady and a fellow in the street and I didn't deliberately expose myself that day.

Turning then to the following day and the abduction of Lesley, he explained how, driving down Broad Lane from Charlotte Street towards Oldham Road, he had seen a girl standing on the left, opposite to a pub on the right-hand side. He had stopped and wound his window down, but he could not recall what he had said to get her into the car, only that she had got into the front. He had driven off and she had started shouting, and he had hit her with his hand. He again explained the route he had taken, to the lay-by, and then taking her up the grass banking to a flat place. He then detailed how he had begun to play with himself and had then laid her down, so that they were side by side.

[I] held her with one hand and used my left hand to wank with. She was laid facing me and I was laid on my right-hand side. I shot between her legs over her knickers. I did not remove her knickers. I had a knife in my pocket and I took it out and stabbed her in the throat. She was still crying. I got a hazy feeling and I can't remember where or how I stabbed her. She slumped away from me and I don't remember what happened after that. I left her where she was and I didn't bother to look. I got back into the car and drove back home. I didn't tell my mother what I had done. I put my knife back into my pocket and I wiped it on to her clothes or something. I can't remember what. I was a bit hazy then.

At 5.35 p.m. the statement was finished, and signed by Kiszko and the officers. He was placed in a cell and, at last, the services of a solicitor were engaged for him, namely Albert Wright of Hartley, Thomas, Wright & Sons, Rochdale.

By this time Ronald Outteridge had arrived in Halifax to liaise personally with the investigating officers. He was on hand with Jack Dibb to receive the first reports from the laboratory. Contrary to what Kiszko had said, there were no semen traces on either the tissues from the car, his trousers or a rag taken from under Kiszko's pillow. These initial reports were met with understandable disappointment, but Brian Damper went on to announce to Dibb and Outteridge that there were semen traces on the handkerchief found under his pillow. Moreover, the semen was devoid of sperm heads. Kiszko was incapable of producing sperm, and, it was believed, the murderer of Lesley Molseed was also believed to be infertile. To complete the picture building up, Damper reported that traces of blood had been found in the nail nick of the lock knife on which further blood grouping tests were being carried out.

The officers took time to review the position, examine where the forensic evidence was leading and assess where the case should go from this point, but at that moment DSupt Wheater joined them to announce that Kiszko had retracted his confession. Wheater had been left sitting with Kiszko for some time, their silence only intermittently broken by Kiszko asking questions about when he could go home. The superintendent reports that it was at 6 p.m. that Kiszko suddenly said, 'What I said was lies. I want to go home to my mum.' Wheater had been stunned, and had asked Kiszko if he realised what he had said, 'Yes,' replied Kiszko, 'I want to see my mum.'

By 6.20 p.m. on Monday, 22 December Kiszko had seen and spoken with Albert Wright, telling him that he had only confessed so that he could go home to his mother, in the belief that the police themselves would prove that he was not the killer. At that time Dick Holland went to Kiszko, to be told by Mr Wright that Kiszko wished to make a further statement retracting what he had said. Kiszko said that that was correct. 'I only made the other (statement) so that you would let me go home.' 'Are you suggesting,' said Mr Holland 'that I promised you something if you made that first statement?' Kiszko replied, 'No, I just thought that if I told you that you would let me out.' He and his solicitor were quite clear when they told both Holland and Jack Dibb that they had no complaint to make about Kiszko's treatment in the police station.

A second statement was taken at 6.30 p.m. In it Kiszko retracted his admission concerning 3 October, but maintained as accurate his account of 4 October. As for 5 October, he adhered to his account of going out in the car that day – thus leaving in place, in any event, the prosecution's later argument that he had lied as to whether or not he had gone out at all on that Sunday – but denied going near the M62 or picking up or killing the girl. The statement was concluded at 7.25 p.m. and was signed by Kiszko and by Mr Wright and Mr Holland.

Whether Stefan Kiszko thought that this retraction statement would bring about his release from custody is unclear, but Mr Wright knew that it would not, and Mr Holland clearly had no intention of releasing his suspect. In the course of the evening of 22 December Holland had Kiszko examined by Dr Edward Tierney, the police surgeon for Greater Manchester police, Rochdale division. The experienced police officer was now looking to support his admission evidence with more tangible forensic, medical and scientific evidence, and Dr Tierney concluded his examination by taking samples of plucked and cut head and pubic hair, skin shavings, two blood, saliva and urine samples. Dr Tierney made the unusual request of a semen sample, but Kiszko, who was proud of his recently acquired ability to ejaculate, willingly complied with the request without demur. Finally the doctor took a penile swab, following which Kiszko was returned to his cell.

The following morning, at a little after midnight, the medical examination at an end, Dick Holland again saw Kiszko. Mr Wright had left, and whilst Kiszko was now undoubtedly suspected of murder (indeed, was now believed to be the murderer), and whilst Mr Holland administered the caution, it was not thought appropriate to bring Mr Wright back to the police station for the interview which DSupt Holland then conducted, at 12.15 a.m. on Tuesday, 23 December.

He began by asking Kiszko, again, about the number ADK 539 L, and again Kiszko was unable to provide an answer. 'I have ascertained,' said Mr Holland, 'that the owner of that vehicle [. . .] has only been over to Ripponden three times, once on the afternoon of the murder. How could you have got that number written down if you did not take it down on the journey when you had the girl Lesley Molseed with you?' On the face of it, this was a fairly telling, albeit only circumstantial, piece of evidence against Kiszko. Considering it rather more carefully, however, it added little to the case. It did not follow that Kiszko had to have written the number down on 5 October. He could have written it down on one of the car-owner's other two trips to Ripponden, or he might have recorded it at any other time in any other place that that car had been. Kiszko habitually wrote down car numbers, for the reason he had already explained to Holland. He wrote down the number of any driver who drove in a manner which offended him. For example, on 10 April 1975 Kiszko had reported to a PC Kenneth Bell that vehicles had been trying to force him off the road. He had kept a note of three such vehicles and it was apparent that he, thereafter, habitually noted the number of any vehicle which was, in his opinion, being driven dangerously.

A further interview then took place in the cell area of the police station. Bearing in mind that Kiszko had made a full statement of admission, and had then, when enjoying the benefit of the services of his solicitor Mr Wright, retracted that admission, what happened next is extremely surprising. The interview consisted of only one question and one answer:

Holland   From your first statement you have described the effects of the drugs and if you were hazy and can't remember how do you know that what you told me in the first statement is untrue?

Kiszko   I am all of a blue. I have told you the truth. I remember the girl by the shop in Broad Lane and taking her to the moors. I must have stabbed her. That's how I showed you the bone-handled knife.

It has never been doubted that Holland accurately noted the contents of this brief interview. Yet the interview remains, for all its brevity, truly remarkable. Stefan Kiszko had admitted and then retracted an admission to killing Lesley Molseed. There appears to be no reason whatsoever why he should then go on to admit the murder again, and certainly no reason was given by him or by Holland in the record made by the detective superintendent. If Kiszko was making an admission in these circumstances, why did the superintendent not go on to ask him further questions, in particular, about the circumstances of the killing and the reason Kiszko had retracted his earlier admission and was now admitting the killing again? Why was this interview not followed by the making of a formal, signed statement, which, with Kiszko's signature affixed, would support what Holland was now recording as having been said? Why had Holland not – as had been done before – brought another police officer into the room to hear Kiszko make this fresh admission, so that there could be no doubt as to Holland's veracity when he gave evidence of it? Why did Holland not invite Albert Wright back to the police station so that he could witness his client's latest admission? It has never been explained why Holland – however confident he was at that stage – faced as he was with one retraction statement made in the presence of a solicitor, left the matter on the morning of the twenty-third at one question and one answer.

It is clear that Holland, at this stage, was satisfied that Lesley Molseed's killer had been caught, for he directed his enquiry team to withdraw all other lines of enquiry. McFadzean was sent to the Inland Revenue office where he searched Kiszko's desk, recovering a blue and white felt-tipped pen, a comb case and a novel. Detective Sergeant Merrick and Detective Constable Peckitt went to 25 Kings Road. In the garage they found an exposed film and some white Solvite paste powder. The garage also yielded some curtains, rugs, shirts and two knives. Samples of the materials were taken. At the police station Kiszko's clothing was taken from him, and, in return, he was given the clothing of the suspected murderer, a white, paper boiler suit.

Dibb and Holland were now satisfied that they had sufficient evidence on which to charge Kiszko with murder, and arrangements were put into effect for him to be transferred to Halifax in Dick Holland's private car, in the company of Akeroyd.

There was to be one final and macabre act before the investigation of Stefan Kiszko on 23 December was at an end. At ten fifteen that night, long after daylight had gone and long, therefore, after anything of value could be seen, DSupt Holland and DS

Akeroyd drove Kiszko up to the lay-by adjacent to where the body of Lesley Molseed was found. It was not along a route directed by Kiszko. Nothing of evidential value seems to have been obtained either on the journey or at the lay-by. But the car was stopped and, on that dark winter's night at the terrible place where Lesley had died, Kiszko started to shake and he held his hands in a praying position. 'I can hear voices, can't you?' said the obviously frightened young man, before this bizarre detour was brought to an end and the journey resumed to Halifax where, at ten minutes before midnight on Tuesday, 23 December 1975, in the presence of Albert Wright and Inspector Slocombe, DSupt Dick Holland charged Stefan Ivan Kiszko with the murder of Lesley Susan Molseed. He was cautioned, but he said nothing, leaving it to Mr Wright to utter on his behalf, 'No reply.'

On Christmas Eve, Wednesday, 24 December 1975, Stefan Kiszko was brought before the Halifax Magistrates' Court and the charge against him was read out in public for the first time.

The court at Halifax is of Victorian design: blackened stone on the outside, dark-brown woods forming the seats and panels on the inside. The prisoner is brought to the rear of the court by police van, then escorted to the cells until it is his turn to be brought up' in this magnificent building, the use of that word is entirely appropriate. The dock into which Stefan Kiszko was brought towers above the rest of the court, being some twelve to fifteen feet above the ground. The public seats were full, and all eyes strained upwards to see the imposing yet humble figure of the accused man. He stood, almost slumped in the dock, his appearance of shabbiness in dramatic contrast to the uniformed officers who, sentry-like, acted as his escorts. His head was bowed, and he spoke only once, to confirm his name, his answer lost in the sheer size of the courtroom. Given that Rochdale was resounding, not only to the peal of Christmas bells, but to the clarion calls for the hanging of Lesley Molseed's murderer, there was little prospect of Kiszko being granted bail. A petition favouring the restoration of hanging and a referendum on the restoration of capital punishment for child murders had been organised by Mrs Pat Conroy, an aunt of Lesley's, and, within a week of the child's death, had raised 10,000 signatures. It is perhaps fortunate for Stefan Kiszko that those calls were to fall upon deaf ears during the remainder of his lifetime.

The Prosecution of Stefan Kiszko

In 1975 there was no independent prosecuting authority, such as the Crown Prosecution Service (CPS), and each police force employed solicitors to prepare and pursue cases. Nevertheless, in certain cases, notably murder, there was a duty on a police force to notify the director of public prosecutions (DPP) of the charge and the evidence. The director's authority was required for such a case to continue, and the case would become his responsibility. It followed that Holland was obliged to prepare a file on the case against Kiszko, for submission to the DPP.

It was clearly never intended that the prosecution case would rest on Kiszko's confession alone, although the fact that Dick Holland had chosen to charge Kiszko with murder by 23 December indicates that he at least had the greatest confidence in that confession. In truth, there was little more to the case against Kiszko than the confession, by the time the charge was put to him. This had to be a concern for Holland, for a confession without support from the evidence could end up being worthless. He needed corroboration, especially if (as he had done in the police station) Kiszko recanted the confession when the case came for trial.

The evidence of the girls concerning the events of 3 and 4 October and 5 November, although incorporated into Holland's file for the DPP, was in no way capable of proving murder. Indeed, had the defence objected to the admission of that evidence at the trial, it is quite possible that the trial judge would have refused to allow it to be admitted, since it was extremely prejudicial to the defence, purporting to show, as it did, the propensity of the accused to commit offences against young girls. The enquiry into motor vehicles had produced nothing of value. There was no eye-witness evidence as to the abduction or the killing. They had, it is true, found sweets and balloons in Kiszko's car, and he also admitted possession of two knives, but even those items added little to the weight of evidence against the suspected man.

As to the incident of 3 October 1975 Colin Peers, who was one witness out of a possible seven, had described the man as having a pair of binoculars. Binoculars were recovered from Kiszko's bedroom, so Peers' evidence would be corroborated by the finding of the binoculars. Holland would also make reference to finding other knives, the 'girlie' magazines and the evidence that Kiszko masturbated.

As to 4 October, the evidence was slightly stronger, with Kiszko owning a parka similar to that described by the witnesses, the identification of Kiszko's house in Crawford Street and the description of the car as being 'gold', where Kiszko drove a car which was 'spice', but in simple terms was gold- or bronze-coloured. In particular, there was Maxine Buckley's identification, on 5 November, of Stefan Kiszko as the man involved on 4 October.

At best, however, this amounted to evidence that Kiszko had indecently exposed himself on 4 October, an offence aggravated by his conduct on other occasions. It fell far short of proving murder.

Holland had witness statements concerning sightings of Lesley on 5 October, and from those sightings it was possible for him to extract a number of witnesses, the totality of their evidence being such as to nearly match the description given by Kiszko in his 'confessions' to the route which he had taken, and the place where he had abducted Lesley. This was crucial evidence, for a confession which is supported by prosecution evidence gains substantial strength, whereas, quite obviously, a confession the content of which is diametrically opposed to the prosecution evidence may have little probative value.

Other statements supported the police contention that Lesley had probably been abducted by twelve noon, and Holland went on in his report to deal with the finding of the body by David Greenwell, at a location within the West Yorkshire boundary, which had brought about the involvement of the police and, in particular, Holland himself.

There then followed the scientific evidence: the post-mortem report of Professor Gee and the forensic examination by Ronald Outteridge of the scene and of Lesley's body, clothing and possessions. Of particular note was the light semen staining on Lesley's knickers, which would accord with Kiszko's confession that he 'shot between her legs'.

In dealing with the registration numbers written down by Kiszko, Holland would note that two of the numbers had never even been issued, although one, ADK 539 L belonged to a Renault car owned by a Mr Derek Hollos, who had driven past the murder scene at 2.30 p.m. on Sunday, 5 October. Mr Hollos and his wife, who had bought the car in February 1975, were to give statements going as far as possible to exclude any possibility of having had contact with Kiszko other than on 5 October. The previous owner, a Mr Albert Oldham of Rochdale, had owned the car between November 1972 and January 1975, but could recall no incident where his car registration number might have been taken by another motorist.

Naturally, the final part of the file submitted by Holland concentrated on the investigation of Stefan Kiszko: all that was known of him and all that had been said by him, both at his home and in the interviews and statements made at the police station. Emphasis was made of the lies told by Kiszko, which were, it would be alleged, probative of the truth contained in his ultimate admissions. Of particular relevance was Kiszko's assertion that he had first driven his car, and left his home, on 12 October 1975, having been discharged from hospital on 15 September: that assertion would be juxtapositioned with his admissions regarding 3 and 4 October, and of the murder itself on the fifth. In accordance with the maxim that it is the lie followed by the truth which is corroborative of a case against a defendant, stress would be placed on the various denials and false assertions, and indeed Kiszko's retraction statement, when compared with his verbal and written admissions of indecent exposure and, more particularly, of murder.

So it was that Dick Holland required some tangible evidence to support the admissions he had received. He wanted fingerprints or blood-stains, he wanted fibres or hairs. He wanted the evidence that could not be obtained from eyewitnesses or from Kiszko alone. He wanted what has come to be known in every good crime story as 'The Forensic Evidence'.

Work on the scientific side of the investigation had, of course, begun from the moment of the discovery of Lesley's body. Ronald Outteridge at the end of extensive and exhaustive examination of a substantial number of samples and exhibits, reported to Holland that there was not found upon Stefan Kiszko, or any of his possessions seized by the police, anything which could be undoubtedly said to be Lesley's blood, although there was extensive blood-staining at the scene of her death, and upon her clothing. He had examined a large number of items recovered from Kiszko, including no less than five knives, two penknives and a pair of scissors. His extensive array of tests was able to prove nothing more than that on the one lock knife, which had a blade 3¾ inches long by ½ inch wide, there was a trace amount of blood, but he could not say even what animal that blood had come from, still less what group the blood belonged to. It was as far as one could get from proving that the knife had been used to kill Lesley Molseed. It would be surprising if a 'frenzied attack' of the sort suffered by Lesley did not give rise to a copious spray of blood, so that one might expect blood-staining on clothing worn by the assailant. No trace of blood was ever found on any clothing belonging to Kiszko. Of course, it would be extremely easy to dispose of (rather than attempt to wash clean) any blood-stained clothing, but if Kiszko had done that, why had he not also disposed of the knives, which it could be suggested had been used in the attacks, and, in particular, the lock knife with the blood-staining? Why too was there no trace of blood in Kiszko's car: if he had driven away from the murder scene with blood on his hands or clothes, surely some trace would be left in the car, unless it too had been subjected to scrupulous cleaning?

Outteridge then turned, however, to the semen staining upon Lesley's underwear, from which there was a possibility that the blood group of the man who had ejaculated on to her could be discovered. Again he was obliged to report that attempts to identify blood group secretor substances in the semen stains on the underwear had been unsuccessful. It therefore appeared that there was nothing upon Lesley which could point to Kiszko, nor was there anything on any of the possessions of Stefan Kiszko which could show that he had ever been in contact with the dead girl.

Nothing, that is, until Mr Outteridge examined Lesley's jumper, vest, skirt and socks. From the first two garments he recovered two pale-yellow wool fibres. From Lesley's skirt, a bright-yellow wool fibre, and from her right sock an orange rayon fibre. When Stefan Kiszko's car was examined, there was a carpet on the floor. That carpet piece, the trial would be told, had come from a stair carpet which Stefan's aunt, Alfreda Tosic, had fitted in her home some years earlier. There had been a remnant which Mrs Tosic had given to Stefan to use as a mat in his car. The remnant of carpet contained pale-yellow and bright-yellow wool fibres and orange rayon fibres, which enabled Mr Outteridge to say that his findings were 'consistent' with Lesley Molseed having been a passenger in Kiszko's car.

It was a link, but it was a tenuous one. A fibre of wool is not a strand of DNA. A carpet may be commonplace, and the trial judge was at pains, in fairness to Kiszko, to make this point clear to the jury when he advised them to 'bear in mind that carpet fibres are not particularly unusual either in shade or variety and very considerable quantities of this carpeting must have been manufactured'.

Thus it was that, perhaps because of the limits of forensic science, perhaps for other reasons, the forensic evidence in the case against Kiszko was limited to a relatively weak connection between Lesley and the car, based on the carpet. There was virtually nothing from the power of science to incriminate Kiszko.

The report to be submitted to the DPP, quite apart from containing an assessment of the case against the accused, had also to consider the antecedent history of the accused and the possible defences which would be open to him. In particular, there would need to be consideration of any circumstances which might go to reducing the charge of murder to one of manslaughter as, for example, where there was evidence of some provocation or where the known facts of the defendant's mental state enabled a defence of diminished responsibility to be put forward. In such circumstances (which did not at that stage pertain to the Kiszko case) a guilty plea to manslaughter might be acceptable to the Crown.

The police in the Kiszko case had to consider possible lines of defence, and, if Kiszko was to deny the killing at all, he would need to adduce alibi evidence, that is, evidence that he was elsewhere at the time of the commission of the offence. To that end officers had interviewed both Charlotte Kiszko and Alfreda Tosic since these two ladies would be the most likely alibi witnesses called by Kiszko.

Charlotte Kiszko spoke fondly of how Stefan would use his car at weekends to take her and her sister to garden centres or would drive them up to the moors to dig peat for the garden plants. As to the events of the weekend of 3 to 5 October 1975, Charlotte remembered Stefan receiving his injections on Friday, the third, but was unable to remember exactly what he had done on the Saturday or Sunday, but she confidently asserted that '[he] has not been out of my sight for longer than half an hour'.

Alfreda Tosic was interviewed by DC Whittle. She recalled that Stefan had a hospital appointment on 3 October. She also recalled that on either 5 or 12 October she had gone out with Stefan and Charlotte in Stefan's car to the garden centre at Royton, a trip she was able to describe in some detail, including the fact that they had returned to the Kiszko house for coffee, and had heard a fire engine go to a nearby house. This detail enabled the police to prove that Mrs Tosic was speaking of 12 October, as fire officers were able to confirm their attendance at a fire in Crawford Street on 12 October, and that no emergency calls were made for that area on Sunday, 5 October.

To Dick Holland's doubtless satisfaction, neither woman was capable of providing Kiszko with an alibi for 5 October. Despite Charlotte's assertion that Stefan had never been out of her sight for more than half an hour, it was clear that both women had a poor recollection of the relevant dates.

The report completed, Holland ordered that all ongoing enquiries and actions be abandoned. One series of actions related to a man who had been eliminated as an indecency suspect at an earlier stage, but who had been actioned for interview. This man, who lived in the nearby Todmorden area, had disappeared on the day Lesley's body had been discovered, and did not return for several weeks. He was, the police had noted with interest, the owner of a light-blue/green Morris 1000 van, a vehicle he had disposed of. He had not been eliminated from the enquiry, but charging Kiszko, the submission of the report to the DPP and Holland's order to cease all further actions meant that the man would not be 'eliminated' from the enquiry, but rather that the enquiry would be wound up leaving him an untouched loose end.

Holland was confident that Stefan Kiszko was Lesley Molseed's killer, for he had Kiszko's confessions and, despite the retraction statement, the substance of the admissions, including the admission made after the retraction, powerfully indicated guilt. Whether Kiszko would be convicted of murder or of manslaughter remained to be seen, for Holland was aware that, in his interviews, Kiszko had, at least, sown the seeds of a diminished responsibility defence by his references to his medical treatment and to going 'hazy'.

The confidence of Dick Holland and his men was shared by the residents of Turf Hill and of Rochdale. People spoke of how strange Kiszko had been. Sheila Buckley said that they had thought all along that he was the killer. The community's hatred and loathing of what Kiszko had done to the frail, waif-like Lesley Molseed was transferred in his absence to his undoubtedly innocent mother, Charlotte, who found herself increasingly ostracised. Forgetting that there still existed a presumption of innocence in the English legal system, the mayor of Rochdale led the accolades for the investigating team, by sending them a letter of congratulations which was followed by a civic reception for key officers in the investigation.

The darkness which had blighted the October investigation was replaced by blinding euphoria that the killer had been caught. For many the trial was regarded as a mere formality prior to conviction and a deserved life sentence for the defendant.

CHAPTER TWELVE

Oliver Laurel

As the police and lawyers continued with their preparations of the case, Stefan Kiszko remained in the background, held on remand in one of the country's most notorious prisons.

When the pear-shaped, knock-kneed tax clerk with the soft, high-pitched voice joined the hard cases at Armley Prison in Leeds he was, unsurprisingly, regarded as a curiosity. He was 'christened' Oliver Laurel, because he had the girth of Oliver Hardy and the permanently perplexed air of Olly's comedy sidekick Stan Laurel. He even displayed a nervous habit of lightly fingering his thinning hair.

What saved Kiszko at that stage from the traditional reception for what prisoners called 'nonces', sex offenders, was that he was unconvicted, and it was difficult to believe that this ambling oaf could have dragged a child to the back of beyond and stabbed her savagely. The inmates of the Yorkshire prison, untainted by the local fervour following the Molseed murder in Rochdale, were prepared to believe – as they so frequently are – that Kiszko had been fitted up by the police. After all, not a few of them had been arrested in their time by men serving under Dick Holland, and so were always prepared to think the worst of those policemen. To them, Kiszko had been fitted up because the police had made him confess to a crime he said he didn't do, a confession which he had retracted once his brief had got through to him. The prisoners needed to know little else at this stage.

'Oliver Laurel', unaware of his new identity, seemed oblivious to most of those around him, as he had always seemed to be, whether at school, college or work. He was seemingly un-perturbed about the enormity of his situation. It was not stupidity but immaturity. He had been in his favourite armchair by the fireside, contemplating his first Christmas with mother in their new home. Now, three days later, he was in jail, for the first time in his life. In two days it would be Christmas Day and he had never been away from his mother on Christmas morning. His preoccupation in Armley was not with his own predicament, but with that of his mother. She would be fretting for him, and that concerned him. What must have been going through her mind as her beloved son had been standing in the dock of Calder Magistrates' Court, wearing a white paper boiler suit given to replace his own clothes and flanked by two police officers and handcuffed to one of them.

It was standard procedure for a man charged with murder to appear in chains. Stefan recalled with a shudder the memory of his mother and Aunt Alfreda at the back of the oak-lined court-room, holding hands, pale and listening to the prosecutor outlining the gravity of the charge to the magistrates that he, Stefan Kiszko, had on the fifth day of October 1975, murdered Lesley Molseed.

Anthony Kilory, the clerk of the court, had asked Stefan if he was Stefan Ivan Kiszko and he had nodded in agreement. He understood the gravity of the charge, but not why they believed he was the murderer. He had made a confession, but they had shouted at him and then offered him orangeade and said he would be home for Christmas. He had signed the papers handed to him by the police officer, sheet by sheet, and he had put his name at the bottom of each piece of paper as it was handed over, all the while thinking about his fireside chair, and how he would soon be sitting there, sipping sherry with his mother. But then they had taken him to a cell at the police station. They had not let him go home. They had not been men of their word.

Stefan had uttered only four words at that two-minute first court hearing: '25, Kings Road, Rochdale', in response to the clerk asking him for his home address. There had been no application for bail by his solicitor.

Within five minutes of the magistrates remanding Kiszko in custody, he was leaving the court building through a back exit, ushered away with an escort of six policemen, added security, to prevent his escape, or to protect the accused. DCS Jack Dibb and DSupt Dick Holland left by the front door, applauded as heroes by the few people gathered outside. They took to their official car to be whisked back to police headquarters. Stefan Kiszko was loaded into a van and taken to Armley Prison in Leeds. Stefan had never been to Leeds in his life, but this was to be no adventure in Yorkshire's first city. Stefan was headed for the 'house on the hill', the gloomy, dark, foreboding Victorian prison, situated just outside the city centre. At night, cars heading out of Leeds towards the

M62 motorway which Kiszko's father had helped to lay, could see the looming shadow of the prison against the lights of the suburb of Armley, and in the day, parents driving past with their children would point out Armley and say,

'Be good, or that is where you will end up.'

25 December 1975 was a forlorn Christmas Day for mother and son. Stefan sat silently in his cell, unable to join in with the remand prisoners' dinner.

Charlotte Kiszko had endured a sleepless night. The tree downstairs had lost its lustre. The unopened presents around the base served only to emphasise the separation. In the night, Charlotte had occasionally sworn out loud in her broken East European accent. She had picked up some choice language in the hard school of the cotton mill. She could lip-read a range of expletives in four different languages. There were no shrinking violets in the mill, but the women workers had team spirit, loyalty to each other and a sense of fair play. Charlotte woke on Christmas morning wondering whether her son had enjoyed such fair play. He was languishing in a jail cell thirty miles away across the Pennines.

She stared blankly at the Christmas cards strung along the walls of the rear parlour. She ignored the tree, and the presents. She went to Alfreda's where the elder sister was caring for her housebound husband. Alfreda Tosic put her own problems behind her, for they were secondary to her duty to her sister: she knew Charlotte was all alone save for her, and Alfreda missed and worried for her nephew in much the same way as Charlotte. The sisters made plans for their first visit to Leeds on Boxing Day. There was no bus service that day, so a neighbour took them. In all the sisters were to make another fifty-seven return journeys to Leeds between Boxing Day 1975 and the end of Stefan's trial at 4.10 p.m. 21 July 1976, a total of 3,420 miles and, apart from that first journey, always by bus.

Both Charlotte and Stefan were bolstered by faith. Charlotte, of course, was utterly convinced of her son's innocence, and that would suffice. When Stefan told the jury that he did not do this terrible thing, she believed that would be enough. They would believe him, and he would come home. She shared Stefan's unswerving conviction that the system of British fair play and justice would soon see him freed and returning home. Stefan continued to believe that it was the police who would prove that he was innocent of the crime with which he had been charged.

Mother and son sought hard to reassure each other and, at that time, neither gave any thought to the possibility that things might not proceed as they believed.

Stefan wrote to Charlotte prolifically, and she equally to him. Paramount in their thoughts was the need not to distress each other. Charlotte did not reveal her inner turmoil and Stefan kept his more miserable days a secret. They maintained a mutual buoyancy, writing thousands of words of blandness, underpinned with an apparent confidence that justice would eventually prevail, and Stefan would be tending his roses by July.

Kiszko was more candid in letters to a colleague at the Rochdale Inland Revenue, Mrs Brenda Lord, who befriended Charlotte when Stefan was sent to Armley on remand. He penned his first letter to Mrs Lord in February 1976, after Charlotte had told him of Brenda's kindness. No one else outside the family had been so kind. Neighbours had been cordial but the immigrant East European workers of the cotton mills had shunned the Kiszkos, believing Stefan had disgraced the community which had successfully integrated with Rochdale's indigenous population, through hard work and law-abiding behaviour.

Christmas without mother was still on Stefan's mind when he wrote his first letter to Mrs Lord on 7 February 1976.

Dear Brenda
I hope you had a nice Christmas. My mother spent hers crying her heart out. And of course I spent mine here in prison. Yes, my mother and I have not had such a nice time in the past with one thing or another. As soon as things were looking better, something had to come along and mess it up again. I was looking forward to the office party on the Monday when the police came on the Sunday morning, December 21st and here I am in Her Majesty's prison for a crime which I have not committed. I am missing my mother very much and mum is missing me too. The only thing I am wishing for at the moment is to be reunited with my dear mum. With it being the first Christmas and New Year in our new home, mother and I were really looking forward to spending it together.

Kiszko referred to his stay in hospital for treatment to his broken ankle and the treatment for anaemia:

The doctors said there was no hope for me coming out of the hospital alive, but I made it. How I regret to this day that it did not come true. Possibly the police would then have got the right murderer. I really would not mind being back at work either, but what can you do but wait patiently for the time when I can go home.

I shall be celebrating my 24th birthday on March 24th here in the company of HMP Armley.

A week later, Stefan wrote of his disappointment that he would not be able to see his Uncle Peter for the first time in his life. Uncle Peter, his late father's brother, lived in Australia and had planned to visit Rochdale on 22 May:

I was looking forward to seeing him so much, but now with me locked up for something I have not done, he has had to postpone it.

On 27 February Kiszko wrote again to Brenda Lord:

I have always been in the good books with my mother and Aunt Freda and I love them very much. No-one realises how it breaks my heart that mum has to go through something like this knowing that I am innocent and locked up. I did so want to see how the garden was progressing this season because most of the work has been done by my mother and my aunt. I am glad to hear you liked the sweetheart plant in the front room. If it could talk it could tell a long story because it is as old as I am.

I have been moved from the small cell to somewhere where I can watch TV but it is still not like being in our nice house with my Dear Mum. Occasionally, I let my memories wander to the days when Dad and Grandma were still alive and the happy days we had together on holiday in Austria. I can't but help let some tears flow.

On 8 March Kiszko wrote, thanking Brenda for her kindness to Charlotte, but it was clear that he was despondent, particularly regarding his mother:

I am not doing badly but I am missing my dear mum. I am missing being at home with her and taking her for a ride in the car. I feel very sorry for her. I am hoping that this affair will soon be over and happiness can be restored to the Kiszko household. Please also express my kind regards and best wishes to all the staff of HM Inspector of Taxes, Rochdale 1.

Five days later Kiszko's letter contained strong protestations of innocence:

> My conscience is clear. Thank you for being so kind to mum and myself . . . any place is better than this. But slowly and surely, and if justice is done, I should be freed and allowed to go home as I know my conscience is clear and that I did not commit the crime with which I am charged.

> STILL ON REMAND.

Stefan's letter of 3 May 1976 contained lightness of mood and firm indications of his optimism:

> Dear Brenda,
> Mum said I am beginning to look like Cyril Smith. She is exaggerating, but I have put on some weight. I am still far away from looking like Cyril. I hope my ordeal will be over by June 9th. The trial is due to last two weeks. I know I have not done this awful murder so I see no reason why I should not be found not guilty. I hope there will soon be a happy ending.

On 25 May Stefan wrote to Brenda Lord about his Uncle Peter, who had made the trip from Australia despite Kiszko still being in prison.

> [Uncle Peter] is stopping for a while and will be attending the trial. If all goes well, the trial should be over just in time for me to get home for mum's birthday and possibly uncle will still be there so we can spend some time as this is the first time in my life that I have seen him. Uncle is the spitting image of my late father, though he is not quite as stout.

On 16 June, Kiszko wrote his last letter before the trial. The letter returned to Kiszko's theme of belief in the justice system. So strong was his conviction of his own innocence that he could not conceive of a situation where the system he so admired could let him down.

> As you know my uncle from Australia is here to watch 'British justice at its very best'. What I mean is that if justice is done, I should be a free man to return home.

The letters written by Stefan Kiszko in the period between his arrest and his trial reveal a man who was, first and foremost, devoted to his mother, and as concerned for the effect that the criminal charge was having on her as its undoubted consequences for him. A constant theme of his letters, of course, was the protestation of innocence. From the moment of his so-called confession, Kiszko never again remotely averted to the possibility that he might in some way be responsible for the death of Lesley Molseed. There is not even the hint, in any letter or conversation, of his suggesting that he may have had some involvement in what he himself came to describe as 'this terrible crime', nor any suggestion that some 'dark forces' might have caused him to act in a way totally contrary to his natural character. Brenda Lord became Kiszko's only friend and confidante outside his immediate family, yet even she received nothing even approaching an admission from him.

Evident in Kiszko's letters, although they were simply written and limited in the topics covered, is the fact that this was a man who had had an education and was of reasonable, ordinary intelligence. The grammar is adequate, the spelling correct and the phraseology appropriate, and they illustrate how wrong it is to regard the writer as being in any way intellectually deficient. Stefan Kiszko was simple, in that he lacked complication or sophistication but he was not mentally underdeveloped. Such mental inadequacy as Kiszko had was in his maturity, character and personality, and not in any way in his intellect.

The final aspect of Kiszko's letters, perhaps their most dominant theme, was his unswerving faith in the so-called British system of justice, and his belief that that system and that justice would prevail, and would not merely secure his acquittal, but would prove his innocence. Such faith undoubtedly stemmed from his parents, and in particular from Charlotte. Charlotte Kiszko, who had come to England to flee injustice and oppression, had experienced only fairness and integrity since she had come to this country, and she had cause to believe that the faith she had shown when she had first arrived remained valid. Nothing had happened to her or to Stefan to contradict that firmly rooted conviction.

All that, however, had clearly changed for Stefan since his arrest in December 1975, and what is remarkable about the man, even when allowance is made for his 'simplicity', is that he retained his faith in the justice system, in particular the police. Kiszko knew that he was on remand charged with murder because of confessions which, he was to allege, had been obtained because he had believed that by assisting the police he could rely on them to allow him to return home and to pursue Lesley's actual killer. That he could continue to assert in his letters to Brenda Lord his belief that 'the system' would bring about his freedom, is, perhaps, remarkable. On one hand it reveals his very basic and uncomplicated nature, even, perhaps, his gross naivety, but on the other hand it confirms that he was very much his mother's son, an immigrant's child, who enjoyed liberty where his parents had known only oppression and subjugation.

As his trial approached, Kiszko's letters continued to express his gratitude to Mrs Lord for her support, his protestations of innocence and his expressions of confidence that 'it' would all soon be over and he would be home again with his mother. Never once did he refer to the possibility that 'it' would not be over, but that he could be convicted.

CHAPTER THIRTEEN

The Trial of Stefan Kiszko

The DPP accepted the recommendation that Kiszko be tried for murder and the case had progressed relatively swiftly through the Calder Magistrates' Court at Halifax, where Mr Wright had accepted a committal to the Crown Court without contesting any of the evidence. Kiszko remained a remand prisoner in Armley Prison whilst Mr Wright prepared his defence and the Crown's solicitors assembled the prosecution case.

The case of Regina v. Stefan Ivan Kiszko, which was listed to start at the Leeds Crown Court on 7 July 1976 was, on the face of it, an apparently straightforward case. For all that it involved one of the most heinous forms of murder – the abduction and killing of a young girl, with a sexual overtone – it was, at first glance, a relatively simple case of its type. A cursory reading of the prosecution papers revealed a case based, virtually entirely, upon the admissions made by Kiszko to the police. There was a small amount of forensic evidence to link the victim with Kiszko, the lies told by Kiszko to the police, the registration number and the incidents of 3 and 4 October and 5 November, but the thrust of the case against Kiszko was the verbal and written admissions he had made.

The defence case, also, would have the appearance of simplicity. The only way in which an acquittal could be obtained would be by running an alibi defence and, at the same time, proving[1] that the admissions made were not the truth.

The seemingly simple trial was in the hands of a formidable array of lawyers. For the prosecution, Peter Taylor QC. Educated at Newcastle-upon-Tyne Royal Grammar School and Pembroke College, Cambridge, he had been a barrister since 1954 and a Queen's Counsel since 1967. He was the leader of the North-

---

1 Strictly speaking, of course, the defence did not have to prove the alibi or that the admissions were untrue, since the burden of proof rests on the prosecution throughout a criminal trial, save in certain circumstances. Thus, in truth, it was for the prosecution to *dis*prove the alibi and to *prove* the admissions.

Eastern Circuit and was destined, within five years of this trial, to become a High Court judge. In 1992 he would be appointed the Lord Chief Justice of England, the highest ranking judge in the English criminal law. With him, Matthew Caswell, who today remains an eminent and highly respected member of the Bar. Upon Caswell fell the burden of vetting all the evidence available, identifying strengths and weaknesses in the Crown's case and giving a structure to that case for use by his leader. Pitted against such talent was a defence team comprising David Waddington QC[2] and Philip Clegg. David Waddington, educated at Sedbergh and Hartford College, Oxford, had been at the Bar since 1951 and a Queen's Counsel for four years at the date of the trial. He was also a Conservative MP and would rise to high political office, and, thereafter, to the governorship of Bermuda. His junior was Philip Clegg, a barrister of only nine years at the date of the trial, but who would himself later be a judge.

Presiding over the trial was Mr Justice Park, aged 65, a product of Blundells and Sidney Sussex College, Cambridge who had spent nearly forty years in the practice and administration of the law, the last ten of them as a judge of the Queen's Bench Division of the High Court of Justice.

These five men were, if not the best of English lawyers, then certainly amongst the best. They gathered together in the Town Hall at Leeds, the then home of the Leeds Crown Court, in the splendour of the Victorian building, to determine the fate of a civil servant from Rochdale. That fate would lie in the hands of seven men and five women, plucked from the streets of Yorkshire in order to do justice in the case of an 11-year-old girl from a town across the Pennines, with which few of them would have any familiarity.

But the injustice done to Stefan Kiszko was, at least in part, in the early stages of construction some time before those twelve people were sworn in. Long before that July morning, decisions had been taken by the lawyers representing both the Crown and Kiszko that would determine the pattern of the trial.

On 28 April 1976 written advice was submitted by Matthew Caswell, who had read all the six thousand and more statements taken by the police, to the DPP, covering twelve areas of the prosecution case as he saw it.

---

2 Albert Wright had originally retained the services of the prominent and highly respected George Carman QC. Mr Carman, however, was involved in a trial which would not finish before 7 July, and therefore Mr Waddington was retained in his stead.

The first matter was Caswell's opinion that the incidents of 3 and 4 October 1975 were admissible as what is called 'similar fact evidence', that is, evidence to prove the commission of a crime by reference to earlier acts of the accused person which are similar to those alleged. Such evidence is not admissible if it merely shows propensity, but is relevant if it goes to an issue in the case. The similarity came from the masturbation and the presence of a knife. The masturbation aspect of the case, in the sense that that was the only sexual element to the crime, was particularly unusual. Kiszko had confessed in accurate detail to the incident of 3 October. Caswell believed that the similar fact evidence would go to support the confession, and would also negate any alibi, as it was expected that the alibi would be based on Kiszko asserting that he had not, on 5 October, sufficiently recovered from his foot injury or the treatment given up to 15 September. Caswell was also anxious to introduce the evidence so as to link in the injection given to Kiszko on 3 October and the assertion by Maxine Buckley, made on 5 November after she had encountered Stefan, that he had exposed himself to her on 4 October.

It had originally been thought by the police that the earlier incidents could not be used in the prosecution of Kiszko for murder. The prosecution had, therefore, produced edited statements from a number of witnesses, in which reference to those incidents was deleted, nor had they caused to be served on the defence any statements from witnesses such as Ann Marie Storto, Sheila Woodhead, Beverley Mullins, Debbie Brown, Colin Peers, Sarah Lord and Alfred Sutcliffe, whose evidence was concerned only with those dates. Now Caswell advised that all those statements together with unedited versions of the other statements be sent to the defence.

In normal circumstances the question of admissibility of similar fact evidence would be a matter of law for the trial judge to determine. As it was, Caswell's proper concerns as to admissibility and his careful exposition of the argument in favour of the admission of the evidence in this case would prove to be un-necessary, since the unusual defence tactics caused that similar fact evidence to be introduced by agreement between prosecution and defence.

There were a number of other statements held by the police, and Caswell advised on the service of those. Later rules of procedure would have required the prosecution to disclose to the defence any statement which was not to be relied on by the Crown at trial. These rules as to 'Unused Material' not being in operation in 1975, meant the prosecution could be selective, disclosing only what they considered advantageous to their case. It is not suggested that Caswell acted in any way improperly, given the rules then in existence.

There were two statements by Debbie Brown, but Caswell advised disclosure only of the statement referring to the man having a knife. He also advised investigation of whether Kiszko had a scar on his left leg, before disclosure of Miss Brown's statement that the man she saw had such a scar. Caswell also advised that Miss Storto be asked whether the man had a knife, before disclosure of her statement saying, 'as far as I know he wasn't carrying anything'.

It was Kiszko's own doctor, Dr D'Vaz, who described Kiszko as having a waddling gait, but Caswell had no wish to rely on the evidence of a defence witness to substantiate the children's evidence that the man they saw had had a peculiar gait. Dr Tierney, the police surgeon, had described only that Kiszko was flat-footed. Caswell asked for a further statement from this doctor as to the manner in which Kiszko walked.

Caswell identified the principal areas of prosecution evidence as being:

i Kiszko's admission that he masturbated in public, invariably in the presence of young girls;

ii the confession to murder (although Caswell saw weaknesses in relying on the confession, not least of which was the defendant's 'persecution complex', as evidenced by the taking of car registration numbers);

iii the identification by Kiszko of the lock knife as being the murder weapon, this being the knife which had blood on it and which fitted the wounds. Caswell, cautiously, required expert evidence to exclude Kiszko's other knives as possible murder weapons;

iv the carpet fibres;

v the admission of wiping the knife on the deceased, which was consistent with the known facts;

vi the paper with ADK 539 L written on it, although Caswell regarded this as being 'of lesser significance'.

Conversely, junior counsel for the Crown was sufficiently experienced and realistic to see that there were weaknesses in the case:

i   the absence of substantial forensic evidence;

ii a confused picture painted by the multiplicity of witnesses, whose statements exceeded 6,000 in number. There was, within these statements, a 'mountain of contradictions and irrelevancies'. Caswell advised that some of these be disclosed, out of fairness to the accused, but he was concerned, in particular, that the defence would be able to assert with some confidence that other cars had been in the lay-by at or about the material time, and Caswell's apprehension was exacerbated by reference to the – still untraced – Morris 1000.

iii Caswell was concerned about Kiszko's admission of indecent exposure in Castlemere Street on 17 November. There was no statement from a witness or complainant, and Caswell was perfectly aware of a defence line to the effect that, if Kiszko falsely admitted committing an offence on one date, how could the jury be sure that his confession to the murder was genuine, and was not merely another 'crank' confession. There were statements from a Leslie Eccles and a Janet Barrett of indecent exposure incidents in Pilsworth Road and Ansdell Road, and Caswell, being unfamiliar with the area, asked the police to clarify where Castlemere Street was in relation to those two roads.

With hallmark expedition, Dick Holland dealt with the requests made by Caswell. Further statements were taken: Dr Tierney described Kiszko as having 'a definite woddle [*sic*]', Professor Gee excluded the other four of Kiszko's knives as possible murder weapons and the two indecent exposures referred to by Miss Eccles and Miss Barrett were found to have no connection with Kiszko's admission at all. Holland quite fairly informed Caswell that he had doubts over Debbie Brown's claim to have seen a knife, and that he had more confidence in Ann Marie Storto's account that she did not see a knife. He provided a statement from Maurice Helm, the milkman who had admitted urinating in the street, but added that he had not provided the defence with that statement, and he also provided statements from Catherine Burke and Debra Mills.

Stefan Kiszko adamantly denied any involvement in the killing of Lesley Molseed, as he did in relation to the indecency incident on 3 October. His case was, 'I did not do it', and the defence case would rest upon an assertion of alibi. To this end Albert Wright wrote to the DPP on 13 May 1976, saying:

> [T]he defence propose to adduce evidence to establish alibi. The accused will say that he was not at or near the scene of the crime on or between the days of 5th to 8th October 1975 inclusive, *but he cannot recollect his precise whereabouts at any material time.*[3]

The letter went on to refer to Charlotte Kiszko as an alibi witness, and that she would say that:

> [Stefan Kiszko] was never away from home on the material dates for any period long enough for her son to have committed the crime for which he is indicted.

The alibi notice was sufficient for the purposes of the law, in that it clearly stated that Kiszko would say that he was not there (i.e. at the scene of the crime) but it was deficient in any detail, failing to assert that Kiszko was at a particular place at the material time. Moreover, it had informed the DPP, and, therefore, Taylor and Caswell, that Kiszko could not remember where he was at the material time. It is also noteworthy that the alibi notice covered only the period 5 to 8 October 1975, and not the preceding two days. A further alibi notice dated 30 June 1976 contained substantially more detail as to the account which would be given by the defence, and the relevance of these two alibi notices was of some importance in the trial to come.

The prosecution case was based, almost entirely, upon Kiszko's verbal and written admissions to the police. If the jury believed those admissions, then they would convict him. The defence, therefore, were obliged to do their utmost to ensure that the jury did not accept those admissions as being truthful or reliable. There are two ways in which this can be achieved in a criminal trial.

The first entails an argument before the judge in an attempt to persuade him to exclude the evidence of the admissions, that is to say, to order that the jury should not hear the evidence of the admissions at all. The process, called a *voir dire*, usually involves the judge hearing, in the absence of the jury, evidence from the

---

3 Authors' italics.

THE TRIAL OF STEFAN KISZKO

police and from the defendant as to the circumstances in which the admissions were obtained, followed by argument as to admissibility, after which he will make a ruling. Should he rule that the evidence is inadmissible, the jury will hear nothing at all about the admissions. In many cases the admissions represent the only evidence which the prosecution has, and, if it is ruled inadmissible, the prosecution would, in such a case, inevitably choose not to proceed.

The exclusion of evidence in this way can only be attempted with any prospect of success in limited circumstances, namely where there is an argument that the admission was made because the police have acted improperly or without justification, in the sense that they have obtained an admission from the prisoner by threats or inducements. It has long been the law that an admission made because the prisoner was in fear of the police, or because the police offered him some form of inducement to confess, is an admission which is not made voluntarily and which should, therefore, be excluded. Thus a threat to beat a man up unless he confesses, or an offer of bail to a man should he choose to admit an offence, would both render any confession thereby obtained inadmissible.

If a defendant was to argue that he had only admitted an offence because a police officer had, for example, offered him bail, the typical *voir dire* would involve the relevant police officer giving evidence as to the circumstances in which the confession was made, with appropriate cross-examination by defence counsel, and the defendant then giving evidence of his version of events, with appropriate cross-examination by the prosecutor. It is, literally, a trial within a trial, with the judge alone determining the issue of whether bail was offered and whether the defendant made the confession because of the offer. He alone determines admissibility in this case.

The second method of dealing with a confession is in the trial proper. Instead of having a *voir dire*, the confession is left untouched until the moment in the trial when the relevant police officers give evidence about it. They can then be cross-examined in front of the jury to show that the confession was obtained by threat or promise.

The *voir dire* method has the advantage that, if it is successful, the jury never gets to hear the confession and, if there is no other evidence, the trial will end at that point. The disadvantage of this method is that if, as is frequently the case, the judge rules the confession admissible, then, whilst it is open to defence counsel to cross-examine the police officers again, in the trial proper, to the effect that they had offered an inducement or threat in order to obtain the confession, the officer has by then had the opportunity to 'rehearse' the cross-examination. He will not be taken by surprise by the suggestion made, and he will have prepared his answer carefully. What is the disadvantage of the *voir dire* is, obviously, the advantage of dealing with the confession only in the trial proper: the element of surprise is retained. The disadvantage of that method, however, is that the jury has heard the confession and, without paying too much heed to questions of voluntariness, may choose to believe the admission to be the truth.

The defence in Kiszko's case elected to deal with the issue of his confessions by using the second method. That, in itself, cannot be criticised. Judges are often less willing to find against the police than are juries. Judges hear so frequently the complaint from defendants 'I only confessed so that I would get bail' that they might be forgiven for having become, on occasions, jaded or cynical. It would invariably be the case that a judge would require evidence of some strength to corroborate the defendant's claim of a threat or inducement: so that a defendant who was in fact bailed only minutes after making a confession which he claims was made in response to an offer of bail, or a defendant found to be injured after making a confession he claims had been beaten from him, would obviously be in a better position to have his confession excluded.

The criticism of David Waddington's handling of Stefan Kiszko's alleged confessions is based, not upon his decision not to have a *voir dire*, but upon the unusual tactic he did employ. Rather than simply cross-examine the police officers, and call Kiszko himself to give evidence to the effect that the confession was involuntarily made and/or untrue, the defence in this trial took a most curious – and dangerous – route.

Quite apart from confessing to killing Lesley, Kiszko had also admitted indecent exposure on 3 October (the 'Youth Club Incident') and the further incident on 4 October (which he had claimed in his statement had been nothing more than his shirt flap accidentally coming out of his trousers). The defence decided – and it must have been the decision of David Waddington QC as leading counsel for the defence – that they would seek to show that the girls who had given statements about these two incidents had been lying. If the girls had lied about those incidents then it followed, ran the argument, that Kiszko must have been lying when he admitted to those incidents. If he was lying about those incidents, then he was probably lying about the murder.

It was an interesting argument in logic: why would a man lie in making admissions about an offence of indecent exposure but then tell the truth in confessing to a murder? But it was an argument fraught with danger. The corollary of the argument was, of course, that if the jury were satisfied that the girls were telling the truth about the incidents, then they would probably be sure that Kiszko's admissions to these matters were truthful, and if he was telling the truth about the indecent exposure then he was probably telling the truth about the murder. But a second, and far more serious, risk with the course proposed was this. By introducing the evidence of the matters in October 1975, the defence alerted the jury to the possibility (subject to the final view of the jury concerning Kiszko's role in those matters) that Kiszko was a man with a propensity for committing sexual or quasi-sexual offences against young girls.

Caswell's opinion that the judge would have ruled admissible the evidence of the girls concerning the events of 3 and 4 October and 5 November 1975 was never put to the test, because of the defence tactics, but it is perfectly possible that the trial judge would not have permitted the prosecution to introduce that evidence, because those incidents had no relevance to the charge of murder.

The course taken by Waddington was not merely curious, but highly risky; he alone bears responsibility for the admission of evidence which would not otherwise have been called, and which was, potentially, so damaging for his client. The danger arose not merely from the issue of proclivity or propensity. The proximity of the other alleged offences, in time and geography, to the abduction and murder of Lesley, would tend to lend weight to any prosecution argument that the killing was the culmination of a sequence of offending by Kiszko. That argument probably could not have been advanced without the allegations of indecent exposure, and the defence had opened the door for Peter Taylor QC, and the Crown's counsel would surely make use of the opportunity presented to him.

It is still more difficult to see the wisdom of Waddington's second defence strategy. The defence of Stefan Kiszko to the charge of murder was always, 'I did not do it.' He never said that he had been provoked into killing Lesley Molseed, he never claimed to have suffered a mental blackout, he never sought to convince anyone that he was insane. He did not look at the strong evidence against him and, having weighed up his prospects of an acquittal, instructed his lawyers to see what could be done to reduce his culpability. There is no indication whatsoever that Kiszko instructed his counsel to approach the prosecution to see whether they would accept a plea of manslaughter based on diminished responsibility, nor that any such approach was made. Kiszko never, ever, admitted killing Lesley Molseed, other than in his alleged admissions to the police in December 1975.

David Waddington, in spite of Kiszko's repeated denials of the killing, decided that a second defence would be placed before the jury. He would run, in accordance with his instructions, the primary defence of alibi. He would seek to disprove the prosecution case that Kiszko had abducted the child and killed her, by trying to prove the confessions untrue or involuntary, and by adducing evidence that Kiszko was at a place other than the scene of the killing on the afternoon of 5 October. But he would also introduce a fall-back defence, namely that of diminished responsibility.

The defence of diminished responsibility, introduced by the Homicide Act 1957, provides that where a person is proved to have killed another, but is able to show that,[4] at the time of the killing, he was suffering from such abnormality of mind as substantially impaired his mental responsibility for his actions in killing, that person shall be convicted of manslaughter, not of murder.

The introduction of this second defence was a baffling and reckless tactic. It was baffling because it required the defendant to be saying to the jury, 'I killed the deceased but my mind was impaired at the time of the killing.' Since Stefan Kiszko strenuously denied killing Lesley, it is impossible to see how this defence could be put forward. There continues to be some dispute as to whether Kiszko ever authorised his counsel to run the defence of diminished responsibility, and David Waddington continues to assert that he was so authorised. But it remains virtually impossible to comprehend how Kiszko if he had understood the logic of the defence fully could have authorised it. If it was adequately explained to him that the defence involved an admission of killing, then Kiszko could not have approved of it, since he was adamant that he had not killed the girl. For all Stefan Kiszko's weakness of personality, he was in no way intellectually deficient: he had had a

---

4 The defence represents one of the rare occasions in English law where the burden of proof is on the defence to prove its case.

grammar-school education and was a civil servant with the Inland Revenue.[5] Those close to Kiszko remain to this day absolutely clear that Kiszko at no time authorised the defence lawyers to run this defence.

Moreover, the running of this defence alongside a complete denial is, quite obviously, intellectually illogical. If a man denies the killing of the deceased, how can he argue that he *did* kill the deceased, albeit under a disability or impairment of the mind. And even if that conundrum can be resolved on an intellectual basis, it is extremely difficult to see how the two defences can be put before the jury, whilst hoping to retain any credibility whatsoever for either.

It is, it would seem, nothing short of impossible. One way of describing such an attempt would be to say that 'You can't have your cake and eat it,' but it was put far better by prosecuting counsel when he accused the defence of riding two horses. In his closing speech Peter Taylor QC, speaking of the two defences in those picturesque terms, submitted to the jury, 'They are just not horses to be ridden together.'

The effect of the decisions taken by David Waddington was to transform substantially the case which Peter Taylor began to open in the crowded courtroom on Wednesday, 7 July 1976. Such simplicity as had once existed was now replaced by a complex web of interlocking and overlapping issues, from the credibility of children, to the conduct of the police, from the habits of a meticulous tax clerk to the technicalities of forensic science. The facts would run from the streets of Rochdale to the moorland of the Pennine hills and the gloom of a police interview room. And, dominating the case entirely, the physical and mental condition of Stefan Kiszko.

The Crown Court at Leeds, and its predecessors the Leeds Courts of Assize and of Quarter Sessions, were no strangers to murder trials, whether sensational or mundane. The trial of Stefan Kiszko, save for those intimately involved with it, was simply another, albeit lurid, murder trial taking place within the striking halls of the Leeds Town Hall. Not for nothing did Peter Taylor, Matthew Caswell, David Waddington and Philip Clegg address each other as 'My Learned Friend', for, if there was not actual friendship, there was a mutual respect and courtesy which could

---

5 Dick Holland was later to recount how Kiszko had done DCS Dibb's tax return whilst he was sitting in a cell in the police station.

not lie well with the adversarial activities which would be carried out in court. These men had come to try to win a case. They were not instructed to find out the truth, nor was that the court's function. In English courts, only one side will win, the side with the best evidence, the side which best attacks the other side's evidence, the side with the best advocate, the side with the best tactics . . .

In accordance with the advice given by Matthew Caswell and the action taken by Dick Holland, the defence was presented unexpectedly on that first morning, and with the trial just about to begin, with a mountain of statements and documents. A random collection of statements of witnesses – including Maurice Helm and Emma Tong – who had been abandoned by the Crown and early statements of prosecution witnesses which had been refined or amended. Thousands of pieces of paper for Waddington, Clegg and Wright to read and digest, and with the judge anxious to begin proceedings immediately. There could be no question of adjourning this trial to allow the defence time to review all this material. Kiszko's lawyers were obliged to depend on hope: hope that they could read all the material whilst the trial progressed, without losing an opportunity to use any of the material, and hope that there was really nothing in this material that could be of use to the defence. So the trial of Stefan Kiszko began.

'All persons having anything to do before My Lords the Queen's Justices, draw near and give your attendance.'

With that call the clerk of the court gave moment to the proceedings before Mr Justice Park, who entered in a swathe of red cloth and white fur trim, his white gloves and now-ceremonial black cap tightly grasped. Automatically the judge's clerk initiated the process of swearing the jury, who entered the jury box where they would hear the case of the Queen against Stefan Ivan Kiszko. A plea of 'Not Guilty' having been entered by Kiszko, the courtroom was in silence as Peter Taylor QC rose to his feet.

Peter Taylor opened the case for the Crown with a thumbnail sketch of what was to come. With some immediacy he told the jury that Kiszko's abnormal development had caused an absence of sexual urge, and that the injected treatment for his abnormality had brought about a 'sex urge which manifested itself in relation to young girls, and to exposing himself'. There had been a developing trend of such behaviour in the days immediately prior to, and culminating in the abduction and killing of Lesley Molseed.

That child had been picked up in Kiszko's car, then driven to a lay-by. She had been taken up on to the moor and then repeatedly stabbed. 'The motive was clearly sexual,' said Mr Taylor, 'but it was unusual, not merely because of the age of the girl but because there was no sexual interference of her or displacement of her clothes.' He concluded this briefest of introductions with these words, 'It seems she was to the accused a sex object whom he required to be there while he abused himself. That completed, he killed her and left the scene.'

An introduction of such brevity is typical of prosecution openings in cases which have a deal of complexity about them. They enable the jury to focus, immediately, on the case which the Crown will put forward. They give nothing more than the thrust of the prosecution case, providing a skeleton upon which the Crown will hang the flesh of the evidence. With the jury's attention assured, the prosecuting QC was able to turn and develop his thesis.

He spoke of the lengthy investigation which had followed Lesley's disappearance, and how the trail had led to Kiszko because of the other acts which he had allegedly committed against young girls. Mr Taylor wove into the fabric of the events of 3 and 4 October the medical history of the accused man, suggesting that the treatment's intentional production of a sex urge might also have had the consequence of introducing into Kiszko an element of aggression. He made no reference to any indecent exposure on the Friday night. Indeed, he made no reference to the evidence of Kitty Burke and Patricia Hind when he dealt with the events outside the youth club, perhaps a curious omission given that the statements of those two girls would be read to the jury as uncontroverted evidence. Of the Saturday incident, Mr Taylor told the jury how Maxine Buckley and Debra Mills had seen Kiszko expose himself by lifting up his parka coat, and that Maxine had recognised Kiszko as a man she had seen before, at a house on Crawford Street which she described in some detail. 'You will hear that that description fitted exactly the house where Kiszko lived at the time,' Mr Taylor told the jury.

Taking the story again to the events of 5 to 8 October, the abduction and killing of Lesley and the finding of her body, prosecuting counsel then linked the finding of semen stains on Lesley's clothing to Kiszko's admissions to the police, where he had allegedly said that he had held her down with one hand and masturbated with the other. Moving on to November, the lengthy investigation into Kiszko, the several interviews at his house and the final chapter at the police station were then outlined. Mr Taylor spoke of the events of Bonfire Night and of the first contact between the police and Kiszko two days later. It was emphasised how Kiszko had first lied by saying that he was still in hospital on 5 October, and had then lied further, when the mistake as to the date of discharge was revealed, by saying that he had first gone out of the house on 12 October. That lie would be proved, said the prosecution, by evidence that on 8 October Kiszko had purchased a new tyre for his car.

Finally counsel moved on to the interviews at Rochdale Police Station, during which Kiszko had first spoken of his injections, and had gone on to admit to DS Akeroyd that he had killed Lesley, before admitting more fully both the killing and the indecent behaviour in relation to the other girls. Quite fairly, the prosecution told the jury that Kiszko had then retracted his confession, saying that, 'I thought if I made a statement you would let me out.' Last, the further admission, and the bizarre early-morning trip to the moors where, shaking and with his hands in a praying position, Kiszko had allegedly said, 'I can hear voices. Can't you?'

For two and a half days, counsel for the Crown meticulously and methodically outlined the prosecution case against Kiszko. If anyone was at the outset of the case inclined to the view that this was merely a 'run-of-the-mill' murder trial, such illusions were surely dispelled by the intricacies of the plot, carefully set out by Mr Taylor. The introduction of the evidence concerning the incidents of 3 and 5 October and 5 November and the two-part defence which would advance a medical aspect to explain the defendant's conduct had brought imbroglio where there had been, many months earlier, simplicity.

High above the court, in the public gallery which looked over the lawyers and jurors below, Lesley Molseed's family had also listened impassively to the opening speech, and when the trial resumed after the weekend recess they were again in place, to oversee the justice which they hoped would be done. It is no criticism of the Molseed family, nor of the family of any murder victim, to observe that when they say they want justice, what they mean is that they want a conviction.

April Molseed sat, with her husband Danny, and with Lesley's father, Fred Anderson, strangely detached from the courtroom, even as her statement was read to the jury. That statement described how Lesley had been sent shopping on the fateful

Sunday, with her shopping bag and her purse and her £1 note, for a loaf of bread from the Spar. How she had been told to go to the second shop, Margaret's, only if the Spar was closed, and how she had not returned by one o'clock. Or two. And how she had next seen Lesley at Halifax Royal Infirmary, on 8 October 1975.

The trial of Stefan Kiszko had several constituent parts. The first stage involved the proof of the killing and the circumstances of the killing. In this there was to be little said of a controversial nature. Matthew Caswell read statements from PC Akerman, the photographer, and PC Green, who had drawn the plans. Now the jury could see the route which the killer and the child would have taken, now could they see photographs of the child, the relevant scenes and, desperately graphically, the post-mortem. The route which Lesley had taken became apparent from a number of statements read to the court, from neighbours who had seen the child that day, and from the shopkeepers who were either closed, or into whose shop the child had failed to come. This was undisputed evidence, as was the evidence of DC Roberts who had made a number of what might be called trial runs from Rochdale to the scene of the murder, in order to establish the duration of such journeys.

Also undisputed was Peter Taylor's first live witness, David Greenwell, who had by accident discovered Lesley's body on a windswept Wednesday morning ten months earlier. He was not cross-examined, but his evidence of stumbling across the child's mutilated body on the barren moor was more dramatic in the telling than it would have been if merely read.

The confessions were pivotal to the prosecution case. Everything else was merely confirmatory, and so Peter Taylor moved swiftly to establish his focal point. He first called DS Mawson and DC Russell to give an account of the initial interviews, where Kiszko had described his movements and actions on 3 and 4 October. Taylor wished the jury to see these interviews as nothing but fabrication and falsehood, for in so doing he would establish Kiszko in their collective mind as a liar, and would lay groundwork for the jury to reject any explanation which the accused would give to them. As against this, Mawson accepted in cross-examination that, at the end of his second interview with the accused the officer was satisfied that Kiszko could be eliminated from the murder enquiry.

Akeroyd, McFadzean and Whittle followed their brother officers into the witness box and gave evidence of the recovery of the knives, the magazines, the balloons and sweets, as well as their own accounts of interviews with the accused, and each then resisted the forceful suggestion from David Waddington QC in cross-examination, that pressure had been placed on Kiszko to admit the indecency offences and, in the case of Akeroyd, the murder itself. From each came a vehement denial that they had put words into Kiszko's mouth, that Kiszko had been subjected to duress, or that the interviews themselves had not been properly recorded. When each had assured Mr Justice Park and the jury that there had been nothing improper in the conduct of the interviews, the stage was cleared for the principal actor in the prosecution cast.

DSupt Dick Holland cut an imposing figure as he strode into court and took the oath with the casual, yet genuine manner which indicates a witness well used to the experience of giving evidence. Like a well-rehearsed double-act, he and Taylor moved through the introductory parts of his evidence: his rank, his experience, his role in the investigation and the format of the investigation itself. He then moved on to the initial interviews already covered by the junior officers, before arriving at the interview which had taken place, with DCI Steele, after Akeroyd had called them in. That interview, at 11.50 a.m. on Monday, 22 December was the first time Kiszko admitted to killing Lesley Molseed in the presence of more than one witness and Holland's recitation of the detail was intended – by him at least – to be the beginning and the end of the case to convict Stefan Kiszko. In clear, stentorian tones Mr Holland read from his notebook the particulars of Kiszko's admission, knowing that it was in the minutiae of the confession that the jury would find the facts corroborated by other evidence, facts which only the killer would know, facts which only the guilty Stefan Kiszko would have had at his command. And Holland explained how he had asked Kiszko to demonstrate how he had killed the child, he himself sitting in a chair to reduce his height whilst Kiszko stood over him, and Kiszko placing his arm over the superintendent's right shoulder with his forearm at his throat, holding a pencil instead of a knife, asking whether that was the position and Kiszko replying 'Yes, but we were lying down.' He spoke of Kiszko explaining that he had wiped the knife on Lesley, indicating the bone-handled knife, the prosecution's Exhibit 54.

Holland went on to deal with Kiszko's admissions in respect of the indecent assaults, more particularly in the written statement taken down by himself as Kiszko sat, shaking, describing what had happened. He was not, added Holland, pressured or intimidated into making that statement. He produced the original statement to the court, noting that Kiszko had signed it in two places, and then read the document in the same clarion-clear voice to the enthralled jury.

At the conclusion of that statement Holland recounted how a solicitor, Mr Albert Wright, had then been provided for Kiszko, and that neither Kiszko nor the solicitor had made any complaint concerning Kiszko's treatment, despite DCS Jack Dibb expressly asking whether they had any cause to complain.

Yet it was, said Holland, that at about 6.20 p.m. Mr Wright indicated that his client wished to retract his earlier confession, with Kiszko saying, 'Yes, I only made [it] so that you would let me go home.' Holland had asked Kiszko if he was suggesting that he, Holland, had offered him an inducement to make the statement, but Kiszko had denied that this was so: '. . . I just thought if I told you that you would let me out.' Holland then read to the jury the retraction statement made by Kiszko in the presence of his solicitor, in which Kiszko denied murder or the incident of 3 October, but maintained his account of the incident in which a carpet he was carrying had caused his trousers to open and his shirt flap to be exposed. Finally he dealt with Kiszko's further admission, made after the retraction statement had been signed.

When Holland had concluded his evidence, when all the interviews and statements were before the jury, when the entire investigation had been laid out for the court like a complicated jigsaw, Peter Taylor took his seat, but Dick Holland remained in the witness box, staunch and upright, for the adversarial onslaught he knew would follow.

His anticipation was swiftly rewarded, for David Waddington showed no mercy as he tore into his cross-examination of the officer who he would have the jury believe was the villain of the piece. 'No' to the suggestion that Kiszko had been subjected to a reign of threats and intimidation. 'No', this was not a timid man, deprived of contact with the outside world, deprived of food for two days, so terrified and, indeed physically sick that he was prepared to say anything to the police just for some relief from his ordeal. 'No' to the suggestion that Kiszko would say anything just to go home, and 'no' to the suggestion that Kiszko had ever been told that, if he would just admit the crime, he could indeed go home.

Holland was adamant that the admissions were entirely voluntary and the details contained in those admissions – whether by description of the scene or by reference to ejaculating over Lesley's clothing – had come from the accused.

Waddington suggested to Dick Holland that the matters contained in the admission were common knowledge in the Rochdale area, but the defence QC took a severe body blow when the officer replied that only five members of the enquiry team, none below the rank of chief inspector, knew that the killer had ejaculated over Lesley's body.

The jury had looked then at Kiszko, and at his counsel, and at the police officer in the witness box. Was this the moment, so early in the trial, when the jury's verdict on Stefan Kiszko was all but decided?

This answer given to David Waddington was what barristers call, in their vernacular, a 'nose-ender', and like a punch to the nose it stings, hurts and drives the fight from the recipient. Waddington's cross-examination tailed off with a few ancillary questions, but when Dick Holland left the witness box the pendulum had swung to the prosecution.

After that, the police evidence was quickly dealt with. DSupt Wheater and DCI Steele gave their accounts of the interviews and Kiszko's admissions, and each officer repelled Waddington's suggestions of duress, undue pressure or the offer of inducements. By now the jury had doubtless formed an initial view of the police, and if Waddington hoped still to dislodge the confessions of his client as formidable pieces of evidence, he was left with a substantial amount of work to do.

The court heard from Professor Gee and from Ronald Outteridge about finding the body and the inferences which they had drawn from the condition of the deceased. Professor Gee described the numerous wounds, in particular a frontal wound to the heart and a wound to the back which had pierced the main artery of the heart, and he commented that one of those wounds – he could not say which – had caused death. All but one of the injuries had been inflicted with only a moderate degree of force, but the one which had transfixed the shoulder-blade had required a substantial amount of force. The number of injuries and the force involved in inflicting at least that final wound could have left the jury in no doubt, had any attempt been made to raise any contrary suggestion, that the person who had struck those blows had intended to kill or at least cause serious injury to the child. The evidence further confirmed that the child had been killed on the moor, rather than that she had died elsewhere and her body brought up to that windswept place.

In cross-examination Gee accepted that his original opinion had been that the murder weapon was of different dimensions to the one taken from the accused, but this was the defence's only profit, for Gee had been called principally to prove cause of death, and this he had done without any dissent from the defence.

Ronald Outteridge told the jury how the cuts to Lesley's clothing corresponded to the bodily wounds, so that, in his opinion, the child had been killed where she was found. He then dealt at length with the results of his own scientific examinations.

The jury were told of the light semen staining found, but the relevance of that staining was simply to provide confirmation of the incentive for the killing suggested by the Crown, namely that there was a sexual motive. The semen was insufficient in quantity to enable the blood group of the ejaculator to be identified, although five slides had been prepared from the semen staining.

He then spoke of the recovery of fibres: two pale-yellow wool fibres from the jumper and vest, one bright-yellow wool fibre from the skirt, one orange rayon fibre from the right sock. Each of those fibres, he told the jury was similar to fibres extracted from the piece of carpet found in Kiszko's car, and the findings were therefore consistent with Lesley having been a passenger in that car.

Turning to the items seized from Kiszko, Outteridge told the jury that he had found semen on the rag and handkerchief found in Kiszko's room, confirmation of Kiszko's admission that he did masturbate. He held up the bone-handled knife and explained that, although he had found blood in the nail nick, he was unable to say from where that blood had come, but, he added, it was the only one of Kiszko's knives which had blood on it.

Waddington made some progress in cross-examination, when Outteridge confirmed that vast amounts of the carpet in Kiszko's car had been manufactured, although the effect of this was dissipated by the professor adding that he understood enquiries to have shown that Lesley had not been in contact with any other similar piece of carpet. He did confirm, however, that he could not say whether or not the blood on the knife was even human.

Taylor now began the process of 'tidying up' the prosecution case.

He dealt with Kiszko's initial assertion that he had not left his home nor driven his car until 12 October 1975, by reading the statement of Derek Beardsworth, who had fitted a new tyre to Kiszko's Avenger motor car on 8 October. Next he read evidence that Kiszko bought a 'girlie' magazine once a month and these two statements caused considerable damage to Kiszko's assertion that he did not drive his car whilst troubled by his ankle injury.

PC Bell gave evidence of his involvement with Kiszko, which began in April 1975 when the defendant had first complained of vehicles trying to force him off the road. Kiszko had kept notes of such vehicles' registration numbers, those being the numbers recovered from the car. PC Bell had dutifully investigated each vehicle. Derek Hollos was the owner of the Renault ADK 539 L, the number Kiszko had recorded in red, and he was called to show how he had passed along the A672 at about 2.30 p.m. on the day Lesley went missing. He asserted that he could recall no other incident which would have brought him into contact with Kiszko, and his evidence was supported by his wife.[6]

Finally, Peter Taylor called the evidence concerning the incidents of indecency. Maxine Buckley, Debra Mills, Michael Rigby, Sheila Buckley (Maxine's mother) and Carole Rigby (Michael's mother) all gave evidence about the events of 3 and 4 October and 5 November. PC Sergeant gave evidence of Maxine's complaint that the man who had exposed himself lived 'at a house in Crawford Street with plants in the window', and how that complaint had lead him to 31 Crawford Street, the home of Stefan Kiszko. Sarah Lord gave evidence that the man she had seen on Friday, 3 October was about 30, five feet seven with dark hair. He was not thin but nor was he fat, and when he walked his shoulders were hunched and he was 'a bit wobbly'. Next came Ann Marie Storto, Sheila Woodhead and Debbie Brown,[7] their evidence as to the Friday night incident being challenged by Waddington only to the extent of establishing that their descriptions of the man did not match Kiszko. Peter Taylor then read Beverley Mullins', Pamela Hind's, Catherine Burke's and Gillian Cleave's statements. David Waddington, despite the need to decimate this part of the evidence if his tactic was to pay off, did not require that any of those girls be called to be subjected to cross-examination.

The prosecution case ended with Mr Taylor reading a statement from the nurse who had administered the injection of Primoteston

---

6 One unanswered question in the case is this: if the evidence of Mr and Mrs Hollos was correct (and the defence did not seek to contradict it), if Stefan Kiszko was, at about 2.30 p.m. on the relevant day, in the process of abducting and killing Lesley Molseed, why would he pause at the lay-by to take down the registration number of a car which was passing by, particularly if that car had caused him no problem?

7 Debbie Brown's first statement to the police described the man as having a scar on his knee, a substantial matter of distinction, since Kiszko had no such scar.

to Kiszko on the Friday, and by calling Dr Tierney, the police doctor, whose detailed medical examination of the accused had included a note of the defendant's physique, his bulging eyes and his unsteady gait.

With the last witness gone, Peter Taylor QC made a slight bow to the judge, 'That, My Lord, is the case for the prosecution.' With a great deal of dexterity the Crown had woven a spider's web of evidence in which to ensnare Stefan Kiszko. Perhaps Waddington had snapped one or two of the strands of that web, but if Stefan Kiszko was to break free completely, the burden – as a matter of fact, even if not of law – now shifted to him to do so.

CHAPTER FOURTEEN

Riding Two Horses

Kiszko's first defence, and therefore the matter to which the defence had first to direct their attention, was that he had not been involved in the abduction or killing at all.

'Alibi' is a Latin word meaning 'elsewhere', and is, in legal terms, the claim, or evidence supporting the claim, that when an alleged act took place the accused was elsewhere. As with virtually all aspects of a criminal case there is no burden on the defendant to prove his alibi; it is for the prosecution to disprove that alibi, to satisfy the jury beyond reasonable doubt that the alibi is false. Unlike most aspects of the defence in a criminal trial, an alibi has to be disclosed in advance. There was in 1975 no obligation on a defendant to notify the court or the prosecution that his defence was, say, self-defence, or that he would or would not give evidence, or that he would or would not be calling witnesses for the defence. But with alibi defences there are very different rules. The defendant is obliged to disclose to the prosecution the terms of his alibi, by which is meant the detail of the alibi and the witnesses who will give evidence to support it. Those matters are incorporated into a document called an alibi notice.

In Kiszko's case there were two alibi notices. The first was dated 13 May 1976, and it simply asserted that the accused denied that he was at or near the scene of the crime on or between 5 to 8 October 1975, but that he was unable to recall his precise whereabouts at any material times.

Despite the absence of any detail, this was, nevertheless, a valid alibi notice. One obvious drawback with such an alibi notice is that the defendant is then in difficulty in asserting an alibi properly so called. He would be open to cross-examination were he subsequently to give evidence that he was at a particular place other than the crime scene.

This, however, was precisely what happened with Stefan Kiszko. The bare alibi notice of 13 May 1976 was followed by a second alibi notice dated 30 June 1976. Given that the original notice expressly stated that the defendant could not recall his whereabouts on 5 to 8 October 1975, it is nothing short of astonishing that the second notice, written only six weeks later, provided a detailed account of Sunday, 5 October 1975. It explained how Kiszko, his mother and his aunt had visited Rochdale Cemetery to place flowers on the grave of his father, how they had then visited a particular shop in Tweedale Street to buy bread and mustard, and how they had then taken Kiszko's aunt home.

It is impossible to overstate the ammunition which this notice provided to the prosecution. The key to the prosecution successfully breaking an alibi is the suggestion that the alibi is invented. The earlier the details of the alibi are given by the defendant, the easier it is for him to assert that he is fully able to recollect his movements on the relevant date, and the more the Crown is obliged to resort to asserting that the alibi is a lie. It is obvious that, where the account changes from interview to alibi notice to alibi evidence, the easier the task becomes for the prosecution. In the case of Kiszko, before a single word of evidence had been given, the prosecution were placed in a position of great strength to destroy the alibi.

The accounts given by Stefan Kiszko showed absolutely no signs of consistency:

1   On 5 November, interviewed at home by PC Shaw and PC Oliver concerning 4 October, Kiszko asserted that he had not driven his car for several weeks because of a bad leg.

2   On 7 November, interviewed at home by DS Mawson and DC Russell, Kiszko said that he thought that he had been in hospital recovering from his leg injury.

3   On 10 November, again interviewed at home by Mawson and Russell, Kiszko said that he had been discussing matters with his mother, and that they believed that he had not left the house all day on 5 October, and that the first time that he had gone out had been on 12 October, when they had visited his father's grave, that being the first time that he had driven his car.

4   On 21 December, in the first interview with DS Akeroyd he maintained that he had not left the house on 5 October because he was weak and could not walk.

Prior to being charged with murder Kiszko's accounts do have some consistency. It was accepted by the police that he had been mistaken about the date of his discharge from hospital so that, excluding that error, Kiszko appeared to be adhering to an account that he had not left the house at all on 5 October. As an alibi, whether true or false, this was an extremely easy account to remember and to sustain, the only relevant witness in support being his mother Charlotte. This then was the alibi up to and including December 1975, that is, within two months of the killing.

But in May 1976, Kiszko, inexplicably, instructed his solicitors that he could not remember where he had been on 5 October. That he could not remember is difficult to understand, albeit that about seven months had elapsed since the date of the killing. There were available, to Kiszko and to Mr Wright, all the interviews and statements with the police in November and December 1975, in which the 'at home' alibi had been put forward. If that apparent inability to remember is difficult to understand, the second alibi notice is, quite obviously, beyond comprehension.

If, as he asserted in May, Kiszko could not recall his whereabouts in October 1975, how was it that his memory became so clear in June, but six weeks later? How was he then able to remember with such clarity events which just a few weeks before were absent from his memory? Kiszko explained this in his evidence to the court. He said that he had had visits from his mother and his aunt whilst he had been in custody awaiting trial, and that in the course of their discussions they had all eventually remembered where they had gone on 5 October. In every possible way this was a dangerous course to pursue. It immediately suggested that Kiszko had concocted his alibi with the assistance of his mother and aunt, although it failed to explain how their collective memories – which were unable to produce an alibi in May – had improved so dramatically in a short space of time, at a date which was further away from the date of the offence. Moreover, the 'new' alibi enabled the prosecution to take a firm line with Kiszko in cross-examining about the complete change from the 'at home' alibi mooted during his interviews prior to being charged.

It is impossible to see any good reason for the change in alibi from the 'at home' alibi, which was reasonably easy to pursue, to the 'cemetery–shop' alibi, which was used at the trial, which depended on the memory of persons other than the accused and his mother, and which was so obviously changed from the account given at the earliest opportunity.

Impossible to explain at all, except by the argument that Kiszko misled the police in 1975, and that he and his mother and aunt were telling the truth when they gave their evidence at the trial. There was certainly no evidence that they had concocted the account.

There was not at any stage any doubt that Lesley's killing was unlawful. No allegation of provocation or of self-defence was raised, nor, obviously, could there have been. Any suggestion of accident or of a lack of intent to kill or cause grievous bodily harm was equally unmeritorious, and could not have survived the evidence of Professor Gee. Thus the only defences which could have been offered to the jury were those raised by David Waddington: did Kiszko do it, and, if he did, was he suffering from diminished responsibility at the time?

As the legal proceedings entered their final phase, the court-room fell silent and the eyes of those assembled swung inexorably towards the dock, as David Waddington pronounced, 'Call Stefan Ivan Kiszko,' and the lumbering figure of the defendant rose to face the ordeal of giving evidence.

He had gained weight in the nine months he had spent in prison awaiting trial, and the awkwardness in his gait and the protu-berance of his eyes were familiar: the jury must have noted both physical features as Kiszko walked towards the witness box. With a prison officer in constant attendance behind him – as if this clumping giant could possibly consider making an escape attempt – the witness took the oath and began to tell the jury his life history.

He spoke of his education and his family. He spoke of his job at the tax office, and of his poor health over the years, detailing childhood ailments and the more debilitating anaemia and hypo-gonadism he had endured as a young man. He told the jury of the injury to his leg, and how that disability had restricted his ability to get about following his discharge from hospital. He told the jury that he had never before been in trouble with the police, and he told them of his car, and the runs which he used to take with his mother and his Aunt Alfreda.

And as for his defence to the terrible charge which he faced, well, that was simple too. He denied being the man at the Kingsway Youth Club on Friday, 3 October 1975, but admitted being in Vavasour Street on Saturday, the fourth, although he repudiated any suggestion that he had indecently exposed himself that day. He explained how, in the process of moving from Crawford Street to Kings Road, he had taken a carpet to Vavasour Street intending to dump it, and had inadvertently caught the roll of carpet on his zip, causing it to come down. Whilst sorting himself out, his shirt flap had come out, or perhaps he had accidentally been exposed, but in any event it was unintentional and he was not aware of any girls in the immediate vicinity.

On the Sunday, he told the jury, he had eaten lunch with his mother between noon and 1.30 p.m., the crucial time covering Lesley's abduction. He recalled – overlooking his account to the police – that this was the first Sunday that he had gone out since his discharge from hospital, and that he, his mother and his Aunt Alfreda had gone to the cemetery to visit his father's grave, where he had placed fresh flowers.

On the way home he had visited the Continental Shop in Tweedale, an establishment run by Maria Baran, where he purchased a jar of German mustard. He recalled an argument taking place whilst he was in the shop, between a young girl and Mrs Baran, concerning some curtains, and Kiszko said that he had intervened in the argument. He had then gone home, dropping Mrs Tosic at her home on the way.

He denied knowing Lesley Molseed. He denied abducting Lesley Molseed. He denied killing Lesley Molseed. That was his defence: I was not there, it was not me. But if the jury was to accept this account, Kiszko had first to climb the hill of explaining why he had admitted the murder to the police.

As to the interviews with the police at his home, Kiszko was to say that he had given false information, but had not done so intentionally. He had been confused, because of his illness. It was true also that he had lied to the police in interview at the police station and, in particular, in his confession. That confession, he insisted, had been put into his mouth by the police officers: he had no idea how Lesley Molseed had been abducted or killed. The police themselves had told him the details of the abduction and killing and he had made the admission because he was terrified of Holland who, said Kiszko, had threatened to beat him up, banging on the table and shouting, 'I know you did it and I'm going to make you fucking admit it.' Kiszko said that he thought that if he told them what they wanted to hear, they would let him go home to his mother, for McFadzean had said to him, 'As soon as we get this wrapped up we can all go home for Christmas,' as if he were dealing with a juvenile being interviewed for stealing apples or breaking windows. And Kiszko, the man-child, had believed him.

Kiszko, displaying his credulity, told the jury that he believed not only this promise, but also that the police would then go on to prove that he was not responsible for the murder. He had painted for the jury, in words, a picture of the classic 'bad cop/good cop' interview technique.

Finally Waddington asked his client to deal with his medical treatment: what effect did the injections and tablets have on him? Kiszko proudly, and without embarrassment, told the jury that he had grown facial and pubic hair and, unlike before, he was able to masturbate and ejaculate. The only side effect was sore buttocks. His plea was simple: I lied to the police when I made the confession. The truth is in my second written statement. I did not abduct Lesley Molseed. I did not kill Lesley Molseed. That is my case.

Waddington sat down. He had made his way through the examination-in-chief, and Kiszko had given his account much as anticipated. Now David Waddington was obliged to leave Stefan to fend for himself: he could offer him neither help nor protection against the cross-examination of Peter Taylor.

Cross-examination of the defendant in any criminal trial tends to be one of the dramatic high points. For the barrister asking the questions he should remember the advocate's maxim 'Cross-examine, don't examine crossly'. In other words, ask your questions carefully, leading the defendant to the answers you want. Do not shout at or argue with the defendant. This is especially true when cross-examining the defendant, for the advocate who tries to bully the witness will find the jury's sympathy slipping towards the defendant.

For the defendant himself, he would always do well to remember that the barrister is at home in the court, and he is generally more adept in handling this situation. He would be wise not to attempt to outwit the barrister, for it rarely works.

Peter Taylor knew his case, and knew the rule to follow in pursuing it. Stefan Kiszko did not, for he attempted to fence with Taylor, to out-smart him, to lock intellectual horns, and he was hopelessly ill-equipped to do so. More seriously, while Kiszko's case depended on him persuading the jury that the confession he had made had been brow-beaten from him by the police, his adversarial stance and his attempt to meet Taylor on his own ground had the effect of displaying the defendant as a man more than capable of handling himself. He described how he was a timid man, frightened and confused in the police station, so afraid that he vomited and was unable to face food, but as he did so he stood erect, and spoke firmly and confidently even when prosecuting counsel's questions were more strongly phrased, even when it was suggested that he was a mere liar and killer. Kiszko did not crack. Kiszko did not admit he was the killer of Lesley Molseed.

In a relentless cross-examination, Taylor asked Kiszko to explain how, in his so-called false confession, he was able to describe so many facts of the abduction and killing which were true. How was he able to tell Holland that the point at which the child was killed could not be seen from the road? How was he able to demonstrate to the detective superintendent precisely how the child was killed, with an arm around the neck and the wound to the throat. There were so many examples, and Kiszko had no answer. Importantly, he agreed that the officers had only noted what he had said. It was not Kiszko's case that the police had invented any part of the 'confession'.

Taylor turned to lies told by the defendant. Yes, admitted Kiszko, he had lied to WPC Shaw and then to DS Mawson, when those officers, on separate occasions, had called at his house, telling them that he had been in hospital at the material time. Taylor went through the many versions of the events of 3 to 5 October, which Kiszko had told at various times. And, at the other end of the time scale, yes, he was wrong when he said he had not gone out before 12 October.

From the lies Taylor moved to the alibi. How, he asked, could Kiszko now, in July 1976, accurately remember the details of his movements on 5 October 1975, when as late as 13 May 1976 his solicitor was writing a letter, purporting to give notice of alibi but saying that Kiszko could not recollect his whereabouts, only that he had not been away from his mother for any considerable length of time. How could his memory have so improved, and why did he not give the account given in evidence at an earlier stage: for example, in his retraction statement in December 1975? Kiszko tried to explain this sudden ability to remember by telling the jury of long discussions whilst he had been in prison on remand, with his mother and aunt, trying to work out what they had done over the weeks between his discharge from hospital and his arrest. It was as a result of those discussions that they had recalled the events accurately. He had not been able to recall the events when first interviewed in November because he was confused due to his illness. Peter Taylor was in no doubt that the entire alibi was invention. 'This alibi has been cooked up at a late stage,' he suggested, to which Kiszko answered, 'No.'

Returning to the theme of his confessions, and the oppressive nature of Dick Holland's questioning, Kiszko insisted that Holland had threatened to beat him up, but he agreed with Taylor that he had not complained to his solicitor, Mr Wright, concerning this oppression.

Finally, Taylor knew that two matters had been kept from the public: that the killer had not removed Lesley's underwear and that that person had also masturbated on to the child. Only the killer would know of those two matters. Kiszko had them both in his confession. Kiszko denied that he was the killer, alleging that the police had said, 'We know you wanked over her,' and so he had put that in his statement.

Taylor sat down, doubtless content that he had not merely outwitted Kiszko so as to show him to be a liar (although that he had certainly achieved) but had, more importantly, made such an impact in cross-examination so as to show Kiszko to have been the killer.

With Kiszko making such a poor impression in the witness box, or with Taylor making such penetrative inroads, could the defence hope that their position could be improved by calling Charlotte Kiszko and Alfreda Tosic, the accused's mother and aunt? Taylor had Kiszko as a liar, notably as to his alibi. He had shown that Kiszko had 'inside knowledge' of the crime – the ejaculation and the fact that Lesley was clothed – and he had Kiszko's verbal and written detailed confessions to the murder. Waddington had the only two living relatives which Stefan Ivan Kiszko had, as his alibi witnesses.

Charlotte and Alfreda both gave evidence supporting Stefan's alibi for 5 October. Charlotte Kiszko's account to the jury was essentially the same as her son's, save in that it appears that she recalled that her sister had not come to Crawford Street as Kiszko himself had said. The difficulty with her evidence arose from statements which she had made to the police in December 1975, which conflicted substantially with the account given in court, a conflict which Charlotte attempted to resolve by an assertion that she was, in December, so nervous and distressed about Stefan's circumstances that she was at that time unable to give an accurate account of his movements on 5 October.

In his cross-examination of Charlotte and of Alfreda, Taylor showed mastery of his craft: he did not put to them that they were lying in their evidence, or that they had 'conspired' with Kiszko to tell a similar story, allegations against two ladies of advancing years which might have cost him points in sympathy, but he gently suggested that they had made a mistake, which was an easy thing to do. He repeatedly suggested that they had visited the cemetery on 12 October rather than the fifth and, despite the vehemence of their denials to this suggestion, the manner in which it was put and the contrast with their earlier recollections in statements made nearer the time did much to dissipate the effect of their evidence.

So too did the appearance Miss Baran, the daughter of the owner of the Continental grocer's shop. She recalled Kiszko coming into the shop – he was a regular customer – some time in early October, on a Sunday round about lunch-time, and that on that occasion there had been an argument with a young girl. Miss Baran's account matched closely with Kiszko's, and she had the appearance of being an independent witness without a motive to lie, but the effect of her evidence was weakened by her admission that she was unable to say whether the incident with the argumentative child took place on the first (5) or second (12) Sunday in October.

Waddington had called all the evidence available to support the alibi. His next move was to attempt to show that the murder could have been committed by some other person.

The first suggestion that another unidentified person had been concerned in the abduction and Lesley's killing, and the most damning from the Crown's point of view, arose out of the reported sighting of a biggish white or cream saloon car in Well-i'-th'-Lane, Rochdale. The defence witness, Mrs Emma Tong, was to tell the jury that she had seen that car in her street at about 1.30 p.m. on the Sunday afternoon of Lesley's disappearance. There was a young girl in the car, in the front passenger seat, who had looked up and smiled at the witness. The view which Mrs Tong had had enabled her to see the child, and she believed the child to be Lesley Molseed.

Again Peter Taylor QC, whilst wishing to denude Mrs Tong's evidence of any value, was cautious not to be seen to be attacking her. Instead of suggesting that the witness was lying, he put it to Mrs Tong that she had made an honest mistake. That she had seen a girl in a blue coat in the car, and, when she had seen the posters of the missing child, had put two and two together and assumed that the child in the car was Lesley. Mrs Tong steadfastly refused to resile from her conviction that the child in the car was Lesley, but she was bound to admit that she had had only a momentary view of the girl's face, and that that had in part been obscured by the hood of the coat which the child had been wearing. Moreover, Taylor was able to establish that the child in the car was smiling, which would hardly be likely if she was the victim of a recent abduction.

David Waddington continued his pursuit of the theory that someone else had committed the murder[1] by calling Thomas Jones and Edith Boulton, both of whom gave evidence that they had driven passed the relevant lay-by at 1.30 p.m. and again at 4.30 p.m. on Sunday, 5 October, at which time, they had seen a green/blue Morris 1000 van parked there, with a tartan rug across the windscreen and driver's window, and that there was no other vehicle there at the time. The first sighting would be at about the time that Lesley, on the prosecution's theory, would have been brought to the place where she ultimately met her death. The prosecution did not dispute the evidence of these two witnesses: they did not have to, for the evidence did not conflict with the possibility that Kiszko had arrived a little earlier or, in particular, a little later, at which time the van might have gone.

The defence case had now dealt with two matters: that Kiszko had not killed the child, and that someone else could have done. They had called their alibi witnesses, answered the confession evidence and put forward evidence capable of raising a suspicion that the murder had been committed by the driver either of the vehicle seen by Mrs Tong or the Morris 1000. The primary defence was complete. The defence could now say to the jury, you cannot be sure that Stefan Kiszko killed Lesley Molseed.

But now Waddington moved on to what can properly be described as the second limb of his defence, namely that if indeed the jury were satisfied beyond reasonable doubt that Kiszko had killed the child, could they be satisfied that he did not do so whilst suffering from a diminished responsibility due to the effects of the treatment he had been receiving for his hormone deficiency. Throughout the trial Waddington had taken any and every opportunity to emphasise Kiszko's medical condition and its effect on the defendant, and whilst he had, in his opening remarks to the jury, stressed that Kiszko vehemently denied the killing, he had also told the jury that they would have to consider the defence of diminished responsibility, which would have the effect of

---

1 The defence, of course, were under no duty to prove this to be the case, still less who that person might be.

Dick Holland, pictured after his retirement from the police force, who conducted the investigation into Lesley's killer which led to the wrongful conviction of Stefan Kiszko. © News Team, Manchester Evening News

(*Opposite top*) The search for evidence on the moorland above the lay-by where Lesley's body was found. © West Yorkshire Police

(*Below*) The police interviewing motorists on the A672 Ripponden Road, 1975. © West Yorkshire Police

(*Opposite bottom*) The lay-by on the A672. © West Yorkshire Police

April and Danny Molseed, 1975. © *Rochdale Observer*

(*Opposite top*) Delamere Road, home of the Molseed family in 1975.
© *West Yorkshire Police*

(*Opposite middle*) The snicket down which Lesley walked: the last place she was seen alive. © *West Yorkshire Police*

(*Opposite bottom*) The Spar shop, at which Lesley never arrived on her errand to buy a loaf of bread. © *West Yorkshire Police*

Lesley Molseed, aged about ten. *By permission of News Team, Manchester Evening News*

Lesley's coffin leaves her home. Danny Molseed is on the left.
© *News Team, Manchester Evening News*

(*Opposite top*) Rochdale schoolchildren line the route as Lesley's coffin is driven to the cemetery. © *News Team, Manchester Evening News*

(*Opposite bottom*) Danny and April Molseed at Lesley's graveside.
© *News Team, Manchester Evening News*

Stefan Kiszko, aged about ten. © *Alfreda Tosic*

(*Opposite top*) Peter Taylor, successful prosecuting counsel at Stefan's trial and (*opposite bottom*) David Waddington, leader of the defence. © *Press Association*

Charlotte (left) and Alfreda after Stefan's funeral. © *News Team, Manchester Evening News*

(*Opposite top*) Stefan and Brenda Lord, to whom he corresponded throughout his time in prison, on the day of his release. © *Brenda Lord*

(*Opposite bottom*) Stefan at home in King's Road on the same day, flanked by his ever supportive mother Charlotte (left) and Aunt Alfreda. © *Rochdale Observer*

Charlotte Kiszko, surrounded by letters of condolence following Stefan's death.
© *Rochdale Observer*

reducing the crime from murder to manslaughter.

The picture now painted of Kiszko was of a man with little education, average intelligence but an abnormal personality. He was fat, socially withdrawn, socially inept, mother-fixated and an unhappy person who was unable to form – and had never formed – relationships. His level of social and emotional maturity was put as being that of an 11- or 12-year-old child.

The jury was first told his medical history. In August 1975 Kiszko had visited his GP, Dr George D'Vaz, complaining of tiredness. The doctor had immediately realised that there was something seriously wrong; Dr D'Vaz gave Kiszko a prescription, and arranged for him to be seen at his home the following day, Tuesday, 5 August, by Dr Gerard Duffy, Consultant Physician.

Dr Duffy found Kiszko to be severely anaemic, and arranged for his immediate admission to Birch Hill Hospital in Rochdale. There, Dr Duffy found Kiszko also to be hypogonadal, in that he had no testicles in his scrotum and an immature penis. The treatment administered for the anaemia was not successful, and Dr Duffy arranged for his patient to be transferred to Manchester Royal Infirmary, on 18 August, where he remained until 15 September.

At the Manchester hospital it was determined that Kiszko was the subject of long-standing hypogonadism and testosterone deficiency,[2] and that the appropriate treatment for the patient would be replacement of the hormone testosterone. This was to be achieved by intramuscular testosterone injections administered once every three weeks. In accordance with the treatment prescribed, Stefan Kiszko was given an injection of 125mg Primoteston at about 11.30 a.m. on Friday, 3 October 1975.

When Kiszko was discharged from Manchester Royal Infirmary on 15 September 1975, the treatment for his anaemia had been so successful that his haemoglobin level had been restored to seventy-five per cent of normal. Doctor Tarsh, a psychiatrist called for the defence, told the court that the result of that restoration would have been to give Kiszko a feeling of physical well-being. A concomitant effect of his hospitalisation had been to cause Kiszko to lose a great deal of weight. He had weighed some seventeen or eighteen stone prior to his illness, but had lost weight so that he was down to fourteen stone when he had left the hospital. Thus by

---

2 The anaemia was explained as being due to a lack of folic acid and an excessive intake of cider, and was resolved by treatment with folic acid.

the middle of September 1975 Stefan Kiszko could properly be described as feeling like a new man.

In addition to the resolution of his anaemia, Kiszko was also receiving treatment for his hypogonadism. Between the ages of 17 and 19 Kiszko had been able to masturbate with the assistance of magazines, but this urge had been lost in the five or six years prior to 1975. The injections of Primoteston he was receiving increased Kiszko's ability to produce male sex hormones: his sexual drive undoubtedly increased. His ability to masturbate and ejaculate returned. The physical and emotional by-products of this treatment had to be seen as combining with the feeling of well-being associated with the improvement in his haemoglobulin level: this man was, in October 1975, a new man, with new urges.

But his mind, according to the medical evidence heard at the trial, remained that of a young boy, certainly in terms of his ability to cope emotionally with his new-found 'manliness'. Dr Tarsh spoke of Kiszko as having a retarded emotional development of both personality and sexuality. He had the personality of a child, and so was unable to cope emotionally with his feelings of well-being and his sex drive. Whereas a young boy's emotional development would usually come in parallel with his sexual development, what happened to Kiszko in the autumn of 1975 was that his sexual development had leapt ahead of his emotional development. He was, quite simply, not mentally ready for what his body wanted to do. The effect of this was that, sexually stimulated, Kiszko would not know what to do. He would not know how to approach an adult woman, and would, according to Dr Tarsh, be more liable to approach children than adults. He would be liable to expose himself, and he would be liable to be aggressive, because some aggression was a recognised side effect of the testosterone treatment.

A plethora of doctors was called by the defence. His GP Dr D'Vaz gave the general medical overview; Gerard Duffy gave details of his hospitalisation, including the transfer to Manchester Royal Infirmary on 18 August; the story was taken up by Dr Peter English from the Manchester hospital, who, in giving his account, was to tell the jury that, on Friday, 3 October 1975, he had given Kiszko 125mgs of Primoteston when Kiszko had attended as an out-patient. A statement was read from Dr Irvine Delamore, under whom Dr English worked, although the statement contained much information which the jury had already heard, even if they had not yet understood it. Dr David Child of Manchester University and Manchester Royal Infirmary provided the next statement, which dealt in particular with Kiszko's hypogonadism which was due to a severe degree of primary testicular failure.

Next came a statement from Dr David Anderson, senior lecturer in medicine at Manchester University which covered, again, the issue of Kiszko's hypogonadism and its treatment by administration of Primoteston. The jury may have been numb as wave after wave of medical jargon swept across the jury box, but even an assembly of twelve laymen could not help but sit up and listen as this part of Dr Anderson's statement was read to them: 'The accepted contra-indication for this (Primoteston) treatment is a history of aggressive and/or deviant sexual behaviour.' Dr Anderson continued, however, by saying that an increase in drive and aggression, and in sexual activity, occurs only where there are existing tendencies. 'They do not result in the arousal of previously uncharacteristic urges.'

Dr Barry Enoch, a Manchester-based doctor specialising in endocrinology, had examined Kiszko in Armley Prison. He had found him to be an intelligent cooperative man who spoke with a high-pitched voice, was unusually tall (6' 2") and grossly overweight. He had scanty facial hair and his pubic hair was of a female distribution. The penis was abnormally small, the scrotum poorly developed and there was no testicle on the left side and only a vestigial testicle on the right. The doctor was able to confirm the diagnosis of hypogonadism and to express his approval of Kiszko's medical treatment. Asked about the effects of Primoteston administration Dr Enoch said that tests had shown a correlation between administration of the drug and an increase in aggression, but no increase in sex drive. He did say, however, that within a day or two of injections erections may appear, although his clinical experiences suggested a longer period of time was involved. Dr Enoch said that Kiszko's anaemia could cause loss of libido, in which case the testosterone treatment might bring about a reversal in that position, but that he had no experience of a man with anaemia as severe as that of Kiszko, so that he was unable to say whether the treatment might have a greater effect in relation to sexuality.

Having established in great detail the conditions suffered by Kiszko, the treatment administered and the effects of those treatments, in general terms as to curative effects and side effects, Mr Waddington then moved on to the specific effect on Kiszko's mind, hoping thereby to raise the defence of diminished responsibility.

There are two essential constituent components of the defence of diminished responsibility. The first is that the mind must be abnormal, but abnormality of the mind alone will not suffice. The defence must also establish that it was the abnormality of the mind which substantially impaired his mental responsibility for the killing. Put simply, the mind defect must have caused or substantially contributed to the killing.

Dr Michael Tarsh told the jury that, whilst Kiszko had no history of mental illness, the account Kiszko gave of recording car number plates was suggestive of paranoia, or at least a paranoid episode. He formed the view that Kiszko was of good average intelligence, although some psychological tests had suggested he was of only low or average intelligence. He was also of the view that Kiszko was suffering from an abnormality of the mind, being a retarded development of personality and of sexuality. The doctor, however, formed the view that Kiszko's personality would, as a result of the improvement in his haemoglobin level following treatment for the anaemia, have become elevated. The anaemia was due to a lack of folic acid, and such a deficiency is said to be associated with a range of psychiatric conditions such as depression and anxiety states. Treatment for the anaemia involved dosages of folic acid, and the increase in folic acid levels would bring with it a feeling of well-being and also a restoration of sex drive. Dr Tarsh considered the restoration of such a drive to be in the nature of a 'profound sexual stimulation'.

The court was told, however, that Kiszko would, in the circumstances, have been unable to control the sexual stimulation, and this was highly material to the defence advanced. Dr Tarsh spoke of Kiszko being 'restored', but he explained this further by saying, 'I would expect him not merely to be restored to normal, but restored to more than normal,' and he spoke (although he accepted the analogy was not entirely appropriate) of a bull, normally quiet and placid, who becomes completely uncontrollable and produces unexpected fits of aggression.

The evidence of the doctor, thus far, enabled the defence to put forward a man who had an abnormality of the mind, and who had been brought to a state beyond his own normality by the treatment he had received. His sexuality was restored, but was restored beyond normality, to be overtaken by a heightened stimulation. This explained the drive which would lead the defendant to want sexual activity and to seek it without reference to normal adult techniques. His inability to form a relationship explained why he should seek sexual activity with a child. It would explain masturbation, it would even explain abduction. Yet at this point in the evidence the defence, having progressed with some ease through the first part of the defence of diminished responsibility, came to something of a halt when the second stage was reached.

What was it that might have caused Stefan Kiszko to kill the child? Dr Tarsh rejected out of hand the suggestion that Lesley had been killed in order to silence her. The degree of violence done to the child was inconsistent with merely killing to cover up what an offender had done. If that was so, then the fact that the violence was disproportionate to 'need' meant that it had been done through a burst of uncontrollable aggression. There was, however, nothing in the personality of Kiszko which could lead to a conclusion that he was prone to such aggression.

Dr Tarsh laboured under the difficulty, of course, that Kiszko had given no account of the killing which the doctor could assess to ascertain whether it was an act done in a moment of uncontrollable aggression. The only 'account' of the defendant concerning the killing was that said by the prosecution to have been given to the police. Furthermore, and this was of particular importance to Dr Tarsh, the account which Kiszko had given in his interviews and statements was remarkably sparse in detail. Dr Tarsh commented on this when he was cross-examined:

> If the position had been that I was extracting a confession not so much to prove guilt as to try to explain why, then I would have asked a lot more questions than the chief superintendent asked. I would have focused particularly on the gap after masturbating himself against the girl and before producing the knife.

Kiszko had given no account in his alleged admissions as to why he had killed Lesley. He had not given any explanation of any event which had triggered that killing, nor of any motivation or cause for the extreme violence used. In the circumstances of the Kiszko case, this meant that Dr Tarsh was obliged to speculate.

Dr Tarsh postulated the theory that Kiszko would have been in a state of 'sexual exultation', for only in that state would he have been able to approach Lesley. In that heightened state, the final act, said Dr Tarsh, would have come about in this way:

> I would speculate that some sort of rejection or fighting was going on, or careless words on behalf of the little girl would

have been the sort of trigger to promote this frenzied outburst which clearly there was. So, when you go back in the story the child has signed its own death warrant by something they have said which has triggered.

David Waddington interjected: 'Like, "You are a dirty old man"?' and the doctor replied: 'Something of that sort, or "You ought to be locked up", or something like that.'[3] He then opined: 'I would think he [Kiszko] would become completely overcome, completely uncontrollably angry . . .'

The prosecution did not seek to rebut the defence of diminished responsibility, but merely to cross-examine Dr Tarsh in such a way as to offer assistance to the jury in their consideration of this defence. Thus Peter Taylor re-emphasised the speculative nature of Dr Tarsh's theory, but he also, if anything, assisted in the development of the theory by drawing from Dr Tarsh the critical state of a man's mind in the immediate aftermath of sexual ejaculation, so that that time could well have been the moment at which Kiszko's mind might have 'ripened' to the state where he could be triggered into killing. To this Dr Tarsh said that 'In the immediate aftermath of ejaculation a man can become uncontrollable, he may be violent, all sorts of things are possible. You do not necessarily return to a normal emotional state. Awful things can happen after ejaculation.' Dr Tarsh did emphasise that the injections could cause the accused to engage in masturbation, indecent exposure and violence if moved to anger.

But Peter Taylor was able to use Dr Tarsh in another way. It was the final question in cross-examination which brought about an attractive explanation for Kiszko's denial of the killing.

Mr Taylor confirmed with Dr Tarsh the very close relationship between Kiszko and his mother, and Dr Tarsh agreed that Kiszko would be anxious about the impact on his mother of her son having committed such a crime, so that the pressure on him would be great to keep any guilt away from her. Dr Tarsh at this point provided substantial help to the Crown, which arguably far outweighed any assistance he had given to the defence, when he said:

[I]f the jury take the view that the actual offence is such that they are certain that he was responsible for this . . . the only sensible motivation that he would have in maintaining the

3 The jury would have to consider, of course, whether a girl of Lesley's maturity and background, who had been abducted and dragged on to the moors would have had the confidence to say any such thing, after her abductor had masturbated on to her.

opposite would be this relationship with his mother and the shame which he himself would have in telling her that he had done this dreadful thing after all . . .

The final defence witness was Albert Wright, Kiszko's solicitor, who gave evidence of his knowledge of the murder prior to his being engaged to act for the defendant. Mr Wright told the jury that, amongst police officers and lawyers in Rochdale it had been common knowledge that the crime was sexually motivated. He himself had spoken with a police officer of a rank below chief inspector in which the officer confirmed that semen had been found on the body. Mr Wright spoke of what he believed was commonly known in the small town, but when cross-examined by Mr Taylor he was obliged to concede that he knew of no media coverage detailing the fact that the killer had masturbated over the lower clothing of the victim, and that her underwear had not been disturbed.

David Waddington then closed the defence case, but there was one final matter of evidence. Designed to show that Charlotte Kiszko and her sister were mistaken witnesses as to the date, Peter Taylor was able to read a statement in rebuttal. It was of the two fire officers who had attended the house fire in Crawford Street, which Kiszko's mother and aunt had claimed was on the same day as their trip to the cemetery with Stefan, namely 5 October. The statements showed that the house fire had been on 12 October. One week after the killing of Lesley Molseed.

With the evidence now complete, all that remained was for the advocates to make their closing speeches and the judge to sum up. There was a sense of anticipation in the courtroom as the trial moved into its final stages.

The effect of a closing speech can never be over-estimated. Many a case has been won or lost by the most singular opportunity of an advocate to display his skill, and whilst barristers may differ in the manner of their final speeches, all would agree that it is a vital stage in the trial process. A trial may have taken days, or even weeks, and the closing speech may be concise or verbose, but the crucial aim of that speech should be to bring the jury's attention to the most salient features of the case advocated. To do that a lawyer may select and emphasise the most positive features of his case or the weakest points of his opponent's. He may seek to answer the arguments of the opposing counsel or he may simply dismiss those arguments peremptorily in favour of repeating his own. Or he may hand to the jury a 'tag' on which to hang their decision.

Peter Taylor QC certainly used this technique, when he accused the defence of 'riding two horses'. The defence, he claimed, argue 'I didn't do it, but if I did it was only because of diminished responsibility.' Those arguments, said Mr Taylor, were two horses which could not be ridden together.

He submitted that the evidence that Kiszko had killed Lesley Molseed was overwhelming. The confessions of Kiszko were couched in terms and detail which only the killer could use and know. He poured scorn on the evidence of Charlotte Kiszko and of Alfreda Tosic, who had given evidence to support the alibi defence, saying that they were so involved with Kiszko that they had led themselves to believe that what they generally did on Sundays was what they had done on Sunday, 5 October. Relying on the bond between mother and aunt and accused, prosecuting counsel took the line that a person who repeats a lie often enough may ultimately believe it to be true. So convinced were the sisters that Stefan Kiszko could not be guilty, they had persuaded themselves of the truth of his alibi.

But of greater importance was the medical evidence. Had Kiszko been a 'normal' man with a normal medical background and a normal sex life, the jury might find it difficult to believe that Kiszko was the man who had committed this offence. 'What you have here,' said Mr Taylor, 'is the absolute opposite. You have here someone who is just the sort of person who might have acted in this way at this time.' Referring to the psychiatric evidence, the prosecution reminded the jury that, in the last six weeks prior to the killing, Kiszko had become physically and sexually a new man, and that some rebound would have been expected. 'Unhappily, the rebound landed on Lesley Molseed.'

Peter Taylor made little effort to persuade the jury that this was not a case of diminished responsibility. 'I do not seek to urge one view or the other, but to leave it to you to decide,' he said. He put before the jury the arguments and evidence on both sides.

He first sought to draw a relationship between the injections and the behaviour of the accused in the time immediately preceding 5 October. On the side of the defence, he pointed to the evidence that the injections could lead to aggression, to the admissions to the police that Kiszko had indecently exposed himself, and to the evidence of Dr Tarsh that Kiszko was suffering from diminished responsibility. But against that, said Mr Taylor, was Kiszko's evidence that the injections did not create in him 'uncontrollable urges' and the evidence of Dr Enoch that his own research had shown no connection between treatment for hypogonadism and indecent exposure, nor that the aggression caused by the treatment ever amounted to more than bad temper and irritability. He went no further in the argument one way or another, but his concluding words were clear: 'The only point I put to you in any positive way on behalf of the crown is this – one way or the other, there is certainly no room here for a verdict of not guilty.'

It was, perhaps, a curious speech. Having told the jury that the defence were riding two incompatible defences, the implication being that the jury should reject both, one might have expected prosecuting counsel to nail his colours firmly to the mast, and to pursue with vigour a conviction for murder. But Taylor was content, in effect, to leave to the jury only the *extent* or degree of Kiszko's guilt. That he did so is, perhaps, a testament of fairness, or an indication of the subconscious view of many, that a man as apparently normal as Stefan Kiszko could not have done this terrible deed unless overwhelmed by some paradoxical abnormality on 5 October 1975.

The defence felt no such restraint, and David Waddington QC began his closing speech with an attack on the Crown's apparent indecisiveness of attitude as to the defence of diminished responsibility, claiming that the Crown itself was riding two horses in saying, in effect, 'Members of the jury, you can convict of either murder or manslaughter as long as you convict.'

An ingenious argument was to follow. If the jury was to accept that Kiszko had killed Lesley Molseed, then they had to reject his evidence in the witness box and *accept* what he had said to the police. Since he had told the police that he had acted only because of a great sexual urge, the jury would have to accept that, and would therefore be a long way towards finding diminished responsibility. Affixing himself with some vigour to the diminished responsibility defence, Mr Waddington said that 'commonsense and the medical evidence pointed only one way'. It was only after the injections that Kiszko had acted in the way the prosecution had suggested. 'Does not commonsense tell you,' submitted defence counsel, 'that there must be a connection of some sort between the condition he was suffering from, the treatment he had for this condition, and his actions on 3, 4 and 5 October?'

The defence urged the jury to consider the combination of factors, the administering of the drug, the anaemia from which Kiszko suffered, and the emotional immaturity of the man.

Whereas in the normal man the sex urge and the emotional equipment grew and developed in parallel, 'What happened in this case is that this man grew sexually in a flash and he could not possibly have had the time to grow up emotionally at the same time.' That imbalance between the emotional and the physical created a circumstance in which the accused was not able to exercise the will power to control his physical acts.

If the jury concluded that Kiszko had killed Lesley, they were urged to find that he did so only as a result of diminished responsibility.

It is interesting to note that the first part of Mr Waddington's speech dealt with diminished responsibility, giving at least the appearance that this was the horse which the defence most preferred to ride. But the other mount was not ignored. The jury was reminded that no witness claimed to have seen Kiszko's car at the lay-by. That Lesley had been seen, according to the witness Mrs Tong, in a cream-coloured car, which car and its driver had never been identified. That a blue-green van seen at the lay-by at material times, notably 1.30 p.m. on Sunday, 5 October had never been traced. Mr Waddington then pointed to discrepancies between the 'confession' and the known facts, and, in particular, to the demonstration of the killing which Kiszko had allegedly given to the police. He had shown how the blow had been struck to the left side of the upper chest, whereas Lesley had been struck, in fact, to the right side of the neck.

But in conclusion, whilst inviting the jury to acquit completely, David Waddington returned to the verdict which the defence lawyers seemed most to seek: 'If you reject his evidence and find that he killed her, then you must accept his written statement, and view it in the light of the medical evidence.' Having done that, submitted the defence, the jury should conclude that Stefan Kiszko was guilty not of murder, but of manslaughter by reason of diminished responsibility.

The final words of the advocates having been spoken, nothing more could be done by those in an adversarial position to affect the outcome of the trial. Now they, and all who had an interest in the case against Stefan Kiszko, could only sit and listen to the closing words: words which would come from the Honourable Mr Justice Park.

CHAPTER FIFTEEN

Innocence?

As the barristers concluded their part in the trial, whatever fears Kiszko harboured he believed that he would be acquitted because he could not conceive of a system which would not operate other than with impeccable fairness. Throughout his trial he believed that the police themselves would prove his innocence.

In this he was, at the very least, naive. His naivety may well have been based on a lack of understanding of the nature of the English legal system. The epitome of that system, the man on whom Stefan had come, ultimately, to depend, was the judge, Mr Justice Park. The judge, however, is not there to discover the truth. His task is to ensure that there is a fair trial, by which is meant not merely a trial which is fair to the defendant, but one which is just for both defence and prosecution.

Any assessment of the trial of Stefan Ivan Kiszko must include a consideration of the role of the trial judge, Mr Justice Park, and in examining that role, an opportunity may be taken to appraise the trial as a whole and the roles of the advocates, against the backdrop of the judge's final summing-up. Juries tend to pay great regard to what the judge tells them, and are frequently willing to be, quite literally, directed by them. The judge's summing-up is, therefore, a powerful and influential tool in the administration of justice.

The object of summing-up is two-fold. First, the judge directs the jury as to the law applicable to the case and second, he sums up the evidence in the case. They are two distinct, but equally important parts. The judge begins his summing-up, in virtually every case, by telling the jury that he is the judge of law, so that the jury must accept all of his directions on the law, and he then tells the jury that they are the judges of fact, and that they and they alone determine the facts in the case, and anything which he may say about the facts may be accepted or rejected by the jury as they see fit. The jury, as lay-people, must accept the judge's directions as to law, and almost inevitably they will do so. The 'Law' part of a summing-up tends to be formulaic.

So it was as Mr Justice Park ran through such matters as the burden and standard of proof, the legal meaning of murder and of diminished responsibility, and how a finding of diminished responsibility in the case of Kiszko would reduce his guilt so as to cause a verdict of manslaughter. By the time that he had concluded this part the jury could be in no doubt that it was for the Crown to prove that Kiszko killed Lesley Molseed, for the Crown to prove that Kiszko's alibi was false, for the Crown to prove that Kiszko's confessions were made voluntarily and were true and for the Crown to prove that Kiszko, if he did kill the child, was not suffering from diminished responsibility. And on each matter, the jury had to be sure beyond a reasonable doubt.

It is always less clear how a jury may respond to the judge's summing-up of the facts. The judge will have told the jury that they may agree or disagree with the way in which he sums up the facts. Few summings-up are a full repetition of all the evidence in the case, they are almost always a selection or summary of facts or evidence which the judge believes to be relevant. Almost inevitably, therefore, a summing-up may have the appearance of being slanted, or even biased, even where the judge has strained to avoid showing any particular emphasis.

Mr Justice Park summed up the case to the jury at some length and with what appears at first blush to be a deal of care. A careful reading of the summing-up in the Kiszko case, however, reveals a judge who clearly believed that Kiszko was lying when he said that he had not voluntarily admitted murder, and that the confession had been forced or made under duress. It is apparent from the summing-up that the judge certainly believed that Kiszko had killed Lesley.

An excellent example of the way in which the summing-up was weighted in this respect is the part at which Mr Justice Park dealt with Kiszko's explanations for the confession as being that he, Kiszko, had only admitted killing the child because he was afraid of the police who were conducting the interviews. The judge referred to the way in which Kiszko had coped with the lengthy cross-examination by Peter Taylor QC:

> Do you think he seemed able to look after himself? Do you
> think he appeared to you to be nervous or under great strain
> . . .? Do you think he kept his head, do you think he kept

cool? Do you think he was able when necessary to parry Mr Taylor's questions?

Of course, the jury – as the judge reminded them – was entitled to take into consideration Kiszko's demeanour at any stage in the trial, but merely by directing the jury's attention to the cross-examination by Mr Taylor, the judge was implicitly inviting the thought that the scene in the courtroom and that which had taken place months earlier, when Kiszko was being interviewed in the police station, were somehow analogous, and that if Kiszko was – as the jury had seen – robust in the courtroom, why should he have been so suggestible in the police interview as to invent a false confession. The judge could never direct the jury: 'Well, ladies and gentlemen, this defendant held up well in cross-examination by a skilled prosecutor in the middle of a murder trial, so how can he say he could not cope with two policemen in an interview room?' but by carefully turning the jury to this aspect of the case, the judge achieved the same result.

It is an extremely skilful way for a judge to indicate to a jury the lines along which his mind is working, yet carefully avoid any prospect of the verdict being appealed on the grounds of a biased summing-up.

Another, perhaps less-obvious example came when the judge was dealing with the evidence of the events of 4 October and, in particular, Kiszko's interview by the police at his home on the evening of 5 November. Kiszko, when the 4 October incident was put to him, denied having driven his car for several weeks, a denial which he subsequently explained as referring to the time he was in hospital. In summing-up the judge said of this 'Why, on 5 November, was he denying that he had driven his car for several weeks? Why give a false explanation for his failure to drive it, that he had got a bad leg which is not true?' Questions framed in that way demand an answer from the jury, and the answer to this particular question was, obviously, 'He was lying because he did not want the police to know that he was out in his car on 4 October, the day before Lesley was abducted in a car.' It would have been most improper for the judge to have commented about this particular lie, but he was able to circumvent any suggestion of impropriety by leaving the question in the mind of the jury so that they could for themselves discover the answer which the judge was aware would be detrimental to Stefan's defence.

A favoured expression of judges seeking to make a point to the jury without appearing obviously to do so is, 'It's a matter for you' or 'It is for you to consider.' It tends to be added to a comment made by the judge in such a way as to appear that he is saying, 'I think X, but it does not matter what I think, it is what you think that matters.' An example in Mr Justice Park's summing-up was when he was dealing with the evidence of Mrs Tong, who claimed to have seen Lesley, alone and smiling, in a car which could not have been Kiszko's. In an effort to lessen the efficacy of this pro-defence point, by the suggestion that Mrs Tong was mistaken and the girl could not have been Lesley, the judge said:

> [I]t is for you to consider . . . if the driver of [this] car had in fact abducted this little girl he would not be likely to have left the little girl alone in the car for some two or three minutes time . . . you will have to ask yourselves do you think Mrs Tong really did see Lesley or was it some other little girl.

A further device, used to great effect by Mr Justice Park, is to give two options, one of which is heavily weighted as being the judge's view, the other ridiculed as being highly improbable. Examples of this are found towards the end of the summing-up, when Kiszko's explanations for the confessions were being dealt with.

Having dealt with Kiszko's explanation as given when cross-examined, Mr Justice Park said:

> Well, members of the jury, you will have to ask yourself whether those explanations carry any weight with you at all or whether he was just answering things on the spur of the moment when he was giving evidence before you in the witness box.

Then, dealing with Kiszko's answer that he had confessed because he thought the police would let him go home to his mother, the judge added: 'Well, you have to ask yourself whether he really did think that after confessing to a brutal killing that the police would let him go home.'

In that one comment, by ridiculing the root of Kiszko's defence to the killing, namely the explanation for his false confession, the judge implicitly commented to the jury that the defendant's explanation for the confession was a nonsense. He nailed the point a few moments later:

> [Y]ou may ask yourselves is the real reason why he made the confession the one that he gave at the end of the interview

when Holland asked him if he wanted to make a statement and he said 'Yes, I want to get it all sorted out.'

The summing-up of the facts began with a lengthy repetition of Stefan Kiszko's good character, upbringing, education and employment, and of the substance of the medical evidence so far as it concerned Kiszko, of his condition and his treatment and the consequences and side effects of that treatment. He was putting the defendant into the minds of the jury, and he did so with a concluding remark as to the cumulative effects of the medical treatment on Kiszko when he said: 'Members of the jury, in view of all that evidence it is clear, isn't it . . . that on 5 October this accused was a person with a sexual problem,' and, observing that the killer of Lesley almost certainly had access to a car and that Kiszko himself did have a car the judge concluded that:

> on 5 October, this defendant fell into the category of persons who might have committed this offence: certainly a very large category, a person with a sex problem and a person with a car.

The jury, if they were to make the giant step from this massive category of persons who might have killed Lesley to being satisfied beyond reasonable doubt that it was Stefan Kiszko who had killed her, had to make that step upon evidence and not upon prejudice or supposition. The learned judge made this quite clear when he advised the jury – and in this he was surely correct – that the main question for them to decide was whether Kiszko's confession that he had killed the girl was a true confession, in all the circumstances of the case. Mr Justice Park told the jury they could only find that he *was* the person who killed the child if they were satisfied beyond a reasonable doubt that his confession to the police was made voluntarily and was true, and, in order to decide whether the confession was true the jury should consider the totality of the evidence, including:

i the evidence of the girls concerning the events of 3 and 4 October and 5 November;

ii the evidence of the police and of Kiszko himself concerning the making of the confession;

iii the knife recovered from Kiszko which had blood on it;

iv the orange and yellow fibres found on Lesley, which

matched the piece of carpet in Kiszko's car;

v a felt-tip pen found near the body, which was the same type of pen as used by Kiszko in his work;

vi the note found in Kiszko's possession, bearing the registration number of the motor car belonging to Mr Hollos, which had been driven past the lay-by below the murder scene, on Sunday, 5 October;

vii the alibi evidence provided by Kiszko, his mother and Alfreda Tosic;

viii the evidence of Mrs Tong.

The judge summed up each of these matters in turn, but he placed particular emphasis on the evidence of Mrs Tong. He invited the jury to consider, not whether Mrs Tong was deliberately seeking to mislead the jury, but whether she had simply made an honest mistake. But if Mrs Tong was correct, then the confession of Kiszko had to be false, and Mr Justice Park recognised this when he said: 'Members of the jury, if you came to the conclusion that Mrs Tong *may have seen Lesley in that car*[1] then that is the end of the case for the prosecution; you would have to acquit the defendant.'

As to the evidence called in support of the alibi, the judge again took a gentle approach to Mrs Kiszko and her sister, echoing with unfortunate and inappropriate clarity the prosecution submission that Mrs Kiszko and Mrs Tosic, devastated by the gravity of the charge brought against Stefan, and unable and unwilling to believe that the allegation could possibly be true, had tried desperately to remember what had happened on 5 October 1975, and had ultimately convinced themselves that the account which they gave to the court was true. In an attempt to offer some assistance to the jury, Mr Justice Park drew attention to statements made by Charlotte and Alfreda.

From those statements it was apparent that Mrs Kiszko and Mrs Tosic were, in December 1975, unable to provide an accurate account of the events of 5 October or, more particularly, that they were unable to recall whether the particular events they described took place on the fifth or the twelfth. The point was obviously made to the jury that the evidence of these ladies, who had been

---

1 Authors' italics. The use of the word 'may' is a clear indication that the defence did not have to prove that Mrs Tong *had* seen Lesley in the car, but that the Crown had to prove beyond any doubt that it was *not* Lesley.

unable to have a clear recollection in December 1975, and who had both then been able to give a broadly similar account in their evidence in July 1976, was at least open to suspicion, although it was emphasised that the suggestion was not of deliberate dishonesty but because they were so convinced of Stefan Kiszko's innocence.

It was the confession, however, which the judge believed to be central to the determination of the case, and he dealt with the course of events leading to the confession and the circumstances of the confession in some detail.

There had been six interviews, but it had not been until the final interview that Kiszko had made his confession. The judge reminded the jury of Kiszko's evidence concerning this interview. Kiszko said that he had been placed into a room at the police station at 10.30 a.m., and he had remained in that room until he was finally allowed to sleep shortly after the 1.45 a.m. interview on the Monday morning. He had left the interview room only to go to the toilet, and he had been sick on several occasions. He had refused all food and hot drinks offered to him, and had drunk only water. 'I felt terrible,' he said, adding poignantly, 'I wanted to go home to mother.'

The crux of his evidence, however, was his explanation for, as he now put it, lying to the police in the interviews, and his reply merits verbatim repetition:

> During the interrogation when I was telling what was my story they wouldn't believe me, so I started telling lies and that seemed to please them and the pressure was off so far as I was concerned. I thought the police would check out what I had said and find it was untrue and would then let me go. Akeroyd spoke much louder than he did in the witness box and on occasions slapped his hand on the table. Sometimes I answered questions quickly. There were some pauses, but never for very long, but they asked the questions over and over again.

Kiszko's evidence in respect of the interviews continued by reference to alleged pressure by the interviewing officers. 'McFadzean said, "As soon as we get this wrapped up we can all go home for Christmas".'

The gentle inducement which Kiszko had attributed to DC McFadzean and the alleged loud voice and slapping of hands on the table by DS Akeroyd were, however, as nothing when compared to the allegation he made against DSupt Holland. Kiszko told the court that, at the first interview at which that officer had been present, at 6.45 p.m. on the Sunday evening, the detective superintendent had sat in front of him and said, 'I'm going to get the fucking truth out of you one way or another,' and he had been poking the frightened Kiszko on the shoulder. 'I was feeling very nervous and worried,' said Kiszko in his evidence.

Stefan Kiszko's account of the interviews on the Sunday could have been summarised in this way. He was frightened, nervous and tired and he wanted to go home to his mother. He had not eaten, nor had a hot drink. He had vomited on several occasions. He had been offered the opportunity to go home, he had been threatened by loud voices, and he had been poked in the shoulder by a senior officer uttering threatening obscenities. In the face of such pressure he had told lies and, seeing that those lies eased the pressure on him, he had continued to lie.

However, Mr Justice Park invited the jury to consider Kiszko in the following terms:

> Members of the jury, you have seen him in the witness box. You saw him there for a long time, I think a whole day. How did he appear to you to be? Do you think he seemed able to look after himself? Do you think he appeared to you to be nervous or under strain although he was being cross-examined with great skill by Mr Taylor on this very serious charge? Do you think he kept his head, do you think he kept cool? Do you think he was able when necessary to parry Mr Taylor's questions?

Kiszko, in evidence, confirmed that he had indeed confessed to the killing. His explanation for doing so was that he had admitted the offence because 'I was sick and absolutely terrified. I didn't want to face more questioning and a little while after Holland had left I told Akeroyd I had picked up the girl and killed her, but it was not true. I said it in order to get the police off my back. They were quite happy with what I had said and started to calm down a bit.'

How does one make up, as Kiszko claimed he had done, a false confession? Kiszko had said that all the details in the admission came from the police officers. He had said that he had picked the girl up in Broad Lane, and he said that this came from Dick Holland saying to him, 'Isn't it Broad Lane where you picked her up?' His explanation for the admission that he had ejaculated on to the girl was that Holland had said to him 'We know you wanked all over her.'

Kiszko had said that he had stuck the knife in the girl's neck. He said that Holland had asked him, 'Where did you stab her, in the neck, in the chest or in the back,' and he had chosen neck. But he went on to say that when Holland had asked him to demonstrate, using a pencil against the squatting police officer, he had demonstrated a cutting motion across the throat, not, as had been reported, a stabbing motion. It was chance that he chose the neck out of the three offered sites of injury. It was also chance, according to Kiszko, that he had been able to provide a description of the place where the murder had taken place which came so close to that of the actual murder scene.

The judge, in summing-up, asked the jury to consider whether Kiszko's explanation for confessing to the murder of Lesley Molseed could indeed be right. Did Kiszko really think that after confessing to a brutal killing the police would let him go home? The jury's verdict suggests that they too found such an idea incredible. It suggests that they could see no circumstances in which an entirely innocent man would confess to a terrible and cruel murder. But who on the jury (all men and women of good character) could imagine the ordeal of being held and interviewed by experienced police officers investigating the murder of a child? Who on the jury could possibly step into the shoes of Stefan Kiszko and imagine how he or she would respond in that same situation? And who, if any, of those twelve ordinary people, remembered cases that had gone before where false confessions had been made by people subsequently found to be innocent of any charge. Was there not one man or woman upon that jury who was able to remember the case of Timothy Evans, convicted and hanged upon his own confession to the murder of his baby daughter, Geraldine, a crime almost certainly committed by the multiple-murderer John Christie?

The defence response to the confession was in two parts. First and foremost it comprised Kiszko's own evidence that the confessions, verbal and written, were fabrications created out of his own sense of fear and desire to be left alone and to go home. The second part, more difficult for the defence lawyers to execute, was to cast doubt upon the evidence concerning the events of 3 and 4 October and 5 November, which meant, in terms, destroying the evidence of the children who had been the victims of those events.

The prosecution relied upon the evidence of the girls, not in order to pursue any argument that a man who would expose himself to children would be the sort of person to abduct and kill a child, but in order to show that Kiszko's confessions were true. The prosecution argument came to this: a man exposed himself to the girls on 3 October, and Maxine Buckley said that it was Stefan Kiszko who exposed himself to her and Debra Mills on 4 October. Miss Buckley was able to say that because she had, on 5 November 1975, identified the accused. In his interviews with the police, Kiszko had admitted indecent exposure on 3 and 4 October. In his written statement he had repeated his admission of indecent exposure on 3 October, but had substituted for his admissions concerning 4 October the account that he had accidentally caught his zip in the carpet. The Crown's argument was that the evidence of the girls was confirmed by Kiszko's admissions, and if he was telling the truth about those matters then he was telling the truth about the killing.

The defence position was, naturally, the opposite of this. They submitted that not one of the girls who described the man who committed the alleged indecent exposure on 3 October was able to provide a description which fitted the accused or his car, so that had Kiszko ever been tried for that offence, he would have been acquitted had the only evidence been that of the girls. That being the case, the confession of indecent exposure on 3 October was false, and it was a false confession for the reasons Kiszko had given in his evidence. The extension of the argument was that, because the confession to 3 October was false, the confession to the 5 October killing, which was to be found in the same written statement, was also false, or at least there should be serious doubt thrown upon it.

The judge directed the jury that there was no evidence which identified the defendant as being the man responsible for the indecent behaviour on 3 October. He told the jury that none of the children who had described the events of 3 October had given a description 'which really began to represent a description of the defendant, who you may think was not very difficult to describe'. He went on to invite the jury to consider whether the failure of the girls to describe the defendant as the man responsible for 3 October cast a doubt upon the reliability of the defendant's confession to the events, not only as to that night, but also as to the killing? He went on to ask them to consider whether, if Kiszko's admissions as to 3 October were believed by the jury, that helped them to come to a decision as to the veracity and reliability of the rest of his confessions and admissions.

The events of 3 October thus became crucial to the case, as being the starting point of the jury's quest to know the reliability or otherwise of the confessions, but the summing-up, at least, failed to address this issue sufficiently. The judge had set the issue in this way:

1 The children have failed to describe (much less identify) the defendant as the man responsible for the indecent behaviour on 3 October.

2 Does this failure assist you in determining whether Kiszko was telling the truth when he admitted being the man on 3 October?

3 If Kiszko was lying when he admitted being the man on 3 October, does this help you decide that he was lying as to the remainder of his confessions?

4 If Kiszko was telling the truth when he admitted being the man on 3 October, does this help you decide that he was also being truthful as to the remainder of his confessions?

There is no criticism of the questions posed at three and four above, but there is a substantial difficulty with the first proposition and the following question.

So far as 3 October is concerned, it was not merely a case of the children failing to describe Kiszko as being the man responsible. It was most certainly that the children had described a man who *was not Kiszko* as being responsible. Glaringly obvious from the descriptions given. Kiszko's car was a bronze Avenger. It was not yellow, nor green, nor a Ford Escort, nor did he have a dog. He was not, as many of the children had described, over 30 years of age, and he was not plump: he was fat, being around eighteen stone. He did not have a scar on his leg. There was no evidence that Kiszko had owned or wore a flat cap, a beret, a trilby or a knitted cap.

Crucial to this aspect of the case was the evidence of Maxine Buckley. Although she admitted that she could not see the man properly, Maxine gave a description to the court of a man with a big build – he was 'very wide' – and she too spoke of the green car with a dog. However, in the statement that Maxine made to the police on 9 October (six days after the event) she described the man as being 'not very tall, *but he was thin*'.[2] She spoke then of the man wearing a black beret, and of the dark-green car with a dog. It cannot be the case that Maxine was describing Kiszko in that statement, since on any possible view Kiszko could not be described as thin. But of even more importance, Maxine, who had identified, on 5 November, Stefan Kiszko as being the man responsible for the events of 4 October, said in her statement that she did not think that the man whom she saw on Saturday, 4 October was the same man as she saw on the Friday, *'because he was much heavier built. He was about 20–30 years, 5'10"–6' tall, well built.'*[3] In her statement of 30 December 1975 she added to this description by saying that he had staring eyes and very pale smooth skin, and that he walked funny, with his feet sticking out at the sides.

It is thus abundantly clear that Maxine Buckley did not think that the man on Friday night was Stefan Kiszko, and that she believed that the man on the Saturday night was him. It is highly unlikely that she could have been mistaken as to the differences between the two men, and had she wanted to actually lie, common sense dictates that she would have lied to say that Kiszko *was* the man who had indecently exposed himself on the Friday night.

It is therefore almost certainly the case that the children's evidence was to the effect that the man on the Friday was not Stefan Kiszko. If that is right then the judge's propositions in summing-up might have been better expressed as follows:

1 The children have described a man other than the defendant as the man responsible for the indecent behaviour on 3 October, so that it is unlikely that Kiszko was that man.

2 Does this description of a man other than Kiszko assist you in determining whether Kiszko was telling the truth when he admitted being the man on 3 October?

3 If Kiszko was lying when he admitted being the man on 3 October, does this help you decide that he was lying as to the remainder of his confessions?

4 If Kiszko was telling the truth when he admitted being the man on 3 October, does this help you decide that he was also being truthful as to the remainder of his confessions?

---

2 Authors' italics.
3 Authors' italics.

It is a substantial change in the way the questions should have been framed. If Kiszko was not the man on the Friday night, which, taken together, the evidence of the children – and in particular that of Maxine Buckley – tended strongly to suggest, then Kiszko almost certainly *was* lying when he admitted being the man on 3 October. The questions framed at three and four remain unchanged, but the answers to those questions might well have been different had the jury been directed that the children were almost certainly pointing the finger away from Stefan Kiszko as the man on 3 October.

Finally, and somewhat circuitously, the judge was to direct the jury that Kiszko's admissions as to 4 October were capable of confirming Maxine's evidence, a curious proposition given that her evidence was being put forward by the Crown as confirmation or corroboration of those very admissions. If Maxine was truthful and accurate and Kiszko's admissions were true and accurate, then, of course the one would confirm the other. But if either was inaccurate or untrue then there could be no element of corroboration. This direction was clearly of a 'chicken and egg' nature, and cannot have been overly helpful to the jury.

Kiszko's statement concerning 4 October was a curious matter. The defendant, having apparently admitted this allegation of indecent exposure in interview, then recanted the admission when he came to make a written statement and substituted instead the story of catching his zip in the carpet. This too was the account that he gave in evidence to the court, albeit that he was only able to say that that incident took place in late October, which did not match, at all, with the 4 October or 5 November. The Crown called that story 'absurd', but it does raise an interesting conundrum.

The Crown's case was that the admissions in the interviews were the truth, and that the truthfulness of the admissions derived some support from the girls' evidence, and from the content of the admissions bearing such a close resemblance to the alleged facts. Yet the Crown also submitted that, at least in the written statement concerning 4 October, Kiszko was telling a plain and absurd lie. If the Crown were right in that respect, it seems that they had to argue that the admissions were completely true, except that Kiszko was clearly a liar, at least regarding 4 October. It does appear to be a very difficult proposition to accept: that Kiszko would lie to the police as to a minor indecent exposure, but would be telling the truth about the far graver crime of murder.

Nor does this offer assistance to the defence. Kiszko's account, in general terms, was that he made false admissions to the police, because of fear and his desire to be out of the police station. If Kiszko was correct, then it appears inexplicable that he would admit the grave crime of murder because he was afraid of the police, and yet would retain the courage and presence of mind to deny a relatively trivial offence such as that of 4 October. Surely if he was brave enough to make denials in respect of one allegation (which he continued to deny) then he would have sufficient fortitude to deny the murder.

A further doubt arises because of a change in Maxine Buckley's accounts, in respect of her description of the man involved in the incident of 4 October. Her statement of 9 October was entirely silent on the manner in which the man walked, but the statement of 30 December said that 'He walked funny, with his feet sticking out at the sides.' PC Peter Sergeant, the officer who attended on 4 October said in his statement that the girls had given him information which had caused him to look for a man who 'shuffled' as he walked. Whilst the officer's statement, if correct, does enable an argument to be put forward that Maxine had on 4 October made some reference to a peculiarity in the way the man walked, there is a difference between saying that a person 'walked funny, with his feet sticking out at the sides' and that that person walked with a 'shuffle'. Moreover, the officer's statement still does not explain why Maxine's statement of 9 October, made at a time when a full description of the wanted man would be most clearly in her mind, and most needed by the police, omitted a most peculiar feature of the description she allegedly gave. Given that omission from Maxine Buckley's 9 October statement, and noting that Debra Mills made no reference in either of her statements to the manner in which the man walked, the statement of PC Sergeant in respect of the girls referring to the 'shuffle' of the man's gait does little to clarify the issue. The statement of PC Sergeant was itself dated 14 January 1976, nearly a month after the flat-footed and waddling Stefan Kiszko had been arrested and charged with the murder of Lesley Molseed.

The addition of material in Maxine Buckley's statement of 30 December which tended to identify Stefan Kiszko by reference to his address and by reference to an unusual walk is a matter which any defence counsel, seeking to cast doubt upon this child's evidence, should have seized upon.

As has been seen, in his first interview Kiszko's retort to the allegation concerning 4 October was that he had been at home with his mother. He subsequently claimed that he could not, in fact, remember where he had been on 4 October, but he then went on to make admissions of offences of indecent exposure, including an admission that he had committed such an offence on 5 November, Bonfire Night.

That admission of itself is important. Maxine Buckley never alleged that Kiszko had exposed himself to her on 5 November and, indeed, there had never been received by the police a complaint from any child about such an offence on that date. Kiszko's admission to this indecent exposure was a confession to one of three incidents about which the police had received no complaint. It is possible, of course, that those offences were committed but that nobody complained to the police, as does sometimes happen. Alternatively, however, it is possible that Kiszko was confessing to offences which had not been committed, and if that is right then it tends to lend credence to his assertions at the police station in his retraction statement and at the trial, that he had made confessions only because by doing so he was making the police 'happy' so as to relieve the pressure on himself. How is such a position to be clarified, since clearly it is crucial to the resolution of the case?

It is not clear that Kiszko ever admitted indecent exposure on 4 October. In the interview in which he admitted indecent exposure on 5 November he was asked by DS Akeroyd: 'Am I to take it that the little girl [Maxine Buckley] was telling the truth when she said that she saw you and identified you [on 5 November] as being the man that exposed himself to her on 4 October?' To which Kiszko replied: 'Yes, I was at the bonfire, but I am a bit hazy. Can I have time to think?'

The interview ended at that point. It is not at all clear to what Kiszko's 'Yes' was addressed, and it must be questionable whether he was thereby admitting indecent exposure on 4 October, or was merely prefacing his admission as to 5 November, namely that he was at the bonfire. The next time that he was interviewed about 4 October he had told DSupt Holland the story about the carpet. Mr Holland had then told Kiszko that each one of the girls had identified him as being the man who exposed himself on 4 October,[4] and had then put to Kiszko the suggestion that Kiszko had indecently exposed himself on that date, to which Kiszko had replied, 'Well, perhaps I did. I can't remember. Things keep going hazy.'

---

4 This was not correct. Only Maxine Buckley had made that identification.

It seems abundantly clear that Kiszko's confession as to Friday, 3 October was inaccurate and untruthful, for he admitted indecent exposure when no such offence was alleged, the descriptions given by the children did not match Kiszko at all, and Maxine Buckley's evidence and statements tend to suggest that the man involved was a different man to the one who did expose himself to her on the following day. The position as to Saturday, 4 October was nowhere near as clear-cut. Whereas Maxine Buckley undoubtedly identified Kiszko on 5 November as being the offender of 4 October, hers is the only such identification. As the law stood in 1976, the judge should have directed the jury to look for corroboration of her evidence, and whilst it is arguable that such corroborative evidence did exist, the nature, reliability and strength of that evidence is itself open to doubt. Kiszko's accounts to the police and his evidence are so confused and unclear as to leave open any number of options. On balance, they tend to fall short of an acceptably complete confession, but the account concerning the carpet appears ludicrous and unbelievable, so that if the jury had to balance that story with the evidence of Miss Buckley it is perhaps unsurprising that they preferred the latter. Kiszko's evidence, wherein he moved the carpet incident to a date late in October serves only to further confuse the issue.

It is important not to lose sight of the purpose of the evidence of the other allegations of indecent exposure or confrontation. The defence sought to adduce that evidence in order to show it as being inaccurate in respect of Kiszko, so that the jury would consider his confessions as to those incidents unreliable and, in so doing, would be obliged to find his admissions as to the abduction and killing of Lesley unreliable. This was the gamble which David Waddington took, when he sought to have that evidence introduced, knowing that if his gamble backfired it would inevitably allow the jury – however carefully they were directed not to do so – to draw the inference that a man who exposes himself to children is a man who may then be likely to abduct and kill a child.

With the benefit of hindsight it is perhaps easy to regard David Waddington's gamble as having failed, because Kiszko was convicted. Such a view is unfair: Waddington showed that Kiszko was lying when he admitted the incident of 3 October and, almost certainly in respect of his admission to other indecent exposures which had not been committed, and that enabled the defence to mount a successful attack on the reliability of Kiszko's admissions in respect of Lesley. The only alternative method of preventing the jury from relying on the admissions to murder had been the *voir dire*, but the prospects of Mr Justice Park excluding the admissions on the basis that they had been made only because of pressure by the police, and because Kiszko wanted to go home and believed he would be allowed home if he admitted his offending were negligible. Mr Justice Park's view was evident in his summing-up.

By drawing attention to the fact that Kiszko had handled cross-examination very well, Mr Justice Park was implicitly suggesting that it was unlikely that he would have yielded under the pressure of the police interrogation. If that was the view of the judge, then there could have been no prospect of success for the defence on a *voir dire*.

A second passage occurred much later in the summing-up, when the trial judge was dealing further with the confessions, and with Kiszko's explanations for making them, namely his belief that if he made admissions the police would allow him to go home to his mother. The trial judge commented: 'Well you have to ask yourselves whether he really did think that after confessing to a brutal killing that the police would let him go home,' and a little further on '[Y]ou may ask yourselves is the real reason why he made the confession the one that he gave at the end of the interview when Holland asked him if he wanted to make a statement and he said, "Yes, I want to get it all sorted out." '

Finally the judge invited the jury to consider what happened after Kiszko had made his confession and had been allowed to see his solicitor, Albert Wright. In the presence of his solicitor DCS Dibb asked Kiszko if he had any complaints about the way he had been treated in the police station. No complaints were raised, and the jury were directed in the following terms: 'Well, members of the jury, that surely was the moment for [Kiszko] to say, "I have been bullied and brow-beaten. I have been terrified by Mr Holland and I have just made a long statement which is totally untrue," but he said nothing to that effect at all.'[5]

The above passages clearly illustrate that, had the reliability and admissibility of the confessions been left in the hands of the trial judge upon a *voir dire*, the ruling would, almost certainly, have been in favour of admissibility. Given this, it is wrong to criticise David Waddington QC for his decision to avoid the *voir dire*, and to take

---

5 A few moments later, however, the judge was directing the jury as to Kiszko's retraction statement.

his chance with the jury, whatever the gamble involved. He had to try to persuade the jury that the confessions were unreliable and involuntary, and to do so he had to *show*, and not merely *assert* unreliability, hence the tactic of reference to the other alleged incidents. Given the evidence concerning 3 October, the gamble should arguably have paid off.

The defence of Stefan Ivan Kiszko, although described as 'riding two horses' comprised three parts. The first part was a complete denial of any involvement in the abduction and killing of Lesley. The second part, ancillary to the first, was to show that the confession was unreliable and should be rejected by the jury. The final part of the defence was the completely separate matter of diminished responsibility.

Throughout the prosecution case the task of the defence lawyers was directed entirely to the second part of their defence, the rejection or disproving of the confession. Since there was so little in the prosecution case apart from the confession which could possibly prove Kiszko's guilt, the lawyers were able to focus almost exclusively on the confession. This, as has been seen, meant attacking the evidence concerning the other alleged incidents and, simultaneously, attacking the police officers who had obtained the confession. It is obvious, however, that the matters of alibi and of diminished responsibility were virtually untouched until the defence case began in earnest.

The final issue dealt with in the summing-up was that of diminished responsibility, the defence which appeared to be so incompatible with a complete denial of involvement, but which it appears remained to the end the defence most favoured by David Waddington QC.

The diminished responsibility defence, however attractive it may have seemed to Kiszko's lawyers – given the nature of their client, his oddity, his emotional underdevelopment and his ties to his mother – carried with it some undesirable but unavoidable dangers, the most immediately apparent of which was that which Peter Taylor QC had referred to as 'two horses which cannot be ridden together', that is, the paradox of arguing 'I didn't kill her, but if I did I only did so because my mind was impaired.' A second, and equally obvious danger was that by putting forward to the laypeople of the jury Kiszko's personality and mind, in their entirety, that jury might draw the inference that a person with that sort of mind was particularly likely to commit the type of offence alleged. It is the danger of a jury acting upon propensity or a perceived propensity, neatly encapsulated in the summing-up by Mr Justice Park's observation '[O]n 5 October this defendant fell into the category of persons who might have committed this offence . . . a person with a sexual problem and a person with a car.' The jury were to hear evidence that Kiszko had not had a relationship with a female, had not kissed a girl, had a poor ability to form any sort of relationship with adults, had a personality which lagged years behind his real age, and a sexuality which was rapidly advanced by the treatment he received for hypogonadism. This was the sort of man who, with a rapidly advancing physical sexuality was likely to develop sexual urges and desires which his personal, emotional and developmental immaturity was unable to be able to satisfy in any 'legitimate' way. The only possible outlet for his urges would be in someone from whom he could take satisfaction without the need to give anything in return, certainly in the sense of a mature approach and a developing relationship. This was the sort of man, stereotypically, who would lure a child with sweets and toys, and take his sexual satisfaction as he wished. Indeed, the fact that the only sexual aspect of the case was that the killer had masturbated on the child tended to improve the chances of Kiszko fitting into the profile – especially the stereotypical profile – which the jury had to consider. Lesley's underwear was undisturbed. Kiszko was a masturbator. He had never had intercourse. He would, therefore, be likely to masturbate if aroused by the girl. This was the clear and obvious danger in the defence revealing the fullness of the accused's mind and personality, but that was a risk which had to be taken if the diminished responsibility defence was to be mounted with any prospect of success.

For the defence to establish diminished responsibility they must prove both an abnormality of the mind and that that abnormality substantially impaired the defendant's mental responsibility for the killing. Put simply, the mind defect must have caused or substantially contributed to the killing. To achieve this duality of proof in Kiszko's case was a profound difficulty, since the degree of violence done to the child strongly indicated that it had been done through a burst of uncontrollable aggression. There was, however, nothing in the personality of Kiszko which could lead to a conclusion that he was prone to such aggression.

If Stefan Kiszko did kill Lesley, the theory postulated at the trial was that he could only have done so if there had been a catalyst or trigger for such excessive violence as there was. It was here that the defence ran into enormous difficulties.

The defence of diminished responsibility is run, usually, where there is no doubt whatsoever that the accused has killed the deceased, so that the jury's choice is between a verdict of guilty of murder or guilty of manslaughter by reason of diminished responsibility. The defence is necessarily established by the psychiatrists concerned examining the defendant's account of the killing. Where, as in the case of Kiszko, the accused denied the killing, the psychiatrist has no factual base upon which to found the theory. There is no factual account, and so the psychiatrist is denied knowledge of the catalytic event which caused the person to kill. Of course, there was a factual account given by Kiszko, that being the admissions that he made to the police. It would appear that Dr Tarsh was not minded to come to any conclusion based on that account, perhaps in part due to Kiszko's denial of the veracity of the admissions, and because of the paucity of detail in the so-called confessions.

Thus the defence of diminished responsibility was left by the defence as resting in the hands of speculation. Did the jury think that words of the sort described by Dr Tarsh had been said by Lesley, so that she did sign her own death warrant? It required speculation by Dr Tarsh to create a workable theory, but it then required equal speculation by the jury: the jury, who had sworn to try the defendant on the evidence, who had heard not one word from Kiszko which might have enabled them to believe that any such expressions had come from Lesley, who had heard only that Stefan Kiszko denied any involvement with the child at all.

It is patently clear from the summing-up that Mr Justice Park believed that Kiszko had killed Lesley, and that the whole of the defence to the killing was a nonsense. It was not an unfair summing-up, not obviously so, but it was a summing-up laden with weighted questions and carefully constructed observations, the import of which was, clearly, that Kiszko had done the killing.

The prosecution, of course, had argued with some determination that Kiszko had been Lesley's killer, but had not gone on to argue quite so vociferously against the defence of diminished responsibility. Indeed, they had called no evidence on the question of diminished responsibility, and Mr Taylor had cross-examined Dr Tarsh in a way which was more inquisitorial than adversarial. He had taken the opportunity to explore Kiszko's state of mind in connection with the confessions, in order to find some support for their veracity, but he had taken some care with Dr Tarsh to make clear that the Crown really had no strong views on the second defence. It was quite apparent that Crown counsel saw his task as being to prove the killing, and then to leave it to the jury to determine whether that killing was murder or manslaughter. The defence's closing speech, whilst not conceding at all that Kiszko was the killer, suggested to the listener that the primary defence was manslaughter by reason of diminished responsibility.

In the light of those positions it would have been somewhat unwise for the judge to take any dogmatic standpoint on the question of diminished responsibility. He certainly was unable to argue with the uncontradicted evidence of Dr Tarsh, that Kiszko was suffering from an abnormality of the mind. The view that the learned judge in fact seemed to take is best reflected in the following passage, with which he brought his summing-up to an end:

[Y]ou approach the question of whether the accused was suffering from diminished responsibility in a broad, common-sense way. You are entitled to take into consideration all the evidence in the case, not just the evidence of the doctors. I wonder if I might invite you to be on your guard against allowing your emotions to sway your judgement on this matter. This was a crime against an innocent defenceless child of the utmost brutality and in the course of his evidence in the witness box the defendant may have revealed himself to you as untruthful, dishonest, perhaps cunning, yet there is no question at all that up to the time of his treatment in hospital he, being a man in name only, stunted physically and in the development of his personality, he had never done anything wrong, he was a law-abiding, inoffensive member of the public holding down this job in the Tax Office, dutifully taking his mother and aunt out in the car; that appears to have been his only recreation. He had never shown the slightest violence towards any living creature and then on 5 October, two days after receiving this second injection, he abducts and kills this child in a frenzy.

These were powerful words, and a reading of them may suggest that the judge himself, believing that Kiszko had killed Lesley, had the greatest difficulty supposing that he could have done so in the ordinary course of his life, so inconsistent was this savage killing with the harmless man who had sat, impassively, throughout the course of the trial. To this extent it seems clear that the judge, reserving his best until last, was willing the jury to find Kiszko guilty, but guilty only of manslaughter.

The summing-up took the whole of Tuesday, 20 July 1976. With breaks, the judge had spoken for about five hours. The following morning, after a very brief résumé of the manner in which the jury should approach their task,[6] the jury were sent out to reach a verdict in the case against Kiszko.

At a little after 2 p.m. the jury sent out a note to the judge, asking for a law book so that they could look up the law on diminished responsibility. The jury was brought back into court and the judge, quite properly, told them that he could not provide them with such a book. Instead, the judge summarised again the law and the material evidence on the issue of diminished responsibility, and the jury were then sent out to resume their deliberations. It was 2.33 p.m.

At a quarter past three, the jury having spent nearly five hours trying to achieve a unanimous verdict, the judge called them back into court and directed them that he could now take a verdict upon which at least ten were agreed. This was the time at which the court felt able to accept a majority verdict, and, in fact, the fore-woman of the jury informed the judge that they had already come to that point. But the rituals and regulations of the law demand that the jury retire once more after they have been told that a majority verdict is acceptable. Mr Justice Park told the jury that they had to go out of court and 'try a bit harder to reach a unanimous verdict'. It is a mandatory direction, even if it is pointless. The jury retire, then go through the motions of seeking to reach a unanimous verdict, then, with their majority verdict already decided, they, counsel, the public and the staff of the court troop back once more into court. The judge, red-robed and ermine-clad, enters and bows to the lawyers and to the jury, before the defendant is brought into the dock.

The clerk of the court rises and his voice is heard: 'Have at least ten of you agreed upon your verdict?' and the forewoman answers that they have.

'On the count of murder, what is your verdict? Please only answer "Guilty" or "Not Guilty".'

There is a pause and the courtroom is silent.

'Guilty,' she replies, but before there can be the commotion in

---

6 As to which see Chapter 17, dealing with Kiszko's appeal against conviction.

the room, so beloved of cinema drama, the clerk speaks again.

'Is the verdict of you all or by a majority?'

'By a majority.'

'How many of you agreed to the verdict and how many dissented?'

'Ten agreed and two dissented.'

And then it is done. Did the two dissenters say guilty of manslaughter only, or did they, perhaps, say not guilty at all. It matters not, for the verdict is guilty of murder, and for that the sentence is known.

Twenty years earlier a black cloth square, the infamous black cap, would have been placed on top of the judge's wig before the then mandatory sentence is passed. Thank God, for this defendant, that times have passed and change has come.

'Stefan Ivan Kiszko, the sentence for the crime of murder is fixed by law. You will go to prison for life.'

Kiszko said nothing. He rose, gathered up the file of papers he had brought into court throughout the trial, and lumbered noisily down the steps leading from the dock.

Charlotte Kiszko remained seated, impassive and stern-faced.

Danny Molseed, sitting with his wife April a few feet from Charlotte Kiszko, broke down in tears.

In the court the case was drawn to a close. Mr Justice Park publicly thanked Maxine Buckley, whose 'sharp eyes . . . set this train of enquiry into motion'. Praise too for the West Yorkshire and Greater Manchester police, 'for their great skill in bringing to justice the person responsible for this dreadful crime'. The officers were to be commended, and the judge named in particular DS John Akeroyd and DSupt Dick Holland.

The jury filed away. The lawyers gathered up their papers and chatted amongst themselves or scurried away to prepare for their next case. Police officers carefully gathered up the exhibits to take back to Halifax Police Station, where they would be boxed and stored with the mass of documentation and reports and statements in the case. The tools by which the conviction had been secured, cached for a future paradoxical use.

In the bare cells below the courts, oblivious to the praise being heaped on others for their skill and bravery, oblivious to the tears, oblivious to the majesty of the law ending one trial, preparing to hear another, a fat man sat, incredulously, at the beginning of his sentence of life imprisonment – for a crime which he did not commit.

CHAPTER SIXTEEN

Prisoner 688837

Whilst Stefan Kiszko had been on remand at Her Majesty's prison, Armley, he was innocent-until-proven-guilty, not convicted and, therefore, was eligible for privileges. He was entitled to extra visits. He was able to wear his own clothing and to enjoy food and cash taken in by his mother. He was handled with a modicum of respect by the authorities.

But at 4.10 p.m. on Wednesday, 21 July 1976 all that changed. When the jury at Leeds Crown Court decided by its 10:2 majority that Stefan Ivan Kiszko was a murderer, and Mr Justice Park decided that Kiszko should go to prison for life, there was an instant and devastating transformation in Kiszko's thus far sheltered life and status in the prison regime.

He was now a convicted man, and the previous privileges were removed from him at a stroke.

Standing, motionless in the dock, as the judge pronounced the final, inevitable words, 'Take him down,' Kiszko was gripped by both arms and led down the steps from the back of the dock and left, handcuffed, in a cell. When they were ready the prison officers put Kiszko in the back of a dark-blue van and drove him back to Armley. Stefan was not merely a convicted prisoner, but a Category A prisoner, a menace to every little girl in the land and destined to be kept in top security.

At the prison he was booked in. His clothing was removed and he suffered the humiliation of a medical examination. Charlotte's little boy bent over whilst they examined parts even his mother had not looked at since he was an infant. His suit, shirt and tie were bagged and locked away, to await the day of his release, and he was handed regulation prison garb of blue, shapeless trousers, blue striped shirt and slipper-like shoes.

Kiszko was read the prison rules and given a number which would remain with him wherever he went in the penal system. The tax clerk and mother's boy was now Prisoner 688837 Kiszko.

Stripped of his belongings and of his confidence in the British judicial system which he and Charlotte had formerly held in such high esteem, Stefan Kiszko was now a very confused and a very vulnerable man.

Gone now was the earlier jocular tag of Oliver Laurel, which he had enjoyed whilst the inmates and prison officers had given him the benefit of the doubt prior to his trial. He had not looked capable of the savagery ascribed to the killer of Lesley Molseed, nor had he the appearance of a man who would act with such evil. But now he had returned from Leeds Crown Court a convicted man, convicted of a truly heinous crime, and carrying the label of a paedophile, who had repeatedly plunged a knife into the frail body of an undersized, innocent child, having sexually gratified himself over her clothing. And Waddington's tactics of introducing the indecent exposure evidence and of running the diminished responsibility defence, meant that every inmate with access to a newspaper knew the supposed pervertedness of this particular prisoner, and that, suffering from an underdeveloped penis and negligible testicles, he was a half-man who had had to take his pleasures from a child. Stefan Kiszko was the lowest of the low amongst the inmates.

Inside Armley there were men who would willingly return to Kiszko the pain the jury had found that the fat man had inflicted on that child. It might take time, but time they had in plentiful supply on the top security wing. Of all this Kiszko, ever unworldly, had no idea as he was booked in. He was completely unaware of the threat that lay in wait for him on the landings and in the bathrooms of the prison. Alone in his cell on a warm July evening in that hottest-of-the-hot summer of 1976, Kiszko sat, preoccupied with thoughts of his mother. How would she cope with this new anguish? Not merely separated from her son, but apart from him at the time that he had been branded by the courts, sex killer, child molester, pervert. Aunt Alfreda was there to offer support, but she had her own burdens and responsibilities as her ailing husband became more ill and ever weaker. And in any case, thought Stefan, even Aunt Alfreda could never give Charlotte the support that a beloved and adoring son had to offer.

Over the next three weeks, Kiskzo's bewilderment gave way to anger as he pined for his mother and the familiar comforts of home. In the last letter he had written to Brenda Lord he showed the confidence that he then had, that the jury would see through the police lie. Those sentiments had changed when, on 8 August

1976, he wrote to Mrs Lord for the first time since the trial.

Dear Brenda,

What can I say after I put my faith in British Justice? Well, all I can say is that it stinks to high heaven, at this stage anyway. I am very sorry for my dear mother and all my friends and workmates. This has cast a black shadow over everyone. I was really amazed by some of the articles in the Rochdale Observer, particularly the one by Alan Tweedale, called Kiszko the loner. It hurt me to think that after so many years of my dad being dead that it was really necessary to bring something about him into the article. I sincerely hope the actions and enquiries of Cyril Smith MP[1] will bring something to light and possibly my freedom again. It seems strange, but there must have been some hokey pokey rat among the fish somewhere because the police chiefs that were the heads of this murder enquiry one after another decided to retire.[2]

I am still adamant about my INNOCENCE, whatever anybody may think after what they had read in the newspapers and heard on the radio and TV. I just hope they will do me the same justice when I prove my innocence. Now that I have been so wrongly condemned the guilty man, I am sorry to say that I am not allowed any gifts, so it is no use sending me any money because I am unable to touch that as well.

So all the condemned man can really say is thank you very much for your letter. I would like to ask you a favour and that is if you would be so kind as to visit mum occasionally so that she is not entirely forgotten and without anyone as company. I know that it has not been easy to grasp as to why would a man in his right mind sign a confession statement to murder but after being ill as I was a couple of months ago and after the way the police had been going at me, you see the public get the wrong image of the police they watch a programme on TV like Dock Green[3] and they think all coppers are polite, patient and courteous as George Dixon. Well believe me, they are far from being like anything you see on TV. On Sunday December 21st right round the clock until the early hours of

---

1 The then Liberal Member of Parliament for Rochdale.
2 This was a delusion. Stefan increasingly sought to explain his predicament by ever more elaborate conspiracy theories that were without any foundation. This is an early example.
3 *Dixon of Dock Green* was a film and television series of the 1950s and 1960s. Sgt Dixon was the epitome of the honourable British 'bobby'.

Monday morning they just gave me some time to rest and then carried on and on again. I think anyone who was so ill and still not 100 per cent up to the mark would more or less have signed his execution warrant if need be. As funny as it seems, I thought after that, I had a good chance of getting home to mum.

But you see, if you walk out of hospital away from the death bed, which I was lying in last year, something had to come along and spoil the Christmas and New Year 76 for Charlotte and Stefan at their new home but that didn't mean as much as spoiling these two people's happiness after what they had been through but the police officers involved in this fiasco were able to down their pints, pulling the wool over the publics eyes that the right person was behind bars and god knows when or who will be next. I am sorry to have gone on a bit too much but I am only trying to set out a clearer picture of this bungle of British Justice.

This letter, reproduced in its entirety, shows the anger which had begun to develop in him, the bitterness he felt at the 'System' and the certainty he had that he had been 'set up' or framed by the police. His rantings against the system and the police were early precursors to his later attacks on those he was convinced were out to 'get' him.

Prisoners get used to life in jail. Even those sent to prison for crimes which they claim they did not commit soon settle into the habits of a prison existence. The prisoners' slang, the limited visits, the 'system' which is known only to the prisoners themselves. Stefan Kiszko did his best, at first, to settle down into his enforced lifestyle. He came to know that the inmates called all men who committed offences against children (which were usually sexual) 'nonces', and that he himself was a nonce: the lowest form of prison life. To be a nonce was to be loathed by all. To be a nonce meant brutality and bullying and a thousand different forms of ill-treatment from one's fellow inmates. And there was no escape. Quite apart from the literal absence of escape routes, Kiszko quickly understood that the only thing worse than a nonce was a nonce who grassed to the warders.

The grim reality of being a convicted child murderer dawned on Stefan after he had spent a month and two days of acclimatisation at Leeds. On 23 August 1976 he was transferred to another West Yorkshire prison, the high security Wakefield

Prison, yet another intimidating fortress for a timid clerical worker whose only previous experience of incarceration had been in the Rochdale Tax Office from nine to five, five days a week. On arrival, again the ritual ordeal of being searched and medically examined and then escorted to his new cell as the word spread that a new sex offender, a new 'nonce' had arrived on the wing. On his first venture from his cell Prisoner 688837 waddled straight along the landing into the open arms of a welcoming committee, whose five members attacked Kiszko, cutting his mouth and bruising a knee and an ankle. Kiszko was taken to a medical officer for patching up. He was not seriously hurt and had got off relatively lightly, but the prison officers knew that he had received only a taster, with much worse likely to come. The prison records detailed the assault but, naturally, there were no witnesses to be found. It was the first time in his twenty-four years that Kiszko had been struck. Not even as a child had there been a need for physical chastisement. He had never been smacked because there had never been any need. Stefan had been a model of good behaviour.

On 10 September 1976 Kiszko wrote to the probation service, returning, as he so often would do, to the theme of his innocence.

Dear Sir/Madam,

I wish to point out that I remain firmly adamant about my innocence and will fight this conviction to the bitter end, because it is only the injustices of 'British Justice' that has brought this wrongful conviction against me. At the present moment I have no serious problems but I have written to my solicitor Mr A Wright of Messrs Hartley Thomas and Wright to come to see me. Up to date my solicitor has been reluctant to come since my conviction. An appeal has been lodged but I have some matters that I would like to discuss with him. I would therefore appreciate it if you would contact him and inform him that his client would be grateful to see him as soon as possible.

    I remain,

Yours faithfully,
Stefan Ivan Kiszko (Mr)
Presently at HMP Wakefield
Previously at 25 Kings Road, Rochdale, Lancs, from November 6th 1975 to December 21st 1975.

Following that first attack and in order to protect their new charge, the authorities arranged for Kiszko to be placed on what is usually called Rule 43, meaning segregation from the other inmates. The men who were on Rule 43 were those most hated by other inmates, those most vulnerable to other inmates, those who were the weakest and the most despised amongst the prison community. Kiszko's arrival on Rule 43 had a certain inevitability about it, but even amongst his co-prisoners on Rule 43 he was at risk, for even amongst the other sex offenders he was the lowest form of life, a child sex offender who had killed his victim.

He had not, of course, been abandoned. His dutiful and loving mother, Charlotte, travelled by bus with sister Alfreda to visit Stefan as often as they were allowed under prison regulations. In the seven months that her son had been on remand awaiting trial, Charlotte had made fifty-seven visits or nearly nine a month. Now she was limited to a permissible two visits a month. She herself was sick with a debilitating lung disease, but as long as she could walk to the bus stop nothing would prevent Charlotte from seeing her son. Mrs Kiszko received some sympathy from her new neighbours in Kings Road but, paradoxically, little from the East European immigrant friends from the old neighbourhood. They believed that Stefan's crime (and they were not prepared to believe that he had been wrongly convicted) had tainted their law-abiding community. They had slowly won acceptance in the town over thirty years, despite some sporadic rumblings about taking jobs from indigenous Rochdalians at a time of rising unemployment. They had been welcomed when mill jobs were plentiful and had rewarded the town by working hard, buying their own homes, learning English and adapting to the ways of their neighbours. Now, having integrated and assimilated, a child murderer from their own community had brought unwelcome attention, causing that community to stick out where it had tried to blend in.

Charlotte was shunned, but she now lived in a better part of town and she held her head high, telling anyone who would listen that her son had not killed Lesley Molseed. He had been with her and with his Aunt Alfreda when the child had been abducted. He was a timid boy and the police had got a confession from him with threats.

Charlotte was not backed by the solicitor Albert Wright. He, like the rest of the defence team, was in no doubt that Stefan had killed the child, albeit he felt that there was some force in the diminished responsibility argument. Cyril Smith MP listened with his usual courtesy to Mrs Kiszko, but for him too the evidence was there. Unsupported but certain in her own mind that her son was not responsible for the child's death, Charlotte was determined to prove his innocence. She was banking on an appeal hearing, but, whilst awaiting that, she vowed to appear cheerful whenever she wrote one of her twice-weekly letters or made one of her visits to the jail. She was determined that Stefan should not see her sadness, her illness or her growing immobility. Equally was Stefan determined not to bring his mother down with his own problems. He hid from her his fears and the bouts of depression he was suffering, finding a conduit for his emotions in the letters he wrote to Brenda Lord.

Mrs Lord had become the only person to whom he would be fully open and his letters to her contained his outpourings of frustration and anger. By October he had been in Wakefield and segregated for two months, and despair was beginning to creep into his letters, as his previously held faith in what he called British justice continued to dwindle. He wrote to Mrs Lord in reply to her letter of 29 September, telling her how depressed he had been the previous weekend, which had been the sixth anniversary of his father's death. 29 September would have been Kiszko's seventh anniversary with the Revenue, and that too was a date which had struck him. Kiszko spoke of his mother's cheerfulness on a recent visit, but that he knew that she was putting on a face for him, and he returned to the theme of his wrongful conviction by writing:

> You were able to see and hear how unfair British justice is and I am sorry to say that if perjury is allowed in the courts of British justice then many more innocent people are going to be convicted but then it is more like mum says, there is one law for the rich and one for the poor. Cyril Smith MP took up an investigation but seems to have let it slide, but he may do something now. Really and truthfully this is bitter punishment for someone who KNOWS he is innocent but whoever wanted it this way, in the way of REVENGE, got what they wanted.

The Rochdale probation service became the major support for Charlotte and Stefan, with visits to Kings Road by a schoolteacher and part-time probation officer called Maggie Buckley. It was Maggie Buckley who soaked up Charlotte's growing frustration, a frustration which would often turn to anger, when the five foot tall woman would berate the 'System' with a stream of expletives and the rich language which she had learned in the cotton mill. On one visit Charlotte had ranted in tears and pummelled Maggie

Buckley's chest, before slumping, spent, in her armchair. It was a side of Charlotte which Stefan had never seen, and never would.

He wrote again to the probation service in November 1976 in a letter revealing that the fight had not gone from the man, however despondent he might become:

> Regarding your comments about my property, strictly speaking and per Archbolds book of the law,[4] the police are somewhat breaking the rules, but for this I have a solicitor and I am sure you must agree that some of the comments I raised at your visit are founded.
>
> I am somewhat perplexed at the working of this country's legal profession and its 'British Justice', for which this country has such great pride and honour. But there seems to be a law for the rich and a law for the poor.

> Yours faithfully,
> Stefan Ivan Kiszko (Mr)
> An innocent condemned man.

Full-time probation officer Jim Schofield inherited the Kiszko file in the spring of 1977. He read the post-sentence report compiled by a colleague, Vin Short, who had since moved on. At that time Stefan was feeling unwell and the first signs of a deteriorating mental state were becoming apparent. In a letter to Brenda Lord Kiszko's handwriting had deteriorated, for which Stefan apologised. He had not written to her since October 1976 and he explained this to her: 'I have been very unwell. I have not fully recovered from this, hence the shaky handwriting for which I must apologise. Thanks for being good to mum and taking her out in your car.'

Jim Schofield was aware of Stefan's mental health problems when he made his first visit to Wakefield Prison in May 1977. He believed that Kiszko was a man who was failing to accept his guilt, and he felt obliged to make the prisoner aware that the probation service was not there in a campaigning sort of way, *à la Rough Justice*, but was a welfare service, offering assistance only in that respect, maintaining contact between the prisoner and his mother. Jim Schofield had no reason to believe that Kiszko was innocent,

---

4 Kiszko was referring to *Criminal Pleading Evidence and Practice*, the criminal lawyer's 'bible' and colloquially referred to as 'Archbold', after its first editor J.F. Archbold. First published in 1822, copies of the voluminous and complex text are frequently found in prisons where inmates refer to the book for guidance on their own cases, becoming, in the process, 'jailhouse lawyers'.

and it was part of his task to coax Kiszko into acknowledging his culpability for the crime of which he had been convicted, and, thereafter, to help Kiszko plan for his future and his eventual release. Schofield was aware that an appeal against conviction was in process, so he resolved not to push Kiszko too hard into acknowledging guilt for what had happened eighteen months before. They spoke about the appeal application and how long Kiszko might have to serve if the appeal failed, a question Kiszko raised and Schofield was unable to answer. Kiszko was emotionally unstable, Schofield knew, and he was wary of Stefan's reaction if he speculated on what the sentence recommendation might be. Instead, Schofield turned the conversation to ways in which Kiszko could reduce the stress of being on Rule 43, such as applying for an educational correspondence course, which provoked a half-grimace, half-smile from the man opposite the probation officer, causing the meeting to end inconclusively.

On 11 May 1977 Kiszko was assaulted for the second time. Warders heard cries and, when they investigated, they discovered that Kiszko had been hit over the head in an attack which was logged as 'brutal'. The investigation which followed was unable to establish what had happened, or who was responsible, but Kiszko was taken to Pinderfields Hospital in Wakefield where three stitches were put into a laceration on the back of his head.

In August of that year Jim Schofield was contacted by Brenda Lord and her husband Donald. They were becoming increasingly concerned about Charlotte, who was often hysterical when she called at their home. Schofield understood that he had to make Charlotte face up to the reality of the situation, although he was mindful that the appeal made this a delicate matter. He found Charlotte sad and confused on his first visit to 25 Kings Road, although she continued to keep the semi-detached house impeccably clean and tidy. Her sadness quickly gave way to hysteria, as she protested her son's innocence to the probation officer. She shouted that she was getting so little help from people and she claimed that the police had tortured her son, speaking, somewhat mysteriously and excessively, of Stefan's bloody and torn shirt. The mystery was that Stefan himself had never alleged, nor had there ever been any suggestion or evidence, that he had been 'tortured' or assaulted by the police. Charlotte protested that, at Stefan's trial, one of the jurors had been seen drinking with the police. Again there was no evidence of this having happened. Jim Schofield recorded that Charlotte was desperate, felt totally inadequate and also alone, and was very tearful. Wisely, the probation officer decided that it would be pointless and dangerous to attempt to begin the process of persuading Charlotte to face up to the actuality of the situation, and that it would be better to await the outcome of the appeal. Charlotte spoke of approaching the National Council for Civil Liberties and Schofield, attempting to be helpful to this desolate woman, promised that he would find the NCCL address for her.

Schofield decided to contact Albert Wright, the family solicitor. He knew Mr Wright as a veteran of the local magistrates' court, where he enjoyed much respect from the bench.

Albert Wright was almost dismissive of Kiszko's appeal, saying that his client could not have it both ways: at his trial, held Wright, Kiszko had agreed with his defence team that they should pursue the defence of diminished responsibility, now he was saying that he had not killed the girl. It was clear to Schofield that Albert Wright thought Stefan Kiszko to be guilty, notwithstanding that he had obtained legal aid for Waddington and Clegg to pursue an appeal against conviction for the murder.

Jim Schofield felt helpless, and so it was the least that he could do to assist Charlotte pen a letter in support of her son's appeal. Through the criminal appeals office at the Royal Courts of Justice in the Strand in London he obtained the reference number which had been ascribed to Kiszko's appeal, 4332A176. He then sat with Charlotte and together they composed a letter to the Registrar of Criminal Appeals. It was necessary to write to the registrar because it is he who instructs counsel in criminal appeals, not the solicitor who instructed the barrister in the original trial. Thus the barrister conducting the appeal receives communications through the registrar.

The letter read:

Dear Sir,
I am the mother of Stefan Kiszko and I have certain information below which I would like communicated to my son's barrister.
1   Confessions – Stefan made a confession to the police. This confession was made, I believe, under undue pressure at a time when my son was not fully aware of what he was doing. It was also made before he was given an opportunity of seeing or speaking to someone of his choice, either a member of his family or a solicitor. He has stated to me consistently that his

confession was a lie and that it was made only under extreme provocation by the police.

2   Evidence was given regarding a prowler around Kingsway Youth Club, who was identified in Court as Stefan. Mrs Joan Chadwick of 16 Lomond Terrace, Turf Hill, gave evidence to the solicitor that she saw and spoke to the prowler on that date and that the man was definitely not Stefan.[5]

3   I have heard from Mrs Bidney of 9 Mary Street, Rochdale, the mother of a police officer that her son, who saw Stefan in the police station, said that Stefan was in no condition to know what he was saying when he made his confessions.[6]

No one has been able to positively identify Stefan as being in the company of the murdered girl. The main evidence consisted of fibres found on the body which came from the aunt's carpet. Some of her carpet was in Stefan's car, but not at the time the murder was committed. At that time he had small pieces of a similar carpet. Those carpets used in evidence were not in Stefan's car on the 5th October. The police were told which carpet he had in on that date but didn't take it. The carpet which was in Stefan's car was taken to the solicitors and is still in his possession. This carpet is a common design bought locally.

4   Alibi

On October 5 1975 Stefan and myself visited his aunt's. The three of us went to the cemetery where his father and grandmother were buried. On the way he mentioned the need to replace a car tyre. This was replaced and the receipt was sent to the solicitor.[7] On the way back, we called into a continental store on Tweedale Street owned by Mrs Baran who is able to recall the day, Sunday. She offered to act as a witness but was not called. It was claimed that this was a last minute alibi but the solicitor was informed in plenty of time for the trial.[8]

5   It was alleged by a witness that on two separate occasions Stefan was seen to expose himself in public. On the first

---

5 Mrs Chadwick was not called as a witness at the trial, nor was she referred to in either the first appeal or the subsequent investigation and second appeal.
6 Neither Mrs Bidney nor her son were called as witnesses at the trial, nor were they referred to in either the first appeal or the subsequent investigation and second appeal.
7 Charlotte was wrong about the date on which the new tyre was fitted. It was Wednesday
8 October, as the receipt (introduced by Taylor at the trial) showed.
8 Mrs Baran was not available at the trial, because she was on holiday.

occasion, the night of November 5th 1975, when he was alleged to have exposed himself, he was actually at home, then 31 Crawford Street in the company of myself, Mrs Ferentschuk of 267 Ashfield Road and two neighbours of his aunt.[9]

On the second occasion [. . .] when he was again alleged to have exposed himself in front of the same witness he was actually at work in his office on the fifth floor and was actually seen by Mr Oldham who worked in the same building.

6   The police found a car number written on a paper in his possession and at the time of the trial he couldn't remember why he had it, but since he has remembered that he jotted down the number when the car in question was blocking his car near his office and he argued with the owner about it. This happened late in 1973 and no doubt the owner of the car at the time could be traced.[10]

Charlotte's letter was duly sent, but it would appear that no action was taken on it. Its content was, in any event, fraught with difficulties, not least of which was the question of why that content had not been adequately acted upon at the first trial.

Stefan Kiszko's mental condition was being logged by prison staff. One handwritten entry gives a most revealing insight into Kiszko's deterioration: 'Talking beneath his breath at times about special messages on radio which worried him about his mother. Could either be schizophrenia or could be acting up.'

Four days later his mother telephoned the prison to voice concern about Stefan's mental state. She feared that he could be having a nervous breakdown. Subsequent entries in the log about Kiszko's periods of silence indicated first the belief that the prisoner was mute of malice, that is, simply refusing to speak and then, contradictorily, that he was suffering from catatonia whereby he was unable to speak. The continuing deterioration in his mental state resulted in him being placed in strip cell conditions because, in total contrast to every element of his upbringing and therefore contrary to his known character, Stefan was soiling himself, his clothes and his furniture. One log entry had the decency to

---

9 Although Mrs Tosic did give evidence at Stefan's trial, she did not give an account of 5 November. No 'alibi' evidence was called as to 5 November nor was any such evidence referred to in the first appeal or the subsequent investigation and second appeal.
10 This last suggestion by Charlotte was one not taken up for several years.

question whether the prisoner's withdrawn behaviour might in some way be the aftermath of the extensive assault on Kiszko shortly after his arrival at Wakefield.

It was in 1977 that Kiszko was first given tranquillisers, known in prison argot as 'the liquid cosh'. He was treated with oral and intramuscular major tranquillising drugs, but did not tell his mother, who was puzzled and angry when she sent her son a calendar and received it back by return of post. Charlotte complained to the only person in authority who would listen to her grievances, Jim Schofield, who replied that he did not know why the calendar had been refused, but he tactfully and gently suggested that it was not good therapy for a prisoner serving a life sentence to have a calendar on his cell wall. By November 1977 Stefan's mental state was drifting further away from normality, and he was described in his prison file as being unable to think or act for himself and that he had to be shown how to perform the simplest of tasks. Later he was treated with Flupenthixol, a major tranquilliser which was used in small doses for the treatment of depression.

In December 1977 Stefan was certainly thinking for himself and, somewhat paradoxically, was able to laugh at himself when he wrote to Brenda Lord when he was fearing another Christmas away from his mother. He said that he had sought consolation for his lonely Christmas by buying himself a box of chocolates for Christmas Eve. He then spoke about how he was occupying his time:

> I am doing an educational course which I am really enjoying and is so time consuming. As far as being athlete of the year, well I do have some mishaps but I like playing volleyball. I don't enjoy the exercise much but it is all good fun and we have a laugh now and then.

Coming from a man who had never in his life played any sport and was physically ill-equipped for any sort of exercise, this seemed a substantial and dramatic improvement. Equally, when Kiszko wrote of 'having a laugh' this too was in a marked contrast to the loner who had no friends and was never regarded as a person able to join in the fun and games of others. Kiszko even told Mrs Lord that he had been encouraged to lose some weight but added, not without humour, 'I have given it up as a bad job.'

It is not known whether Stefan Kiszko made a New Year's resolution as 1977 came to a close, but it is more than clear that the beginning of 1978 brought a new persona, one which was in stark contrast with the Stefan Kiszko of old. Kiszko appeared to refuse to be the good-natured oaf who would take any sort of ribbing. The boy who had absorbed all bullying at school, the clown who endured the daily mockery of other inmates finally hit back at another inmate and, perhaps, at the prison regime. He threw a bucket of water over another captive in the segregation unit. This was the first act of violence in his life. The reason for the attack was never recorded, but it heightened the belief that Kiszko was developing catatonic schizophrenia. Consequently the daily delivery of the 'liquid cosh' was maintained.

It had been nearly two years since Kiszko had been convicted, and it may have been as a demonstration against the tardiness of the appeal system that he began what IRA prisoners had labelled a 'dirty protest'. He refused to wash or feed himself. Again he refused to use the toilet and soiled himself. Each time he did so the jailers would not find it particularly difficult to force the mild-mannered Kiszko into changing and washing the dirty clothes, and cleaning himself up. Kiszko's rebellion was betrayed by his overwhelming desire to please, and so the warders demanded that he bathe himself after each instance of soiling. Kiszko duly obliged them, and they believed that he would not have the resilience to keep up his protest for anything more than a few weeks.

Kiszko was sent to see the prison welfare officer, Miss Boyle, and it became clear to her that Kiszko's failing mental condition was being aggravated by the long wait for a decision on his appeal hearing. Yet in his continuing correspondence with Brenda Lord Kiszko chose not to reveal much of his mental decay, nor of his brush with the authorities at Wakefield. In correspondence throughout 1977 Kiszko continued to rage against the police, whom he now perceived to be his enemy. In letters to Mrs Lord he made allegations of police conduct in cases other than his own, revealing how his animosity towards the police was already beyond his control.

Charlotte Kiszko would never have tolerated her son being anything other than fastidious but she would never know of his 'dirty protest'. The prison authorities dealt with Kiszko and the probation service did not betray client confidence by informing Charlotte. Making her aware would only have served to exacerbate her own festering frustration with the judicial system. She was already at fever pitch, as Maggie Buckley would vouch for following visits to see Charlotte, during which she would listen to the now-ageing woman's ranting protestations of her son's innocence and the judicial system's abandonment of him. It must have been difficult for Mrs Buckley not to have queried Mrs Kiszko's mental state.

It was not only Maggie Buckley who was on the receiving end of Charlotte Kiszko's ire. Charlotte became upset and angry with everyone who called, although there were never many visitors to her tidy little home. Even in her anger and frustration, Charlotte proved that she was able to hold on to her sanity by remembering her inbred East European hospitality, ensuring that any visitor, whatever time of day, was offered a tumbler of sherry.

Charlotte ignored her fibrosis and byssinosis to make the eight-hour return bus journey to Wakefield in the company of the ever-loyal Alfreda, the trips funded by pension and disability allowance. She was, at the same time, taking legal advice on her incurable lung disease caused by inhalation of cotton fibres, and she was suing for compensation.

Stefan Kiszko was becoming increasingly impatient, in particular with Albert Wright, a fact he made clear in his letter of 1 March 1978 addressed to Jim Schofield:

> I am fed up, sick, perplexed, you name it, because I cannot even raise a reply from my solicitor. The last letter I got from Mr Wright giving me some idea as to what was going on was November 8th 1977. I ask you, is this professional etiquette?

Stefan's understandable frustration – especially if he was correct in his calculation of the five-month silence – may have been misdirected. There had been no communication from the solicitor because he had no news to communicate, but only a matter of weeks after Kiszko penned his letter of complaint his concerns about Albert Wright were put very much into the background, as both Charlotte and he were independently advised that Stefan's appeal against his conviction was, at last, going to be heard. For the Kiszko family it was a time of anticipation and optimism, with spirits raised as they had not been since the trial of 1976. Charlotte and Stefan believed it was now merely a question of being patient until the hearing, which was due to be in May, and then they would be reunited again.

Kiszko wrote to the probation service as he eagerly anticipated his appeal hearing in May. He convinced himself that the evidence heard at his trial was linked to new reports in the *Rochdale Observer* of a sex attacker in a white car. He was clutching at straws: the police had rejected the earlier evidence as mistaken. The white car was a mirage, the letter a misguided rant:

The 'Rochdale Monster' with his white car has returned. You may recall that, when the police were looking for Lesley Molseed's murderer, they were looking for a white car and its occupant. They were never traced. I have informed my solicitor of this new development. My appeal hearing has been set for Thursday 25th May and I am waiting to see what counsel for the defence and their instructing solicitor have to say about this new occurrence.

It is very apparent and plain to see that the police never did their job right in the first place and an innocent person has to suffer instead, as in so many cases.

I am disgusted to say the least when I recall the things that took place at Rochdale police station whilst the Yorkshire officers were 'guests' there.

A few days ago, a letter came out of the blue from my solicitor Mr Wright and it is somewhat of a miracle because it is hard to get anything out of him. When you next visit me, I will show you this letter and explain why this solicitor annoys me. The letter is dated the same day as Wednesday's Rochdale Observer with the front page article headed 'Police hunt sex attacker' in which the white car is recalled three times. I think this prompted him to write. [. . .]

The 'Rochdale Monster' with the white car I am sure is Lesley Molseed's murderer. Well if the truth is found out and I am freed, what do I get? A 'we are very sorry for the mistake' letter or a golden handshake, because nothing in the whole world can bring back those days my mother and I have been parted and the hell we are living through.

I am adamant about my innocence.

Yours faithfully,
Stefan I. Kiszko,
formerly with HM Inspector of Taxes, Rochdale.

For those who cared about the welfare of the family, the forthcoming appeal was viewed with dread. Although an overturning of the conviction would be welcomed by Jim Schofield and the Wakefield Prison authorities, so far as the welfare of their respective charges was concerned, each viewed with trepidation the prospect of the appeal being unsuccessful, and each feared beyond measure the harm which would result to the mental condition of the mother and son were Kiszko not freed by the Appeal Court.

CHAPTER SEVENTEEN

The First Appeal

After the trial which resulted in Kiszko's conviction, his legal team of Mr Wright, Mr Waddington and Mr Clegg continued to work on his behalf. Although they were not convinced of his total innocence, they did believe that the jury had come to the wrong decision, but only in respect of the ultimate finding. There was little doubt among the defence lawyers that Kiszko had killed Lesley, but they believed that he had done so whilst labouring under a diminished responsibility, so that a verdict of manslaughter ought to have been returned. However, when an appeal was launched to overturn Stefan Kiszko's conviction in the Court of Appeal, Criminal Division the lawyers held their views in private, and the appeal itself attacked the conviction in its entirety, not merely as to the failure of the jury to convict of manslaughter.

On 25 May 1978, very nearly two years after he had begun the life sentence imposed after his trial, Stefan Kiszko's appeal against conviction was heard. Strictly speaking it was not an appeal against conviction that came before Lord Justice Bridge, Mr Justice Wien and Mr Justice Eastham, but an application for leave to appeal against conviction. There is no automatic right to appeal against conviction in England, it is necessary to apply for and be granted leave to appeal. If leave is granted, the matter goes on to be argued as a full appeal. If it is refused, that is an end of the matter as far as the defendant is concerned.

An application for leave to appeal must set out the grounds on which permission to appeal is sought. It is often said that it is better to take one very good point on an appeal, rather than to bombard the Court of Appeal with a large number of points, of varying quality. That point seemed to have passed by Kiszko's legal representatives, for whilst they did have what Lord Justice Bridge described as 'the matter perhaps of most substance', David Waddington also took two very inferior points (described by Lord Justice Bridge as being 'of a purely technical nature'), thus, perhaps, diminishing the importance of his primary ground.

It is perfectly proper for an appeal to be based on allegations of incompetence of, or error by, the barrister who conducted a trial. It is highly unusual, however, for such arguments to be put forward by the trial barrister himself. Yet at least two of the grounds of appeal put forward by David Waddington amounted, in effect, to criticism of his own performance in the trial of Stefan Kiszko, in one case directly and in the second by implication.

It appears that at a late stage in the trial a member of the jury had been in a public house close to the court during a luncheon adjournment. She had overheard a conversation between an employee of the Leeds Borough Council's prosecuting solicitors department and another person, in which the former had informed the latter that Kiszko had been advised by his own counsel to plead guilty. This conversation was relayed to the trial judge who, in accordance with common practice, had called all the barristers in the case into his room to canvass their views on the effect of this matter upon the trial.

In criminal trials it does occur, from time to time, that a member of the jury, some way into the trial, brings a difficulty to the judge's attention. A juror should have no personal knowledge of any of the parties in, or circumstances of a trial. It is obvious that, were it otherwise, the juror might end up reaching a decision based on his or her personal knowledge, or feelings towards a party, rather than upon the evidence he or she has heard. Were it to become apparent that a juror had such knowledge, before the trial began, that juror would be excluded from the jury. However, it does occasionally happen that it is only in the course of the trial that a juror suddenly becomes aware of having such knowledge. In such a case the judge will certainly canvass counsel for their views, and will usually act upon the views of the defence, if those views are reasonable and forcefully made out. Defence counsel has three options. He may elect to continue with a full jury of twelve, in spite of the knowledge of one of the jurors, he may ask that the relevant juror be excused, and continue with a jury of eleven or, in an extreme case, he may ask for the whole jury to be discharged and the trial aborted. It is always a difficult decision to make. If the trial has been going well for the defence, no barrister would wish to abort that trial and start again, with the risk that a second trial may be very different. On the other hand, the risk of a juror being in some way undermined in his impartiality is one which can never be underestimated. Discharging that single juror may be a compromise solution, but it carries its own difficulties. Counsel cannot always be sure that the juror has not already shared his 'personal knowledge' with his fellow jurors, and, even if he has not (and it is usually impossible to determine, accurately, whether he has spoken with his co-jurors or not in such a case), proceeding with only eleven jurors may not always be to the advantage of the defendant. The larger the jury, the more chance there is of disagreement between jurors and, if the mood of the jury upon retirement is generally favourable to the accused, the more likely it is that an acquittal will result. Reduce the number of jurors and one reduces the prospects for disagreement and, perhaps, of acquittal.

Mr Justice Park, the trial judge, had expressed the view that he saw no reason why the trial should not proceed and, indeed, no reason why the juror who had overheard this conversation should be discharged. Thus his view was that it mattered not that this juror had heard a person stating that the defendant's barrister had advised him to plead guilty. The juror might have been forgiven for thinking that (whether this was right or not is immaterial) if the defence barrister has advised the accused to plead guilty, that means that the barrister himself does not believe him to be other than guilty, so that he was probably guilty. Such a thought process is obvious.

Lord Justice Bridge, however, thought otherwise, as he made clear in the course of his judgement:

> No doubt [the trial judge's] view was based on the almost self-evident proposition that in these circumstances any intelligent juror would have realised that the advice [Kiszko] had been given by his counsel was to plead guilty to manslaughter on the ground of diminished responsibility.

This view was fundamentally flawed. The reported conversation was to the effect that defence counsel had advised Kiszko to plead guilty. It was not, 'plead guilty to manslaughter', or any variation on 'plead guilty'. Kiszko was not charged with manslaughter and was not on trial for manslaughter and, although it is not clear how far the defence case had progressed at the time of this particular incident, it was probably clear to the jury that the prosecution did not accept that Kiszko was, at the time of the killing, acting in circumstances giving rise to a defence of diminished responsibility, nor that he was guilty of anything other than murder, and were not seeking any verdict other than one of murder. How Lord Justice

Bridge came to the above-stated view is impossible to tell, but his following words give, perhaps, some clue, and indicated quite clearly his own opinion of the case against Kiszko, for he continued: '*for in truth the invitation to the jury to acquit him altogether was from the outset a perfectly hopeless prospect*'.

Mr Justice Park had not, however, decided this problem without asking for counsel's submissions and, in particular, those of David Waddington, who took the view that the trial was, at that point, going well for the defence, to the extent that he was confident that a verdict of manslaughter by reason of diminished responsibility would be achieved. He took the view that that confidence might not be attained again, in the event of the trial being aborted and there being a re-trial. He did not object to the trial continuing, with the full jury remaining, and this is what had happened.

It is obvious that, defence counsel having raised no objection to the trial continuing with the juror in question still in place, there could be no appeal based on the submission that that juror should have been excluded. Instead, David Waddington took as his first ground a failing on his own part, in that the decision to proceed had been taken without consulting Kiszko himself. Waddington, with Philip Clegg, his junior counsel, had taken the decision to proceed. They had not asked Stefan what he wanted to do. It was a failure on the part of Waddington, and yet he came to the Court of Appeal and sought to argue that his own failing had created an unfair trial. It was put in this way: that the decision to proceed or not was not one within the authority of counsel to deal with, without specifically obtaining the instructions of the client and his consent to the proposed course of action.

This, of course, was an interesting argument for the defence to proffer, in any event, bearing in mind Stefan Kiszko's personal view of this trial. His instructions were, 'I did not kill Lesley Molseed.' It was not Stefan Kiszko who averred 'I did kill Lesley, but I was labouring under an abnormality of the mind such as to enable me to rely on the defence of diminished responsibility such as to entitle me to a verdict of manslaughter.' That defence was the creation of the legal advisors. Meritorious or not, it was not one to which Stefan is known to have given his specific consent. Whilst the juror may have overheard a conversation to the effect that Stefan's barristers felt that he should plead guilty, and whilst Lord Justice Bridge interpreted this as meaning that Kiszko should plead guilty to manslaughter on the grounds of diminished responsibility (which, of course, involved an admission that he had killed this young girl), Kiszko himself did not, of course, enter any such plea. It may thus be inferred that Stefan did not seek for himself a verdict of manslaughter, but that his legal advisors incorporated the seeking of such a verdict into their strategy for the trial, without Stefan's specific consent or instructions.

It was therefore unusual, to say the least, that David Waddington could raise the absence of Stefan's consent on a relatively minor issue, as a ground for arguing that the trial was unfair, the verdict unsafe and unsatisfactory, when on the far more important issue – the very nature of the defence which was to be run – there was an area of doubt about the degree of agreement over the defence tactics.

Lord Justice Bridge did not hesitate before rejecting the submission, on the basis that this decision was one which was entirely within counsel's authority to make. His conclusion was terse: 'There is nothing at all in that first point.'

The second ground was a little more complicated, and its source was the summing-up in the trial. The first stage in a judge's direction on diminished responsibility is to explain what is meant by that defence, and on that Mr Justice Park had directed the jury with impeccable accuracy. The second stage is to direct the jury that, unusually in the English criminal law where the burden of proof rests, almost without exception, upon the prosecution, it is for the defence to establish that the accused was suffering from diminished responsibility at the time of the killing.

The third stage is to tie together the elements of murder and of diminished responsibility. The judge directed the jury thus:

> [Y]ou must first decide whether the Crown have proved so that you feel sure that the accused killed the girl. If you reach a unanimous decision that that case has not been proved then of course you will acquit him, but if you unanimously reach the decision that he did kill the girl then you must consider the second matter and you must decide whether on the balance of probabilities the accused at the time of the killing was suffering from diminished responsibility, and if you are satisfied in that way your verdict will be one of not guilty of murder but guilty of manslaughter.

The direction to this point had been faultless, but the judge went on to make what was later described as a clear slip of the tongue, when he said: 'However, if you are unanimous that he killed the girl but not unanimous that he was suffering from diminished responsibility at the time then your verdict would be guilty of murder.'

Peter Taylor QC, for the Crown, interjected to correct the judge, saying:

> My Lord with respect I would have thought your Lordship meant (if the jury) were unanimous that [Kiszko] was not of diminished responsibility rather than that they were unanimous that he was.

This was, however, not strictly correct. Mr Justice Park's direction had been accurate, if convoluted, for what it amounted to was a direction that if the jury had been made sure by the prosecution that Kiszko killed Lesley, but had not been made sure by the defence that Kiszko was suffering from diminished responsibility, they must find him guilty of murder. In order to find Kiszko guilty of murder the jury did not have to be sure that he was not of diminished responsibility, for that would be to put the burden of proof (or, perhaps more accurately, to put a burden of disproving) upon the Crown, and Section 2 of the Homicide Act 1957 makes it perfectly clear that this is not the case: the burden is on the defence to *prove* diminished responsibility, it is not on the prosecution to *disprove* diminished responsibility.

The correction of the learned judge had, however, come from counsel for the Crown. David Waddington had, thus far, said nothing, nor did he say anything until Mr Justice Park addressed him, to ask his views on Taylor's interjection. His reported reply was: 'I was not going to say anything my Lord but I suppose that is technically correct.'

Such a response is difficult to comprehend. Peter Taylor QC had made a mistake or had at least further muddied the waters, in correcting the accurate, if not entirely clear, direction of the judge,[1] but in making that correction he had, doubtless inadvertently, arguably made the prosecution's task more difficult, for he had quite feasibly confused the issue of burden of proof, by ascribing to the prosecution a burden which, in law, was not the prosecution's. It is unthinkable to consider that Waddington was seeking to take advantage of the error by Crown counsel, and no one would

---

1 It would almost certainly have been better for the judge to have directed the jury in these terms: 'If you are sure that he killed the girl, but you are not satisfied, on a balance of probabilities, that he was suffering from diminished responsibility, then you must find him guilty of murder. In other words, unless you think it more likely than not that he was suffering from diminished responsibility, then he is guilty of murder.'

ever suggest that that was the case. What other explanation merits consideration? Was he simply not concentrating at that time? Was he confused by the lack of clarity in the terminology being used, for if he was, how could the jury have been expected to understand? Why did David Waddington say that he had not intended to say anything, but then agree that Peter Taylor was 'technically correct'?

It is equally troubling that the three judges hearing the application for leave agreed with Peter Taylor, describing his correction of Mr Justice Park's 'slip of the tongue' as being 'entirely accurate' when it was Mr Justice Park who was accurate and Mr Taylor who was not.

The direction having been 'corrected' by Peter Taylor, Mr Justice Park left it to the jury. They retired, but came back after several hours to seek clarification on the law governing diminished responsibility. The trial judge's answer had been to repeat his direction.

At 3.15 p.m., when the jury had been out for nearly five hours, the trial judge had the jury brought back into court, and directed them that he could now accept a majority verdict in the following terms:

> [If you are not able to reach a unanimous decision] then I will accept a verdict upon which at least ten of you are agreed and that means this, if at least ten of you are agreed that the accused did not kill the girl then you would acquit him. Alternatively if at least ten of you have agreed that he did kill the girl *and at least ten of you agree that he was not suffering from diminished responsibility* then the verdict will be one of murder.

The words in italics served to re-emphasise the so-called corrected version of the original direction, namely that the burden was on the prosecution to prove that the defendant was not suffering from diminished responsibility, before a murder verdict could be reached. The trial judge continued:

> The third alternative is if ten of you are agreed that the accused did kill the girl and ten agree that he was suffering from diminished responsibility at the time then the verdict would be one of manslaughter.

David Waddington took his second ground of appeal from this tangled mess of legality. He firstly criticised Peter Taylor's correction, not on the basis that it was, as we have seen, wrong, but on the ground that it had been 'insufficiently explicit to remove [the effect of the judge's initial misdirection] from the jury's mind. If it is right that the judge's initial direction was not, in fact, a misdirection, then this ground of appeal was patently absurd. In any event, the court hearing the appeal saw no merit in this argument.

There was, however, a follow-up to this. David Waddington argued that, whereas the directions on diminished responsibility given during the judge's summing-up had been inaccurate, and insufficiently corrected by Peter Taylor, the later direction, given in the midst of the judge's directions as to majority verdicts was impeccable, but the jury had not had sufficient time to assimilate it, because they had already reached a majority verdict, even though the judge refused to take that verdict until after the jury had been sent once more to try to achieve unanimity. Lord Justice Bridge was to give this argument, attractive though it was, no truck, for he rejected this ground on the basis that, even in the short time the jury had been out after the judge's majority direction, they had time to absorb his 'impeccable direction' on diminished responsibility, and to reconsider their (already reached) majority verdict with this direction in mind.

It was an ingenuous rejection of a not-unattractive argument, but it reflected the mood of the court, and provides ample illustration of the dangers of taking a number of 'technical' points in an appeal, rather than concentrating on one's best argument.

And so the court came, finally, to 'the matter of most substance'. It was a very simple submission. The applicant argued that the totality of the evidence in support of diminished responsibility, which had not been controverted by any evidence called by the Crown, meant that the verdict of murder was unsafe and unsatisfactory, because the evidence led to a conclusion, on a balance of probabilities, that the defence of diminished responsibility was made out, i.e. the jury simply got it wrong.

It is worthy of note that, whilst Lord Justice Bridge considered this ground to be 'of substance', and whilst David Waddington addressed some time towards arguing it, and the court some time towards rejecting it, it was an argument which, even if successful, would have achieved no more than the substitution of a verdict of manslaughter for the murder conviction. As he had done in the trial, so he did in the application for leave: David Waddington pinned his, and Stefan Kiszko's, hopes, on an argument, primarily, for a verdict of manslaughter. He attempted to *limit the degree* of Stefan's guilt, whereas Stefan denied *any* guilt. Waddington therefore did little or nothing to establish Kiszko's innocence.

The rejection of this third ground of appeal illustrated the difficulty David Waddington had, not only in advancing the appeal, but, more importantly in advancing the defence of diminished responsibility in the first place. That difficulty arose from only one source: Stefan Kiszko. It was difficult for Waddington to advance diminished responsibility because Stefan did not want to advance that defence. For him there was only one defence, and that was 'I did not do this act, I did not kill this child, I am not guilty of anything.'

It was correct that no medical evidence had been called by the Crown to controvert that evidence called in support of diminished responsibility. The defence had called Dr Tarsh, who had based his opinion that the accused was suffering from diminished responsibility upon the primary medical evidence: the condition of Kiszko before his treatment for anaemia and hypogonadism, what that treatment had been and the likely effect of that treatment upon Kiszko. But, thereafter, Dr Tarsh had been placed in a difficult position, because, unlike doctors in ninety-nine cases out of a 100, who give evidence in support of a defence of diminished responsibility, Dr Tarsh had not had the benefit, the advantage, of hearing from the defendant his own account of his motivation for the attack.

And so it was that Dr Tarsh had had to consider diminished responsibility against a background of stout denial by his 'patient'. He was able to put forward the defence at all only, in the first instance, by assessing the pre-condition, the treatment, and the likely effect of that treatment, but he was still unable to conclude that those matters would lead Kiszko to kill her, particularly with grossly excessive violence. In order to reach such a conclusion the doctor had had to speculate as to an intervening cause. This he had done, for he said that had the girl said something along the lines of 'You dirty old man' or 'You ought to be locked up', then those words might well have triggered the amount of violence to which she was subjected.

There lay the problem. There was no evidence whatsoever that the girl had said anything of the sort. Had Kiszko admitted the killing then he might, perhaps, have given evidence that she had spoken some such words which had caused him to launch into a violent frenzy, but his only evidence had been, of course, a blanket denial of any involvement in the offence.

The court considering the application rejected the submission because of the absence of evidence supporting Dr Tarsh's theory. Whilst they agreed that there was cogent evidence of an abnormality of the mind, this alone did not establish diminished responsibility, for that defence was only established if it were proved, on the balance of probabilities, that that abnormality of mind substantially impaired the defendant's mental responsibility for his acts in doing the killing. In the absence of any evidence of any catalytic act on the part of Lesley, it was not possible to make the transition from abnormality of mind to diminished responsibility. The medical evidence of Dr Tarsh could not stand alone, it required the jury to be satisfied that Lesley *had* said something like 'You dirty old man', and there was, quite simply, no evidence that she had said any such thing. The Court of Appeal, quite rightly, found that the jury was entitled to reject diminished responsibility because there was no evidence that anything had been said or done by Lesley to provoke a violent reaction on the part of the defendant. The jury were entitled to look at all the circumstances of the case and this, said the court, they had clearly done.

This third ground thus fell alongside the two technical grounds, but it, along with the first ground, provided a clear illustration of David Waddington's approach to the pursuit of this case. It may well be said that his approach was to 'go it alone'. He had not consulted Stefan about the potentially tainted juror. Perhaps that was of little consequence, for Stefan was certainly not conversant with the ways of the court, whereas Waddington was, undoubtedly, an experienced and capable lawyer. Stefan would almost certainly have taken whatever advice his barrister had given him, and that advice would have been to carry on with the juror in place. The fact remains, however, that Waddington did not ask. Of far more relevance was the decision taken by David Waddington, who, as the queen's counsel was leader of, and held responsibility for, the defence team, to run concurrent defences which were, by their nature, incompatible. Lord Justice Bridge described this dual defence as giving the defence: 'the difficult task of inviting the jury to consider two quite separate issues in relation to which the defences advanced were really quite inconsistent with each other'.

Not only were the defences incompatible, they were also mutually self-defeating. It was impossible to have it both ways. The difficulty was, however, more fundamental than that. The dangers of running a dual defence were undoubtedly damning for Kiszko, but it is unclear whether those dangers were ever fully understood by him, or whether he was ever given the choice of running one, or other, or both defences. It seems certain that he never expressly approved the defence of diminished responsibility. Save for the police interview in which he allegedly admitted the killing, Kiszko had not given any account, to his solicitors, counsel or Dr Tarsh, which was suggestive of him acting whilst under an abnormality of the mind such as to give rise to the defence of diminished responsibility. Had he done so, Waddington would undoubtedly have brought that account out at the trial. He must have realised that he could not run diminished responsibility without Kiszko giving evidence of what had happened on the moor. It seems difficult, in all the circumstances, to believe that Kiszko ever had explained to him, or gave his consent to, the defence of diminished responsibility.

What is clear is that David Waddington and Philip Clegg elected to run the two defences side by side. They failed in the trial and they failed in the application for leave to appeal. The dual defences died in the Court of Appeal on 25 May 1978, never again to be resurrected.

The rejection of his appeal devastated Kiszko. His confidence had been high: confidence in his lawyers, confidence in their arguments, confidence in the Court of Appeal, and confidence in what he continued to believe was the great system of British justice. When his appeal was rejected, his hopes were utterly confounded, his confidence decimated. He had believed that he would be quickly acquitted and released, but now faced the prospect of an indeterminate period of incarceration, with his prospects of early release hampered by what he recognised as the awfulness of the crime. He could foresee only years of imprisonment where bullying and violence and rejection would be his daily bywords. Hope was now an alien concept, and with his rapid decline from confidence to futility came a deterioration in his mental condition.

Equally devastated by the failed appeal was Charlotte, not merely because of the implications for Stefan, nor that she could not have him with her, but because by rejecting Stefan's appeal, the court had confirmed what was in the mind of Rochdale: Charlotte Kiszko's son was a perverted child killer. Ostracisation and alienation were to follow. Unable to vent their anger on the killer of a child of one of their number, the community rounded on Charlotte as the symbol of the object of their hatred.

Unperturbed by verbal abuse and public humiliation, Charlotte

Kiszko continued to protest her son's innocence, with her sister Alfreda as her sole ally.

But Charlotte did not protest that her son was mad, mentally ill, unbalanced or anything of the sort. Her protestation was that Kiszko was innocent. He had not committed the crime alleged against him. That was to be her only ground of appeal.

But it was to be another thirteen years before anybody listened.

CHAPTER EIGHTEEN

Prisoner 688837, Continued

In May 1978 Jim Schofield picked up the *Manchester Evening News* and read that Stefan Kiszko's appeal against conviction had been rejected by the Court of Appeal. His disappointment for Stefan was far outweighed by his immediate concern for Charlotte, and the effect that what she would see as the court's confirmation of an injustice done would have on her already-shaken faith in the justice system and those who she believed were its minions. To an extent, that included Schofield himself.

Kiszko had not been brought up to London to hear the appeal being argued, and in a letter to Jim Schofield of 16 June 1978 Kiszko revealed his bitterness:

> I heard the outcome of my appeal on the radio. Only through the kindness of a principal prison officer ringing the court of appeal was the matter confirmed. To be honest, I am disgusted with this sort of treatment and am contemplating making a very serious complaint, because no one, not even Mr Albert Wright is going to pull the cotton-wool over my eyes and when the going gets rough wash their hands of the matter. I have no copy of a letter from my solicitor or barrister to say what happened at the appeal hearing.
>
> Yours faithfully,
> Stefan I. Kiszko (Mr)
> An Innocent Civil Servant.

It was becoming apparent to Charlotte that no one, apart from her and her sister, believed Stefan to be innocent, and she made this point to Maggie Buckley when the probation officer called shortly after the appeal decision was announced. As was becoming common, Charlotte was hysterical, shouting, swearing and drinking. She raged that she would never give up and would appeal to the House of Lords. When Mrs Buckley gently tried to explain to her that an appeal could only be mounted in the House of Lords where there was a point of law of general importance, Charlotte snorted in reply, 'Point of law? What is the point of having a law when my son is not allowed to prove his innocence?' It was a comment she was to make, long and loud, to anyone prepared to listen. But many believed she was simply unable to accept the reality of her son's situation.

Stefan responded to the failed appeal with a short-lived dirty protest. His true feelings were revealed in a letter to Brenda Lord. Having thanked Mrs Lord for her continuing support, Stefan's introductory politenesses were replaced by an attack which was wholly without foundation or truth and yet was both vicious and venomous:

> I can think . . . of a few people who are very happy about the way things have turned out. I gather a lot of people have had a lot to say about my case behind my back. But consider what I am going to tell you. Initially, what sent the Yorkshire Task Force to the door of our new house was a report that had been given by the husband of Pat Jones' friend, Brenda Oliver, who worked with us at Lonsdale House. Yes, her husband Richard started this whole thing off. Brenda Oliver's husband always used to be at the garage, where I bought petrol, drinking with Cyril instead of doing his patrol duty. I am sure that June Jordan, Mabel Kitchen and others will back me up on the fact that our dear police inspector's wife did a good job of telling everyone what had happened at the scene of the murder. This was done one evening when we were going down in the lift and home. The things said were only to be known at Inspector level and no wonder her husband had to resign.
>
> You know Brenda, in the past two years I have really found out who my faithful friends are. Even those Rochdale police officers who used to come to our house at Crawford Street and drink tea with my late father don't want to know now.
>
> Mum's spirits are quite high. She doesn't have to hang her head in shame because she knows I am innocent.

It was apparent that Kiszko saw conspiracy everywhere, and every amateur psychologist who came into contact with the prisoner was able to see the creeping paranoia which now dominated his thoughts. Jim Schofield contacted Albert Wright, who informed the probation officer that, now that the appeal was over, Kiszko could seek the return of belongings taken by the police when they visited Crawford Street during December 1975. When Schofield passed this information to Kiszko, he found that the prisoner was compiling a dossier of grievances against Albert Wright, and this report was to be added to that dossier.

Schofield found Stefan in angry mood, because he had received what he perceived to be a discourteous letter from Rochdale MP Cyril Smith. It was, Kiszko acknowledged, in response to a rude letter which he himself had sent the MP, and Schofield agreed to write to the MP with Kiszko's apology, in an attempt to defuse the situation. Stefan and the probation officer then sat down to construct a list of belongings which Kiszko maintained had been taken by the police after 21 December 1975, which included a cash book, two watches, premium bonds, a silver necklace, binoculars, keys, a partly exposed film and camera, a white jumper, check jacket, check coat, imitation leather gloves, a wallet, car documents, car keys, driving licence, sunglasses, a 1975 diary and various knives. This was the property he asserted should be returned to him after the refusal of his appeal.

Maggie Buckley reported that Charlotte was calming down, but she felt that she was walking on a knife edge and could easily be pushed off. Charlotte now wanted the address of the European Court of Human Rights. So certain was the loving mother that only she and Alfreda could be relied on to support Kiszko, that she intended to write a letter to the Human Rights Court, expecting them to take up her son's case without any interference from lawyers.

Stefan, too, seemed to set aside his anger. He became more at ease with – or resigned to – his situation, as letters written to Jim Schofield and, later, to Brenda Lord, evidence.

To Jim Schofield he wrote, on 5 July 1978:

I am keeping reasonably well and I hope I will live through this ordeal of injustice. However, I have a very promising letter from the secretary of the organisation 'Justice' who are looking into my case. The secretary states that Mr Clegg, barrister of Manchester, for whom I have great respect, has been very helpful in the matter and so I am continuing my fight for justice and freedom.

By the way, have you seen the papers today and the article about a policeman. The headline reads 'Web of Lies Puts PC in Jail'. Someone told me policemen don't tell lies!

Meanwhile the Rochdale monster is free as a bird and I am doing penance for something I have not done. I have been on Rule 43 since August 1976. Being in prison is of no benefit to me or my future.

Writing to Brenda Lord in September 1978, Stefan, with an air of melancholy, wrote:

It is hard not to think of the old days at home and at work when one is almost always confined to a cell, but the knowledge that I am innocent is one of the things that keeps my spirits up, until the day justice is done.

That glimmer of optimism quickly disappeared as depression set in again and Stefan's handwriting, always an indicator of his mood swings, deteriorated again. Jim Schofield wrote that Stefan was suffering from paranoia, now complaining that he believed the medical profession was deliberately neglecting the health of his mother. Schofield attempted to break down the depression by telling Kiszko that he was spending too long brooding over his mother's letters, reading them over and over again until he came to believe they contained things that were not there.

Jim Schofield, of course, still had no reason to believe that Stefan Kiszko had not killed Lesley Molseed, and it was always the probation officer's intention to try to persuade Kiszko to accept his guilt and, perhaps, even to make a confession, retrospectively, in jail. At that time it was clearly established that without a confession a prisoner in Kiszko's position would not be eligible for parole. Schofield, however, was sufficiently experienced to know that to raise the question of admissions of guilt at this stage could only further unbalance Stefan.

Charlotte's strength was now beginning to break through what she herself had recognised as demonstrations only of weakness and self-pity. Slowly her anger and frustrations were being replaced with a gritty determination to prove her son innocent. She told Maggie Buckley that she had been to Wakefield and had scolded her son for being negative, insisting that he get to grips with himself so that his sentence might at least appear to go faster. As he had always followed her before, so Stefan stepped into the path his mother was beating now. She had lit a spark within him and, ten days after she had remonstrated with him, Stefan was making enquiries about renewing his driving licence. Heartened by his client's new-found positive attitude, Jim Schofield contacted the

DVLC at Swansea and was told that, whilst it was unique in the experience of the licensing authority to receive an application for renewal from a long-term prisoner, there was nothing to prevent it. Kiszko then made his application and, in due course, his new license was sent to 25 Kings Road where, like his car, secure in the garage, it could await his return home. Charlotte had locked the car away in the garage, evidence of her belief that her son would return to drive it, one day.

Charlotte was grateful for Jim's intervention, and gave him a potted plant as a Christmas gift, along with books for his children. She also told the probation officer that Stefan would not harm a worm, let alone a small girl, and that she, Charlotte Kiszko, would herself prove her son's innocence.

Christmas, of course, was a painful time for Stefan, triggering memories of so many wonderful Christmases at home with his mother, and causing him to recall vividly the Christmas of 1975, when he had lost his freedom. As he approached his fourth Christmas in captivity, Stefan's melancholia returned, displacing the optimism of only a few months before and imbuing him with negativity and depression. His latest complaint was that he was not allowed to close the room door during visits, and he made carping remarks about petty rules and officialdom. Jim Schofield took a leaf from Charlotte's book and tried a new approach. He gently ticked Stefan off for feeling sorry for himself and pointed out that he would not win sympathy in a court, still less in a jail, by whingeing. No one wanted to be locked up, but the public believed him to be guilty, and were not hanging on to his every whim. Kiszko responded that he understood that, and he took it in what at first appeared to be good part, but he told Jim Schofield that he had, as a last resort, petitioned the Home Office.

Although this petition represented a last hope for Stefan Kiszko, for Jim Schofield it looked like another opportunity for his charge to be disappointed and with disappointment there would surely come another downturn in Stefan's mental well-being. If the petition failed, as Schofield believed it surely would, then he feared that Stefan would become permanently psychotic. He was already becoming obsessed with the idea that officialdom – They – had conspired to put him behind bars and wanted to keep him there. His Christmas letter to Brenda Lord illustrated his bitterness:

> I am still cooped up in here and it isn't going to be much of
> a Christmas, but no doubt everyone else, including the

murderer, will all be enjoying the festive season. I am waiting patiently until something is done about my petition to the home office.

This letter contained one of the few references Kiszko ever made to the 'real' murderer. It is not a feature of Kiszko's writings that he would ever refer to the man, who he firmly believed existed, who had killed Lesley Molseed, nor indeed to Lesley Molseed or her family. Whilst Jim Schofield could properly criticise Stefan for feeling sorry for himself, never in Kiszko's letters does there appear a hint of sympathy for the Molseed family, who were also experiencing their fourth Christmas in another kind of jail, namely the prison of loss that had encaptured them since Lesley's death in 1975. It is a reflection of Kiszko's melancholy that he had become so self-centred, which was inconsistent with the character he had always displayed when a free man.

A further letter to Brenda Lord amplified Kiszko's increasingly bizarre conspiracy theory, which extended everywhere. He told Mrs Lord how the police probably thought that he was the killer because they had found Leslie Thomas' sexually explicit book *Virgin Soldiers* in his desk drawer, but Kiszko believed that the book had been 'conveniently left' in the drawer 'by someone who used the desk while I was absent ill'. Yet in a further letter to Mrs Lord one week before Christmas he was slightly more upbeat when he wrote:

> Sorry I sounded a bit off in my last letter, but I am a bit fed up with being incarcerated. I miss my dear mum and everyone at work. The conviction will not have given the office a good image. Inquiries are continuing in my case and I hope there will be some better news in 1979.

He remained articulate in his first letter of the New Year and, whilst complaining that he was 'cheesed off with being locked up in this semi-mental asylum' Kiszko was able to find a touch of humour, when writing about Brenda Lord's amateur dramatics society and also her having sustained a broken hand: 'The stage when it is set up must look good for your pantomime, so I hope you will not break your hand again falling off the stage.'

He quickly returned to his own concerns when he added:

> During the time you are incapacitated why not pay my poor mother a visit. She is suffering from the pressure of worrying about me in this place and the exaggerated newspaper articles that one reads.

Mum has bought me a superb new watch, a gold plated Sekonda which is keeping time very well. It is psychologically soul destroying being in prison, but do not let that alarm you. I miss mum's cooking and working for some money.

Remember you visited me at Armley with only 20 minutes to talk. Well here you get 2 hours, so I do hope you will oblige me with your presence and we can have a good chat, reminisce over old times, have a laugh and bring the house down. They always say that he who laughs last laughs longest and no way is Stefan going to snuff it this time. I have been too close to that in the 27 years I have been on this earth. I hope you have the time to write to a lonely lamented heart.

With being on Rule 43 I cannot watch TV, but I can hear it blaring away in the background. My radio and reading matter and various correspondence fills up the time adequately. I am starting an English course which should give the psychologists some fun.

I wish you well in your pantomime. I wish you were my fairy godmother and granted me a wish to be back at home with my mother. By the way, Gracie Fields sings a good song, 'Red snails [sic] in the sunset, carry my loved one home to me.'

Stefan refused to attend religious services after he was struck by another prisoner in the jail chapel. He did not report the assault, the third against him since his arrival at Wakefield, nor did he tell his mother or Brenda Lord. The assault report emerged later, but staff put it down to Kiszko being difficult. He became more obsessive about what he believed was the conspiracy against him, causing the probation service to fear that it would lead to a total mental breakdown, now that all avenues of appeal appeared exhausted. Jim Schofield told Stefan that there could be no reason why there should be a conspiracy by authority in general, but Kiszko was now convinced that he had been singled out for a government experiment. He told Schofield that the government wanted to find out how a civil servant such as himself would react in a top security jail, particularly when the civil servant was innocent of the serious crime of which he had been convicted. It was a delusion which seemed to uplift Kiszko, for he developed it into a theory that, as he was part of an experiment then he remained, strictly speaking, a civil servant, and he felt that he should, accordingly, be in receipt of his monthly salary, plus back pay owing since his conviction. Still worse, so far as any rehabilitative process was concerned, Kiszko came to think that Schofield himself was part of the conspiracy, and he urged the probation officer to admit it. He insisted that Schofield draw the charade to an end. Schofield wrote in one of his reports: 'I understood the obsession. It was a defensive mechanism. He felt that no one would listen to him and he had to find a reason for that.'

During 1979 the image of a conspiracy festered in Kiszko's mind, and he became convinced that it was now a national conspiracy against him. He extended his theory that he was a government guinea pig still further, explaining that there had been no murder at all and that the trial was a charade, a mockery and was rigged so that his reaction to the prison regime could be monitored. He began to write to the Inland Revenue about his salary. It was in fact true that, even three years after his conviction, he was still, technically, an employee, but under suspension. In July 1979 the Inland Revenue finally informed Kiszko that his employment was being terminated. He then fretted that his mother would become financially destitute, the more so when she told him that the roof of the house had developed a leak which needed repair.

The termination letter from the Revenue seemed to cause his obsession with conspiracy to abate, but he then explained that he believed he would be free by Christmas, despite being told that this was a wholly unrealistic expectation. It was, by now, obvious that Kiszko was suffering from prison psychosis, a mental state common in those inmates locked away indefinitely whilst protesting their innocence, yet unable to find anyone to share their beliefs. In 1979 Kiszko was examined by an experienced forensic psychiatrist at Wakefield, who found him to be showing a schizophrenic-like reaction with false ideas about innocence. His treatment was stepped up and, in addition to a hypnotic drug he was prescribed a major oral tranquilliser. The same psychiatrist later described Kiszko as having very odd reasoning, adding that his condition very much resembled schizophrenia.

Towards the end of 1979 Kiszko began to realise that his expectation of being home for Christmas was not coming to fruition, and he returned to a state of depression. Jim Schofield, seeing deterioration again, judged the time to be right to attempt to persuade Kiszko to accept that his incarceration was not going to be short-term.

Schofield visited Charlotte at home on New Year's Eve, and was greeted with a glass of fortified wine. She was calm, even philosophical about Stefan's imprisonment. She continued to express quiet determination to prove her son's innocence, telling Schofield, 'If he had murdered the child then I would have been able to accept his imprisonment, although I could never have rejected him.'

Throughout 1980 Stefan's psychosis deepened and his conspiracy theory again became prominent in his ramblings. He now imagined coded messages on BBC Radio Two's *Jimmy Young Show*, which he believed were all part of the testing of a civil servant's resolve behind bars. He explained that every time Jimmy Young, or one of his political guests said 'I beg your pardon' it was a cryptic message for him. In a letter to Brenda Lord he asked her: 'As a matter of interest, do you ever get round to listening to the radio? Something surprising seems to be going on. Let me know if you agree.' In another letter, however, he again managed to find humour when he wrote: 'We had a Venus fly trap (plant) which caught so many flies that it died from over-nourishment.'

This lay in stark contrast to what next appeared, for Kiszko hinted in this letter that he might be approaching the point where he would accept culpability for the crime of which he had been convicted: 'Even if I was guilty, it was the medication I was on, but as I am not taking it now, I can't be a danger anymore, so I should be released.' This paragraph contains a mere insinuation that Kiszko's agenda might have changed: from the essentiality of proving his innocence to the priority of securing his release.

But the calmness of this letter belied the undercurrents of anger, frustration and, in lay terms at least, madness which were filing into his system. When he spoke, he would wave his arms about 'like a mad professor' as one person put it. He talked about his childhood, claiming that his parents had argued so much that he had had to act as a referee. This was the first time that Kiszko had spoken of his parents in anything other than idyllic terms, leaving listeners wondering if he was now beginning to tell the truth about a childhood which had been less than happy, or whether these sayings were demented inventions.

Overall, Stefan's mental decline had been measurable as a steady downward progression, until there had come a dramatic plunge at and around the time his appeal had been in apparent suspension before it was eventually rejected. It was apparent to his probation officer that if a halt was not called to the plummeting mental condition then the prisoner's prospects for parole would substantially diminish, indeed, one would query whether he would ever be released. Jim Schofield tried, gently, to coax Kiszko into an acceptance of, at least, the sentence he faced, so that he might look towards some future parole application. Stefan, in turn, became quite inquisitive about the meaning of parole, as though he was beginning to think that it represented his only hope. The paradox of parole for a man serving a life sentence, so far as Kiszko was concerned, was that it required an admission and acceptance of the crime of which he was convicted. At the time Kiszko was serving his sentence, there was simply no prospect of release on parole until he admitted that he had killed Lesley Molseed, a confession which would, of course, be entirely inconsistent with the protestations of innocence he had made continually since his retraction statement in December 1975.

In the event, such considerations became somewhat immaterial when he expressed resentment at a prison psychiatrist who had tried to persuade him to accept his guilt, as did the prison welfare officer. It appears that, whatever Kiszko's mental state and however great his desire to return to his mother, he found himself unable to make the gigantic step from innocent man to admitted killer. Indeed, if Kiszko had found himself unable, over a substantial period of time, to admit guilt to his mother, aunt, Jim Schofield or his legal advisors then it can be regarded as highly optimistic for a prison psychiatrist to have assumed that he would have had the capacity to coax a confession from this unfortunate man.

Kiszko was becoming increasingly wild and unpredictable in his actions and words. It is possible that he had reached a stage of believing it was time for the victim to fight back. In any event, he made wild statements about authority in general, and his fixation with his conspiracy theory reached such heights that he began to suspect that his beloved mother was part of the plot against him. The fact that he was lashing out at the mother for whom he had always had an obsessive love was the most worrying sign of his mental decline, although he never behaved with any aggression towards her when she visited him, and she was never to know that she herself was a player in the theatre of conspiracy which Kiszko was directing. He believed that the initials 'EH' and the numbers eight and five were significant. An official who had been involved in compiling transcripts of the murder trial had the initials EH, the fifth and eighth letters of the alphabet. Lesley Molseed was abducted on the fifth day of October, and her body had been found on the eighth day of that month, which in Kiszko's tortured mind gave weight to both the conspiracy theory and the relevance of the letters and numbers.

In March 1981 Kiszko was found fighting with another prisoner during exercise. It was a significant turning point, for Kiszko was, for the first time in his life, an active participant in a fight, and not merely a passive victim, running for cover when attacked. He received medical treatment for a graze to his face. Seven months later he was put on the punishment block for unauthorised possession of a pair of scissors found during a routine search of his cell. He was also in unauthorised possession of a pair of prison greys.[1] The greatly overweight prisoner explained that he had taken the greys to hold together his bed, which had collapsed.

These matters had no bearing, however, on the decision which was taken to move Kiszko to another jail. Category A inmates were routinely moved for security reasons, and on 11 November 1981 Kiszko was transferred to Gloucester Prison, the first of many moves which would pepper his period in prison. The probation service had argued against such a move, saying that Kiszko was in need of psychiatric treatment and that such a move, taking him even further away from his mother, would only exacerbate his paranoia. It was to no effect, and Kiszko's transfer brought increasing hardship for the ailing Charlotte Kiszko and her sister Alfreda. They had thus far made fifty-seven visits to Leeds before and after Stefan's trial, followed by ninety-three return trips to Wakefield in the five years and three months that Stefan had been a prisoner in that jail.[2] Most of the 200-mile journeys to Gloucester were made by the elderly ladies using public transport but occasionally they were given a lift by Brenda and Donald Lord.

Probation officer Jim Schofield also did not abandon Kiszko when he moved to the new prison. He made a trip in March 1982 to be told by the prison welfare officer that Kiszko was 'quite mad'. A prison psychiatrist diagnosed depression, although it was later asserted that Kiszko was manipulative (an assertion which was not wholly unreasonable, since most prisoners, even those with complete control of their sanity, learn something of the art of manipulation as a necessary weapon in the fight for prison survival). Kiszko's sad fixation with his mother's role in the imagined conspiracy was stronger than ever. 'Waving his arms around rather like Magnus Pyke,' recorded the probation officer. Kiszko accused his mother of being 'one of the people keeping me locked up'. He continued to believe that he was employed by the Civil Service,

---

1 The seriousness of this offence arose from the reasoning that possession of extra clothing indicated that the prisoner might be storing supplies for an eventual escape.
2 The pair were to make a further 157 trips to penal establishments around the country, a total of 308 return trips of varying distances in the sixteen years of Stefan's incarceration.

and that he was being monitored behind bars. He returned to the theme of his parents, saying that he had been an unwanted child and that his father had been a drunkard. He claimed that his parents had a tape-recorder hidden in the kitchen ceiling and would make him sing after switching it on, later selling the songs to Barry Manilow to make money out of their son's talent. He described his mother as being two-faced. Thankfully, she was never to hear this remark, although even she was able to see, on one of her visits to the prison, that her son was evidently ill. Kiszko was no longer well enough to hide his illness from his mother. He would only speak to her in Ukrainian, something he had never done before, although she would answer him in English.

On the journey home in Jim Schofield's car, Charlotte gave an indication of her own precarious state of mind, showing great distress as she blamed the police and judiciary and even the witnesses for the prosecution at the trial for her son's illness. Charlotte was now, as had become common for her, shouting and swearing, but Jim Schofield could not help but feel sympathy for the woman. She truly loved her son, she genuinely believed him to be innocent, she desperately wanted him home and she was at the end of her tether, feeling, above all, that no one cared for their plight. In the days following that harrowing visit, Charlotte felt isolated and depressed and her resolve to free her son was unimaginably weakened. She too complained of hearing messages from the radio, although she had retained sufficient strength of mind to realise that they were imaginary.

In his correspondence with Brenda Lord, Stefan's handwriting had deteriorated sharply and he was far less articulate. He was clay modelling, making a windmill for his mother and he was cutting elastic for underpants in the workshop. There was an air of resignation when he wrote: 'Unless the end of the world comes I will make the best of things until I am released.'

In general the letters were mind-numbing and progressively illegible. He claimed to be keeping well, ever anxious to keep the truth from Brenda and from his mother, but the content and style of the letters told Mrs Lord a different story.

As 1983 arrived and Stefan entered his eighth year of imprisonment, he was still being given the label 'quite mad' by the welfare officer, who could be forgiven for expressing this layperson's diagnosis, having witnessed more incomprehensible outbursts. His erratic behaviour and growing aggression did little to persuade onlookers that they were in the presence of an innocent man, and the probation service, which had tried and failed to obtain any form of admission from Kiszko was now told that there was little hope of their client being considered for parole in the near future.

In April 1983 the prisoner once thought of only as kind and gentle was found struggling with another prisoner whilst grasping a pair of scissors. He was disciplined and confined to his cell for three days. At visiting times he began to swear, although he was instinctively able to restrain himself in front of his mother. Stefan at other times spun out obscenities which shocked hardened prison staff, who had never before heard the former tax clerk swear. He stuck to the conspiracy theory by asserting that his mother's only interest was to keep him in prison.

By April 1984, a year later, Kiszko had become such a caricature of madness that he sickened the experienced Jim Schofield, who found him swearing incessantly, thumping the table, shouting and foaming at the mouth. It occurred to Schofield as he made the long drive back north that his client might never now be sane enough for release.

In May 1984 Stefan was transferred to Bristol Prison, where an assessment by a forensic psychiatrist concluded that he was suffering from schizophrenia and recommended that he be admitted to one of the special hospitals at Broadmoor, Rampton, Ashworth or Park Lane, But after only seven months at Bristol Kiszko was unexpectedly transferred back to Wakefield, where a psychiatric examination on admission brought a view which was staggeringly contradictory to that formed at Bristol only months before. The prisoner was not found to be suffering from any mental illness, and a special hospital admission was therefore inappropriate.

By the following year, however, Kiszko was back on a 'diet' of minor and major tranquillisers as understated and odd remarks such as 'appears mildly suspicious' began to appear on his prison record. A new probation officer made a visit to Wakefield and, after meeting the man formerly regarded as a 'gentle giant' he reported that he had found Kiszko to be seven feet tall with a glandular disorder. It is, perhaps, a measure of the former tax clerk's decline that he was being given, as occupational 'therapy', the tasks of sewing buttons on shirts or ruling lines in books.

In the following two years Kiszko continued to be tranquillised, until in 1987 the prison doctor was forced into reconsidering the assessment made on his re-admission to Wakefield in late 1984. He found the prisoner to be suffering from a mental illness, basing this opinion on Kiszko expressing beliefs of persecution, talking to himself and having incoherent speech. On the same day as this report was filed, another doctor logged a report of a sensitive and paranoid personality, whilst the view of experienced prison officers was that their charge was developing a psychotic state.

After ten years of incarceration medical opinion was still inconclusive and contradictory as to the precise state of Stefan Kiszko's mental health.

Further deterioration in 1987 at last resulted in positive steps being taken, when in August he was transferred to HM Prison Grendon Underwood in Aylesbury, a prison which specialised in the incarceration and treatment of the mentally ill. This excellent facility suffers primarily from being dramatically undersized for the substantial numbers of mentally ill prisoners who fall short of the severity of illness requiring admission to one of the special hospitals. It is, unfortunately, the only facility of its type within the prison service. At Grendon Kiszko was treated on the hospital wing for paranoid psychosis. He was considered by specialists to be possibly manic, since he would suddenly fly to a state of elation, where he would display grandiose delusions. So severely ill was Kiszko, according to the staff at Grendon, that consideration was again given to the merits of a transfer to one of the special hospitals, providing, if nothing else, a further illustration of the continuing uncertainty and disagreement about what should be done with him. Of course, much of the uncertainty inevitably arose from his diverse symptoms, and the variation in his state from time to time. One illuminating comment from a prison psychiatrist neatly encapsulates the situation: 'How ambivalent we psychiatrists are about whether Stefan does or does not suffer from a process of schizophrenia.'

Kiszko's pathetic – but continuing – protestations of innocence served only to confuse the psychiatrists, for another 'expert' explained these declarations as being a contradiction of his known guilt, based on 'a psycho-dynamic need to believe his innocence and an inability to contemplate therapy'.

After a five-year gap, Kiszko resumed correspondence with Brenda Lord. His last letter had been written in 1984 and was barely legible, and although Brenda had faithfully continued to write, Stefan had been unable to respond. So it was that the letter to Mrs Lord, written, in April 1989, in a trembling but legible hand, began poignantly:

Dear Brenda,

Sorry for the delay in answering your letters, but I have been lost for words. As you know it has been 15 years since I was in society. The Home Office must be bent and corrupt not letting a virgin out of prison at the age of 37. Writing to you is part of my campaign for freedom, or do you suggest that I write to the Queen and ask for a pardon? I am at my wits end trying to work this out, so I can get out of prison. I wish prison was something of the past and not the present. Is there any way you can help?

One month later, in May 1989, Kiszko was transferred from Grendon Underwood back to Wakefield. His prescription of tranquillisers was being gradually withdrawn, but this was in the face of contradictory recordings of his mental health. One logged comment was 'distressed, upset, frightened, with pains all over', whilst another recorded at about the same time read simply 'No complaints'.

By the summer of 1990 Kiszko was showing more disturbed behaviour and at one stage it was recorded that he was striking out at a ghost who he believed was attempting to sexually abuse him. Later he claimed to be receiving VHF radio signals. He swore incessantly on another visit from Jim Schofield and, asked why he swore so much he replied: 'No one listened to me for fourteen years. Perhaps if I swear now they will take notice.' Kiszko rambled about Margaret Thatcher and talked about 'getting the boys from the IRA' or from Mars to 'sort you all out'. Despite such dramatic outpourings and obvious signs of mental imbalance, the psychiatric services were unable to provide a categorical diagnosis of his mental state.

Kiszko had stopped writing letters to Mrs Lord. She had not received one for over a year but in September 1990 Kiszko wrote to her a letter most noticeable for its obviously rambling and often incomprehensible style:

I always remember my younger days in Austria where I would not dare to drink a quarter of wine, but had to put up with an eighth. Now I know why Queen Victoria was reigning this country they were all alcoholics. I know you would like to take me for a ride in your car and I would like to see the little village near Bristol called Staverton. I can take my bag and do some shopping there. When I next remember you when I am drunk, then I am sure my Russian Elite friends can cope with everything when I go to the Ukrainian Club with my mother Charlotte.

When I get out of prison I must ask you to meet an old colleague of mine called Sharafat Saddiqui ha ha ha. No mistakes made. I know you are a good comedian yourself and could even tell me a joke about a Blackpool donkey.

My mother is very distressed and cannot turn to the bottle from Austria or Yugoslavia. I know the boss at the tax office is Mr Morris or Mr Archibald. I hope I will soon be in re-employment.

By the end of 1990 the on/off question of a transfer of Stefan Kiszko to hospital was again under consideration. A Section 47 form was signed for him to go to a medium-secure unit, but the Home Office insisted that he be treated in conditions of maximum security which caused further delay until, on 15 March 1991, Stefan was finally transferred to Ashworth Hospital, Merseyside, under Section 47 of the Mental Health Act 1983.

Stefan Kiszko had been a prisoner since 1975, and it had been on Christmas Eve of 1976, after a year of incarceration, that prison records had first tentatively hinted that he might be suffering from schizophrenia. Fifteen years of transfers around the country, accompanied by learned debate between the various medical practitioners who had dealt with him had failed to provide a sure diagnosis. What role that delay had played in the mental deterioration of a man once regarded as a mild-mannered, gentle and harmless mother's boy, to the point that he would now reside in the place designed to take the country's most dangerous mentally ill prisoners can now only be a topic of speculation. Was it the very fact of Kiszko's incarceration that had rendered him 'quite mad', or was it the fact that he was never regarded as a likely candidate for parole, notwithstanding that he had served longer than other convicted murderers who were released after a much shorter time inside. Was it his immovable belief in his own innocence (bolstered by the support of the tenacious and dogmatic Charlotte) or was it merely the failure of any other person to consider that he might be telling the truth when he declared that innocence? Was it the persistence of those who sought to persuade him to admit his crime or was it simply an inevitable consequence of an underdeveloped and fragile personality dealt the most enormous wrong by a system of justice and a society in which he placed so much faith?

Whatever or whoever was to blame, at 39 Stefan Kiszko was now defined no longer as a prisoner, but as a patient, a form of words which took nothing away from the fact that he remained immured by the state and unlikely to be released. On admission to Ashworth he was noted to be overtly psychotic, having auditory hallucinations, grandiose delusions and persecutory ideas. He was socially withdrawn although not disruptive, and he drank excessive amounts of water. An unequivocal diagnosis was at last made. Stefan Kiszko was schizophrenic and the treatment to be administered was, again, major tranquillising drugs.

Yet on 1 May Kiszko was able to write to Brenda Lord from his bed on Tennyson Ward. His handwriting was unrecognisable to his oldest friend as he wrote:

> I am glad I am out of Wakefield and *now things are moving towards the parole board*[3] . . . I hope you can write soon. I would hope since my last letter that we have not fell out as I used some sharp words that would have given you a clearer picture of the situation.

The letter is notable not merely because it contains the delusionary expectation of parole, but because, paradoxically, it was written more in the style of the Stefan Kiszko of old. It was, however, to be the last letter of a fifteen-year friendship. Whilst Stefan Kiszko's mind had been savaged by the effects of his long imprisonment, such that his release from involuntary incarceration was neither likely nor practical, other minds had been concentrated on the facts surrounding his 1976 conviction, and there seemed to be a very real prospect of a further appeal being launched against the conviction which had stolen his liberty for the fifteen years which had passed since he first wrote to Brenda Lord.

---

3 Authors' italics. Kiszko's transfer to Ashworth rendered any possibility of parole so remote as to be negligible.

CHAPTER NINETEEN

A New Legal Team

Following the failed first appeal in May 1978, as David Waddington returned to other cases and other public duties, there was a significant development when Philip Clegg, Waddington's junior, revealed his own feelings. In a reply to a letter from Tom Sargant, the Secretary of Justice, Clegg wrote:

> Personally, I have always had lurking doubts as to the view that Kiszko was in fact the person who killed Lesley Molseed. I doubt whether many would share those doubts in light of the fact that the prosecution based its case in the main on the confession statement. Further, there were matters which, while in themselves proved little or nothing, lent considerable force to the claim that the confession was true.

For the first time a representative of the criminal justice system was openly supportive of Charlotte and Stefan. Having stated what was a commonly held perception of the strength of the prosecution case, namely the confession, Clegg highlighted two key matters which raised the lurking doubts to which he had already made reference:

> The Defence called Mrs Tong at trial and I found her a most compelling witness. The prosecution and judge accepted her entirely as an honest and careful witness. The prosecution sought, successfully it would seem, to suggest that she had made a mistaken identification because she had been so affected by the horror of the little girl's death and her desire to help.

Philip Clegg's second doubt emanated from the Kiszko confession statement in which he had admitted the two indecent exposure offences of 3 and 4 October 1975.

It was quite apparent from the evidence of the children

involved on October 3rd that Kiszko was not the person who exposed himself to them. This lends some credence to Kiszko's claim that the confession was a mere subterfuge designed to appease police wrath and to secure a return home to his mother.

The letter continued:

Had these been the sole matters upon which my doubts were based, bearing in mind all this was laid before the jury, I would not suggest that this was a case in which Justice ought to involve itself. However, I am now informed that, since Kiszko's conviction, there have been a number of cases where children in the Rochdale area have been sexually attacked by a man with a white car. It is vitally important that an eye should be kept on developments in the latest series of attacks. Later, when the current offender has been brought to book, enquiries should be made.

The Justice Group, a campaigning group based in London with a special interest in cases where a miscarriage of justice is alleged, had been brought into the case by Charlotte Kiszko who, despite the debilitating effects of her lung disease, persistently pestered the authorities to reconsider her son's case. Her absolute belief in his innocence never wavered and, when Albert Wright had said to her after the appeal had been lost that there was 'nothing else that could be done', Charlotte had retorted by swearing at him, vowing to find a 'real lawyer'. She had tried various sceptical solicitors before happening upon Tom Sargant at Justice.

Sargant's interest in the case and Clegg's 'lurking doubts' letter had been Charlotte's first signs of progress, yet, paradoxically, the first real hope emanated from Charlotte's own adversity. Through legal action sponsored by the textile workers' union, Charlotte was seeking compensation for her industrially contracted disease of the lungs. She was represented by solicitor John Pickering, who was handling a number of similar cases involving byssinosis around 1980. Pickering was based in a converted Victorian home in cobbled Church Lane in nearby Oldham, but, on receipt of Charlotte Kiszko's case he travelled to Charlotte's own modest home to see his client, quickly appreciating that she was suffering from severe byssinosis. With great confidence he took on her case although, in the manner of most actions in the civil courts, progress was slow, and it was to be almost three years before

Pickering won the out of court settlement of his client's case, which in turn would provide a significant springboard for her campaign to secure her son's freedom.

On Pickering's advice she accepted the offer of settlement of £40,000, and when the cheque arrived he suggested that he post it on to Charlotte, but she insisted that she pick it up that very day. Pickering was surprised, but thought the lady did not trust the post, and probably wished to take it straight to her bank or building society so as to be sure the money was safe. It was a bitterly cold February day but Charlotte met her sister Alfreda and together the two women travelled by bus from Rochdale to Oldham where Pickering was based. They stepped from the bus, linked arms and proceeded to Pickering's office, where the solicitor handed over the cheque. Holding the piece of paper aloft, as if to emphasise that justice cost money, Charlotte declared 'This will prove my son's innocence.' In that moment, she stood in the same shoes as the sister of Derek Bentley and the mother of Michael Hickey: a woman with an unwavering conviction as to the innocence of a man she could not help but love.

Pickering was not aware of Mrs Kiszko's other battle and asked what her son had done. 'Nothing,' she snapped, and then, with eyes burning with an intensity the solicitor would remember long after that day, she told the entire story of Stefan's conviction and the fact that he had been framed and jailed for life for a crime of murder which he could not have committed. Could not, because he had been with her and Alfreda that day; could not, because he was Stefan, her only son, her devoted son, who had never had one ounce of malice in his entire body. The money she had just received would be used to bring about Stefan's freedom, explained the doting mother, and she asked John Pickering if he would fight for Stefan as he had fought for her.

The solicitor explained that he did not specialise in criminal law and that she needed a specialist to fight a case such as this. He was able only to advise her on a man he believed was suitable for the task, and then he watched as Charlotte placed the cheque into her bag and rose to leave. Pickering offered to call a taxi for her, but nothing as trivial as a cheque for £40,000 was about to change this indomitable woman and her long-established ways. The money was needed for Stefan, not for fripperies and frivolities: she and Alfreda would use their bus passes.

The solicitor rose from his seat and could only watch in admiration as the two ladies again linked arms and marched out into the February sleet to head with renewed determination towards the bus stop.

Once home, Charlotte's priority was to telephone a Mr Campbell Malone, the solicitor whom Pickering had recommended and said could be trusted. Pickering had been concerned that Charlotte might fall into the clutches of a less-than-scrupulous big city lawyer, whose eyes would gleam at the sight of the compensation cash which Charlotte would naively offer to anyone prepared to fight her corner. She was prepared to spend every penny of the £40,000 to win Stefan's freedom, a devotion which Pickering could understand and appreciate; but he could see circumstances in which that pot of gold would be drawn on and drawn on with little to show for the expenditure, until Charlotte had little left in reserve and Stefan was no nearer to freedom. Without specialist criminal knowledge Pickering could not know whether Charlotte's fight could ever be successful, and it pained him to envisage a situation where her son remained imprisoned for life, and Charlotte's compensation for her own suffering was gone. It was for that reason that he had steered her towards Malone, a criminal law specialist operating from Salford and a friend and neighbour whom Pickering had know for twenty years. He could not say whether Malone would win the case, but he trusted him to try his best without taking advantage of the woman.

Charlotte telephoned her new solicitor that day at the offices he shared with his partners, and immediately poured out her troubles to a bewildered Malone. His confusion emanated from his difficulty in following the conversation due to her thick European accent, which forty years in a Lancashire mill had done nothing to eradicate, and also because of her tendency to talk rapidly, interspersing details of the case with a repeated and plaintive cry: 'Please, please, please Mr Malone, help my son!' Malone asked Charlotte to write him a full and detailed letter explaining the position. He then spoke to Pickering and, after the two lawyers had picked over their personal recollections of the killing of Lesley Molseed, Malone asked his friend for his opinion of the woman and her case. What Pickering told him of Charlotte Kiszko's character and what Malone had heard from the woman himself persuaded him. She had not been ashamed to plead for his help, and that in turn had made it impossible for him to resist her intensity. He had been impressed by her sheer determination and had been moved by her raw passion for her son and the injustice done to him. 'Mr Malone,' she had said, 'if I thought my son Stefan had done this I would never reject him, but I would not try and get him out before he had done the sentence he deserved.'

Malone's professionalism enabled him to retain an open mind. Too often had he heard the cry of innocence uttered by the palpably guilty, but the sincerity of this woman who was prepared to spend her own money and not rely on legal aid to pay for her fight, made him confident of her sincerity. He told Charlotte that he would take the case, but he made her no promises save that he would take no fees for the time being.

Malone began by speaking to Tom Sargant at Justice, and to a BBC investigative journalist called David Geen, who hoped to make a programme about the case. Geen suggested that house-to-house enquiries in Rochadale might prove the type of carpet fibre found on Lesley Molseed's clothing and matched forensically to a piece in Kiszko's car was very common in the area.[1] Surprisingly, Charlotte was able to provide the exact carpet sample, which had remained in Kiszko's Hillman Avenger, locked in Charlotte's garage awaiting the return of the owner. Malone asked two law students, Ged Towey and Linda Grindley to take the sample round hundreds of homes in Rochdale, a task carried out diligently but which was to yield nothing of value, for very few houses possessed a matching carpet. This first line of attack was a failure.

Malone spoke to Philip Clegg who reiterated that the Kiszko case had troubled him more than any other in his career and that he felt that Kiszko had been badly served by the judicial system, which may well have contributed to a grave injustice.

Several weeks after Pickering had handed the case to Malone, and Malone had made his initial contact with Charlotte, Malone decided to resign his partnership with Casson & Co. in Salford and set up in business as a sole practitioner for himself. His decision was in part influenced by Malone's partners not seeing the Kiszko case as an economically attractive proposition, nor could they see a future in the case. They did not object to him taking the Kiszko file with him to his new practice, which Malone did, impressed by both Charlotte and by Philip Clegg and his doubts. The case, however, had come to a standstill, with no tangible new evidence uncovered.

Malone saw that it was time to take a new direction, and he took on more personal responsibility for the case. The papers con-

---

1 In fairness, this point had been made quite adequately in Kiszko's trial. Although no evidence had been called to *prove* that the carpet was common, the point had been conceded by the forensic scientist Outteridge.

cerning the case were with the BBC which had been considering making a programme about it. The decision had been not to make the programme, but the papers were left at the BBC studios where Malone and Geen were able, by special permission, to examine the file at will. Malone arranged to meet Philip Clegg. The meeting took place in Clegg's chambers in Manchester in February 1986, where Clegg, Malone, Geen and Sargant discussed the way forward. It was agreed that one line would be to look at alternative candidates for the 1975 murder, and they would examine the records of convicted sex offenders who, by reason of their *modus operandi* could fit the profile of Lesley's abductor, one of whose characteristics was the abduction of young girls for sexual purposes.

Malone decided to hire a private investigator, an enterprise which Charlotte was willing to fund, but he took it upon himself to begin by visiting Kiszko in Wakefield Prison. This meeting took place nearly ten years after the murder, a fact not lost on Malone. Nor could he be anything less than aware of Kiszko's predicament, noting in his diary that his client was 'clearly ill' and that he 'gabbled'. Malone explained to Kiszko what it was that he, Geen and Sargant were looking at, but he was careful not to raise any false hopes which might result in further deterioration in Stefan. He explained that he had hired a private eye, Peter Jackson, with whom Malone had worked before and whom he regarded as a dogged and reliable investigator. Kiszko appreciated the efforts being made for him, but failed to appreciate the stark contrast between the substantial materials and facilities available to the West Yorkshire police who had put him in prison, and the tiny team of Malone, Geen, Sargant and Jackson who were trying to get him out. Perhaps it was as well.

Peter Jackson was a former serviceman and policeman who knew Rochdale well. He began by re-interviewing defence witnesses but his one success was, in real terms, quite minor, in that he saw Stefan's GP, Dr D'Vaz, and took him to the lay-by. The doctor, aware of Kiszko's ankle injury, considered it virtually impossible for his patient to have even climbed the steep banking, still less to have dragged a resisting child up there with him.

Philip Clegg was asked for an opinion as to whether there was sufficient material assembled to warrant petitioning the home secretary. In his written advice, Mr Clegg began where any legal assessment of the case would begin, an assessment of the prosecution case. He said that he considered the prosecution case at trial to be 'compelling' and advised that it was important to consider the strength of that case before attempting to undermine it.

The only evidence capable of establishing Kiszko's guilt were his oral and written confessions, which the jury had implicitly decided were both voluntarily made and true. This was the thrust of the Crown's case. The confessions contained certain information which could only have been known to the killer:

  i   four knives were seized from Kiszko's home. He was asked to show the police which had been the murder weapon. The knife Kiszko selected was the only one of the knives to have traces of blood on it;

  ii in both confessions Kiszko had said that he recalled 'sort of wiping the knife on her or her clothes', an admission which tallied with the forensic evidence;

  iii Kiszko had admitted that the girl's underwear had not been removed, and that he had ejaculated between her legs, both admissions fitted the known facts, and these were facts which Dick Holland had specifically ordered be kept from all but the most senior officers involved in the investigation;

  iv Kiszko had provided in his confessions a very good description of the scene where the child had been killed and her body abandoned.

In addition to the confessions and the details contained in them, there was additionally:

  i   the carpet fibres found on Lesley's body which matched fibres in the carpet in Kiszko's car;

  ii a felt-tipped pen found at the murder scene which was the same as the pens Kiszko used at work;

  iii the piece of paper found in Kiszko's car on which he had written the number ADK 539 L, which was the registration number of Mr Hollos' car. Mr Hollos had driven past the murder scene on Sunday, 5 October 1975. Kiszko was unable to provide an explanation for why he had written the number down.

These were matters in the prosecution case which Mr Clegg had quite rightly observed had to form the starting point of any attack on the conviction. For the purposes of this part of his report Mr Clegg ignored the girls' evidence concerning the indecent exposure allegations or the possibly damaging effect of the evidence introduced by the defence as to Kiszko's medical conditions, which were necessary to enable them to run diminished responsibility, but which had a concomitant effect of making Kiszko appear to the jury as, as Mr Justice Park had put it, 'a man with a sexual problem'.

'Such was the case for the Crown,' reported Clegg, 'that it was and remains a powerful and compelling case.' Clegg then went on to make, with remarkable courage and frankness, an admission that he and David Waddington had made an error of judgement in the construction of the case.

> There was a considerable body of evidence which tended to suggest that at the time of the offence Kiszko was suffering from the side effects of treatment he had recently received for hypogonadism and anaemia. So beguiling was this evidence that the Crown would have accepted a plea to manslaughter by reason of diminished responsibility, had it been tendered. By insisting that he was not the killer Kiszko made such a plea impossible to tender. Nevertheless, it was here, with hindsight, that the defence team, *myself included*,[2] made an error of judgement.
>
> Instead of forgetting about diminished responsibility and running alibi for all its worth, we endeavoured to preserve the manslaughter option by inviting the jury to say first and foremost that they could not be sure he was the killer but, failing that, to consider diminished responsibility. These pleas are mutually exclusive. I felt it was a case of trying to have our cake and eat it.

However, Clegg recalled that, before his trial, Kiszko had given five variations of his alibi and the only independent alibi witness had been unable to say whether it was 5 or 12 October when Kiszko was in her shop. This had not helped the defence team or Kiszko.

He admitted another defence error of judgement in not asking for a retrial after the woman juror had overheard a remark that 'even Kiszko's barristers had tried to get him to plead guilty'. Clegg

---

2 Authors' italics. Clegg was not unwilling to share responsibility for the fault in the presentation of the defence case.

wrote: 'Personally, I cannot imagine anything more prejudicial and I am still of the opinion that we should have sought a discharge of the jury. This point was taken on appeal but did not seem to find favour with the court.'

He added:

Having read what I have said about the strengths and weaknesses of the prosecution and defence cases, it may be wondered why I have always harboured a feeling of disquiet about the correctness of the jury's verdict. It can be summed up in one phrase – Mrs Tong. This lady's evidence is in my view central to any chance of a successful reference.

Clegg explored the possibility of evidence being omitted which did not 'fit' a suspect like Kiszko, and said:

The principal danger that arises where there has been a crime as emotive as the killing of a child, is that the police are under enormous pressure from the public to find the culprit as quickly as possible. The temptation to overlook evidence which does not fit a likely candidate's involvement and to look for evidence which does fit, must be strong. I suspect something of this nature may have occurred in this case. I gained the impression at the trial and still hold it, that the turning point for Detective Superintendent Holland was the discovery that the registration number on Kiszko's scrap paper belonged to a car which had passed the lay-by. Thereafter the confessing starts and, somewhat disturbingly, there is nothing in the confession which does not fit with what the police have already deduced. I would have found the confession more compelling had it contained substantial matters of narrative hitherto unknown to the police.

In accordance with the opening comments in his advice, Philip Clegg returned to the theme that no appeal could succeed unless it could cast doubt on Kiszko as being the killer of Lesley Molseed, and he declared his firm view that the Kiszko case was going nowhere until it could be shown that there was a:

compelling possibility that the murder was committed in a different manner to that confessed to and/or that someone else committed it. This may seem an impossibly tall order but I do not feel that the attainment of this goal is without hope.

The advice was not merely a statement of the obvious. Clegg rightly took the view that any new evidence would have to be dynamic and highly probative if it were to overcome the best evidence available in any criminal trial: the defendant's detailed confession to the crime, backed with sufficient detail to show it to be genuine and made voluntarily. This the Crown had, as it were, in the bag.

Clegg advised that new enquiries should concentrate on four areas:

1 The Alibi

Geen had established that Mrs Baran was now able to say that it was certainly 5 October when Kiszko had called into her shop, by reference to her own recent birthday, and the fact that on that particular day she was waiting for her brother to call with her birthday present. Clegg advised that any evidence supporting Mrs Baran would be of great value.

2 The White Car

Possibly the best evidence called by the defence in the original trial, Mrs Tong's account, that she had seen Lesley in a white car was of such value that even the trial judge had told the jury if they believed her to be right, Kiszko had to be acquitted.

Philip Clegg emphasised the importance of Mrs Tong, commenting that he had always been amazed that such an important piece of evidence should have been disclosed by the Crown only on the morning of trial and wondering if there was any other evidence that had not come to the attention of the defence.

Apparently there was, for the journalist Geen had been told by Holland since the trial that the police were in possession of a further statement from a person who had seen somebody behaving suspiciously near a white van, in Stiups Lane at about the time when Lesley would have been walking there. Holland said he had been prepared to release the statement but that the DPP had stepped in and refused disclosure. Mr Clegg was unable to see any reason for this order from the DPP, save, perhaps, sensitivity to the 'snooping' of the media. Clegg went on to state that if the statement was one which could tie up with Mrs Tong's evidence then it would lend powerful support to Mrs Tong's identification of Lesley and, at a stroke, 'the foundations of the Crown's case against Kiszko would have been seriously disturbed': Clegg naturally advised that the statement in the hands of the police be obtained, and he also sought any other references to a white car, including an old statement from Mrs Sandra Chapman to the effect that she had seen a similar car parked close to the murder scene at dusk, the time of day likely to be chosen to commit murder on the deserted moors.

3 The Blue Van

There had been, in the initial investigation when led by Dibb, a number of suggestions that there had been a blue/green Morris 1000-type van of the sort used by the GPO, parked in the lay-by at 3.50 p.m. or thereabouts on Sunday, 5 October. This vehicle had never been traced, although the police had expressed in the media from an early stage their desire to find it. The trial judge had wrongly believed it to be the defence case that the driver of this vehicle was the killer. In fact the defence argument had been that the killer was very unlikely to draw up in the lay-by with his victim and then kill her close by when there was an occupied vehicle close to the scene whose occupants could have seen or heard any commotion connected with a sex killing on the moorland immediately above the lay-by. If no car – particularly no car similar to Kiszko's – had been in the lay-by when the blue van was there, it would go a long way towards proving the confession wrong in a particular and significant respect, thus undermining the entire confession.

In this part of the advice Clegg can be seen to be pursuing a similar line to that which had already failed once. Undermining the confession was, of course, crucial to undermining the Crown's case as a whole. However, if the van had been there for, say, an hour or less, the scope for the Court of Appeal to say that Kiszko could have arrived on either side of that hour was obvious.

What appears most obviously missing from this part of Clegg's advice is any suggestion that efforts should be put into investigating the driver of the blue GPO-style van.

4 Fibre Evidence

Clegg reconsidered the fibre evidence which, as the Crown conceded, was never the strongest point in the prosecution case because they could not say the fibres were common. Clegg, however, now went further. He stated his amazement that no fibres had been found on Lesley's anorak and, of perhaps more importance, he questioned how it had been that, when Lesley had never removed her clothes, one of the carpet fibres had got on to her vest, especially since the carpet in question was in the footwell of the car. Clegg wanted to know from where else fibres had been recovered and, in particular, to what extent those fibres had been found 'inside', that is, inside her vest, jumper, sock or skirt. The barrister postulated the theory that the fibres found could have got into the garment while it was being washed or stored in a drawer with other garments or items containing the fibre.

Clegg's advice came down to the investigation of seven points:

1 show the evidence of Mrs Baran related to 5 October 1975;

2 show that Mrs Tong did see Lesley in the white car;

3 show that, between 2.10 p.m. and 3.50 p.m. on 5 October, no car remotely like Kiszko's parked on the lay-by;

4 demonstrate that the distribution of fibres on Lesley's clothing was inconsistent with her acquiring them in the car, given that she never took off her anorak;

5 refer to the fact that, on any view, Kiszko confessed to an indecent exposure on 3 October 1975 for which he was clearly not responsible;

6 refer to the inevitable prejudice which must have been caused by trying to run alibi and diminished responsibility together;

7 refer to the inevitable prejudice which must have been caused by what the lady juror overheard in the public house during the trial.

'If all these goals can be attained,' wrote Philip Clegg, there would be 'a powerful case for reference under Section 17'.[3]

At a further meeting held in 1988 and attended by Clegg, Malone, Geen and Sargant it was agreed that limited progress had

---

3 Section 17 of the Criminal Appeal Act 1968 provided for references to the Court of Appeal by the home secretary. This section has been repealed by the Criminal Appeal Act 1995 which provides for references by a Criminal Cases Review Commission, the commission exercising the powers formerly vested in the home secretary.

been made by Peter Jackson, whose findings thus far had been helpful but insufficient on their own to force the Home Office to refer the case back for appeal. Malone considered that a new impetus was required.

Campbell Malone decided to consult a barrister with whom he was friendly for a fresh review of the evidence. Jim Gregory was a flamboyant barrister specialising in criminal law and a neighbour of Malone in the moorland town of Todmorden on the Lancashire–Yorkshire border. He was also in the same chambers as Philip Clegg. It was a true test of friendship, for Gregory agreed to review the papers with no guarantee of being paid, just as Clegg and Malone had done initially.

Gregory agreed that something else was required to give the petition a realistic prospect of success. He began to look at the mechanics of the trial, including the concern over the juror's eavesdropping of the public house conversation, which he felt had not been properly addressed at the 1978 failed appeal hearing.

Jim Gregory wanted to meet Kiszko, but by the time they met, on 1 August 1989, Stefan was so disturbed as to make his recollections of the trial and his instructions to the defence team unreliable.

Over the next few months Gregory set about drafting a petition to the Home Office. There were many late-night meetings with Malone, in which drafts were rejected and amended and arguments and disagreements over wordings were resolved. The two lawyers had a fundamental disagreement as to what should be at the heart of the petition. Gregory believed that its thrust should be based on the Kiszko defence team's errors as he did not believe the updated evidence would take the petition anywhere. Malone believed that the Home Office would not refer the case back to the Court of Appeal on the basis of misjudgements by Waddington and Clegg. Malone had previous experience of appeals based on barristers' errors, and all had been in vain. Malone believed that only updated evidence would give the Home Office justification to refer the petition to appeal. It would give the civil servants at the Home Office something else to focus on.

Eventually the lawyers agreed to produce a compromise petition, combining the so-called fresh evidence with the mishandling of the murder trial and the first appeal. In later years Malone would reflect that he and Gregory had made the same oversight as Wright, Waddington and Clegg had done fifteen years earlier. They had analysed where Waddington, Clegg and Wright had gone wrong, but had then walked in the footsteps of their predecessors. They were moths, dancing round the flame of real or imagined errors of counsel at the first trial, but in the brightness of that light they were blinded to the crux of Kiszko's case. He was not guilty; he did not kill her. And in their blindness they did not even see the question: How could a man with Kiszko's condition of hypogonadism be sterile and yet be said to have left fertile semen on the body of Lesley Molseed?

Gregory and Malone agreed that they had finally got the theme and the wording right. The petition was ready to be submitted. The two men shook hands on it, and Malone went home, a man well pleased at the progress which was at last being made. He sat down and switched on the television set where, incredibly, the announcement on the BBC news was of the appointment of a new home secretary. It was David Waddington QC MP, who would remain in the post of home secretary from 26 October 1989 to November 1990, and would be a member of the cabinet until 1991.

Immediately Malone telephoned Jim Gregory, the barrister's words of incredulity echoing his own emotions. What powers had acted to appoint, on the very day when the draft petition to the home secretary had been given the two lawyers' seal of approval, a new home secretary who was, in his former life as an active Queen's Counsel, to be criticised in the petition document? The appointment of Waddington might be thought likely to intimidate the Home Office officials who would first receive and review the petition, so much so that they might consider it imprudent to offend their new superior, and bury the petition under a pile of other matters until a more appropriate time. This initial reaction of Malone and Gregory was soon replaced by a more positive attitude. The appointment might have benefits for Stefan, in that it might make it less likely that the petition would be overlooked. No new home secretary, particularly one with Waddington's background of 'active service' in the courts and his reputation for integrity, would wish to open himself to accusations that he had used his position of power to cover up an injustice, of which he himself – albeit unknowingly – had been a part.

It was decided to send the petition immediately, but Malone elected first to give notice to the new secretary of state that there would soon be coming in the post the first grumblings of doubt about the Kiszko case since the end of the 1970s. Malone wrote to the Home Office what, despite its subtle tone, he later described as a 'shameless flyer'. Dated 2 February 1990 and sub-titled 'Stefan

Ivan Kiszko. Wakefield Prison. Prisoner No. 688837' the letter
read,

> Dear Sirs,
> We have been consulted by the above named, and also by his
> mother regarding his conviction in 1976 for murder.
> Although we did not act during the trial we have, for several
> years, been carrying out investigations into our client's con-
> viction, initially under the guidance of Mr Philip Clegg, who
> was junior counsel to Mr David Waddington QC, who de-
> fended Mr Kiszko at his trial.
>
> Following Mr Clegg's relatively recent appointment to the
> Circuit Bench, we have instructed fresh counsel and have
> recently received his advice.
>
> As a result of that advice, we have now instructed him to
> prepare a petition to the home secretary based on the infor-
> mation now available to us and also on the conduct of the
> trial. The purpose of the petition is to persuade the home
> secretary to refer the matter to the Court of Appeal.
>
> Before doing so, however, we consider it appropriate to
> write to enquire whether or not there is any review currently
> being undertaken regarding Mr Kiszko which might lead to
> his early release. We have in mind, should Mr Kiszko be
> released, the importance of him being rehabilitated into a
> stable home environment and we have also to bear in mind
> the fragile nature of his mother's health.

The Home Office had been forewarned that the petition would
be accompanied by an appeal for urgency, but the Home Office
resisted any temptation to parole Kiszko as a gesture of goodwill,
thereby avoiding the petition, with all the cost implications of that
procedure and also thereby avoiding any possible embarrassment
to the home secretary. The immediate reply which Malone had
requested was that Kiszko's earliest review date was to be in
December 1992, nearly three years away.

The final draft of the petition was submitted on 18 June 1990,
accompanied by a letter in which Malone suggested that a meeting
with Home Office lawyers might be helpful. The Home Office,
however, was not to be rushed into an early decision on the petition
on the grounds that that petition was critical of the serving home
secretary for his role as advocate in the original trial. By September
1990 no response to the petition had been received, and in an
attempt to put pressure on what he perceived as lackadaisical

bureaucrats, Campbell Malone wrote again, stressing the importance of a prompt decision because of Charlotte Kiszko's growing frailty. The Home Office was doing in the Kiszko case no more nor less than they would have done in any other case where a reference is sought. They were taking the usual amount of time to thoroughly investigate the content of the petition. This became quite apparent when, Campbell Malone having once more written in October 1990, a reply was eventually received from the C3 Division of the Home Office, which had been written on 8 November 1990. The letter expressed sympathy with Malone's desire for a speedy response, and acknowledged why Charlotte's frailty added to the urgency of the case, but it continued:

> You will appreciate . . . that before the Home Secretary refers any case to the Court of Appeal he must consider all the circumstances of the case very carefully in order to be satisfied that proper grounds pertain for so doing.
>
> The current position on Mr Kiszko's case is that enquiries are now being made on some of the matters raised in your petition. You may be assured that as soon as the results have been seen and examined, they will be considered against the framework of the case as a whole, and the Home Secretary will not hesitate to act if he considers that any intervention on his part is warranted.
>
> Yours sincerely,
> T McCarthy

The letter was a model of civil service verbiage. Stripped down to its essentials it did not impress Malone at all. The reference to 'enquiries . . . into some of the matters in the petition' rankled. He felt that the Home Office should have been investigating all the matters raised in the petition, not merely some. Unwilling to be patient, he considered it appropriate to apply more pressure. As he was later to recall, 'I felt we had to push up the stakes and let them know we were unhappy and determined.'

Malone approached a barrister he knew well and had previously instructed. Stephen Sedley QC was one of the country's leading authorities on judicial review, and Kiszko's solicitor considered that Sedley would be able to provide the final turn of the key which would open the doors of the Court of Appeal. Mr Sedley advised the solicitor on the appropriate approach, and Malone acted with haste on the advice given. No more the polite and oblique technique, instead, a direct-attack strategy was implemented, intended to put the home secretary on the spot by calling into question whether he felt compromised by his unique position with regard to the Kiszko appeal. On 12 November Malone sent off a letter which, couched in the terms advised by Sedley, was likely to make an advantage out of Waddington's position. A home secretary without connection with the case might find it easier to reject the application for a reference, and Malone hoped that, with Waddington as Secretary of State, the converse would be true. The letter was a carefully worded exercise in brinkmanship, striking a delicate balance between deference and offensiveness. To be too abrupt, harsh or threatening might result in the entire file being consigned to the bottom of the fullest 'pending' tray. On the other hand, were Waddington to feel that Malone's frustration was such that the press might find entertainment in the home secretary's discomfort, it would be no bad thing for Kiszko. It would be completely improper for details of the actual petition to appear in advance of any Court of Appeal hearing, but a leaked report of a new home secretary under scrutiny for his response to an appeal petition allegedly critical of his performance in a murder trial had definite and immediate news potential. The lawyers decided that to irk the home secretary might just encourage a little more haste, and therefore the letter to the Home Office read as follows:

> I am becoming increasingly concerned – and my client and his mother even more so – at the length of time it is taking for the decision to be reached on the petition for referral of Mr Kiszko's conviction to the Court of Appeal.
>
> I have consulted Leading Counsel about this and the problem, which will be apparent to you, of the present Home Secretary's role as counsel in the trial and appeal. As to the first of these matters I am advised that the Home Secretary is compellable by mandamus[4] to consider and decide on an application for the exercise of his power under Section 17, where there has been an unreasonable delay on his part in coming to a conclusion on it.
>
> It is possible, however, that one reason for the delay is the Home Secretary's previous part in the case. You have not, in our correspondence to date, explained what, if anything, it is

---

4 Mandamus is a power of the Crown called a prerogative order, which is exercised by the High Court, whereby public bodies and officers may be ordered by the court to take action.

proposed to do about this. In the ordinary way, as I understand it, the Home Secretary would personally take the decision
on referral under Section 17, no doubt after obtaining all the
advice he considers necessary.

In the present case, the Home Secretary will be the first to
appreciate that there is a particular need for a visibly disinter-
ested decision to be made, even though it will be necessarily
made in his name.

It is not for my clients or me to say what is the right
procedure, but I would be glad to learn from you not only
when a decision can be expected, but, in the particular circumstances of the case, by whom it will be taken and on the
basis of whose appraisal or advice.

Let me make it clear that I do not for a moment anticipate
a decision taken in less than good faith. My concern is only to
point out the conflict of interest with which my client's
petition unavoidably faces the present Home Secretary and
to know how it is proposed to solve it.

Yours faithfully,
C J Malone.

It took precisely nine days for the reply from Mr McCarthy at C3
to arrive at Malone's office. Mr McCarthy noted Malone's concern
over Waddington's previous involvement in the Kiszko case, and
continued:

The powers afforded to the Home Secretary by Section 17 of
the Criminal Appeal Act 1968 impose a duty on him to
consider claims that a miscarriage of justice may have
occurred. It must be for the Home Secretary to determine
the proper manner in which to conduct an investigation of a
case of alleged wrongful conviction. Each case is individual,
and is considered on its own merits, and you may be assured
that once a full examination of Mr Kiszko's case has been
completed, if the Home Secretary is satisfied that proper
grounds exist for his intervention, he will not hesitate to take
appropriate action. We are making enquiries with the police
with regard to Mr Kiszko's conviction and, while I cannot
give you any firm estimate of the likely duration of these
enquiries, there will inevitably be some delay before the case
can be considered in full.

The letter was cause for celebration at Malone's offices in Broad

Street, Salford. Stephen Sedley's advice had enabled the key to be given a half-turn. The revelation, delivered in a low-key manner, that 'enquiries were being made through the police' was indeed splendid news. The delay was now explained and, in the circumstances, could not be bettered. Only five months after the petition was submitted the police were involved. This petition was not thrown in a government dustbin, not even half-way down some departmental filing tray. It had already been considered briefly, it had raised enough hackles to stir interest and now it was proceeding with sufficient pace to satisfy the most impatient lawyer. As Malone was to reflect in later years, it was not bad going, all things considered.

CHAPTER TWENTY

Some of My Best Friends are Policemen

Monday, 26 November 1990 commenced for DSupt Trevor Wilkinson in its usual, unremarkable fashion. A review of the weekend revealed nothing of substance requiring his immediate attention. A consideration of his schedule for the forthcoming week was more noticeable for the gaps and the absence of any major criminal investigation to keep him occupied. A discussion with his immediate superior and divisional commander, Chief Superintendent Tom Moran showed that, apart from both men having spent a pleasant weekend without interruption by police business, Calderdale remained a generally quiet area so far as serious crime was concerned.

Rather than high drama there was standard office procedure. Wilkinson obtained a cup of coffee and his morning's post from the divisional offices secretary Angela Boyer. He exchanged chit-chat with her while she selected his pile of mail. It was readily apparent that most was merely the usual string of directives, opportunities for courses and internal police documents which made up the trivia of Wilkinson's life, but there stood out a large, brown envelope, heavier than anything else, and when Wilkinson opened it before leaving Boyer's desk, he saw that it contained a large file, and the name at the head of the file was Stefan Ivan Kiszko.

After the petition was served on the Home Office Mr Tom McCarthy from the C3 Division wrote to Chief Constable Peter Nobes of the West Yorkshire police, enclosing a copy of the document for his perusal. The home secretary, in considering what course of action to take, required the views of the West Yorkshire force, not least because of the allegations made against Dick Holland. The force was also asked to interview witnesses, old and new. Within the West Yorkshire force it had been the Calderdale

267

division which had been responsible for the initial investigation into Lesley Molseed's death, and when West Yorkshire's assistant chief constable Tom Cook met with the head of CID, Detective Chief Superintendent John Conboy, Mr Cook determined that it should be the Calderdale division who should carry out the investigations required by the Home Office, in response to Gregory's petition on Kiszko's behalf.

The decision was logical, given Calderdale's knowledge of the Molseed Case, albeit fifteen years earlier, but it was also arguable that to ask that division to investigate matters which included allegations against its own officers was a course fraught with danger. Quite clearly, had the officers charged with the new investigation found nothing further in the case, accusations of 'whitewash' would inevitably follow, and yet it would also be testing the loyalties of the investigating officers to require them to find fresh evidence, including evidence which might be used to support allegations of serious misconduct against colleagues and superior officers.

It was therefore an investigation of some delicacy and requiring a deal of tact and caution. The file was directed to be dealt with urgently, and the man placed in charge of the investigation was DSupt Trevor Wilkinson, of Halifax police.

Like the Molseed case itself, Wilkinson was a trans-Pennine transfer. He had been an officer in the CID of the Greater Manchester police at the time of Lesley's murder, and that force had played a substantial role in the investigation of her death because Rochdale was within the GMP's jurisdiction. Wilkinson had had some knowledge of the case, although the GMP role in the investigation had been substantially less than that of the West Yorkshire force, which had claimed jurisdiction because of the location of the body.

Promoted a year earlier, Wilkinson had transferred to the West Yorkshire police bringing twenty years' experience gained from the investigation of crime in the Greater Manchester area. He also brought with him a willingness to use scientific techniques which were within West Yorkshire police's artillery. Wilkinson's final qualification for the role were his own personal ambitions and the knowledge that this, potentially high profile, matter was an opportunity to make a name for himself in the county's police.

He would not be afraid to take that opportunity, even if, as he suspected, the investigation would achieve nothing to the benefit of Kiszko, but would more likely obtain further evidence to support the man's guilt. 'Rough justice' was the catch-phrase of the times, with a bandwagon waiting to be leapt on by anyone with a grudge against the police. The police had to be seen to take these cases seriously, but inevitably, more often than not, the justice that was found was not of the rough variety. He hoped that this would be so, aware that, were it not, he would become responsible for bringing embarrassment and shame, and perhaps criminal charges, upon brother police officers. He could not allow that thought to influence his actions, for he was aware that attitudes within the criminal justice system were changing, and that the police had also to be open to change. This was happening. Accountability was the watchword: taped interviews, codes of practice under PACE, supervision of junior officers, all intended to place the actions of the police under readily available and fully documented scrutiny.

Conversely, Wilkinson was enough of a 'copper' to know that, if evidence existed which would prove Kiszko's innocence, and that evidence was found during his investigation, this would mean that a killer had roamed free for fifteen years, and was still doing so.

Clutching the envelope containing the Kiskzo file, Wilkinson closed his office door and spread the papers on his desk. The first page was a minute dated 23 November 1990 from Detective Chief Superintendent John Conboy, the operational head of West Yorkshire criminal investigations department. It was addressed to Wilkinson and it was marked 'Confidential'. In the half-page which followed, Wilkinson read of discussions between ACC Tom Cook and Conboy himself, as to the 1975 murder of Lesley Molseed. The assistant chief constable had decided that a thorough investigation of the case be undertaken by Wilkinson. The investigation was to be detailed, but urgent. DCS Conboy was to receive regular updates as the enquiry progressed.

The nature of the enquiry Wilkinson was to glean from a letter of T. McCarthy of the Home Office to the chief constable of West Yorkshire, dated 7 November 1990, and from the petition drawn up by Jim Gregory which was annexed to the Home Office letter. The letter was merely a summary of the Kiszko/Molseed case, and there were annexed the statements of Dr D'Vaz and Maria Baran. It was, thought Wilkinson, fairly routine stuff, and he read nothing in the summary or the additional statements to cause him to think differently. He was curious, however, to see what the letter meant when it referred to Kiszko's 'extensive criticism of defence Counsel'. For the detail of that he opened the petition.

Headed 'Petition of Stefan Ivan Kiszko, Pursuant to Section 17 of the Criminal Appeal Act 1968', Gregory's document ran to seven pages. By way of introduction it outlined the character and history of Kiszko and gave some detail of the murder and its investigation. It mentioned Mrs Tong and it explained how Kiszko had confessed the crime but had steadfastly protested his innocence since that confession. The petition then analysed the case both for and against Kiszko before going on to criticise the process of the trial and, in particular, defence counsel's handling of that trial, notably the twin defences, the decision to allow the evidence of indecent exposure to be given at the trial and putting Kiszko's medical history before the jury which was, on any view, a double-edged sword. The matters raised in the Court of Appeal in the first appeal were repeated.

Wilkinson felt that he had yet to read anything of concern. There was a suggestion that the police had been oppressive in obtaining the confession, but the essence of the petition seemed to question whether Kiszko had been adequately represented and had received a fair trial. Such matters did not determine guilt or innocence, although they might concern the Court of Appeal. Certainly there was nothing in David Waddington's conduct of the defence case that could require a police investigation.

It was only when Wilkinson moved on to paragraph ten of the petition, dealing with fresh evidence, that he began to take a professional interest in the case. The so-called 'white-car' evidence had been described by Mr Justice Park as crucial, but Philip Clegg, junior counsel for the defence at Kiszko's trial and now a circuit judge, had told Jim Gregory that they had received Mrs Tong's statement only on the morning of the trial, and therefore without sufficient time to explore it further. They had also received, that day, the statements of Sandra Chapman and Donald Gledhill, and neither of those witnesses had been called, because there had not been the time to check their evidence against Mrs Tong's. Wilkinson realised that, had those three statements tallied in detail, Mr Justice Park would have summed up the evidence with even more force than he had done for Mrs Tong alone. Moreover, the police officer recognised, as had the judge, that if Tong was right, and Chapman and Gledhill were right, Lesley Molseed had been alive after the time at which Kiszko was alleged to have killed her, and was in a car quite unlike that driven by the convicted man. It was also quite apparent that the police had not managed to trace this white car and its owner:

that, in itself, caused a distant alarm bell to ring.

Wilkinson broke off from his reading. He had just seen that the police did have information concerning the sighting of a white car at the time and about the place of Lesley's disappearance, but had refused to disclose that information. The defence ought to have known of the existence of this information. Why had the defence not pressed for disclosure of the source of information? Why had they not sought an adjournment when they had received the Tong/Chapman/Gledhill statements, which were crucial to the primary defence of denial of the killing?[1] Although these queries implied criticism of the defence lawyers, they also questioned whether the police were even-handed in the case. In 1990s England there would have been no justification for a failure to disclose a source of information such as this.

Wilkinson scribbled a note concerning the white car: it was the first note he had written since opening the brown envelope.

The petition moved on to the alibi, noting that Anne Marie Griffin had given evidence that Kiszko had been in her mother's grocery shop at 1 p.m. on 5 October, but that the child had given her evidence badly. There was, however, annexed a statement from her mother, Maria Baran, confirming the alibi and detailing the police action, which included the advice that she would probably not be needed as a witness, so that it did not matter that she was due to be on holiday during the two weeks of the trial.

Wilkinson wrote a second note: to check whether Griffin and Baran had indeed made statements to the police.

Finally there was the statement of Dr D'Vaz, which explained how Kiszko had suffered a Potts fracture of his ankle, was overweight and had an awkward gait. The doctor said he could see no way in which Kiszko could have climbed up the banking to the scene of the crime. Wilkinson again made notes: Did the doctor make a statement in 1975? Who had shown him the lay-by? Had the lay-by changed since 1975? And the officer wondered why, as Dr D'Vaz made clear, he had not been called to give evidence.

The petition continued with a rigorous attack on Waddington's conducting of the trial, dealing with the dual defences and the juror incident in particular, as well as the failure to call Mrs Chapman and Mr Gledhill to help prove Kiszko's innocence, and

---

1 Wilkinson was unaware, at that time, that an application for an adjournment had been made by Waddington and turned down by the trial judge.

it concluded by setting out the principal grounds of appeal as being:

i   the pursuit of a defence of diminished responsibility without the express instructions of the defendant and in clear contradiction of his defence of alibi;

ii   the failure to conduct a 'trial within a trial' on the issue of the admissibility of the confession;

iii   the failure to seek the discharge of the woman juror who had overheard a court official saying that defence counsel had advised Kiszko to plead guilty;

iv   the failure to consult Kiszko on the issue of the juror.

Gregory had also asserted that fresh counsel ought to have argued the appeal, and he sought leave to adduce fresh evidence in the form of statements from Mrs Baran, Mr and Mrs Chapman, Mr Gledhill and Dr D'Vaz.

Certain that there were a number of matters which he could usefully investigate, Wilkinson decided that he would conduct the investigation with the assistance of one colleague only. It did appear to him that everyone associated with the trial and appeal was satisfied that Kiszko had been the killer of Lesley Molseed. He was not aware of how far his investigations would challenge that assumption. Wilkinson's preliminary view was that the Kiszko case pointed more to the inadequacies of lawyers than it did to any failings on the part of the police. He allowed himself a wry smile as he wondered whether any complaint of a miscarriage of justice by reason of the inadequacy of representation by David Waddington QC would receive the same media attention as an allegation of miscarriage of justice as a result of police error.

Wilkinson left the Kiszko file to attend a meeting at Wakefield police headquarters concerned with mundane matters of police administration, the lot of the senior officer, but as he left that meeting he encountered DS Tony Whittle, and fell into conversation with him. Whittle raised the Kiszko investigation, telling Wilkinson that he had worked on the case which had been 'sewn on' – proved, in police jargon – by the forensic evidence. Wilkinson left Wakefield wondering how he could have just read a confidential document and then, on the same morning, been engaged in a conversation about the confidential re-investigation by an officer who had worked on the case and who might well be touched by that investigation. Incidentally perhaps, he stored in his mind the assertion as to the 'sewn on' forensic evidence, and determined that that too would require investigation.

As if to indicate that he was not to be tarnished with any label of bias, Wilkinson's first move was to make contact with Kiszko's solicitor, Campbell Malone, to assure him that an investigation was taking place and to inform him that the police would need to interview people, such as Maria Baran, who were regarded as defence witnesses. Malone did not dissent. Wilkinson, perhaps with a premature assumption that he had already gained the solicitor's confidence, then asked whether the lawyer's client would cooperate with the investigation. Wilkinson was particularly keen to take advantage of the technique of DNA testing, the so-called genetic fingerprinting, which had not been available at the time of Stefan's trial. The technique would require a blood sample from Kiszko, but Wilkinson felt duty bound to advise the lawyer that, when Kiszko's blood was checked against the semen samples taken from Lesley's clothing, the result might as easily show Stefan to be the murderer as prove his innocence. Unlike any of the evidence at Kiszko's trial in 1976, DNA testing did not lie. Malone agreed immediately, although he was somewhat puzzled, because he had understood that the exhibits from the original trial had been destroyed. However, he was as adamant as his client that Stefan Kiszko had not killed the girl. They had nothing to fear from any DNA testing: the test would clear Stefan's name. It was as simple as that.

Malone then wrote to Stefan at Wakefield Prison to tell him of the police enquiry, but his client's reply indicated that Kiszko was more concerned about a proposal to transfer him to Ashworth Mental Hospital in Merseyside than with the news of police involvement. He wrote simply, 'I hope you and the detectives are getting somewhere.'

Malone found Kiszko very agitated when he visited him in March to obtain signed consent to the provision of blood for the police tests. Malone then took the authorities to Wilkinson's office in Halifax, and from there he went on to Charlotte's home in Rochdale. Malone had visited Mrs Kiszko many times, and each visit was the same. The frail, elderly lady would grip his arms and say, 'Please, please, please Mr Malone, get my son out of jail.' Malone always left feeling moved, a shade embarrassed and more determined. When he told her of the new police enquiry Charlotte

Kiszko advanced from the gripping of the lawyer's arms to embracing him fully.

The day following his meeting with Malone, Trevor Wilkinson drove five miles to the small town of Sowerby Bridge. He pulled into the yard of the town's stone-built police station, his objective, to pull Detective Sergeant John Mackerill from his routine duties. Although Mackerill did not know it, Wilkinson had faith in the sergeant's abilities and integrity, and he wanted him as his right-hand man for the investigation. In the two-hour meeting that followed, the two officers discussed the appropriate approach, and determined that the starting point was to find the original murder file and examine the confession. The other priority was to visit the forensic science unit to establish whether any of the exhibits from the case had been preserved. Wilkinson felt that, were any exhibits still in existence, advances made in the use of DNA fingerprinting might quickly wrap up the Kiszko case by proving the conviction to be right, however it had been achieved.

Mackerill went immediately to the local police headquarters in Halifax, in search of the murder file. With a certain amount of frustration he discovered that, whilst the file had been stored in Halifax for fourteen years since the trial, it had been moved two months earlier to Todmorden Police Station, 100 yards from the office of solicitor Campbell Malone. Even more frustrating was Mackerill's discovery that Lesley's blood-stained clothing had been destroyed, on the grounds that it was a potential health hazard. That is the usual fate of blood-stained materials.

At Todmorden Police Station, in an attic where it had been housed during some decorative works, Wilkinson and Mackerill found the Kiszko file, which Wilkinson removed. He spent the next five days studying the wealth of papers.

On 3 December the two officers drove to an appointment at the forensic science laboratory in Wetherby, where they were met by Robin Falconer, a forensic scientist, who had been a junior technician when the original tests were carried out in 1975 and 1976. Falconer had confirmed by phone that the laboratory still had the original file and boxes of samples, bringing a sense of relief to Mackerill who had been so disheartened by the loss of Lesley's clothing. Ronald Outteridge, the man who had supervised all the tests, had long since retired, but Falconer remembered him well.

Wilkinson took charge when they met the scientist and, having explained the new investigation which was to be mounted, asked

Falconer if it would be possible to carry out DNA testing on the original samples, notwithstanding their age. Falconer assured him that certain tests were still feasible, but that he remembered Kiszko's semen as being sterile, and there had been no sperm heads in the semen stains found on the child's clothing. This was a major blow to Wilkinson, as he knew that seminal fluid alone did not carry DNA characteristics, but that the DNA strands were carried in the sperm heads. If there were no sperm heads, there seemed little point in carrying out fresh tests.

Wilkinson could recall no forensic evidence being in the file which had been sent to the DPP, concerning the comparison of semen samples. In fact it was unusual for semen samples to be taken from offenders, and when Wilkinson asked Falconer why this had been done, he was told that it was probably to 'tighten up' the fact that no sperm heads had been found on Lesley's clothing. This was a disappointment in that it made DNA comparison impossible, and it still left unanswered the question of why the file to the DPP was silent.

The officers nevertheless examined the files held by the laboratory. Wilkinson, who never claimed to be a scientist but was quite sure of his abilities as a detective, saw something which caused him to pause, and then he felt sure that the investigation would not prove as straightforward as he and Mackerill had at first assumed.

As they turned to a section of the file dealing with semen staining on the girl's corpse, Wilkinson saw a handwritten jotting, to the effect that the semen staining had a + H sperm count. In other words, that the semen found on Lesley's clothing contained sperm heads that could be classified. Falconer, however, had told them that Kiszko was sterile, and they had believed that the seminal staining on Lesley's clothing was also free of sperm heads. Wilkinson put to Falconer that he had been wrong, and Falconer naturally admitted this possibility and agreed that this meant that DNA testing was now possible. Just as hopes were elevated, however, they came tumbling down again when the officers read in the same file that tests carried out on the handkerchief by Kiszko's bed showed his semen to be devoid of sperm heads, just as Falconer had believed. Extensive testing had been carried out on the semen on the handkerchief, according to the files. Yet, despite all the testing, no evidence concerning the comparison of the semen was apparent on the file sent to the DPP. Wilkinson thought it strange that so much effort had gone into attempting to find sperm heads.

The laboratory notes showed that a phone message about the handkerchief test had been relayed to the Rochdale murder room at a time when Ronald Outteridge was with Dibb and Holland, whilst Kiszko was being examined by Dr Tierney. Wilkinson knew from the file that Tierney had taken semen samples from Kiszko at Rochdale, but there were no test results on the official police file. Why was there no mention of the apparent discrepancy? Wilkinson made a mental note of this question, and instructed Falconer to secure the forensics file and keep it in a safe.

After examining the file, Falconer sorted through boxes of forensic slides, searching for those slides of the semen staining from Lesley's clothing. He was, however, unable to find the five slides for which he was looking, despite rechecking the file for the slides' reference number. He promised the officers that he would check the file against all the slides and make a search of the file store to ensure that there was not another box of slides.

As the two officers made their return journey to Halifax, Wilkinson thought that this was not merely a question of confirming the confession by DNA testing. Kiszko's medical condition in relation to his inability to produce sperm heads would have to be explored in some depth. Why had the sample been taken from Kiszko: it was the first case in twenty-five years as a police officer in which Wilkinson could recall such a sample being taken. And why, he continued to muse, if this unusual course had been taken, was there no record of the results of forensic tests carried out? And why were the five slides missing? And, finally, what did it mean if there were sperm heads on the semen sample found on Lesley's clothing, but none found in Stefan Kiszko's sample? Did it merely mean that a DNA comparison could not be achieved, or would it have some more substantial relevance?

With a certain amount of prescience, Wilkinson decided that he needed the assistance of a larger team to re-evaluate the entire case file. The files contained a vast amount of material which had to be considered swiftly. Kiszko's medical condition, in particular in relation to his ability to produce sperm was another matter requiring consideration, and the two fields could not be handled with sufficient expedition by only two police officers. He doubled his team to four, by bringing in Detective Inspector Desmond O'Boyle and Detective Constable Alison Rose. They reconstructed the original materials and documentation on which the original enquiry had been based, bringing in a fifth assistant in the form of a now-retired policewoman who had been part of

SOME OF MY BEST FRIENDS ARE POLICEMEN

the original murder team, who agreed to help.

In an attempt to give a quasi-legal framework to his task, Wilkinson tried to obtain a transcript of the trial and of Kiszko's failed 1978 appeal against conviction. He was unable to obtain the full transcript, which had been destroyed, but the public records office in London was able to provide a transcript of Mr Justice Park's summing-up, the value of which was that it contained a thorough review of the evidence which had convicted Kiszko. Other members of the team were assigned to trace the original witnesses and, in particular, the girls who claimed to have been able to identify Kiszko as the man who had indecently exposed himself to them, and those witnesses who had seen a white car in the lay-by.

There would not, Wilkinson knew, be opportunity to interview three witnesses at least. DCS Jack Dibb, DS John Akeroyd and DS Kenneth Godfrey, each of whom had played crucial roles in the initial investigation,[2] were now dead.

But, above all, Wilkinson's thoughts on how best to conduct his investigation inevitably and inexorably came back to the medical evidence and, in particular, the seminal fluid. He had received a major disappointment. Robin Falconer had contacted Wilkinson to inform him that, despite thorough searches, he had been unable to locate the five missing slides. The relevance in one respect was immediately apparent. There could be no DNA comparison of the semen found on Lesley and Stefan Kiszko's. There would be no quick 'fix' to this investigation. Wilkinson had examined the original file to the DPP and such of the original court papers as were still available, and nowhere was he able to find an indication that the conflict arising from the laboratory semen tests had been brought to the attention of the court.

Wilkinson went first to his station commander, Chief Superintendent Tom Moran, and was then referred on to ACC Tom Cook, and Wilkinson did not hesitate to proffer his opinion that material evidence had not been put before the jury, evidence which might have gone a long way towards proving that Stefan Kiszko had not killed Lesley Molseed. What had started as a courtesy to Kiszko's new lawyers, what had been anticipated as a mere exercise in confirmation of a man's guilt, had now taken on the volume of

---

2 It was to Akeroyd that Kiszko had, allegedly, blurted out his initial confession, when he and the officer had been alone in the police station. Gregory had been the exhibits officer in the case.

a major enquiry, and an enquiry shadowed by the possible revelation of police non-disclosure. It might have been tempting for Cook to appoint a neutral officer from another force to head up the enquiry, in order to preserve the integrity of the investigation, but he knew Wilkinson to be a recent import from Manchester, without any connection to the original murder squad, and so the assistant chief constable elected to remain with the officer who had detected the first cracks in the case against Kiszko, and trust him to carry out the investigation with honesty and principle.

Wilkinson left headquarters at Wakefield to return to his home station in Halifax. His professional life was now committed to the fat, waddling former tax man from Rochdale. It was a commitment which was to last for three years.

The fresh year of 1991 brought fresh impetus. Wilkinson's team visited Rochdale, and walked the route which it was supposed Lesley had taken on the way to her death. With plans and photographs from 1975 the officers were able to establish that little had changed physically since that year, and they were able, without difficulty, to find the house on Delamere Road, Vavasour Street, the shops Lesley had visited and the Kingsway school. The Molseeds still lived at Delamere Road. Charlotte Kiszko remained at Kings Road. Even the infamous lay-by remained largely undisturbed. It seemed as if time had not moved on, except for the people concerned.

With a full and adequate knowledge of the locations involved, the team now felt able to re-interview witnesses in a professional manner and with the ability to appreciate if any subtle changes in account were given. With all preparation in place Wilkinson set five principal tasks for his officers:

1 consider the medical evidence, both as to Kiszko's reproductive abilities and as to whether there was any merit in the assertion of Dr D'Vaz that Kiszko's physical/medical conditions at the time of the offence precluded him from abducting and killing Lesley;

2 investigate the sightings of the white car;

3 investigate the sightings of the blue van in the lay-by;

4 consider the alibi evidence, particularly that of Maria Baran;

5 check the veracity of Kiszko's signed statement.

What was clear to Wilkinson was that the areas of the petition dealing with the manner of the conduct of the defence were of no consequence to a police investigation and he was able to discard such matters from his considerations.

Dr David Anderson was a specialist in hormone treatment who, in 1975, had been treating Kiszko with Primoteston. The doctor had given the police a statement at the time of the trial, but he had not been called to give evidence. He was now a professor of endocrinology at Hope Hospital in Salford, which is where detectives Wilkinson and O'Boyle met him in February 1991. Although Wilkinson's experience of academics in general was that they were aloof and uncommunicative, in Professor Anderson's file- and blood sample-laden office the officers were given a cordial welcome. When asked if he remembered the Kiszko case the doctor astounded the police officers by leaping to his feet, announcing, 'Remember it, I'll never forget it. They crucified me in the press.' He was able immediately to locate his file on the Stefan Kiszko case, producing it from a desk drawer with a flourish, and then proceeding to empty its contents on to his desk.

There were a number of newspaper cuttings from the trial, each with a variation on a criticism of the professor. THE DOCTOR WHO TURNED MILD-MANNERED TAX CLERK INTO A MONSTER was one example, but the others were all along the same lines. Professor Anderson explained to the detectives that such was the press vilification that he was unlikely ever to forget the Kiszko case. He had been blamed in the press for prescribing testosterone to Kiszko, because he had been blamed in court for the same thing, and yet he had not been given the opportunity to appear in the witness box, to defend himself or to explain that the drugs he had prescribed to the defendant would not have had the effect ascribed to them. Those drugs could not have turned Kiszko into a savage sex monster. He had come to court and had spoken to both prosecuting and defence counsel, but he had not been called. The prosecution doubtless believed that he would remove an important strand of their case against Kiszko: that he was a sex-crazed monster. The defence, conversely, were probably afraid that he would remove part of their case as to diminished responsibility. The doctor had not been called because his evidence did not fit with the lawyers' arguments. What it fitted was the truth as Stefan expressed it: he was no monster; he did not kill the child.

Anderson explained the effect of the drug Primoteston. It could have made Kiszko more aggressive, but it would not have made him into a person who could have killed a child in a frenzy. The tendency was for the drug to exacerbate an existing aggressive tendency, not to create an aggressive tendency which had hitherto been absent. Professor Anderson considered that, in his absence from the courtroom, he had been misrepresented, and he would welcome an opportunity to put the record straight. In answer to Wilkinson's question as to whether the testosterone treatment would enable Kiszko to produce sperm heads, Anderson said that fertility was not relevant to the treatment at the time, the objective being to enable the patient to obtain an erection and to ejaculate. However, he thought it unlikely that Kiszko would ever be able to produce sperm. He told the officers that Kiszko had been examined by Dr Childs on 20 August 1975, and that the doctor had been unable to feel Kiszko's testes. In such cases where the testes cannot be felt in the scrotum the patient's sperm count is generally zero or very low, less than 500,000 per millilitre.

Wilkinson then asked the professor if he had been aware in 1975 that sperm had been found on the body of the child, and that Kiszko had produced semen which was free of sperm. The professor was shocked by this revelation, and declared that, had he been aware of those facts he would have said that it was extremely unlikely that it was Kiszko's semen on the child.

Professor Anderson was asked about his dealings with the police in 1975, and he asserted that the police had visited him at his work at the Manchester Royal Infirmary. He had told the officers that Kiszko had been referred with anaemia and was in a poor physical state, and was suffering from hypogonadism, a condition where the testicles are defective. He had prescribed Primoteston for Kiszko's hormone deficiency. Wilkinson then relayed to the professor a draft statement purporting to have been made by him. Anderson claimed never to have seen this statement, and that he had never signed such a statement. The statement had the doctor saying that testosterone caused a change in behaviour patterns and was usually accompanied by the person becoming aggressive and/or sexually deviant: in fairness to the police, the statement went on to state Dr Anderson's belief that the treatment would result 'only in an increase or potentiation of existing tendencies and not the arousal of previously uncharacteristic urges'. It went on to say, however, that it was possible for a man to ejaculate after a certain period of time, but only with a very low sperm count. Anderson said that he would not have signed this statement, as he did not fully agree with its content, and that whoever had composed it had misunderstood what he had said. A subsequent statement which took into account Anderson's objections was later signed by him.

At that point the officers chose to leave Professor Anderson, having asked him to keep their discussions to himself. As Wilkinson and O'Boyle drove back across the Pennines, Wilkinson considered the implications of the professor's account. He was a witness who could have destroyed the defence of diminished responsibility, but he was also a witness who denuded the prosecution case of its required feature of frenzied violence perpetrated against the child. He was a witness who added weight to the growing thought in Wilkinson's mind that there was a sinister undercurrent to the case of Stefan Kiszko: an undercurrent visible in the failure of police officers to get a witness to sign his statement, and in the evidence concerning sperm heads which was, potentially, completely fatal to the conviction of Stefan Kiszko.

It was, of course, the evidence concerning sperm which troubled Wilkinson the most. The semen sample from the child contained sperm heads. Kiszko was believed to be unable to produce sperm. How far was this true? Could Kiszko have produced a low sperm count (as found on the corpse) so soon after producing a completely blank or sperm-free ejaculate, such as was found on the handkerchief taken from his bedroom? Was it possible for the beginning of an ejaculated semen sample to be devoid of sperm, but then the middle or final part to have a small or low sperm count? Wilkinson could pose these questions, but he knew he required expertise to provide answers, and therefore an additional expert opinion would have to be sought.

Whilst Wilkinson and O'Boyle were exploring the medical and scientific aspects of the case, Mackerill and Rose were engaged in the more mundane, day-to-day task of checking civilian witnesses. Their labours speedily brought results.

They investigated first the white car, since the defence had suggested there was fresh evidence concerning it, and they re-interviewed Mrs Emma Tong, who despite attaining 82 years of age, remained adamant that the girl she had seen in the white car sixteen years earlier had been Lesley Molseed. The fact that Kiszko had been convicted had not caused her to change her mind. Nevertheless, the officers were obliged to conclude that, whilst Mrs Tong's sincerity could not be doubted, her evidence added nothing fresh to the case. The jury had clearly disbelieved her, almost certainly on the ground that her age meant she was mistaken.

DS Mackerill interviewed Leslie and Sandra Chapman, who claimed to have seen a white car at the lay-by on the Sunday afternoon. There was ambiguity between the Chapmans as to the direction in which the vehicle was facing, and Mackerill was obliged to conclude that this evidence was unhelpful and, in any event, did not amount to fresh evidence because Matthew Caswell had prepared a schedule of all sightings of all vehicles in the lay-by, which contained these sightings. It was not for the police to comment whether the defence had sight of this material in time for the trial. That they had the material at all was the only matter which the police felt obliged to deal with. They did observe, however, that the schedule had included Christopher Coverdale, who had seen a man assisting a small girl up the embankment. The girl had fitted Lesley's description, but the man described bore no resemblance to Kiszko. The defence had not called Coverdale as a witness at the trial.

There was even less success with the blue van. It had been investigated thoroughly and extensively in 1975 without success, and the defence had been aware of all steps taken in this respect. It was not a matter which the defence had chosen to pursue at the time of the trial. There was no fresh evidence available in 1991 concerning this vehicle.

Mackerill and Rose then turned their attentions to Kiszko's alibi. They re-interviewed Anne Marie Griffin, who had given evidence at the trial that Kiszko had been in her mother's shop on a Sunday afternoon in early October 1975. She had been unable to say whether it was 5 or 12 October, enabling her evidence to be easily dealt with by the Crown. However, she now claimed to be sure that it had been the fifth, by reference to an argument she had had with her mother and to an argument she had had with her boy-friend on the Saturday before. She also recalled her brother calling at the shop on the same Sunday, the day being her brother's birthday. Miss Griffin told the officers that she had discussed these matters with her mother, and that they had contacted the police who had not been to interview them until July 1976. She conceded that she had been unable to say whether the date had been the fifth or the twelfth, but blamed this on the police who had not asked her for detail, but only wanted to know the date. Likewise at the trial she had not been asked to develop in any detail how she had been able to ascertain the date. 'Both the prosecution and defence barrister,' she said, 'seemed to want to concentrate on my statement and cut me off short.' She confirmed that her mother had been on holiday at the time of the trial, that she had kept a diary record of the incident in the shop referred to at trial, and that Stefan Kiszko had been in her shop at between twelve noon and 12.30 p.m. on Sunday, 5 October 1975.

Maria Baran was interviewed at Peterborough on 25 February 1991. She was, perhaps, tainted by having known Kiszko for years and being unable to believe that he was capable of the crime alleged against him. That said, she had a diary entry detailing Kiszko's visit to the shop and, indeed, the conversation they had held. She explained that she was a diarist, and that it was usual to record the visits of friends. Mrs Baran had not mentioned the diary to the police at the time, an omission she limply explained as being due to forgetfulness. She had not remembered the diary even after Kiszko's conviction. It was not until 1984 that she had come across the 1975 diary again and, she explained, she had thrown it away in 1988 – two weeks before Kiszko's new legal representatives had contacted her.

However adamant the mother and daughter had seemed in their support of Kiszko's alibi, the officers were forced to report to Wilkinson that the new statements were tainted by passage of time, by a belief in Kiszko's innocence, by an obvious and admitted discussion between the witnesses and by the loss of the diary. Again, it could not be said that there was strong evidence probative of Kiszko's innocence, and neither statement fell into the category of fresh evidence.

Dr D'Vaz was taken to the scene of the killing and observed that he could see little possibility of Kiszko climbing the embankment. He could not say that such a task would be impossible, but, having regard to Kiszko's injured ankle, awkward gait, flat-footedness and excessive weight, it would have been exceedingly difficult to make the climb. There were alternative routes to the top, but the officers themselves noted that those routes were known only to people living in the immediate vicinity. Kiszko in his confession had said that he had climbed the embankment from the lay-by, and that he had not had to climb high. Dr D'Vaz said that he had not been asked, when giving his 1975 statement, as to Kiszko's ability to climb the embankment, nor had he been taken to view the embankment nor, of course, had he been called as a defence witness at the trial. In one sense there was nothing fresh about this evidence: Kiszko's account of climbing the embankment had been within the knowledge of the defence at the time of the trial, and it was known that George D'Vaz was Kiszko's GP.

As this phase of the investigation came to a close, Mackerill and Rose were obliged to conclude that, as regards the white car, the blue van and the alibi, they had been unable to trace anything which remotely approached the fresh evidence which the defence sought to introduce in the petition. Yet the doctor's assertion, based on a visit to the lay-by which he had not enjoyed at the time of the trial, gave Mackerill and Rose cause to persist in their enquiries.

Rose and Mackerill accordingly turned their attention to the allegations of indecency made against Kiszko, which he had in part admitted, in the hope that by disproving them Kiszko's confession to murder might also be thrown into doubt. In 1975, the girls who suggested that Kiszko had exposed himself to them had been children, teenagers giggling at the man and his 'thingy', excited by the police attention and not really afraid for their own safety. Now the officers would invest a great deal of time and effort in tracing those girls, who were now young women, to establish the degree to which they adhered to their 1975 evidence and, equally, to ascertain the full extent of the discrepancies between the accounts.

Catherine 'Kitty' Burke, now 31, was interviewed at Sowerby Bridge Police Station on 14 February 1991, and, surprisingly, she readily admitted that she had lied to the police in 1975. She maintained that there had been a man standing near to the clinic, but she said that Pamela (Hind) had claimed that night that the man had 'got his thing out'. Burke said that she had not seen an exposed penis, and when asked why she had then made a statement in which she spoke of the man dropping his trousers and exposing himself, she admitted that she had lied, but that she had just gone along with what Pamela Hind had said. She had not given evidence at the trial and she assured the officers that she never would have done so: 'I wouldn't have sworn on no Holy Bible,' she bleated to the police officers, before adding, 'I wish I'd never said owt. Will I get into trouble?' Doubtless with a feeling approaching astonishment, Mackerill and Rose moved on to the caravan site home of Pamela Clark, the former Pamela Hind, who had been Burke's cohort.

Pamela Hind, by then a married woman of 33, had taken Lesley Molseed to the youth club on Friday evening, 3 October 1975. She was a friend of the Molseed family. She was to tell Mackerill and

Rose that she 'must have got carried away' and said, 'I must have just gone along with what Kitty (Catherine Burke) was saying'. She said that she had not seen the man's penis at all, but that Kitty had run up to her and told her that she, Kitty, had seen the man with his penis exposed. She went on to admit that the man had not said, 'Come here let me ram this up you,' as she had said in her statement. She explained the account she had given in 1975 by saying, 'It was foolish but we were young and it was a confusing situation.' Pamela Hind had not given evidence at the trial of Kiszko, but her statement was read to the court. It was therefore undisputed evidence, but sixteen years later the grown-up woman told the police that, had she been called as a witness, she would not have lied, but would have told the truth, and she added, somewhat poignantly, 'After Lesley went missing it wasn't funny any more.'

Burke and Hind, after formal interview, were both cautioned for the offence committed by them in 1975. Both had been children at the time and there was little point in prosecuting them, sixteen years later. The third member of this unreliable triumvirate was Debbie Holt. As Debbie Brown she had, at 13, lied along with her friends: 'As a young girl,' she said, 'I had a vivid imagination and frequently made up stories about things.'

It must be observed, however, that Sheila Woodhead and Ann Marie Storto, both of whom had been 10 years old in 1975, stuck to the accounts they had then given, to the effect only that there had been a man in the shadows outside the youth club, as of course there had been on 3 October: Maurice Helm.

Maxine Buckley, who, through her mother's persistence had been the girl most responsible for bringing Kiszko to the attention of the police, now told Mackerill and Rose that she knew Stefan Kiszko, and he had not been the man who had been seen on 3 October.

Sarah Lord, who had given a description in 1975 which did not fit Kiszko, who alone amongst the girls had claimed to have seen a knife and who in 1976 had amended her statement by adding, for the first time, a reference to the man having a 'wobbling gait', claimed to have no recollection of the man's gait or any knife.

Beverley Mullins, now Auxley, who in 1975 had told the police first that the man was wearing a hooded mask with eye holes, then that he had been wearing a beret, was now unable to provide any assistance and, in particular, was unable to explain the differences in description.

Mackerill was obliged to conclude that there was no witness who would now say that a man with a knife had exposed himself to the girls on 3 October. That had been the crux of Kiszko's admission to the police, and it was, in 1991, without corroboration from any one source. Alison Rose had determined that the original statements of the children (including that of Colin Peers who had said that the man had a pair of binoculars) had not been disclosed to the defence to enable them to explore discrepancies and, of greater significance, she was to say that the defence had not been pointed to the statement of Maurice Helm, the milkman who had admitted relieving himself near the youth club, and who may well have been the man described by the various girls. Mr Helm's statement had merely been part of the substantial sheaf of papers handed to the defence on the morning the trial began.

When this information was brought to Wilkinson, it fuelled his growing belief that there had been, not merely a miscarriage of justice, but one in which the police had played a not insignificant part. There seemed to be some sort of cover-up concerning the evidence of the sperm. Anderson had not signed the statement which purported to be his view. Now Alison Rose had established that Kiszko had confessed to an offence which did not take place, and which had been falsely reported before Lesley's death. Dick Holland should have known (although it cannot be said with absolute certainty that he did know) of Maurice Helm's statement when he questioned Kiszko, yet he had permitted the suspect to make what had to be a false admission, and had then allowed that admission to be incorporated into Kiszko's statement and used against him at his trial for murder.

When Wilkinson was apprised of the reviewed evidence he began to believe that Kiskzo's confession was seriously flawed. David Waddington had introduced into the original trial the evidence concerning the indecent exposure. He had done so in order to convince the jury that that offence had not been committed. If the offence had not been committed, then Kiszko's admission to the offence must be false, which would cast serious doubt on the reliability and veracity of his confession to murder. At last, Trevor Wilkinson and his team were, perhaps inadvertently, showing that Waddington's tactic might have worked. On the basis of what Burke, Hind and Holt were now saying, there never was an offence of indecent exposure. Kiszko had, therefore, quite clearly made a false admission. There remained the question of why he had done so and, of equal importance, from where had he got the information to make the admission. If he had not committed the offence, the 'details' of that offence could only have originated from the interviewing officers – Akeroyd and Holland – who at that time had held the statements of the young girls. They had fed the girls' stories to the vulnerable Stefan, who would say what he had to so that he could return home to his mother.

Kiszko's admissions to murder could not be corroborated, especially as the import of the medical and forensic evidence was to the effect that Kiszko could not have been the man who ejaculated over Lesley. Kiszko's admission to the incident of 3 October 1975 was now provably false. And reliance on the 'detail' in Kiszko's statement as having corroborative effect was not appropriate, unless it was possible to show that no such details had leaked from the officers who had been kept privy to every aspect of the case, and all indications were to the effect that this might not have been the case. For example, a police officer from the Rochdale area not involved in the investigation had a divisional disciplinary finding recorded against him for disclosing information about the murder. His wife had been heard discussing the fact that semen had been found on Lesley's body, and the source of that information was traced back to her husband.

In an attempt to resolve, finally, the scientific investigation into the effect of the treatment on Kiszko's ability to produce sperm heads, Wilkinson took advice from Professor Anderson and made contact with Dr Paul Belchetz, a consultant physician and endocrinologist, and an expert on hypogonadism and the effects of testosterone. Dr Belchetz was based at Leeds General Infirmary, and he agreed to examine Kiszko to ascertain whether he had ever been capable of producing sperm.

At this time Wilkinson met Campbell Malone, Kiszko's solicitor, for the first time. It was intended to be nothing more than an introduction, and the officer kept the conversation to small talk, save for asking again whether Kiszko would agree to being examined and to provide a blood test, to which Malone agreed. Wilkinson did not at this stage inform the lawyer how the enquiries were progressing because he was aware that the re-investigation had set rumours running and he had no wish to amplify or encourage them.

To deal with the possibility that the rumours had reached Lesley's family, Wilkinson visited them and explained that the police were making enquiries, and that they should not be perturbed. April Molseed was surprised that Kiszko was still in prison; she believed that murderers were released after far less than the sixteen years Kiszko had thus far served. Whatever time had passed, Wilkinson observed, the Molseed family remained traumatised by their loss.

Wilkinson and O'Boyle passed through the portals of Wakefield Prison, and met the true object of their investigation for the first time: Stefan Ivan Kiszko. Sixteen years a prisoner, sixteen years of victimisation and abuse, sixteen years of unswerving belief in the system which had convicted him, sixteen years of unquenchable belief in his own innocence. 'I did not do it,' he protested to the visiting officers, just as he had protested to anyone else who had been willing to listen to him. But he was no longer the astute and intelligent tax clerk. He was diminished as a man, depleted as a person, and his obviously deteriorating psychological condition gave added impetus to Wilkinson in his desire to bring the investigation to a conclusion.

Mackerill and Rose continued to find success. Derek Hollos, the owner of the car registration number ADK 539 L, which had been found on a scrap of paper in Kiszko's car, and which had seemed to have such a conclusive effect on the mind of DSupt Holland as to Kiszko's guilt, was also traced. Mr Hollos had given evidence that he had driven past the lay-by on the afternoon of the abduction, enabling the prosecution to argue that Kiszko must have noted the number there and then. Kiszko had never been able to explain how he had come to make a note of that number, although he thought he had had an argument with the bespectacled driver of the car in a car park which Kiszko used when he went to work. Hollos was able to lead the police to the previous owner of the car, Albert Oldham. Although Mr Oldham could not recall any argument he confirmed that he had used the same car park as Stefan.

In the spring of 1991 Dr Belchetz received Home Office authorisation to visit and examine Kiszko. On Monday, 6 March 1991 Belchetz, a man more used to the sterility of the hospital and the quiet of the consulting room, met Stefan. The doctor's first impression was of a tall and very fat man, with bad teeth due, no doubt, to Kiszko's liking for sweets. In order to gain Stefan's confidence Dr Belchetz asked for a medical history, and he listened with interest. Kiszko was able to give an accurate chronological account of his illnesses, but this account was interspersed with paranoid and schizoid remarks and neologism. He was friendly and cooperative, occasionally forceful, but the doctor at no time felt threatened.

When the doctor came to physically examine Kiszko he found that his testes were of the size associated with a pre-pubescent boy, the right measuring 3mm and the left, 5mm.

When Dr Belchetz had concluded his examination he was able to incorporate his findings into a report for the police investigation team, but it was, perhaps, a single conclusion which stood out bold from the other matters. In 1975 Kiszko's testicles could not be felt by Dr Childs. When Dr Enoch had examined the defendant in 1976 the testes were scarcely palpable, and when Dr Belchetz had examined the prisoner he had found them to be tiny and of the size found in sexually immature boys. Dr Belchetz's conclusion was that there was no realistic possibility of Kiszko ever having produced sperm heads.

For Trevor Wilkinson, the implications of this conclusion were obvious: Stefan Kiszko could not have produced the sperm heads on Lesley Molseed's clothing. Stefan Kiszko had not ejaculated on to Lesley Molseed. Stefan Kiszko had not killed Lesley Molseed.

The medical opinion expressed to the trial jury differs from current medical expertise about the effects of testosterone treatment. Of more importance, the jurors had not been given the details of the discrepancy between the semen found on Lesley's clothes and the ejaculate produced by Kiszko. For the enquiry to be complete, Wilkinson knew he had to establish, in particular, why the semen and sperm evidence had been kept from the court.

He was virtually certain that Kiszko was an innocent man, and he knew that he had to act fast. First, because after nearly sixteen years' incarceration Kiszko's mental state was deteriorating rapidly and second because, if indeed Kiszko was innocent, then the man who had so brutally killed Lesley Molseed remained at large, and had done so for over fifteen years.

For complete certainty, Wilkinson wanted confirmation of Dr Belchetz's view that there was no reasonable possibility of Kiszko producing sperm. He wanted to retest Kiszko's semen. He visited Kiszko at Ashworth Hospital, Liverpool on 17 April 1991, taking with him DI O'Boyle. The police officers asked for Kiszko's drug treatment, which sedated him and suppressed any sex drive, to be withdrawn long enough for Stefan to be capable of sexual arousal, erection and ejaculation. Two days later they joined Kiszko in his secure room on Tennyson Ward. The officers carefully and patiently explained their mission, unsure to what extent he could take it in, but Stefan seemed to understand, for he told them 'I knew one day the police would prove it wasn't me.' Despite the vast experience of the two detectives, nothing in their past had prepared them for such an expression of blind faith in the police, from a man who had been incarcerated for sixteen years, perhaps by errors or impropriety by the very force of which these men were members.

Kiszko was left alone in his room with a plastic sample bottle. Locked in securely, he attempted to provide ejaculate to order. The officers paced the corridor for an hour until, at last, a knock indicated that he could be unlocked, but when the door swung open, Stefan stood, grasping an empty bottle with a sheepish grin across his face. 'I'm sorry, Mr Wilkinson,' he said, 'it must be blocked up.' Were it not for the gravity and importance of the situation, Wilkinson would have burst into laughter, but instead he tried to provide Stefan with reassurance, and explained again the significance of the task. The door was locked again, and again, an hour having passed, Kiszko emerged with an empty bottle and more apologies. Wilkinson knew he had to show nothing but understanding. Stefan was given time to eat lunch, and then to try again, but by 2.30 p.m. he had still failed to produce a sample. The officers consulted with ward staff and they concluded that tension was causing Kiszko's difficulties. Charge nurse Joseph Brown offered to give Kiszko two sample bottles each night, just before lock-up time. He would then telephone the police with a progress report. All staff were alerted to ensure that no one else offered to supply the samples for Kiszko, and the specimen containers themselves were kept secure all day.

Three days later at 7 a.m. Nurse Brown opened the door to a smiling Kiszko, who was clutching one specimen bottle and proudly announcing that he had produced a sample for Mr Wilkinson. That bottle was taken from him and placed under lock and key, until O'Boyle could drive from Halifax to Liverpool to collect the prized specimen. O'Boyle then delivered it directly to the pathology department of the Halifax Royal Infirmary for examination by scientific officer Martin Roulson and Alan Edwards, a consultant pathologist. The following day the sample was taken for further examination at Leeds General Infirmary. The test results were clear: Stefan Ivan Kiszko was unable to produce spermatozoa.

The samples were photographed in the laboratory for comparison with a normal semen sample, but Wilkinson wanted a categoric assurance before opening the investigation results to a wider stage. A second expert opinion was sought, from an eminent clinical consultant Dr Frederick Chung Wei Wu, a senior lecturer in endocrinology and reproductive medicine at Edinburgh University, and an internationally renowned endocrinologist with over fifteen years' study into male sexual development and fertility disorders, including the use and effects of testosterone treatment for male hypogonadism. In early May Wilkinson and O'Boyle flew to Scotland and presented all the available medical evidence to Dr Wu, including the most recent semen tests, although excluding the opinion of Dr Belchetz.

In due course, Dr Wu compiled a report which opened that it was extremely unlikely that Kiszko would ever have had the capacity to produce an ejaculate containing sperm heads, and it was equally unlikely that two 125mg injections of testosterone would have induced a sufficient degree of testicular function to produce an ejaculate containing sperm heads. The semen sample recently provided by Kiszko was entirely in keeping with this opinion.

The semen found on Lesley Molseed had contained sperm heads, albeit a low (+H) number. Dr Wu's report, of course, was crucial, for it showed not merely that Kiszko could not *now* produce spermatozoa, but that he would not have been able to do so in 1975. It was a conclusive opinion that Stefan Kiszko could not have ejaculated the semen sample which was found on the dead girl.

The officers were now convinced that Kiszko had not killed Lesley Molseed.

DSupt Wilkinson was not, however, prepared to leave the matter there, even if be did have enough, probably, to obtain Kiszko's release. He wanted the investigation to go a little further. He wanted to ask the question, why?

Ronald Outteridge, the forensic scientist involved in the original tests on the semen samples taken from the body and from Kiszko on his arrest, had retired by 1991, and was living in peace in Cambridgeshire. Outteridge agreed, however, to meet with the police at Wetherby. It was intended to be an informal interview, but Outteridge's demeanour alerted Wilkinson. Outteridge was defensive and aggressive under questioning: he extolled the virtues and integrity of Jack Dibb and, when Wilkinson pointed out the apparent anomalies discovered in the forensic finds between the semen found on the clothing and the sample provided by Kiszko, Outteridge began immediately to defend himself. He demanded to know what was being insinuated. Wilkinson desperately tried to calm the situation, assuring Outteridge that no allegations of malpractice were being made, but that it was necessary to examine the forensic findings in order to confirm that the results supported the admissions made by Kiszko.

Outteridge was asked to consult his original notes, and he told the investigating officers that he had been unaware of the defendant's medical background and had attributed no relevance to the absence of sperm in the semen sample he examined. He said that he had not requested a sample of semen to be obtained from Kiszko and he did not know why one had been obtained. He claimed no reports had been transmitted to the police at Rochdale relating to the presence or absence of sperm heads. No report was ever prepared of the examination of the Kiszko semen sample examined by Outteridge. In any event, he continued, he had always thought that any man could, occasionally, fail to produce sperm in semen, although he was not, he added, a medical person. He could not recall who had called for the sample, it had just arrived. Asked why he had not enquired why he was being asked to examine the semen sample from Kiszko, given that there was no DNA testing available at the time, Outteridge said he had not questioned his orders, he had just carried out his tests.

Outteridge's answers were intriguing. He claimed not to have examined the samples for sperm heads. He claimed he had not been told the purpose of the examination. He claimed not to know anything about the police view that the killer had a low sperm count. As Trevor Wilkinson asked Outteridge at the time, why did he not ask what he was meant to be looking for? Indeed, what *had* he been looking for when he examined those two semen samples? In the absence of DNA comparison, comparative features between semen samples were extremely limited. The visible, though microscopic, sperm heads would be the first comparative feature to search for.

Outteridge denied that he had been involved in a 'hunt for sperm heads', and added that there was nothing unusual in the making of fourteen slides of Kiszko's semen, nor of subjecting the semen to centrifugal examination, although both practical exercises could be seen as part of a search for sperm heads. He could offer no explanation as to why the five slides of semen taken from Lesley's clothing had gone missing, asserting that he had last seen them when he produced the evidence at Kiszko's trial.

Wilkinson also took the time to question Outteridge on the carpet fibres, and Outteridge confirmed, as he had said at the trial, that the fibres were not unique and would have been found on several carpets from the same manufacturer. As an isolated piece of evidence it was of limited value, but it did go some little way towards corroborating the assertion that Lesley had been in Kiszko's car. This much was acceptable, but Wilkinson wanted to question fibre transfer the other way: why had no fibres from Lesley's clothing been found in the car, even allowing for the fact that Kiszko would have had opportunity to clean his vehicle before his arrest. Outteridge said that he had only put in the evidence of the fibres because Kiszko had confessed. He accepted that he had been unable to trace the sources of other fibres found on the child. He admitted also that, without Kiszko's confession, the fibre evidence was valueless.

Wilkinson's disquiet at Outteridge's attitude had not abated by the time he prepared to leave. His misgivings were echoed in Outteridge's parting question, 'Where does this leave me now?'

Wilkinson drove back to Halifax with his mind in turmoil. He instinctively felt that Outteridge's account was inadequate, at least incomplete. He knew that he had not been told everything about the semen testing, and why it had been carried out. Time and again his mind returned to the only viable explanation: that Outteridge had been urged to find any trace of sperm heads, once the discrepancy between Kiszko's sample and the semen staining on the body had been discovered. If it had been discovered that there were sperm heads in the sample taken from the body, then it was critical to the case against Stefan to find at least some sperm heads in his semen sample. If that discovery had been made, and if Outteridge had embarked on a critical search for sperm, all fingers of suspicion would point only in one direction: Jack Dibb, who had originally headed the 1975 enquiry. Was Outteridge attempting to protect the memory of Dibb, a man whom he had known and believed to be of the utmost integrity?

In Halifax Wilkinson's team of four assembled to discuss the findings and their implications. The report was a bomb about to explode on the chief constable's desk. At present only the band of four was privy to a secret which, when revealed, would have far-reaching impact, far beyond the fat man who sat in his locked room away in Liverpool. It appeared to be unarguable that the case against Kiszko was, at least, seriously flawed. At best there had been oversight, something missed in a laboratory. At best there was a question of whether the conviction of Kiszko could be regarded as safe. At worst, Stefan Ivan Kiszko was completely innocent, and had been convicted by a coincidental combination of the stupidity of some teenage girls, the inability of the police in

1975 to trace certain leads to a conclusion, a misguided defence team of lawyers, and the concealment of a crucial piece of evidence which proved Kiszko's innocence beyond a shadow of a doubt.

One question still rankled: why had the semen sample been taken from Kiszko at all. This question hovered over the four officers, until an answering light appeared to DI O'Boyle, who suddenly realised that they had failed to ask the very man who had taken the sample from Kiszko at Rochdale, namely Dr Edward Tierney, the police surgeon. Dr Tierney readily agreed to meet DI O'Boyle, and he explained that he had been called to Rochdale to make a routine examination of a man then in custody on suspicion of murder. He had been told that the suspect had a number of health problems, and in the course of his routine examination he had ascertained that Kiszko suffered from hypogonadism and was being treated with testosterone. Tierney knew that hypogonadal men were unlikely to produce sperm heads. He was aware that semen had been found on the girl, and for that reason a semen test on Kiszko could be vital.

Tierney was a meticulous doctor and had kept his original notes. They revealed that he had told the police what he had planned to do and why, and although the notes did not record all the names of the officers with whom he had dealt, Dibb's name did appear. The case had, in any event, stuck in his mind, for it was only the second occasion in twenty-five years as a police surgeon that he had found it necessary to obtain a semen sample from a suspect. He had never been made aware of the test result in Kiszko's case.

This was the last stage in the investigative process. All materials were now gathered in by Wilkinson's team, including the report on Dr Tierney. After a careful review, the team concluded that they had sufficient new evidence to cast serious doubt upon the propriety of the original conviction and, indeed, that they were now probably able to prove Kiszko's innocence.

Wilkinson prepared a report which specified the actions taken and the conclusions which could be drawn. He outlined the results of the investigation and reviewed the other circumstantial evidence presented by the crown at Kiszko's trial. None of these matters had been relied on to stand alone as proof of guilt, but their cumulative effect in supporting the limited direct evidence of Kiszko's culpability, and in particular his confession, could not be overlooked. The sex books, sweets and balloons in Kiszko's possession could support the contention that he wished to abduct and use children for sexual purposes, even though Stefan's own innocent explanation was equally plausible. The felt-tip pen found at the scene could have been Kiszko's, but it had no distinguishing feature to show that it did belong to him. There were cuts on Kiszko's parka, but their relevance must be in doubt when no blood was found on the coat and, given the child's extensive and horrific injuries, it was very surprising that the coat had not received some blood splashing.

Wilkinson's view was that the new forensic and medical evidence cast serious doubts upon the validity of the confession of Stefan Ivan Kiszko, and, in turn, gave credence to his alibi. Kiszko had always denied making or signing the statement voluntarily. He had insisted that the content came from details he had gleaned from the police officers during interviews. He had confessed to relieve the pressure on him and in the belief that he would be allowed to go home.

The view of the investigators was that it was the authenticity of the confession, the very heart of the prosecution's case in 1976 and which had survived Waddington's ineffectual attacks, which now seemed to be in grave doubt. Kiszko had elicited sufficient information during his detention in the police station to make admissions which would satisfy the detectives who were interviewing him, and the method of interview at that time contained ample opportunity for police impropriety.

Dr Tierney's new statement seriously questioned whether the original investigative team were in fact aware of the significance of Kiszko's medical condition in relation to the semen left on the body, and chose, at best, to ignore the facts.

The confession was therefore provably flawed in two crucial respects:

i   Kiszko described an incident concerning an alleged indecent exposure which, by reason of the statements of Burke, Clark and Holt, it was now clear had not been committed, and about which Kiszko could not have known prior to his interrogation;

ii Kiszko could not have been the person who ejaculated over Lesley Molseed.

If the full circumstances concerning the indecent exposure allegation, the presence of sperm heads on the body and their absence in Kiszko's semen had been available to the defence, their attack on the validity and voluntariness of the confession would have been more full and more vital. The full evidence about the sperm heads was not put before the jury and, therefore, the conviction of Kiszko was unsafe.

This was the conclusion of Wilkinson's report, although it must be said that that conclusion, although entirely accurate, perhaps over-complicated the matter. Once it was clear that Kiszko could not have provided the ejaculated semen which was found on the girl's body, then it was proved beyond a shadow of a doubt that he was not the killer. The confession, the indecent exposure allegation, Dr D'Vaz's evidence about climbing grassy banks, the evidence about Kiszko writing down car numbers, even the alibi evidence, all of this was irrelevant. Kiszko was not Lesley's killer. He ought never to have been charged and, if charged, the case ought never to have been committed to the Crown Court. Stefan Ivan Kiszko ought never to have had to suffer a single day's incarceration and separation from his mother. He was innocent.

Wilkinson recommended that Kiszko be released on bail pending an appeal hearing, or that the home secretary declare the conviction unsafe and unsatisfactory and take appropriate steps to have Kiszko pardoned. Wilkinson blamed Kiszko's psychiatric illness on the prisoner's well-founded belief that he was wrongly convicted. Early release was essential to stop further mental anguish. Wilkinson went on to recommend an independent enquiry into the circumstances surrounding Kiszko's arrest and conviction.

Copies of Wilkinson's fifty-page report, with cross-references to the three large volumes of statements accumulated during the investigation by his team of three men and one woman officer, were handed to ACC Tom Cook and DCS John Conboy. Cook and Wilkinson then spent a day discussing the implications of the report.

They then arranged a conference with Chief Constable Peter Nobes and Deputy Chief Constable Paul Whitehouse at West Yorkshire police headquarters in Wakefield. They agreed to send a copy of their report to the Home Office, and that both Kiszko's solicitor and the Molseed family would have to be told the details of the investigation's findings. As to the investigation into this tragic miscarriage of justice, that required the appointment of an independent police force to consider the circumstances of Kiszko's arrest and conviction, and Paul Whitehouse was given the responsibility of establishing such an investigation. Independence would be an essential requirement or the name of the West

Yorkshire force would surface amongst allegations of impropriety, misconduct or worse.

On 22 May 1991 Campbell Malone was usefully employed in representing the usual collection of shoplifters, drunken drivers and street-fighters who make up the daily diet of any solicitor who earns his crust in the Salford Magistrates' Court, when he was given an urgent message to telephone DSupt Wilkinson urgently. The use of the word 'urgently' caused flutters in the stomach of a man not used to being apprehensive, but his uneasiness was quickly replaced by mild euphoria. Wilkinson told him that the police investigative team had completed their report and had submitted it the previous week to the Home Office. He explained that the so-called fresh evidence referred to in the petition had not stood up to close scrutiny, but that their own enquiries had revealed matters of real concern regarding the original police investigation. When Wilkinson said, without going into detail, that the report recommended that the Home Office take urgent steps, Malone was genuinely overjoyed. He was told finally that there had been an unfortunate leak to the London press from the Home Office, and that a press release was to be made at 1 p.m. that afternoon. The time had been chosen to give Malone time to inform Mrs Kiszko in advance.

Malone left court and drove immediately to Rochdale, with what would be the most heartening news that Charlotte Kiszko had received in fifteen years. The effect of fifteen years' incarceration on Stefan was obvious, but the burden of being Stefan's only true friend had weighed heavily on Charlotte, and she had aged and suffered with every set-back in the campaign to free him. Malone knew that, however Stefan took the news, Charlotte would be both overjoyed and relieved that her adamant refusal to accept her son's conviction had not been in vain.

As he was welcomed in to Charlotte's immaculate home, Malone's elation was dampened when he arrived to find Sue Hanson, a representative of Ashworth Psychiatric Hospital who was briefing Charlotte on her son's completed transfer to the hospital from Wakefield. Another bureaucratic move was being explained to the by now-weary mother, and she was accepting the information with no display of emotion. Malone realised that his own news outweighed the gravity of the hospital representative's, and that Charlotte needed to know that the battle was nearing an end. He was to grin sheepishly, as Charlotte Kiszko hugged the towering solicitor in the presence of Sue Hanson. Malone warned her of the impending press release, and advised her that she should refer any enquiries to his office.

From Rochdale, Malone returned to his office to telephone Stefan's psychiatrist at Ashworth, to ask that he tell Stefan of the breakthrough. His next call was to C3 at the Home Office where Mr McCarthy, although unwilling to make any comment whatsoever, said that the matter had been referred directly for the urgent attention of the minister, with an answer on a referral to the Court of Appeal expected within two weeks.

The press release issued by ACC Tom Cook that afternoon was to this effect:

> I can confirm that the West Yorkshire Police have been making enquiries into the murder of Lesley Molseed and the conviction of Stefan Kiszko, at the request of the Home Office. This follows representations made to the Home Office by Mr Kiszko's solicitors. A file has been sent to the Home Office for consideration by the Home Secretary.

Campbell Malone's recollection of that day remains vivid. He remembered visiting Kiszko to find him a very sick man, but the news which he had brought to his client definitely had a therapeutic effect. He says, 'From there I drove to Halifax and was given a fuller briefing on what had been uncovered by Trevor Wilkinson. As the detail unfolded I felt wholly exhilarated. I did not understand the full detail, but I realised there had been a significant breakthrough. I was delighted for Stefan, but at the same time absolutely appalled at what I had heard.'

Malone had not forgotten researcher David Geen and private detective Peter Jackson, whose own dogged belief that there had been a miscarriage of justice had so impressed him. They too reacted with a mixture of pleasure and satisfaction tinged with horror. Once the euphoria had subsided the three men wondered if what had happened so far could have been achieved much earlier. Malone certainly wished that he had carried out certain tasks more quickly. But more pressing now for Malone was the need to consider Kiszko's short- and medium-term future. A priority was to consult his client's doctors to see if and when Stefan would be well enough to be released on bail.

Campbell Malone now began to concentrate on Stefan's fitness for release, and on handling the inevitable appeal hearing. Once confirmation was received that the case was to be referred to the

Court of Appeal, Malone contacted the office of the Director of Public Prosecutions in an attempt to establish what stance the Crown would take at the appeal. He was frustrated by the DPP's unwillingness to discuss the matter with him, although it was indicated that they would not seek to oppose the evidence found by DSupt Wilkinson and his team.

Malone's reaction to the conversation with the DPP was to make the assumption that, as it was the forensic evidence which had brought about the referral, if the Crown accepted the new evidence the Crown's case against Kiszko would be untenable. In those circumstances the Crown would be unable to do anything to oppose the appeal, even if, as the DPP had put it, the Crown would leave it to the court to decide. Malone's reaction was to lodge a bail application, for until that was granted a nagging doubt would remain about the outcome of the case. He was not unduly worried, but the initial euphoria had been replaced by realism and he was aware that he was not yet out of the woods.

Travelling again to Ashworth Hospital, Malone explained the position to Stefan, who was responding well to medical treatment and who was intellectually capable of appreciating that he would soon realise his dream: that he would be released from jail without breaking the vow he had made, never to make a false admission of guilt simply to become eligible for parole.

In a letter dated 16 December 1991 Malone told Kiszko:

The court will, on the 20th of this month, hear an application for bail on your behalf and give directions as to the way in which your full appeal will be conducted.

At this stage it is very difficult to predict how the case will be heard, because the prosecution takes the view that, notwithstanding the fact that much of the fresh evidence has been obtained by the police, it is a matter for the Court as to the weight to be given to that evidence. I am hopeful that the prosecution will indicate that, certainly so far as the new forensic material is concerned, they agree that evidence and, if that is so, I anticipate the hearing of the appeal will be relatively short. If the prosecution give that indication then the prospects are that your chances of bail, subject to a condition that you reside at Prestwich Hospital, are good. However, if the prosecution gives no indication whatsoever, other than that they propose to test all the arguments before the Court, then we must assume every point in our appeal is

in dispute and must prepare for a full-scale battle. If that is
the indication from the prosecution then the Court will be
unlikely to grant bail. I am hopeful that the court and prosecution will take a common sense view of the overwhelming
forensic evidence that is now available, but I must ask you to
prepare yourself for disappointment because it is very rare
that the Court of Appeal grants bail pending an appeal
against conviction, particularly if somebody is serving a life
sentence.

For DSupt Wilkinson, convinced of Kiszko's wrongful imprisonment, the completion of the report was not the end of his task.
His conclusion contained an unavoidable consequence. If Stefan
had not killed Lesley Molseed then who had? He was detailed to
re-open the file on the case.

CHAPTER TWENTY-ONE

The Freeing of Stefan Kiszko

The three files of statements and Wilkinson's report dated 10 May 1991 were sent to the Home Office, accompanied by a letter from Tom Cook summarising the contents of the files. Had Cook's summary been given a banner headline reading KISZKO IS INNOCENT it is unlikely that the secretary of state for the Home Office would have moved with greater speed. It required a mere eighteen days for the Home Office to lodge the paperwork necessary for the appeal of Stefan Kiszko to be put in train with the registrar of criminal appeals.

At the same time, copies of the report were being received by two other lawyers. Campbell Malone got the first inkling of the results of Wilkinson's investigation when he received the report.

Diametrically opposed to Malone, Franz Muller QC read the papers in his chambers in the city of London. He had been appointed by the Crown Prosecution Service to advise on Kiszko's appeal, which would be heard by the Court of Appeal on 1 August 1991. A simplistic view of the case would be to regard the Crown's position as crystal clear. The Wilkinson report made Kiszko's innocence obvious, and the Crown, which had played no small part in securing the conviction in 1976, would be required to do nothing more than agree to his appeal being allowed. Franz Muller, however, would not take a simplistic approach to this, or any other case. He met in conference with representatives of the CPS, and with Tom Cook and Trevor Wilkinson, who had travelled from Yorkshire, bringing copies of their files with them.

It would be a serious matter for the Crown not to seek to defend the propriety of Kiszko's conviction, explained Mr Muller. Before that step could be taken it was essential to resolve any weakness in the medical evidence, particularly as the confession and circumstantial evidence built a powerful case against Kiszko. Wilkinson noted the lawyer's reservations, and responded that three endocrinologists had, verbally, expressed no doubts that Kiszko had always been incapable of producing sperm heads. Professional caution had lead Dr Belchetz to use the expression 'no realistic possibility' and Dr Wu had said that sperm production was 'highly unlikely'. Muller advised certain further points of action for Wilkinson to attend to, to tighten the new forensic and medical findings and to provide a comprehensive analysis of all the statements taken relating to the alleged indecent exposure incident of Friday, 3 October 1975.

Franz Muller met Dr Belchetz, and the question of the effect of testosterone treatment on sperm production was raised. Belchetz recommended that the Crown consult the acknowledged authority in this field, Dr Richard Sharpe of the Medical Research Council reproductive biology unit in Edinburgh. A solicitor from the CPS wrote to Dr Sharpe requesting his opinion on Kiszko's ability to produce sperm heads following testosterone treatment. Sharpe was provided with all the original medical and forensic findings, as well as the new findings, subject only to the deletion of the other doctors' conclusions. Dr Sharpe also had the benefit of the trial judge's summing-up of the medical evidence at the trial.

Richard Sharpe's response was that Kiszko's testes measured 3 to 4 mm in 1975. Normal adult males have a testicular size of 15 to 20 mm, and the expansion in size is what enables sperm to be produced. Kiszko's small testicular size meant that the man had never made sperm and never would. His small testes were due to an abnormality in development as evidenced by his subnormal blood testosterone level and his under-virilisation. A failure of testicular descent before puberty would cause infertility due to azoospermia.

As to the effects of testosterone treatment on hypogonadal patients, Dr Sharpe reported that such treatment had been shown to have no ability to induce sperm production in pre-pubescent boys. It had been possible to administer high doses of testosterone to adult animals so as to induce sperm production, but the doses involved were some ten to twenty times higher than those administered to Kiszko. It was therefore remotely possible that the administration of a considerably smaller dose of testosterone to Kiszko might enable him to produce a few sperm. However, Dr Sharpe regarded this possibility as an irrelevance. The 'root' of a sperm head is a cell called a spermatogonia, which develops through a number of stages before becoming a spermatozoon. The time taken for this development exceeds ten weeks, and that duration is constant and invariable. There is no known way in which the duration can be shortened. The significance to Kiszko was that he received his first injection of Primoteston twenty-four days prior to Lesley's murder. It was absolutely impossible that testosterone treatment could have induced sperm production to the point at which they would have been present in semen ejaculated on to Lesley on 5 October.

Dr Sharpe therefore concluded that the absence of sperm from Kiszko's semen meant that it was impossible for him to have been the source of the semen on Lesley Molseed's clothing. He explained to Wilkinson in a telephone conversation that his concession of the possibility of Kiszko producing sperm was nothing more than an allowance for a freak of nature. He was in no doubt that Kiszko had never in his life produced sperm.

On 20 September Wilkinson attended a conference with Professor Anderson, Jim Gregory and Campbell Malone, at which the full implications of the new findings were explained. Following the conference Anderson produced a further statement which set out his opinion that Kiszko had always been azoospermic and that the sperm found on Lesley's clothing had not been produced by him.

With the benefit of these additional statements Franz Muller was able to express a conclusive opinion to the CPS, that there was no realistic prospect of supporting the conviction of Stefan Ivan Kiszko for the murder of Lesley Molseed.

On Monday, 17 and Tuesday, 18 February 1992 the appeal was heard at the Central Criminal Court in London. Franz Muller QC and William Boyce appeared for the Crown, Stephen Sedley QC and Jim Gregory for Kiszko. Central to the appeal were the medical findings, proving beyond reasonable doubt that Stefan Kiszko had not been Lesley Molseed's killer. The appellant's counsel, however, were obliged to pursue those grounds of the petition which were critical of the then defence team. It was, however, lip service, and the court were able to disparage that aspect of the appeal with the assertion that they had no doubt that David Waddington QC MP, the present Home Secretary, had at all times acted in the best interests of his lay client.

The result of the appeal was a foregone conclusion in view of the Crown's lack of opposition. Indeed, as the prospects of a successful appeal had become apparent medical staff at Ashworth Special Hospital had begun to consider a way forward for their patient should he be 'freed' by the Court of Appeal. In August 1992 a psychiatrist from the medium secure unit at Prestwich

Hospital in Manchester had advised that Kiszko should be taken out of a maximum security environment and into one of medium security should the appeal be successful. In accordance with this advice, on 8 January 1992 Stefan Kiszko was, pending his appeal hearing granted bail, of sorts. He was transferred from Ashworth to Prestwich Hospital, ten miles down the road from Charlotte's home in Rochdale. Her marathon treks around the country were now at an end.

On 18 February 1992 the Court of Appeal allowed Kiszko's appeal against his conviction for the murder of Lesley Molseed. His appeal was not allowed simply because of a mistake in law by the trial judge, or because of any other reason which might cause the Court of Appeal to overturn a conviction as being 'unsafe'. In Stefan Kiszko's case the allowing of his appeal was on one single basis: Stefan Kiszko was innocent. Lord Chief Justice Lane made this abundantly clear when he said:

> [I]t has been shown that this man cannot produce sperm. This man therefore cannot have been the person responsible for ejaculating over the little girl's knickers and skirt, and consequently *cannot have been the murderer*.[1]

On that same day Peter Taylor QC, whose prosecution of Kiszko could not be faulted, was appointed, to succeed Lord Lane, as Lord Chief Justice Taylor of Gosforth, making him the highest ranking judge of criminal law in England and Wales.

Stephen Sedley QC, Stefan's barrister, had, at the conclusion of the successful appeal, applied for his client's costs. He had expressed to the court uncertainty as to whom his application should be made: should it be out of central funds (a central government body, which pays costs where no 'fault' is found in the conduct of the case) or against the police. In asking the court to deal with his application he said that the question of who should pay costs would depend on the court's view of who was responsible for the miscarriage of justice: 'That would depend,' he said 'upon whether your Lordships' view was that this was one of those things or that there has been some failure in the early conduct of the prosecution.'

The Lord Chief Justice replied, 'We think central funds, without any doubt,' and he therefore refused to ascribe blame to any party.

---

1 Authors' italics.

For Stefan Kiszko in Prestwich, it was just another day. He was innocent, and he was technically free, but his mind had endured the punishment of sixteen years' false imprisonment. No one but he could understand how he had suffered. The lawyers could pat each other on the back, or heave sighs of relief, depending on their position. Trevor Wilkinson could rightly bask in the glory he and his team richly deserved for enabling a terrible wrong to be righted. Those who were to be the subject of the Lancashire Constabulary's investigation into the conduct of the West Yorkshire police could consider how that enquiry would affect them.

But for a fat, balding, waddling former tax clerk, left with bad teeth and a befuddled mind after sixteen years' incarceration, who was the recipient of the most gifts that day but was unable to enjoy them . . . it was just another day.

CHAPTER TWENTY-TWO

Who Killed Lesley Molseed?

Trevor Wilkinson's involvement in the Kiszko enquiry showed him the necessity of having sufficient men working on the various actions, and he enlarged his original team of four for the new investigation into Lesley's murder. Throughout Wilkinson's work on the Kiszko case he had retained his responsibilities as a divisional detective, and in that regard he had come into contact with Detective Chief Inspector Bernard Browse, the head of Dewsbury sub-divisional CID. The two men had worked on a number of suspicious deaths and one murder together, and Wilkinson had a high regard for Browse's detective and organisational abilities. He had no hesitation in approaching the detective chief inspector to be his deputy, running the day-to-day aspects of the enquiry and managing the incident room.

Nine months were spent analysing the thousands of actions, reports, documents and statements which made up the bulk of the original murder enquiry documentation, and by the time of the press release informing the country that a new investigation would take place, Wilkinson already had in operation a small team of detectives with clerical and computer support, which had reconstructed the majority of the original enquiry.

Wilkinson started his investigation to try to find Lesley Molseed's true killer with, effectively, a blank sheet of paper. In practical terms it meant nothing more than that the detective superintendent had no preconceived ideas about whom to investigate and how the investigation should be carried out. In real terms, however, the officer had a wealth of information, elicited from both the original and subsequent 'Kiszko enquiries' which could be put to good use. Importantly, the reconstruction of the original enquiry meant that Wilkinson's team could take up the investigation where Holland's team had left off. Holland's team had been lead up an alley by the indecent exposure allegations, that alley leading the police to Kiszko. If Wilkinson began his journey of investigation at the beginning of the alley, he could retain and rely on all that was positive about the Holland investigation, without being misled by what had subsequently been shown to be irrelevant.

The two senior detectives also had an additional line of investigation, unavailable to those involved originally. It is believed that most sex offenders are also serial offenders, and it was therefore considered that Lesley Molseed's killer had either offended since the killing, and been caught, or could be responsible for a series of undetected or unsolved offences. The antecedents of every suspect and witness were therefore checked for relevant convictions since 1975.

While sorting through a box of reports, John Mackerill came across a large manila folder marked 'In the event of re-investigation – The main six suspects'. Mackerill's excitement at finding what he believed to be the alleyways which Holland had chosen not to travel was short-lived. Although the envelope contained a detailed file on six known sexual offenders who lived within the proximity of the Turf Hill Estate and who had not been fully eliminated in 1975, when Mackerill and his fellow team members managed to locate and interview the six men, each was able to be eliminated from the enquiry.

Other leads left over from 1975 were, in descending order of importance, the white car with red primer on the wheel arches, the turquoise Morris 1000 van and the sighting of a man leading a small child up the embankment on to the moors. The first could be crucial, if Mrs Tong was right about seeing Lesley in that car on the Sunday lunch-time, and if there was anything in the accounts of Mr and Mrs Chapman and Mr Gledhill, of seeing such a car at the lay-by that afternoon. The second was important because of the numerous sightings of a Morris 1000 van at the lay-by on the Sunday afternoon, and because of the failure of the police in 1975 to trace that vehicle. The man climbing the embankment with the child was almost certainly the killer of Lesley Molseed, unless she had been abducted and killed by a person who knew the area surrounding the lay-by so well as to be able to find an alternative route to the steep banking. DC Cooper, in charge of the enquiry into the blue van in 1975, believed then and subsequently that the driver had been Lesley's killer.

In an attempt to give impetus to the investigation, BBC's *Crimewatch* programme offered its assistance. Wilkinson supported the making of a reconstruction of Lesley's movements and abduction and the taking of the child to the place where her life was to end. The reconstruction, however, produced no concrete results when the programme was shown.

It was whilst scrutinising a box of documents that WDC Alison Rose read action number 588, which concerned the interview of a Todmorden man by Detective Sergeant David Paxton, prior to Kiszko's arrest. Once Kiszko had been charged with murder the investigation had been halted, and all uncompleted lines of enquiry, including those into this man, were left in abeyance.

It was, to say the least, unfortunate that the enquiry of Paxton had been abandoned. Sergeant Paxton had indicated that he was unhappy about his 'suspect' and that further enquiries should be made. The officer's concerns arose, not least, from the fact that the man had a previous conviction for a sexually motivated offence, but also from the knowledge that he had owned a Morris 1000 van.

The man's name was Raymond Hewlett.

Born in Blackpool on 24 January 1945, Raymond Hewlett was the second youngest child of a family of seven. His father, who was in the armed forces, was a strict disciplinarian who showed little affection towards his wife or his children. He set high standards and had expectations of his children which Raymond was unable to attain. Raymond enjoyed a good relationship with his mother, although her health was poor, which caused him to miss a great deal of his education whilst he cared for her. He left school at 15 without qualifications, then held a short apprenticeship as a welder, a position he abandoned after six months. In 1961, at the insistence of his father, he joined the Scots Guards, an experience he disliked because of what he perceived to be the brutality of the regime. After nine months he was discharged, facing charges for causing disorder, being absent without leave and stealing a regimental bicycle. When his father heard of Raymond's dishonorable discharge, he ordered his son not to return home.

Hewlett spent the next twelve months wandering the country, finally settling in the West Yorkshire community of Todmorden where, at 17, he found employment as a miner and as an agricultural labourer, and where he made his first of many court appearances, for assault.

He married Susan Ginley in 1963. Over the next five years she was to give him four children whilst he was to give her increasingly long breaks from his attentions, as he spent more and more time in prison, for offences ranging from dishonesty to possession of a firearm. He enjoyed a variety of employments, as a fairground worker and then an electro-plater, until 1972, when he committed the offence which had brought him to the attention of the police first investigating the death of Lesley Molseed.

On 19 September 1972 at about eight thirty in the morning, Hewlett's neighbour's daughter, aged 12, was walking to school with a friend. Hewlett drew alongside the girls in a maroon car, sounding his horn to attract their attention. The girl was told by Hewlett that her mother wanted to see her urgently as she was upset, and the girl, believing that her father had attacked her mother, got into the car. After travelling a short distance Hewlett pulled into a petrol station, returning with a large canister which, he said, contained a liquid he needed for stripping paint. He set off again, and the child realised that they were going the wrong way, but Hewlett reassured her by saying that it was a short cut.

At the top of a moorland road the car was stopped, and the girl, realising that something was not right, said she wanted to go to school and attempted to get out of the car. Hewlett grabbed the child, pinning her to the floor and placing a rag soaked with thinners over her face. He told her to be calm, that he was not going to hurt her. Then she lost consciousness. When she awoke she was naked on the back seat of the car. Hewlett told her to dress and said that if she told anyone, including her parents or the police, he would hunt her down and kill her. She was terrified, but when she arrived at school she lied about her lateness and told nobody about the abduction, until later in the day when she confided in a school friend, saying, 'A man has tried to kill me.' The girlfriend insisted that the teachers be told, but even then the girl was not believed, although she was sent home sick. That evening, when the child was put to bed, her mother observed blisters and a rash on her face, and she was unable to sleep, being tormented by the vision of Hewlett's face and the white rag he had used to cover her eyes. By now sobbing uncontrollably, she cried out to her mother, 'Ray next door tried to kill me. I woke up with no clothes on.'

Eventually the child's mother was able to calm her down, and get a clear story of what had happened. That story was duly reported to the child's father who went next door and confronted Susan Hewlett. Raymond was out. The police were called and an investigation proceeded, medical evidence revealing that intercourse had taken place and semen, containing sperm, was present. A white rag dipped in thinners was found on the moor and, after a week of hiding in his attic, Hewlett was arrested when his wife informed the police of his whereabouts. In interview Hewlett insisted that the girl's eyes had been open throughout, and that she had consented to intercourse, but on 15 January 1973 at Leeds Crown Court, he admitted stupefying the girl to enable intercourse. He served twelve months of an eighteen-month sentence before returning to Todmorden.

Armed with this information DS Paxton had visited Hewlett's address only to be told by Susan that her husband had left the area shortly after the discovery of Lesley Molseed's body.

On 7 November 1975 Paxton had been able to interview Hewlett at Burnley Police Station, where he had been held having been arrested for theft. Hewlett told Paxton that he had travelled to Scotland on 20 September 1975 in a car he had stolen from Morecambe, together with his brother-in-law Martin Ginley and two friends, John and Michael Goodall. They had only reached Lachgilfield in Ayrshire when they were all arrested and charged with breaking into caravans. They were remanded in Barlinne Prison until 25 September when they were bailed to attend court on 6 November. He had returned home by train. He went on to say that, on Sunday, 5 October 1975 he was at home with his wife until 2 p.m., when he went out for a walk in Central Vale Park, Todmorden, with a girl named Rosalie Dolan, his under-age lover, though Hewlett kept this fact from Paxton. They had been together in the park until 5 p.m. that afternoon, and Hewlett claimed that he remembered meeting a man who had owned the model shop on Halifax Road. He had gone to the home of a friend, Gerald Shawcross, until 6.30 p.m. when he returned home.

Paxton had considered it suspicious that Hewlett was able to account his movements for the Sunday in such detail, but was unable to provide any particulars of what he had done on the Monday, Tuesday or Wednesday. Hewlett's explanation as to why he had left the Todmorden area so soon after the killing was that he had left for southern Ireland on the following Friday, with Rosalie Dolan, remaining in Ireland until 24 October 1975, when he returned to his wife.

Hewlett had told Paxton that the Morris 1000 van had been obtained in Scotland. It had been a blue ex-GPO van and he had swapped a Hillman Imp for the van, before Martin Ginley had sold the van for £10. He described the van as being scruffy with a tendency to leak oil. It had no rear seats and had a piece of tin riveted to the door on the passenger side. He was unable to say who had the vehicle on 5 October 1975.

DS Paxton had recorded these details in a statement, and he had also been able to establish that Martin Ginley had appeared in court in Scotland on 5 November, and was now detained in Barlinne Prison.

Other parts of Hewlett's story had also received confirmation. Susan Hewlett had told Paxton that their domestic circumstances were troubled, so that Raymond would often go off for weeks at a time. She had limited knowledge of the blue van: she thought that her brother had sold it without Raymond knowing. Rosalie Dolan, then 15, had confirmed Hewlett's alibi. She gave details of several of Hewlett's vehicles, but she made no mention of the blue van. Gerald Shawcross had confirmed Hewlett's visit to his house, although he was unable to recall the date.

All of the above information had been recorded by Paxton against Hewlett's name. He had requested that Ginley be interviewed at Barlinne, since he was not content with Hewlett's account, but when news came through of Stefan Kiszko having been charged, the request to interview Ginley was cancelled.

Hewlett, following his interviews with Paxton, appeared at Wyre District Magistrates' Court for the matters of dishonesty. Sentence was deferred, but he then appeared in Scotland in connection with the matters with Martin Ginley, whom he was soon to join when he received a three-month sentence on 20 November 1975. By the time he was released and could return to Todmorden in January 1976, Kiszko had been arrested, interviewed and charged with the murder of Lesley Molseed.

After discovering this much about Hewlett from the records of the investigation in 1975, WDC Rose went on to research Hewlett's criminal antecedents in the period that Stefan Kiszko had been in jail. She discovered evidence that confirmed her unease, and supported the theory that Lesley Molseed's killer was likely to be a man with a proclivity for sexual offences against young girls.

At 7.45 a.m. on 24 April 1978 Hewlett had made a telephone call to a family home in Stansfield Street, Todmorden. To the 14-year-old girl who answered the phone he claimed to be a union official wishing to speak to her father, but when the child informed him that her father would be at work until 5 p.m., Hewlett ended the conversation and promptly drove to the house in a van. The girl opened the door to him and was informed that he had a parcel for her mother. The girl knew Hewlett by sight, and allowed him in to the kitchen. He asked for a drink of water, and she turned her back on him to get it, but then felt something prodding her in the back. As she turned she found Hewlett pointing a handgun at her face. He told her not to do anything stupid and she would not be hurt, he wanted only money. The girl was terrified and crying, and Hewlett forced her upstairs and made her lie on the bed. He was in the process of undressing her when the child, believing that she was about to be raped, told Hewlett that she was expecting friends to call, and that the neighbours would hear, whereupon Hewlett stopped what he was doing and ordered her to dress, and to tell nobody of what had happened. The threat was insufficient to prevent the girl reporting the offence, and in due course Hewlett was arrested and admitted his guilt, asserting that he had changed his mind about having intercourse and had wanted only money.

At his trial, Hewlett's defence counsel Michael Lightfoot submitted in mitigation that Hewlett had suffered during his previous prison sentence because he had been jailed for a sexual offence. He had continued to suffer, for the same reasons, when he had returned to Todmorden at the end of his sentence. In 1975 he had been implicated as the prime suspect in the savage killing of a girl in Ripponden, an offence of which he was innocent and of which he had been 'exonerated by the police'. He had nevertheless been subjected to such unpleasantness in Todmorden that he had been obliged to move himself and his family to Bacup. Hewlett apologised for the present offence, explaining, through his counsel, that he had written to the girl's parents expressing remorse for the anguish he had caused.

Hewlett was sentenced to four years' imprisonment, serving sixteen months before being released, to move his family to Telford. He found work, but after five months left, citing ill health.

In 1980 Hewlett left his long-suffering wife for a woman named Anita, whom he had met when he had gone to buy a car from Anita's husband. The relationship resulted in two children, and they married in 1982, notwithstanding that Hewlett had subjected her to several vicious physical assaults throughout their relationship. In 1987 Hewlett had assaulted a social worker attached to the family when she had visited the house.

WDC Rose read on. On the first day of January 1988, at 7.30 a.m. Hewlett had kidnapped a 14-year-old girl on a paper-round at knife point on the Valley Lane Estate in Northwich, driving her fifty miles to a quarry near Llangollen, North Wales. 'You know what is going to happen to you now,' he had said, and the girl had said that she did know, that he had no need to use the knife, and that she would comply. She had undressed and Hewlett, having removed his trousers, began to indecently assault her, but without making any attempt to have intercourse with her. After only a few minutes he had rolled off her, telling her to dress. He had then bundled her into the boot of his car and driven a further fifty miles to another quarry, at Festiniog, North Wales, where he abandoned her at ten thirty in the morning.

The girl's absence had already caused a major search to be put into operation. Hewlett, however, had fled back to Telford and then to Ireland, but enquiries at and near his home soon revealed him to be the offender. Forensic evidence provided a link with his car, and semen found on the girl and on her jeans indicated that Hewlett had prematurely ejaculated over his victim, which accounted for why she had not suffered further violation.

WDC Rose read the detail of Hewlett's 1988 offence, knowing that one aspect of the circumstances was of great importance to her investigation. She was alerted by the premature ejaculation, recalling that Lesley Molseed had not been sexually assaulted, but that her attacker had ejaculated over her clothing.

Hewlett had returned to Telford and admitted the facts of the offence, asserting that the girl had willingly gone with him. The character of the girl provided ample contradiction of this: she was highly intelligent and extremely reserved, having had no previous boyfriends or sexual experience.

On 24 June 1988 at Mold Crown Court, Hewlett had been sentenced to six years' imprisonment for kidnapping and indecently assaulting the girl. He had not, however, completed his sentence, for, granted home leave from Stoken Prison in Leicestershire on 6 December 1990, Hewlett had gone, as instructed, to a hotel in Telford, but after two nights there he had absconded and was still unlawfully at large.

The history WDC Rose had read, the method of luring or forcing young girls into cars, the use of a weapon – notably a knife in the last incident – and the premature ejaculation caused WDC Rose to believe that Raymond Hewlett, whatever his alibi for Sunday, 5 October 1975, was a prime suspect in Lesley Molseed's killing. She determined to resume the enquiries started and abandoned by DS Paxton in 1975.

She first traced Martin Ginley who agreed to speak of his friendship with his brother-in-law who, not having a driving licence, was regularly chased by the police, which led him to buy and sell his cars with some frequency. Ginley could not remember Hewlett having a Morris 1000 van, nor could he recall, as Hewlett had alleged, being present when Hewlett had exchanged a Hillman Imp for this van. Ginley said that he had not seen Hewlett after their trip to Scotland until they had met up during Hewlett's three-month sentence at Barlinne. Hewlett had not turned up at the first hearing, when Ginley had been sentenced, but he denied that Hewlett had ever told him of an intention to skip bail or flee to Ireland.

John and Michael Goodall gave WDC Rose different reasons for the trip to Scotland in 1975. It had been their intention to rob a post office that Hewlett knew, but the arrest of the four men for breaking into caravans put an end to that particular plot. Of Hewlett's flight to Ireland with Rosalie Dolan – whose name they did not know – the Goodalls told of how Hewlett had arrived at their house in the early evening on Thursday, 9 October 1975, the day after Lesley's body had been found. He had arrived in a blue Morris 1000 van, similar to a GPO van, in which all four had driven to a housing estate in Rochdale where Hewlett wanted to visit his sister-in-law, Margaret Ginley, the ex-wife of Martin. When they arrived at Mrs Ginley's home Hewlett decided not to make the call, and they had then returned to the Goodall house in Burnley where they had slept in the sleeping bags and a tartan blanket they had brought with them in the van. The following day Hewlett and Dolan had left early for Ireland in the van.

The circle appeared to be close to completion when WDC Rose visited Margaret Ginley. She lived on the Kirholt Estate, opposite the homes of James McGurgon Baillie and William McCondichie, who were close friends of Danny Molseed. The estate adjoined the Turf Hill Estate, and the Molseeds, including Lesley, had been regular visitors to the Baillie household. The idea that Lesley Molseed had gone with her killer willingly, because he was some-one known to her, fitted in with what Margaret Ginley was now telling the police.

Margaret Ginley was able to tell WDC Rose of regular visits to her house by Susan and Raymond Hewlett, and that her daughter Carol frequently visited the Hewletts' house in Todmorden, staying there up to and including 1975.

Carol Ginley told WDC Rose that, following her weekend visits to Todmorden, Raymond would take her home. Sometimes they would travel on Hewlett's motorbike, but Carol recalled at least one occasion on which she had gone home in a light-blue van, similar to a GPO van.

Hewlett, interviewed by DS Paxton in 1975, had denied owning the Morris 1000 van after Lesley's murder, asserting that Ginley had sold it for £10. He had also denied visiting the Rochdale area in 1975. Now Alison Rose had proved both of those assertions to be false: Hewlett had still owned the van at the time of Lesley's death, and he was still visiting Rochdale, and in particular Margaret Ginley, in 1975.

Having established that Hewlett had lied to Paxton, and having been provided with statements made quite willingly by the persons she had interviewed, Alison Rose now believed that the trail led to Rosalie Dolan, the girl who had fled with Hewlett to Ireland in early October 1975, and who had provided to Paxton an alibi for her lover for Sunday, 5 October. Rose knew she had to interview Dolan to establish why the couple had fled, and whether she had provided a false alibi for Raymond Hewlett. Dolan, however, now lived in Australia, but tenacity and pugnaciousness enabled Rose to trace her quarry through local Australian police and, having spoken to Dolan on the telephone, Rose arranged for the police to pay for her to come back to the UK to help in the investigation, which had reached a crucial point.

Rosalie Dolan flew back, and the police provided her with accommodation at a hotel in central Bradford, where she spent her days and evenings in the company of the woman detective constable who had made it her business to establish the truth about Raymond Hewlett.

Dolan readily remembered the alibi provided for Hewlett, and how she, as a 15-year-old girl, had come to provide it. On Sunday, 5 October 1975 Hewlett had arranged to meet his besotted child-lover at Todmorden market place. She had idolised Hewlett. He provided her with a refuge from the strictures of her home life. He treated her like a woman, not a child. How often did a besotted young girl make these claims for her older lover? More suspicious to WDC Rose was that Hewlett had taken for himself a paramour of such tender years, a child half his age, only a few years older than Lesley Molseed . . .

Rosalie Dolan told WDC Rose that she and Hewlett had arranged to meet at 5 p.m., and that he had been late, but that she had waited for him, so devoted and obsessed was she with the man. When he had finally arrived more two hours later he appeared bothered, putting his arms around the girl and asking, 'Will you cover for me with the police?' He had made some reference to the theft of motor cars and she, thinking it all some harmless adventure of which she was honoured to be made a part, had agreed. Hewlett had told her what to say: that if she were asked what they had done this Sunday, she was to tell what they had done the previous Sunday, 28 September 1975. He had rehearsed with her the story she (and he) would tell, explaining that the untruths would be easier to remember if she referred back to the preceding week. He then told her that he might have to go away, and he asked her to go with him. Breathless as the female in love in a Jane Austen novel, she readily agreed. She was included, she was a vital part, she was loved for herself and she was needed for her role. Here was her opportunity to be away from Todmorden and with her lover – it was a heaven-sent opportunity.

Rosalie had been something of a tomboy when she met Hewlett. Her life had been ruled by her father, a strict disciplinarian who had insisted she call him 'Sir'. He had died in 1974 and, thereafter, she had resisted all attempts by her mother to exert the same sort of influence and control over her life. Raymond was a perfect opportunity to expand the rebellious side of her nature. She had met him through a mutual friend, in Todmorden market. They had begun to chat, and she was immediately attracted to him, not least because of his age, which was more than twice hers. He gave the impression that he was separated from his wife, and she began to see him in her lunch breaks, when Hewlett would pick her up in his car and take her to the moors, where they would sit talking. He generally talked: she listened. She knew that Hewlett messed about with stolen cars, but was surprised when a friend told her that he had raped a girl. She asked Hewlett about it, and he had told her that the girl had chased him and, when he had rejected her advances she had made up lies about him. The naive 15-year-old Rosie, unable to conceive of her Romeo committing anything *serious* like rape, had believed his story.

Their attachment had developed into a sexual relationship, with Hewlett taking the dominant role and introducing her to alternative forms of intercourse, such as anal intercourse, which he preferred. Although Dolan had not been a virgin when she met Hewlett, she had never had any previous experience of this kind of sexual practice.

In September 1975 they had run away to Scotland, touring around and sleeping in Hewlett's van. When it became cold at night Hewlett had broken into a caravan, stealing a blanket which they had used to keep warm. Rosalie remembered that blanket as a souvenir of Scotland. It was tartan.

The trip had lasted only ten days before they had returned to

Todmorden where, despite the ire of her mother at her daughter's absconding, the relationship had continued as before, with the couple meeting each Sunday. Rosalie's devotion was a strange puppy love coupled with fierce adult sexuality, and she needed little persuasion when he asked her to run away with him again, on the Wednesday lunch-time that Lesley Molseed's body had been found.

Hewlett had met her from school on the Thursday. She had taken clothes with her that day, and they spent that night with the Goodalls in Burnley before setting off for Liverpool early the next morning. On the journey Hewlett told Rosalie that the police were looking for him, using the cameras which she could see at the side of the motorway, so they travelled on A and minor roads. Although the couple had little money, Hewlett chose to abandon the blue van rather than sell it, and the vehicle was left, with the souvenir of Scotland and her happy memories of that trip, rolled up in the rear.

That evening they had travelled by ferry to Dublin, before making their way to Cork where they had booked into lodgings in the name of Dolan. Hewlett had obtained employment picking mushrooms, Rosalie earned money cleaning and washing for the man in the flat below them. They had been like a married couple. Hewlett even changed her birth certificate so that she would appear to be his wife, a matter which had actually caused her some upset. Unusually, Raymond had been quiet and withdrawn, but that had not interfered with her happiness at being together and away from Todmorden.

After three weeks they had returned to England, ending up in Dover where, the following day, Hewlett had told Rosalie that he was going to store their luggage at the railway station, before going out to find work. She should wait for him at the beach.

As she had on Sunday, 5 October 1975, Rosalie Dolan had waited for Raymond long after he should have made their appointment, but this time he did not return. She spent the night under an upturned boat on the beach, before going to the police for help to get home. Despite his abandoning her, the young girl could not forget her feelings of love for him, so that when DS Paxton had interviewed her regarding 5 October, she had had no hesitation in reciting her rehearsed story.

After she had heard Rosalie's account Alison Rose showed her the *Crimewatch* reconstruction, which depicted the Morris 1000 van seen in the lay-by on 5 October 1975. This was similar to the

vehicle Rosalie recalled Hewlett had owned, then abandoned in
Liverpool. She remembered, with a trace of nostalgia, how she
and Raymond had made love in the rear of the van, their privacy
ensured by the tartan blanket, draped thoughtfully by Hewlett
across the front windows. They would often go for drives in the
moorland areas. Raymond liked quiet areas, especially when he
wanted to have sex. She also was reminded by the video programme of the damage repair to the front passenger door.

Rose took Rosalie Dolan to the Turf Hill Estate, and to the A672
murder scene, and she was able to recall having visited both places,
although she was unable to tell the circumstances of being there.
She was unable to say whether Hewlett had owned a knife, but she
did remember that she herself had owned a pocket knife, which
she had left in the van and never seen again.

Rosalie Dolan's story placed suspicion firmly on Hewlett: she
had shown his sexual preferences; she had linked him to the Morris
1000 van, and she had spoken of Hewlett's tendency to use a tartan
blanket to obtain privacy for the activities inside; she had disclosed
that he had asked her to lie for him. But mostly she had put
Raymond Hewlett's name starkly in the frame, because Rosalie had
shown his alibi to be a lie. Only Raymond Hewlett could answer
the questions of why he had lied about his alibi, where he had
really been on Sunday, 5 October 1975, why he had fled the area
so soon after Lesley's killing, and at the time her body was found,
and why he had lied about his ownership of the blue van, and had
abandoned that vehicle when both money and transportation were
still important to him.

Hewlett's entry on the police national computer had already
been amended to add that, should he be apprehended, the
Molseed incident room was to be notified of his detention.

Hewlett was arrested in September 1991 as he entered Holyhead
port, having disembarked a ferry from Ireland. He was in the
company of a woman and her three children and, as soon as
Hewlett had been detained, the woman's 9-year-old daughter
complained that Hewlett had been indecently assaulting her, entering her bedroom at night before climbing into bed with her,
fondling her vagina and masturbating over her. The mother was
advised to report the matter to the Royal Ulster Constabulary, since
the offences alleged had occurred within their jurisdiction.

Hewlett was returned to Stoken Prison in Leicestershire, to
complete the sentence from which he had absconded in December
1990. In June 1992 Trevor Wilkinson arranged for Hewlett to be

transferred to Armley Prison in Leeds, to facilitate interviewing the prisoner concerning the murder of Lesley Molseed. Once at Armley, Hewlett was visited by DS Mackerill and WDC Rose, who sought his consent to being interviewed at a West Yorkshire police station on the subject of the abduction and killing of Lesley Molseed. Hewlett later agreed to be interviewed in the presence of his solicitor.

At the beginning of his first interview concerning Lesley's death since 1975, Hewlett was faced with a new situation of which he had no experience. His previous criminal cases had started life with an interview by two police officers, sometimes with a solicitor, sometimes without, and one of the officers would make a note of the interview. He would not see that note until it had become part of the police officer's statement. This had been his, and Stefan Kiszko's, experience of police interviews. But by 1992 the provisions of the Police and Criminal Evidence Act 1984 had come into effect. Gone was the notebook, in came the tape-recorder. As he was told right at the beginning of the interview, the interview would be tape-recorded and his solicitor would have access to a copy of the tapes.

The officers led Hewlett through his life story, from birth to settling in Todmorden, allowing him to comment on the effects of his childhood on his later development. His early criminal career and his love of, and marriage to Susan came next, with Hewlett asserting that Susan had let him down, and was going to leave him for another man, staying with him only when he had pleaded with her to do so. His trust in her had, however, been damaged, and his affection was gone. Realising that he had married too young, he had taken to having relationships with other women.

Moving swiftly through the details of his first sexual offence, the officers manoeuvred Hewlett round to his relationship with Rosalie Dolan, and to his friendship with Martin Ginley and the Goodall brothers, covering their visits to Scotland. They made Hewlett aware that Dolan had been flown to Britain, but they did not tell him that they were monitoring how his account tallied with that of witnesses already interviewed.

Ignoring the substantial age difference between them, Hewlett painted a very different picture of his sexual relationship with Rosalie Dolan. She was the dominant partner, prepared to do anything and everything and to enjoy it. She was every man's dream woman. It was true that they had most of their sexual encounters in the back of a van he owned, but that had been a

Vauxhall Viva van, the vehicle in which he had taken Rosalie to Scotland. He denied ever having owned a Morris 1000 van or an ex-GPO van, even in the face of the officers telling him that a number of people had told them about his blue Morris 1000 van. He denied also asking Dolan to give him an alibi for 5 October 1975, saying that he was not even seeing her then. He did, however, concede that he had been interviewed at Burnley Police Station concerning the Molseed murder, by a detective whose name he could not recall. Even when pressed Hewlett continued to deny setting up a false alibi, claiming that he had done nothing wrong that day which would require an alibi. He was dismissive of Dolan's version.

Hewlett was prepared to admit that he had taken Rosalie to the Goodalls' house on the Thursday, then on to Ireland on the Friday. He said that they had travelled by bus, although he admitted stealing cars – sometimes two or three a day. He could not remember details of the bus journey to Liverpool, a matter considered suspicious by the officers, who believed that he had driven there in the blue GPO van, but the remainder of his account of their stay in Ireland, to their return through Dover, tallied exactly with what Rosalie had said.

Pressed by WDC Rose he admitted that each time he had been in serious trouble he had fled to Ireland, but he refused to accept that it was axiomatic that his trip to Ireland in 1975 was due to his having killed Lesley. The facts and details provided by other witnesses were put to him but he angrily replied that he did not care what anyone else was saying.

On 7 November 1975 Hewlett had been interviewed by DS Paxton, whose note of the interview included Hewlett admitting to the ownership of a blue ex-GPO Morris 1000 van, which he had said he had swapped for a Hillman Imp and admissions that, on 5 October 1975 he had spent the afternoon in the company of Rosalie Dolan. When these matters were put to him, Hewlett again denied ownership of the van, saying that he had owned a blue Ford Escort van which he had swapped for a green Vauxhall Viva van, owned by one Frankie Jowett. He claimed that the 1975 statement read to him was a forgery designed to trap him, as he had never owned a Morris 1000 van. When confronted with the statements of his friends, the Goodalls and Ginleys, that maintained that he had owned such a van, Hewlett, unable to accuse them of trapping him, began to stumble on his words, and to appear more uncertain of himself.

The first interview was brought to an end, with Hewlett agreeing to be interviewed the following day at Bradford Police Station. However, at about midnight a message was passed from the prison to the effect that Hewlett no longer agreed to be interviewed and wished to change his legal representation. A further eight days were then to pass before Mackerill and Rose could interview Hewlett again. This time it was in Armley Prison, in the presence of his new solicitor Mr Paramore. At the beginning of the interview Hewlett protested his innocence of the offence, then announced that his new solicitor had advised him to make no reply to all questions. As Mackerill and Rose persisted in questioning him about Rosalie Dolan, his previous offending and the murder of Lesley Molseed, Hewlett sat in stony silence, broken only from time to time by, 'No reply.'

On 13 July 1992 during a further four hours of questioning, this time in Wakefield Prison, Hewlett maintained his 'No reply' stance. The officers, undaunted by the wall of silence, persisted. Rosalie's detailed statement and the allegation of indecent assault made by the 9-year-old when he was re-arrested in 1991 were put to Hewlett, and he was also reminded of the trauma suffered since her attack by his first ever victim. She was unable to make love without seeing Hewlett's face looking down on her, the smell of paint thinners still invading her. She had been unable to form a lasting relationship with anybody, including her own children, and had made twelve attempts to take her life since Hewlett had ruined her childhood.

Hewlett, who received just eighteen months and served only twelve for his crime, remained unmoved.

The following day Mackerill and Rose were replaced by DCI Bernard Browse and DI Desmond O'Boyle. They carefully questioned Hewlett using the approach of detailing what was known from the evidence proving Hewlett's possession of the Morris 1000 van to the lies he had told in his first interviews in 1975 to the fact that a PC Guest, who had worked in Todmorden in 1975 recalled prosecuting Hewlett for fraudulent use of an excise licence on a Morris 1000 van, which Hewlett had denied owning. Throughout, Hewlett maintained a stony silence. Bringing together all the strands of evidence the officers told Hewlett directly that they believed him to be responsible for the death of Lesley Molseed, but even this approach failed to move the suspect. The chief inspector brought the interview to a close by informing Hewlett that, because of their belief that he was involved in the killing of the child he would be questioned again after further enquiries had been made.

It was a mere twenty-four hours later that the original participants assembled again. On 15 July Mackerill and Rose, Hewlett and Mr Paramore sat down in Wakefield Prison for what was to be the final interview of Raymond Hewlett in connection with the crime for which Stefan Kiszko had been deprived of such a substantial portion of his life. No doubt Kiszko's suffering would not have touched Hewlett any more than the torment endured by the 9-year-old daughter of his last partner over a period of several months whilst they had lived in Ireland. Her statement was put to him, including those parts where she had alleged that he had come to her in the night, laid down naked next to the child, lifting her nightie and rubbing his erect penis against her, massaging and fondling her genitals and even attempting to penetrate the infantile vagina with his penis. The child was even aware of liquid emanating from Hewlett's penis, between her legs and over her body. It was an account of brutality that could have come from the mouth of Lesley Molseed, had she lived to give it. But no visible chill ran through Hewlett; he made no answer.

Hewlett was told that a report would be sent to Ireland, in connection with the offences against the 9-year-old, but, thereafter, he was left alone to complete his prison sentence. The police did not return again.

Wilkinson's squad analysed the content of the interviews and re-interviewed all their witnesses to ensure that the accounts on which they were relying were true, in the face of Hewlett's denials and protestations of innocence. They traced Frank Jowett and James Vickers, men named by Hewlett as being involved in the sale of the two vans. Vickers said that, whilst he knew Ginley, he had not sold or purchased any sort of van from him, and he had never heard of Hewlett. Jowett also vehemently denied that Hewlett had sold him a van.

In the half-light of a wintry morning, on 6 November 1992, Raymond Hewlett completed his prison sentence and walked out through the dark-oak gates of Armley Prison, but it was not a walk to freedom. As he stepped across the prison threshold Constables Neil Pickering and John Robinson arrested Hewlett on suspicion of murdering Lesley Molseed. As before, once the caution had been administered Hewlett made no reply, and the officers transported him in silence to Bradford Central Police Station to be detained for further questioning.

What followed, over the next four days, was a series of interviews as intense as permitted by the rigid codes of the Police and Criminal Evidence Act. A solicitor was always in place, and Hewlett could consult with his solicitor whenever he wished. There were regular breaks for refreshment, drinks, food or simply to rest. The interview could be stopped at any time, and the suspect was allowed nine hours of sleep every night. But throughout, the officers ground on, determined to use each legitimate interrogation technique to break through Hewlett's refusal to answer. Officers interviewed him in pairings different to those used before. Different questions were put, or his lies were put to him in a different order, but he was never put off balance, and after thirty-six hours of questioning Wilkinson and Browse had debriefed each interviewing officer to be told the same thing: Hewlett had made no reply. As the first thirty-six hours of detention and interrogation approached their end, interviewing was suspended whilst application was made to Bradford Magistrates' Court for a further period in which to question the accused man. The law grants a suspect such protection, to avoid any possibility of him being kept incommunicado, indefinitely. Hewlett had nothing to contribute to the court proceedings, and his solicitor did not object to the extension. The application was granted and the officers prepared to resume their battle of wills with Raymond Hewlett.

When Wilkinson and Browse returned from justifying to the magistrates the need for a further period of detention, they were greeted by DI O'Boyle who had just returned from Armley Prison, in possession of news which his senior officers had not anticipated.

Whilst the interviewing of Hewlett had been suspended pending the setting of a court hearing for the police application, a telephone call had been received from the governor's office at Armley. Three inmates had come forward offering information which they believed would be of assistance to the enquiry team. O'Boyle, recognising the loathing which 'regular' prisoners had for offenders suspected of sex crimes against children, and aware also that co-prisoners generally make poor witnesses, had been to Armley to interview those inmates.

The first inmate had told of being moved in to share a cell with Hewlett on the first day of Hewlett's questioning. He had met Hewlett at lunch-time, after Hewlett had spent a morning session with Mackerill and Rose. The inmate described Hewlett as being very quiet and withdrawn, and that he would not mention the reason for the interviews. After the afternoon session Hewlett had returned, panicky and scared. The inmate had asked what he was being questioned about, and Hewlett had said that it was for the murder of a middle-aged woman some sixteen years earlier. He had mentioned a name, which the prisoner had forgotten, save that it began with an L. His new padmate had asked for advice, as he had agreed to go to the police station for further interviews, and he did not trust his solicitor.

The inmate said to Hewlett that, if it was serious, he needed to get a good brief and refuse to be interviewed until he had spoken with the solicitor, and he had given his own solicitor's name, Mr Paramore. Hewlett had followed this advice.

After the following interview, the inmate continued, Hewlett had returned to the cell in an agitated state. He was chain-smoking and he had described how one of the interviewers was a woman, who had told him to look into her eyes and tell her that he did not commit the murder. This had disturbed him, and he talked about it continually.

As the interviews continued, Hewlett opened up to his cellmate, doubtless in the belief that the man could be trusted, and oblivious to a fact of prison life of which he ought, by 1992, to have been painfully aware: there was no honesty amongst thieves. Hewlett told his cellmate how he was worried about a Morris or Austin 1000 van which he had owned, a post office van which he had got from a friend who had swapped it for him. It had been parked at the scene of the murder, leaking oil. Hewlett said that he had got rid of the van in Liverpool, thus confirming Rosalie Dolan's evidence. The inmate could not, of course, have known what Dolan had said, yet the details which he said Hewlett had told him matched the police evidence.

Following a further interview Hewlett had returned to the cell, concerned because the police had told him that they were flying an ex-girlfriend back from Australia who could link him with the van. Hewlett had then told the inmate of his trip to Scotland with Rosalie. The inmate had asked Hewlett directly whether he had committed the murder but, despite the same question being put to him several times, Hewlett had not replied, but had sat in silence staring at his cellmate. When he did finally speak it was to talk about the van linking him to the murder, and the girl from Australia linking him to the van. Hewlett was clearly nervous about the interviews, but the inmate was moved from him after that. He still saw Hewlett in recreation times and he had been kept abreast of the interviews. Hewlett had told him that he expected to be re-arrested on release from prison.

A second prisoner had met Hewlett in the prison hospital when Hewlett had attended for treatment. He was depressed at being interviewed by the police for the sixteen-year-old murder of a woman. When the man had asked whether he had done it, Hewlett had allegedly replied, 'Yes.' Hewlett had gone on to explain that the only evidence to link him with the crime was a van which leaked oil. This inmate had tried to reassure Hewlett by telling him that he would have been charged if the police had any evidence, but some days later Hewlett had confessed to being so depressed that he was suicidal.

The third inmate had become Hewlett's cellmate in August, and Hewlett had told him that he was being interviewed for the murder of a woman. He had denied the offence, but told the other man of his possession of a van which was connected to the murder, and which he had abandoned in Liverpool. Hewlett had bragged about his sexual exploits with a 14-year-old girl, speaking about 'good sex' in a van on the moors, and he had also told his cellmate that he had had sex, or had masturbated on someone called Lesley, also on the moors. The inmate believed his cellmate to have been bragging, but he had then formed the opinion that something was not right when Hewlett had again spoken of the 14-year-old, saying that she had provided him with an alibi but the police had brought her back from Australia and she had changed her story.

Hewlett had told this man that his concern about the murder was such that he had attempted suicide on three occasion. He had taken pills prescribed for his depression and ointment prescribed for a foot complaint, but these had merely made him ill, and he had made a noose from bed clothes, intending to hang himself from the cell window.

Hewlett had said that he had thrown the noose from his window into the yard below, a fact which the police were able to confirm when the prisoner whose duty it was to clear up the exercise yard below Hewlett's cell was traced, and confirmed finding a noose made of bedding in the yard, which he had placed in a rubbish bin. The second inmate's account was confirmed by the medical staff, to the extent that they could say that that man had been treated on the same day as Hewlett had received attention for his depression. They also confirmed that Hewlett had been prescribed drugs for depression and ointment for his foot complaint.

Hewlett had told each of the three men that he was in prison for an offence of aggravated burglary, but whether the grapevine had told these three men otherwise or whether a rumour had spread about his previous offending, or that the police were questioning him for a sex offence against a child, Hewlett was marked as a 'nonce' and the prisoners were happy to inform on him for that reason alone.

When the officers, armed with the new information, had resumed questioning Hewlett, he dismissed the new 'evidence' as fantasy, and then resumed his position of non-cooperation. He did, however, tell the officers that samples had been obtained from him, in 1975, for forensic purposes. Hewlett believed the samples had been lost, and he had mentioned this to his daughter, Dawn, when she had visited him in prison.

Officers were dispatched to interview Dawn Griffiths, Hewlett's daughter from his marriage to Susan. Dawn spoke of visiting her father in prison and mentioning to him that the police from Yorkshire had been to see her mother about the murder of a girl in 1975. Following his interviews in Armley, Hewlett had told Dawn that he had been interviewed by the police about this murder in 1975, and had given blood and hair samples which the police had now lost. He had said that the murder had nothing to do with him.

By 3.25 p.m. on Sunday, 8 November 1992, all attempts by the detectives on Wilkinson's team to prise open the door of 'No reply' which had become Hewlett's barrier to solving the Molseed case, had failed. He had not been prepared to speak of his reasons for lying, his ownership of a blue Morris 1000 van or the murder itself. All that he would talk of was matters unrelated to the murder enquiry, and of such ancillary matters he was prepared to prattle endlessly in an attempt to avoid the primary focus of the officers' enquiry.

Wilkinson and Browse, acknowledging that Browse had already tried and failed to break Hewlett, determined that they would make one last attempt. Wilkinson had, thus far, seen him only once, on 6 November, and that had been to ensure that Hewlett was satisfied with his treatment.

Wilkinson opened the interview by approaching the subject-matter from an entirely different direction. It was a direction inconsistent with the words of the caution then in use, namely that the accused did not have to say anything. It was an approach more consistent with the caution introduced in 1995, which was to the effect that an accused's silence could be used as evidence against him. But Wilkinson had already administered the caution and Mr Paramore stood ready to guard against his client being misled, and

Wilkinson was acting in frustration; the frustration of a detective who knows he has got his man, but cannot quite seal the case. The detective superintendent told Hewlett that if, as Hewlett had thus far asserted, he was a genuinely innocent man, Wilkinson wanted to eliminate him from his enquiry. He did not want, said the officer pointedly, another Kiszko-style miscarriage of justice. Hewlett declined to answer any questions, maintaining that position as the two detectives trawled over the same areas covered by the other officers. They again assured Hewlett that their objective was not to convict an innocent man and, at this point, Hewlett caused the interview process to halt. It was a moment of complete silence, the police holding their collective breath, aware that they might be about to progress, terrified to break the atmosphere which Hewlett's brief pause had created. 'I am innocent,' he declared, 'but I will answer your questions, although I do so against the advice of my solicitor and although it may cause me trouble.'

Astounded at Hewlett's apparent about-face, the detectives began again to review the evidence. Hewlett responded to Wilkinson's asking him to explain the differences between his account and the witnesses' account of the alibi with a resounding 'No Reply', and he used the same words when he was asked about the Morris 1000. He did, however, suggest that the statement he was alleged to have made to Paxton in 1975 was a fabrication, and said that if he saw the original he could prove its falsity. He was then shown the original, which rendered him speechless. Having previously said that he did not tell lies in serious matters, and would not do so in a murder enquiry, Raymond Hewlett was unable to account for the content of the statement. He was left to deny that the signature on the statement was his, conceding that it could be his writing but that because he tended to sign his name in many different ways, it could be a forgery.

When he was challenged again about the van, and the evidence which tended to prove his ownership of it, Hewlett now said that he could not recall having owned it. It was the only vehicle he could not remember owning, so he had denied owning it rather than resorting to a rather limp claim of an inability to remember. Having given this explanation, Hewlett seemed to change tack again, moving from the 'No Reply' denial that he had used thus far, to a stance of 'I cannot remember, it was all seventeen years ago.'

As the interview proceeded Hewlett repeatedly changed the subject. At one stage he claimed to the officers that he had now been cured of his previous sexual interest in young girls. He explained this transformation by referring to an incident in Ireland, when he had met a young girl by the side of the road, who had tried to kill herself as a result of being raped. He had taken the girl to hospital, thereby saving her life, and the experience had been a life-changing one, making him realise the error of his ways. He now wanted, he told the officers, to protect and help young girls. Wilkinson, understandably cynical in the light of the evidence, put to Hewlett that the cure had been so complete that right up to the moment of his being re-arrested at Holyhead he had been indecently assaulting a young, 9-year-old child. Hewlett said that he did not want to talk about that.

He refused to acknowledge that he had lied and was cautious not to incriminate himself in respect of the van or the alibi. He attempted to portray himself as the victim of the girls he was alleged to have assaulted, implying that, as he had said of Rosalie Dolan, they had been the dominant party in sexual matters.

When Hewlett realised that the five slides obtained from Lesley Molseed had been mislaid, his confidence grew, and he actually remonstrated with the officers that he could have been eliminated from their enquiries had those samples not been lost.

There had been a time, just for a few moments during the interview, when Wilkinson's hopes had risen. They had not soared wildly. He had not been overwhelmed by optimism, but he had, just for a moment, experienced a feeling that Hewlett was about to break, that his indication of a willingness to talk was a precursor to more detailed answers to the case which had been constructed against him. Hewlett's response to the forensic evidence had caused that moment to end, for Trevor Wilkinson knew that, with Hewlett's confidence on the rise, there would not be another opportunity for the police.

So it was to prove in three further interviews, with Hewlett increasingly cocky and confident, sure in his own mind that no charges would flow from this investigation.

At about 7.20 a.m. on Tuesday, 16 November 1992, Hewlett was released from custody, bailed to re-appear at the police station in February 1993. As he left the police station he turned to DCI Browse. Holding out his hand to the officer Hewlett said, 'No hard feelings,' and walked away.

All the witnesses amassed by Trevor Wilkinson's team, including the prison inmates, signed statements to support the prosecution of Raymond Hewlett. A file of evidence was submitted to the

Crown Prosecution Service special case unit in London. The file was given intense consideration, but at a conference held in January 1993, DSupt Trevor Wilkinson and his trusted lieutenant DCI Bernard Browse were informed that, in view of the absence of an admission from the suspect, the evidence was not sufficient to guarantee that Hewlett would be convicted of Lesley's murder. Unwilling to risk another scenario such as that which had arisen from the case against Stefan Kiszko, the Crown Prosecution Service was unable and unwilling to pursue a prosecution against Raymond Hewlett for the murder of Lesley Molseed.

Raymond Hewlett did not meet his bail condition, to surrender at Bradford in February 1993. Whatever confidence he might have had, he fled the jurisdiction, leaving England for Ireland, the country which had always been his safe haven when he was in, as he had put it, serious trouble.

In Ireland he lived in the Mati Maitheal Commune in Co Donegal where, despite police warnings, he was allowed to look after young children. Eventually he was asked to leave due to concern arising from remarks made by the young children. These caused the commune members to question the trust they had placed in Hewlett.

He then wandered Ireland and had gained further convictions for dishonesty before travelling in the continent, where he obtained casual work. In September 1994, he obtained employment as a candle maker in Saint Pierne Valley, Italy. Whilst in Italy, he met and married an Italian woman, who returned to Ireland with him in 1995, following a failed attempt to gain Italian citizenship.

On 23 April 1995, Gabriella, the new Mrs Hewlett, gave birth to his son, Marco. However, she became homesick and returned to her family home in Turin. When Hewlett later followed her, he was banished by his wife, being informed she wanted nothing further to do with him due to enquiries the Italian police had made of her concerning him.

Hewlett returned to an itinerant lifestyle in the UK. He has never been charged with Lesley's murder.

CHAPTER TWENTY-THREE

Jesus in Heaven

When the Court of Appeal determined that Stefan Kiszko was innocent of the murder of Lesley Molseed, there were no scenes of jubilation on the courtroom steps, with the freed man and his family drinking champagne and giving interviews decrying British justice. Campbell Malone and Jim Gregory were greeted by Charlotte Kiszko at her home in Rochdale, where she served tea and tarts. The atmosphere was not of elation, but of relief. Malone recalls, '[E]ven though it was a happy occasion, it was one tinged with some sadness as we reflected on the wasted years.'

The media, however, were interested, and after consulting with medical staff at Prestwich, Malone brought his famous client before the national press. The briefing was held at the hospital, two days after the Court of Appeal verdict. Stefan wore a jacket, shirt and tie, and walked in with his mother, whom he kissed, for the benefit of the cameras. He was clearly ill at ease and smiled only once. He spoke first of Charlotte:

> My mother has been great. She has been very supportive. That was very important to me. I did not want to lose her because of the crime of which I was convicted. Mum has given me every confidence.

Turning to the deprivations of his imprisonment Kiszko told how he had missed his freedom, the comforts of home and the ability to drive his car, but he did not disguise his suffering when he spoke of 'the years in prison which were hell'. He explained how he had been tormented by other prisoners because of the nature of his crime, but, echoing a theme which had been a constant, he explained that he had derived strength from within himself and said: 'I always believed in my own innocence.' He added: 'I didn't lose faith that I would be acquitted. I always believed the courts would come on my side. I had faith in British justice. I still have that faith.'

Yet he could not hide his bitterness towards those whom he held responsible for his plight, principally the police:

> They just wanted somebody to go down as a mug. In a way, I was framed, because the detectives told me to get it wrapped up in time for Christmas . . . I was under the impression these officers were going to hit me or do something violent.

He said that he had opposed his lawyers running the defence of diminished responsibility, and, turning to the future, he spoke first and foremost of his hope that the real killer of Lesley Molseed would be caught. Of his own future he expressed the aspiration to marry, but it was clear to all in the room that it was unlikely that he would ever do so.

Twelve weeks later Stefan went home on weekend leave, to sleep in his own bed for the first time in sixteen years. His mother had kept the room exactly as it had been when he left, and the Hillman Avenger car, returned by the police, remained unchanged in the garage, although he was not yet well enough to drive it.

The following day some friends took Stefan to Rochdale town centre, a visit made eventful by people either staring at him or stopping to shake his hand. Ironically, the trip was made at the same time as the BBC *Crimewatch* team was filming the reconstruction of Lesley Molseed's abduction.

But it was his home where Stefan was happiest. It was as he remembered it, even down to his favoured armchair being in the same position as it had been in December 1975.

A week later Stefan was allowed home permanently. He was still suffering from mental illness, but it was controlled by medication and, perhaps equally, by his happiness at returning to his mother, and to the peacefulness and warmth of the family home. His car was sold and replaced by a silver Sierra, and Stefan began to drive it on short journeys, to the garden centre or to the shops. A claim was lodged for compensation for wrongful imprisonment, and though an interim payment was made, money alone would not compensate Stefan Kiszko for the wrong he had suffered.

Charlotte noticed that he would spend hours in his chair, staring out of the window, not speaking unless she spoke to him. Dr Kim Armand Fraser, a consultant forensic psychiatrist, had no doubt that indelible damage had been caused to Stefan's mind. Kiszko became increasingly reclusive, and when Dr Fraser interviewed him he found Stefan to be lethargic and tired, with monotonous speech and prolonged eye contact, and he concluded:

> It is hard to comprehend the enormity of what this man has
> been subjected to through wrongful conviction. Aside from
> the 'normal' distress that anyone experiences through the
> deprivation of liberty for sixteen years, he has been the subject
> of two serious assaults early in his sentence and has developed
> the most crippling of mental illnesses, schizophrenia . . .
>
> I am of the opinion that he is showing some of the negative
> . . . symptoms of schizophrenia in terms of his anergia, lack
> of drive and limited range of interests.

Dr Fraser, however, was optimistic that Kiszko's mental state would
improve substantially, until he would be able to take up employment again, and yet he also expressed the view that, were his
mother or aunt to become unable to care for him, Kiszko would
need a paid carer; he would not be able to look after himself.

As 1993 began, Charlotte and Stefan continued to live their quiet
life, consisting of time together at home and trips in Stefan's car
to the shops or to garden centres, often with Aunt Alfreda, as they
had done so many years before. Kiszko was beset with vomiting
episodes, particularly in the morning and especially when he
recalled the days he spent in prison, but, as in those days, he
continued to derive strength and support from his mother.

Charlotte's role in supporting and fighting for her son was
recognised on 14 April 1993, when she attended a dinner
honouring her as Rochdale Woman of the Year. Stefan shared his
mother's pride in the honour, but was not allowed to accompany
her to the ceremonial dinner, it being a women-only event. He
remained at home, watching television and glancing periodically
at the cuckoo clock, which told him that his mother had been out
of his sight for longer than at any time since his release. Charlotte,
meanwhile, revelled in the evening which had seen her chauffeured
to the Avant Hotel in Oldham, to dine on game and leek terrine
and poached salmon, before receiving the award which she
regarded as signifying, finally, her acceptance by the community.
She was enduring increasingly worsening health, but she left the
event determined to return a year later to hand over the title to
her successor.

It was a snapshot of traditional Britain, Christmas Eve 1993. A
small, neatly furnished room, its lighting dim, as if to enhance the
atmosphere of peace. The green fir tree pointed symbolically

heavenwards. Bedecked with tinsel and baubles, its myriad of fairy lights twinkled so much brighter in the half-gloom. Surrounded by gifts, once brightly wrapped, but now opened in accordance with tradition. A solitary, poignant angel stood aloft, wings spread, embracing the scene below, gazing down, beatifically, upon the chair.

The chair. Where the man-child had sat, those few hours ago. His mother looked, without comprehension, at the vacant seat, as if staring upon some ancient royal throne. The king had gone, for surely he had been a king to her. Her only son, her only child. Her boy-child.

He had risen from the chair as he had those eighteen years ago. The same massive frame, the same child-like weakness, but with an age of punishment within his body, within his mind. It was Christmas, and the presents had been unwrapped with child-like excitement. Now he had hopes and aspirations, now he had dreams and ambitions, now Christmas Eve would once again bring peace on earth to this mankind. The angel stood impassive.

She had found him. He had served his life imprisonment, and now the life had gone. His body still and rigid, his face pale, his lungs breathless, his heart unbeating. His forty-sixth Christmas had been his last.

This time she had not been able to watch him leave.

This time she had not been able to say goodbye.

In the autumn of 1993, after having collapsed at home, Stefan was diagnosed as suffering from angina for which he was prescribed medication.

On the night of 21 December Stefan kissed his mother goodnight, as he always did, and went to his own bedroom. There was a crash as the overweight man hit the floor, and Charlotte hurried to his room, placing a pillow under his head and whispering his name. There was no response, and when an ambulance took him to Rochdale Infirmary it was only for him to be pronounced dead on arrival. Charlotte kissed her son's forehead and returned to her home, alone. They had been reunited barely a year, and he had died, eighteen years to the day after he had been taken from his home to Rochdale Police Station to begin the torment which would represent so much of his life thereafter.

When Steve Panter of the *Manchester Evening News* visited Charlotte Kiszko at 9 a.m. on the morning following Stefan's death, he was greeted with her traditional hospitality and warmth. She spoke to Panter of how she had found Stefan, occasionally allowing her inevitable anger to surface. She did not weep freely, but occasionally wiped away a tear with the dignity, strength and fighting spirit which had been the hallmark of her struggle to free her son. Such anger as she had was directed at those who had brought about his imprisonment:

> '[T]here are certain people I cannot forgive for the way they treated my son. There is one police officer in particular who will not only have the jailing of an innocent man on his conscience, but this as well.

But above all Panter was moved by the words of this indomitable woman, when she spoke of her son:

> The police took him away three days before Christmas and now three days before Christmas again, God has taken him ... At least Stefan will go to his grave with his name cleared, and having had some freedom again.

Stefan Kiszko was buried on 5 January 1994 after a requiem mass at Holy Family Church, Rochdale. Father William O'Connor described Charlotte and her sister as 'women of fortitude, who made great sacrifices, showed great love and suffered great heartbreak', and of Stefan he added, 'the world has failed Stefan, but there will be no more pain, no more suffering for him now.'

With Stefan's death, Charlotte's will to live crumbled. What use had she now for his shiny silver motor car? What need had she for the payment of compensation? Her only love in life had been her son. She had surmounted her crippling lung disease to fight for Stefan's release, but as her now-famous grittiness evaporated the illness took hold again. Her solicitor, Campbell Malone, was later to say, 'She did not think she had anything to live for. She had lived for Stefan's freedom and once he had gone, her health visibly deteriorated. She had no reason to live any longer.'

Charlotte's one remaining ambition, that being to attend the Rochdale Woman of the Year Dinner to hand over the title she had received the previous year, was achieved in April 1994. The following month, her life's purpose at an end, Charlotte Kiszko died, aged 70. Before she died she expressed gratitude that Stefan had died before her: she had not wanted him to have to endure more pain, as he surely would have in his bereavement, and she knew that he would not have been able to cope without her.

Innocent? One more victim must always be remembered.

April Molseed holds a black and white photograph, now more than twenty years old. The 3-year-old girl with the gap teeth and curly mop of brown hair smiles out at her mother. The photograph of the child in her favourite dress had been taken the day she had come home from hospital, alive and glowing after the surgery which had repaired her heart, and given back to her the life which would, so shortly after, be stolen away with such terrible violence. The photographic memory still comforts the woman who has never got over her terrible loss, but she is able to remember her daughter's short life with great fondness, and she recalls with vivid accuracy a conversation she had with Lesley some three weeks before the child's death. Lesley, recounting a dream from the night before, had told April that she had been talking to Jesus in Heaven. 'He was dressed in white, whiter than your washing, Mum. I said, "It's lovely, Jesus, but I want to go home".'

Epilogue

DSupt Dick Holland was commended for his 'skilful handling' of the Lesley Molseed enquiry, receiving praise from the trial judge, Mr Justice Park, and from his chief constable, Ronald Gregory. Gregory it was who commented on Holland's 'skill and persistence during trying circumstances in the final interrogation' of Kiszko, that is, in obtaining Kiszko's confession.

Dick Holland had joined the police force in 1953, rising rapidly through the ranks in a service lasting twenty-five years. The zenith of his career was the Kiszko investigation, during which he was promoted from inspector to superintendent. The nadir was the investigation of the so-called Yorkshire Ripper, Peter Sutcliffe. Following Sutcliffe's conviction, criticisms were levelled at the West Yorkshire police's handling of the investigation, and Holland found himself demoted to uniformed duties in Sowerby Bridge. He retired from the force in 1988, proud of his role in the conviction of Stefan Kiszko, and also of Judith Ward, the woman found guilty of the M62 coach bombing.

Ever a strong man, Holland took criticism in his stride, recognising that the police would always be the target for disparaging remarks and rarely recipients of praise. On his retirement, Dick Holland spoke fondly of the force and its integrity saying, 'There is no other organisation more accountable [than the police force].'

After retiring from the force, he became a hospital security chief in Huddersfield. Ronald Outteridge, the leading forensic scientist in the Kiszko case, also retired and moved to live in Cambridgeshire. In both cases the peace of retirement was shattered by the re-opening of the Kiszko case in 1991, in which the roles of both men were brought into the spotlight.

Dick Holland, in an interview with the *Manchester Evening News*, said, 'I did an honest and professional job. I didn't stitch up Stefan Kiszko.'

In July 1994 Holland and Outteridge were formally charged with suppressing evidence in the case against Kiszko, namely the results of scientific tests on semen taken from Lesley's clothing and on the semen samples given by Kiszko. The case against the two men progressed slowly through the magistrates' court at Rochdale, moving inexorably towards a committal and an undoubtedly high-profile trial in the Crown Court. But on May Day 1995 the case was challenged in the magistrates' court, barristers for both defendants arguing before the stipendiary magistrate, Jane Hayward, that the case was an abuse of process. Jane Hayward was a professional magistrate, a lawyer with the knowledge and experience to consider with care the arguments placed before her. The argument was that the case should not be allowed to progress any further, but should be stayed, because the passage of time since the events alleged made a fair trial impossible. The barristers raised the death of Jack Dibb and the loss of vital exhibits and documents as adding to the difficulties of their clients being able to defend the charges.

Jane Hayward listened with care to the arguments on both sides before ruling that proceedings should be stayed against both Holland and Outteridge, on the basis that they could not receive a fair trial. Her judgement stated:

> I have no doubt that the absence of Chief Superintendent Dibb is prejudicial to both defendants. There are two possibilities concerning Mr Dibb. One is, he suppressed information from both Mr Outteridge and Mr Holland and they are in the dock for acts or omissions which are in reality those of Mr Dibb. The second possibility is that Dibb, though doing his best in what he said to one or both of these defendants, made statements to them which would excuse liability on their part.

A serious allegation had been raised against two formerly highly respected men. It was an allegation which would not be determined by a jury, for Miss Hayward prevented that course from being taken. Holland and Outteridge were never convicted of suppressing evidence, the law regards them as innocents.

Campbell Malone and his wife Judith were appointed executors and trustees of Charlotte Kiszko's will. As such, the responsibility fell on the Malones to ensure the wishes of Charlotte were fulfilled. They were also faced with the task of clearing the house at Kings Road of all the Kiszkos' effects.

Campbell Malone later recalled sifting through drawers and cupboards that were as tidy as the rest of Charlotte's well-ordered home. In the months after Stefan's release Charlotte had become close to Campbell and particularly to Judith, to whom she had confided her frustration at Stefan's docility and inertia as he spent days in his armchair simply starting out of the window. This image required Charlotte to recognise that Stefan was ill and that he would never be as he had been prior to his imprisonment. Charlotte threw a protective wall around Stefan, as she had always done, especially when letters arrived from people who had never met Stefan but who knew he had received some compensation for his suffering. Many letters expressed nothing more than genuine sympathy and concern, and several of the writers apologised for being parts of the system that had failed Stefan so badly.

Within weeks of Stefan's release the Home Office made a goodwill interim payment. The amount was confidential, as was the full claim for compensation although it was widely believed to be in the region of £500,000. It would have been greater had Stefan lived. His death meant that 'future loss of earnings' had to be expunged from the claim. Campbell Malone has said that he was 'unhappy' at the final figure, which he has not made public.

When Charlotte signed her will on 22 February 1994 she made specific bequests of £1,000 each to the Rochedale Infirmary and Birch Hill Hospital and the Springhill Hospice Day Care Appeal, a modern development at the end of Turf Hill Road at a spot Lesley Molseed would have passed on her fateful shopping trip.

The remainder of her estate Charlotte left to the man she believed was most responsible for securing her son's freedom: Campbell Malone. Judith was a joint beneficiary. For unknown reasons Charlotte left nothing to her sister Alfreda and the will did not expressly refer to the compensation, which was still under negotiation, but which would become the substantial part of Charlotte's estate.

Campbell Malone lives at Todmorden where he has an office. He has another twenty-five miles away in Salford. After the Kiszko triumph Malone was asked to pursue other rough justice cases, including that of Kevin Callan, released by the Court of Appeal in 1995, and Eddie Gilfoyle, who remains in prison but whose appeal is being pursued by Malone.

Alfreda Tosic lives modestly in Rochdale, frail after recent surgery.

Opposite her settee is a photograph of her, Charlotte and Stefan outside the front door of 25 Kings Road on the day of his return home.

April Molseed lives in sheltered accommodation on the outskirts of Rawtenstall. She lives apart from Danny and has most contact with her daughter Julie, who lives at Littleborough. April lives in quiet reflection. Not a day goes by when she does not think of Lesley.

On 29 April 1997, during the completion of this book, Lord Taylor, the former Peter Taylor QC, who had prosecuted Stefan Kiszko with such fairness, passed away.